D0609417

SPRINGBOK SAGA

A PICTORIAL HISTORY FROM 1891

CHRIS GREYVENSTEIN

DON NELSON, P.O. BOX 859, CAPE TOWN.

OTHER BOOKS BY CHRIS GREYVENSTEIN

Bloody Noses and Crack'd Crowns
Springbok-seges in rugby en krieket (Afrikaans)
This Brutal Glory
The Bennie Osler Story
They Made Headlines

Designed by Peter Ibbotson
Printed by Printpak (Cape) Ltd
Reproduction by Unifoto (Pty) Ltd
ISBN 0 909238 27 8
Set in 10 on 11 Times Roman

First impression October, 1977
Second impression April, 1978
Third impression December, 1978

AUTHOR'S INTRODUCTION

Our rugby history is part of the South African heritage. More than 86 years of triumph and defeat, achievement and humiliation, have gone into the forging of a tradition of which the Springbok jersey is the symbol.

Now we have reached the end of an era; perhaps it should be described as a new beginning. The Springbok legacy is about to be shared with all who live in this land and who accept what was good in the past as a firm foundation on which to build a mutual future.

This book is therefore a tribute to all those who have played rugby for South Africa over the past 86 years.

Every effort has been made to ensure accuracy and to eliminate factual errors which have been perpetuated for many years. The unselfish advice and assistance of Teddy Shnaps, the official statistician to the South African Rugby Board, has been invaluable. He checked the manuscript, provided much new information and spent many hours identifying a large number of rare photographs which otherwise could not have been used. He also supplied the statistical analysis published at the end of the book.

It must be noted that because of the nature of the contents I have not followed the metric system with any consistency and the last part of the book which deals with recent and current players, tours and events is more commentative and less detailed than the rest. All statistics and records are as of July 31, 1977.

The help and co-operation of the following must be acknowledged: Dr. Danie Craven, Alex Kellermann, A. C. Parker, George Gerber, Herman le Roux, Dawie de Villiers, Gerhard Kirsten, Neville Leck, Pieter Coetzee, Robert Denton, Neil Steyn, Johan Volschenk, Louis Wessels, Kim Shippey, Paul Roux, W. Humble, Maxwell Price, Org Potgieter, Andrew Jardine, Sam Mirwis, Brian Crowley and Gerhard Burger.

Without the photographers whose role in recording history is so often ignored, the project could never have got off the ground. For 86 years cameramen have defied the pressures of deadlines, weather conditions and inexplicable hostility from the more petty type of administrator and official to leave us with a graphic record of the game.

The enthusiasm of my publisher Don Nelson and the assistance of Toyota South Africa Ltd. made the scope of the book possible and I am also grateful to my colleagues Robert Ball, who read the proofs, and Peter Ibbotson, who spent so much time on the design and typography.

Finally, I want to thank Iris, Linda and Terry for their patience and understanding.

CHRIS GREYVENSTEIN
Cape Town
July 31, 1977.

BIBLIOGRAPHY

In addition to the files of the Cape Times, The Argus, Die Burger and Die Huisgenoot, the following books were also referred to:

History of South African Rugby Football by Ivor D. Difford (The Speciality Press of S.A. Ltd. 1933)

My Recollections and Reminiscences by W. A. Millar (Juta & Co Ltd. 1926)

The Springbokken Tour in Great Britain edited by J. L. Platnauer (G. E. O. Wunderlich, 1907)

Sports and Sportsmen (Compiled and Edited by the Cape Times, circa 1925)

All Blacks in Springbokland by M. F. Nicholls (L. T. Watkins Ltd., Wellington N.Z., 1928)

South Africa's Greatest Springboks by John E. Sacks (Sporting Publications, Wellington, N.Z., 1938)

Ek Speel vir Suid-Afrika by D. H. Craven (Nasionale Pers, 1949)

Oubaas Mark by Danie Craven (Afrikaanse Pers Bpk, 1959)

Toetsprestasies by Danie Craven (Afrikaanse Pers Bpk, 1953)

Springbok Story by Danie Craven (R. Beerman, 1954)

Danie Craven se top-Springbokke by Hennie Gerber (Tafelberg, 1977)

Giants of South African Rugby by A. C. Parker (Howard Timmins, 1955)

Ringside View by A. C. Parker (Howard Timmins, 1963)

Now is the Hour by A. C. Parker (Howard Timmins, 1965)

Ruffled Roosters by A. C. Parker (Howard Timmins, 1965)

The Lion Tamers by A. C. Parker (Howard Timmins, 1968)

Battle of the Giants by C.O. Medworth (Howard Timmins, 1960)

Beaten by the Boks by Terry McLean (Howard Timmins, 1960)

Springbok and Silverfern by Reg Sweet (Howard Timmins, 1960)

Pride of the Lions by Reg Sweet (Howard Timmins, 1962)

Lions Rampant by Vivian Jenkins (Cassell, 1956)

The Bok Busters by Terry McLean (Howard Timmins, 1965)

The Bennie Osler Story by Chris Greyvenstein (Howard Timmins, 1970)

They Made Headlines by Chris Greyvenstein (Don Nelson, 1972)

Frik du Preez Rugbyreus by Leon Gouws (Janssonius & Heyns, 1971)

The Springboks Talk by Maxwell Price (Howard Timmins, 1955)

Wallabies Without Armour by Maxwell Price (Howard Timmins, 1969)

Le Grand Combat du Quinze de France by Denis Lalanne (Editions de la Table Ronde, 1959)

The Bob Scott Story by Bob Scott & Terry McLean (Howard Timmins, 1956)

Nice Guys Come Second by John Gainsford & Neville Leck (Don Nelson, 1974)

The Unbeatables by Kim Shippey (1971)

Colin Meads All Black by Alex Veysey (Collins, 1974)

The Boot by Don Clarke & Pat Booth (A. H. & A. W. Reed, 1966)

The Lions by Wallace Reyburn (Stanley Paul, 1967)

There Was Also Some Rugby by Wallace Reyburn (Stanley Paul, 1970)

The History of Natal Rugby edited by C. O. Medworth (Howard Timmins, 1964)

This World of Rugby by John Thornett (Murray 1967)

The Barbarians by Nigel Starmer-Smith (Macdonald & Jane's, 1977)

The Unbeaten Lions by John Reason (Rugby Books, 1974)

One in the Eye by Barry Glasspool (Howard Timmins, 1976)

Several editions of the **S.A. Rugby Annual** (edited by Quintus van Rooyen)

FOREWORDS

When Hitler decided to take up the cudgels on behalf of Germany he also decided to study history.

We don't need Hitler, however, to tell us how important it is that the history of any subject tells us what could be done in the future. In other words, history provides one with the basis and the evolution, in our case, of rugby.

Apart from that it keeps fresh in our minds the great players of the past, the triumphs and jubilation on the one side and the disappointments and remorse on the other. It also brings into the present the famous deeds performed by such players on the rugby field. It is only when the past and present become one that the game becomes strong and that the future of our game is ensured.

To delve into history is, however, a tedious and laborious task requiring time and energy and few people are willing to undertake the project dealt with by Chris Greyvenstein in this book. We are grateful to him for what he has contributed to our game and we are also grateful that the past will be revived and that people will do justice to it.

D. H. Craven
President,
South African Rugby Board
August 1, 1977

I regard it as an honour to be associated with a book of this nature, not only because of my high regard for the author, Chris Greyvenstein, and his statistician, Teddy Shnaps, but also because I am proud to be a member of the Springbok Club.

History of any kind is always a valuable contribution to society, if only because the past helps to guide us in the future. The British Lions, for example, only became a world force when they delved back into history and realised that the South African scrum and the New Zealand ruck were the pillars of Southern Hemisphere superiority in the first 50 years of this century.

But the history of South African rugby in the international arena is a particularly notable subject of which we can all be justifiably proud.

The Springboks have had their black moments, even their black years. Who of us who experienced it will ever forget the test series against Willie John McBride's British Lions in 1974!

But in the long run there is not a country in the world that has been able to push us around for any length of time and the stirring deeds of our Springboks in the years between 1896 and 1956 when South Africa was never defeated in any series, both at home or away, is enough to make any contemporary Springbok feel truly humble.

South African rugby is fortunate indeed in that there is an extensive bookshelf recording its story, but Springbok Saga comes at an extremely appropriate time, for it is a permanent record of an era of the past. As I write we are moving into a new age of merit selection that will change forever the face of South African rugby and, in the words of Dr. Danie Craven, will make the Springboks even stronger and more feared than ever before.

I have not had the opportunity of reading all of the manuscript that is going into this extensive book, but judged on what I have seen and the painstaking work that has been put into it, I am sure it will be a magnificent addition to South African rugby literature.

Morne du Plessis
Springbok captain
August 22, 1977

CONTENTS

1. The Pioneers

2. The Golden Era

3. Faltering Champions

4. The Turbulent Years

1/THE PIONEERS

Eager pupils

The first week of July, 1891.

President Paul Kruger had a severe cold and he decided not to address the Volksraad although he later did find it possible to attend a successful test of the new Grusonwerk machine gun in Pretoria.

There was an earthquake in San Francisco, so powerful it was reported to have altered the course of the Colorado River, and part of Prussia was hit by a tornado.

Civil war raged in Chile, press censorship was instituted in India and a financial crisis caused consternation in Lisbon. In Cape Town a Professor Cogan advertised himself as the "world's champion phewnambulist" and offered £5 to anyone in the audience who could pull him off the wire on which he did his ballroom dancing act in the Elite Roller Skating Rink.

But the people of Cape Town had more important things to do in that first week of July 1891 than to bother with Professor Cogan or to worry over the fate of Lisbon, for that matter. They were too busy with preparations for the arrival of the first international rugby team ever to tour Southern Africa.

Rugby football had been played in South Africa from at least as early as the 1860's and with its various offshoots soon withering, the game was firmly established by 1889 when the South African Rugby Board was constituted as the governing body. T. B. Herold, then honorary secretary of the Western Province Rugby Union, was the first to suggest that a touring team from Britain be invited and with the strong support of W. V. Simkins, his president, contact was made with the England Rugby Football Union and after lengthy negotiations the project was approved. Cecil John Rhodes, then Prime Minister of the Cape Colony, offered to pay any possible financial loss and in April 1891 it was duly announced that W. E. (Bill) Maclagan would visit South Africa with a team of 20 players.

A few days before the touring party was to arrive the Western Province Rugby Union organised a trial match to test their strength for the forthcoming games against the visitors. It was a disastrous affair with many of the invited players not showing up because, as the *Cape Times* reported, "the doubtful aspect of the weather and the arrival of the mail mitigated against a strong muster".

The game nevertheless helped to establish that Ben Duff and Alf Richards were in fine form while H. H. Castens kicked well and, according to the report, "put in a decent dribble". A second trials match also failed to satisfy the critics who did not like the "ill-formed scrums and loose footwork" and much fun was poked at an accidental collision between Louw and Castens.

The *Dunottar Castle* docked in Cape Town after a 16-day trip, a new record for the journey at the time, and a large contingent of officials and supporters were there to welcome Maclagan, Edwin (Daddy) Ash, the manager, and the 20 players who were, incidentally, all from England or Scotland. An entire procession followed the team to the Royal Hotel which was festooned with flowers, ferns and a large "Welcome to South Africa" sign.

Eight members of the side had played international rugby before, while four had represented the South of England and two had played for Oxford. The remaining six were all Cambridge "Blues". W. G. Mitchell, reputed to be the best fullback in Britain at the time, Bill Maclagan, R. L. Aston, Arthur Rotherham, Paul Clauss, W. Wotherspoon, R. G. (Judy) Macmillan, W. E. Bromet and Froude Hancock were the best-known players and everybody clamoured to see them.

"Baby" Hancock was huge for his era. He was 6 ft. 5 in. tall, weighed 240 lbs and was described as "useful in the lineouts, but difficult to fit into the scrum".

Shortly after their arrival, Maclagan took his men for a practice to loosen up after the long voyage and the large crowd of spectators was deeply impressed by what they saw.

Of Bill Maclagan the *Cape Times* critic wrote: "He has acquired the acme of perfection as a tackler, can punt with considerable ability and with

W. E. (Bill) Maclagan, captain of the team of "rugby missionaries" who came to South Africa in 1891 to test the strength of the "Colonials".

Overleaf: "Playing football on Camp Ground" is the title Otto Landsberg gave this painting he did of a match between Bishops and Victoria College in 1888. This work by Landsberg (1803—1905) is regarded as one of the earliest graphic works depicting rugby in South Africa and it is reproduced here by kind permission of the owners of the original, the Potchefstroom Museum.

Herbert Hayton Castens has a special place in the annals of South African rugby. An Oxford graduate, he led his adopted country in the first-ever test to be played on South African soil. Castens also captained the first South African cricket team to tour the United Kingdom.

Above: Ben Duff, the Western Province fullback who played in all three tests against Maclagan's men. He was one of the stars of his time.

Left: Alf Richards, an accomplished player who captained South Africa in the final test and was described as the "mainstay of his side".

either foot, and can cover the ground at a splendid pace . . ."

The big centre from Cambridge, R. L. Aston, excited him as much. "He is the best passing man in England and can take the ball when proferred, from almost any difficult position". His summing-up was accurate, Aston was to be one of the biggest successes of the tour and for many years was regarded as the best centre to have been seen in this country.

The visitors were overwhelmed with hospitality – smoking concerts, dinners, a formal ball at Government House, picnics at Hout Bay and Constantia followed in quick succession – and no wonder that Maclagan was compelled to say in one of his after-dinner speeches: "We have enjoyed ourselves, perhaps too thoroughly!"

In the meantime the two Cape Town newspapers were drumming up interest in the first match, Cape Town Clubs against the British team, and the *Cape Argus* predicted that the tour would put South African rugby on trial. "The metal was to be placed in the crucible, the gold to be separated from the dross", S. W. Black thundered in his article.

The Cape Government Railways advertised that first and second class return tickets between Cape Town and Newlands would cost 3/– with admission to the ground included in the price. Wealthier fans who wished to see the match in comfort could enter the ground in their landaus at a charge of 2/6 a carriage plus 2/– for each occupant. It was announced after the match that the gate takings amounted to £400 with the local Union officials declaring themselves well satisfied with the financial aspects.

To Charles (Hasie) Versfeld belongs the honour of scoring the first-ever points by a South African against an international team. His unconverted try, which in those days counted for a single point, also happened to be the only score achieved against Maclagan's side throughout their 20-match tour of South Africa.

The Hamiltons centre was one of the four Versfeld brothers who played against the visitors on the tour and, apart from Hasie, the most famous one was probably Loftus, after whom the vast Northern Transvaal rugby stadium was one day to be named in recognition for his services to the game in those parts.

Town Clubs lost 15–1, but considering the touring team's eventual record of 224 points for (plus two more in the unofficial 20th game against Stellenbosch which the British Isles won 2-0) with only one against, they did quite well. According to contemporary reports, "the play was a treat to watch" with "the leather often in motion". Ben Duff, at full-back for the home team, played particularly well and his brave performance ensured his place in all three tests. Versfeld's try came after a forward rush and this was how this historic moment in the history of South African rugby was described in the *Cape Times*: "Versfeld found an opening, put in a grand sprint and scored a try for Cape Town amidst tremendous cheering. Duff took the kick, but failed to announce the major points".

After the match it was back to another round of dinners and the smoking concerts so popular in those days and it was at one of these functions that Maclagan produced an elaborate gold trophy given to him by Donald Currie, the founder of the Castle Line and later to be knighted, for presentation to the team to give the best performance against them on the tour. Currie, incidentally, made it quite clear at the time that it was to be a floating trophy for annual internal competition and it is therefore not correct to say that Griqualand West who, at the end of the tour, got the cup, had kindly donated it to the South African Rugby Board. The Kimberley rugby authorities simply carried out the donor's instructions. The cup, which was valued at the time at £40, was put on display at Burmester's shop in Adderley Street and caused a great deal of comment.

Two days after the opening match, Western Province did fairly well against the tourists. Led by Duff and with players like Alf Richards, F. H. Guthrie, Barry Heatlie, and H. H. Castens, who had also refereed the Cape Town Clubs game, in the side, they only lost 0-6.

This match took place on a Saturday and on the Monday the British team were in action again at Newlands, beating Cape Colony 14-0. Aston gave an outstanding performance and was praised in the newspapers for "often claiming leather for his side". The youthful Heatlie, destined to become one of the first personalities of South African rugby, did a lot of good work on the defence, but he was criticised for "being slow to get his head in to push". Shades of loose forwards to come in the distant future!

After the first three matches in Cape Town the team left for Kimberley and they soon discovered that the most strenuous part of their tour would be the travelling. The train trip to Kimberley took two nights and a day and even the presence of the irrepressible Barney Barnato, on his way to fortune as a mining magnate, could not relieve the utter boredom and very real hardship the players had to endure. On arrival in Kimberley they were shocked to learn that they would be playing on a sun-baked ground with not a blade of grass on it, "a wretched pavement", one of the players called it. The field was covered with red dust and once a game was in progress, sight of the ball was often lost completely in the miniature sand storms caused by 30 boots scuffling, kicking and pounding. And, as Paul Clauss wrote later: "The hard and gritty ground somewhat damped our ardour; it was no joke tackling or being tackled. The writer can testify to that, as a fall against Griqualand West injured his elbow to such an extent that he had to stand down for seven matches . . ."

Griqualand West, being used to the appalling conditions, gave the tourists a torrid time and only lost by a narrow margin. Maclagan scored a try (1 pt.) and Rotherham a penalty (2 pts.) for the British team to win 3-0. It was on the strength of this performance that Griquas were handed Donald Currie's cup at the end of the tour.

After Kimberley the team trekked to Port Elizabeth where they welcomed the green grass and A. A. Surtees, who had come out from Cambridge on a later boat to join them, with almost equal warmth. The tourists ran rampant on the soft turf and scored seven tries against Eastern Province; Aston, Wotherspoon and Thompson each scored two tries and E. Bromet got the seventh with Rotherham converting all of them to notch a 21-0 victory.

South Africa entered the international rugby arena on the afternoon of Thursday, July 30 when our first representative side met the British team in Port Elizabeth. Our first captain was H. H. Castens.

Very little is known about Herbert Hayton Castens who also holds the unique distinction that after leading South Africa in her first rugby international, he became this country's first touring cricket captain as well when he was placed in charge of the 1894 team to visit England. According to *Wisden's* he was born on November 23, 1864 and died in London on

J. T. ("Chubb") Vigne, who was one of the best of the South Africans in the first test. The tourists had a high regard for him, Richards and Duff.

Above: On Thursday, July 30, 1891, South African players entered the international rugby arena when they met Maclagan's team in the first test in Port Elizabeth. The South Africans were beaten 0–4 and this rare photograph shows a scene from the match.

October 18, 1929. He was, appropriately enough, educated at Rugby and later at Oxford where he gained his full "Blue" by playing for his university in the traditional match against Cambridge in 1886 and 1887. He also represented Middlesex and the South of England. Soon after leaving Oxford he must have emigrated to South Africa where he did much to foster rugby in the Western Province. He played as a forward for Villagers, but also did a great deal of coaching, particularly at Diocesan College.

Castens was described as "a curious, but lovable character" in a letter from a friend to the editor of the *Cape Times* shortly after his brief death notice had appeared. No other details of his personal life could be found, although it is known that he was a good tennis player and "extremely fond of billiards".

He was also a fine wicket-keeper who captained his school in at least one of the annual matches against Marlborough, but the match was something of a personal disaster, Castens being dismissed with the first ball in each innings. He failed to get his cricket "Blue" at Oxford, but did better in South Africa where he scored 165 for Western Province against Eastern Province in the 1890/91 season. Contemporary reports state that he was a good batsman, "handicapped by nervousness".

In 1894 Castens took the first South African cricket team to England and although they won 12 out of the 25 matches including an 11-run victory over the M.C.C. led by the legendary W. G. Grace, the tour was denied first-class ranking and was a financial flop.

The cost of the tour exceeded £3 000 with the gate receipts totalling only about a tenth of that amount and the South Africans were stranded in Ireland at one stage, penniless and unable to get back to London. Philanthropists came to their rescue, but generally the tour was "unhappy" with Castens apparently unable to handle the British newspapermen and not making many friends. His own

The Versfeld brothers who played such a major role in the early history of South African rugby. This photograph, taken by J. E. Middlebrook in Kimberley more than 85 years ago, shows John and Charles standing and Marthinus and Loftus seated in front. Marthinus played in all three tests against the 1891 British team and Charles, known as "Hasie", scored the only try to be notched against the tourists. Loftus Versfeld did much to establish rugby in the Transvaal and the game's headquarters in Pretoria carries his name.

performances were poor and he averaged only 9,19 for 24 completed innings and twice not out.

Although the South Africans lost their first test, Castens did a lot better as a rugby captain than he did subsequently as skipper of the cricket team. He was often prominent with "grand rushes" in a game fought out mainly by the forwards. Ben Duff and "Chubb" Vigne also played well for South Africa and Alf. Richards was described as the best half-back on the field. Generally the British backs were far more sophisticated however and Aston and Whittaker "planted tries" with Rotherham converting one to make the final score 4-0 to Britain. All the points were scored in the first half with the South Africans apparently receiving very good advice from, as one newspaper report hinted, a "well-known backer" while they enjoyed their "lemons and sundry".

After the test the British team had an opportunity to do some hunting and one member of the side had "occasion to give a wonderful exhibition of his speed and dodging powers when pursued by an irate ostrich".

After easy wins at Grahamstown and King William's Town the tour nearly terminated in tragedy. The team had to be taken by tugboat from East London harbour to board the *Melrose* outside the breakwater for the trip to Natal. A strong wind blew the tug across the bows of the steamer, but fortunately it was struck only a glancing blow and the players made it on board the ship without further mishap. Had the tug been struck squarely, they would all probably have been drowned as the sea was rough.

In Pietermaritzburg they encountered the first of two opponents who in the turbulent years to follow, were to gain fame as military leaders. Playing against them for Pietermaritzburg was W. E. C. Tanner who was to command the South African Forces in Flanders in World War I and a week later in Johannesburg, Christiaan Beyers was a member of the Transvaal Country team who lost 22-0. Beyers was to become a general in President Kruger's forces in the Anglo-Boer War less than nine years later. While in Natal, incidentally, several members of the touring team made a pilgrimage to Majuba Hill where the British Army suffered such a devastating defeat against burghers of the Transvaal Republic in 1881.

The team travelled from Natal to the Transvaal in a coach drawn by 10

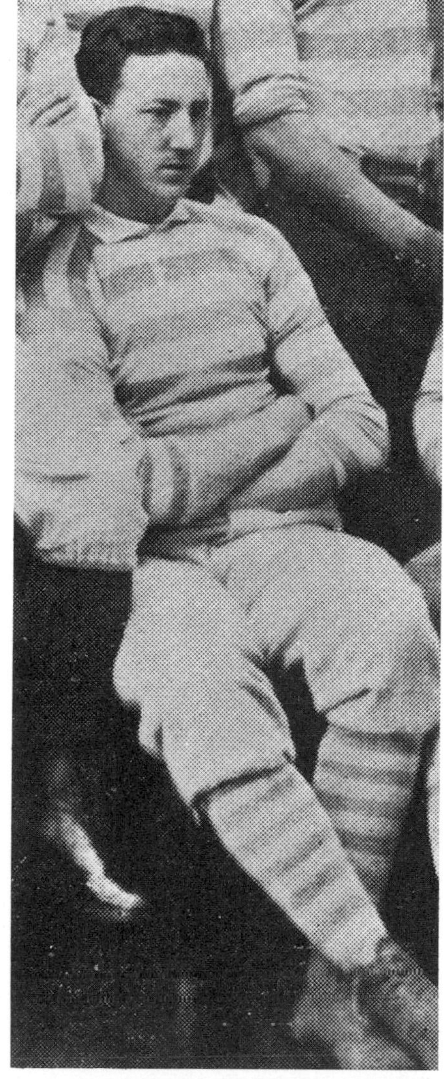

Bill Maclagen as he looked when he played for Edinburgh Academical Football Club in 1878. Thirteen years later he led his team undefeated through South Africa and afterwards predicted a great future for rugby in this country.

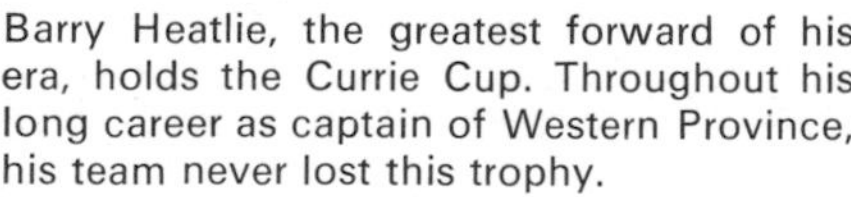

Barry Heatlie, the greatest forward of his era, holds the Currie Cup. Throughout his long career as captain of Western Province, his team never lost this trophy.

P. F. ("Baby") Hancock, massive member of the British touring sides of 1891 and 1896. He was described as "useful in the lineouts but difficult to fit into the scrum . ."

Right: The second test in 1891 took place in Kimberley, on a field described by at least one of the British players as a "wretched pavement". This historic photograph shows a general view of the match. The British team won 3–0.

Below: The third and final test of the tour was played in Cape Town and in this old photograph Alf Richards (extreme right) is preparing to throw in at a lineout. Richards captained the home team who lost 4–0.

R. C. (Bob) Snedden, who succeeded Castens as South African captain and led the local side in the second test. Alf Richards replaced him for the match in Cape Town with the result that South Africa had a different captain for each of her first three tests.

horses and after two successive wins in Johannesburg, played on a ground so bone-dry and in such a dust storm that newspapermen afterwards complained that "it was difficult to discern what was going on", the team paid a brief courtesy visit to President Paul Kruger in Pretoria.

After that it was back into two coaches for the first leg of another body-shattering trip to Kimberley. One coach got through without any problems, but the other lost a wheel and the players had to spend the night on the floor of a hut before help arrived. The team, now thoroughly sick of travelling, managed to beat a Cape Colony side and followed it up with a 3-0 victory over South Africa, this time captained by R. C. (Bob) Snedden, in the second test of the series.

It was customary in those days for the rugby authorities at the venue where the international was to be played, to do their own selection, and it is not surprising that only Duff, Vigne, Richards, Marthinus Versfeld and Japie Louw played in all three tests. The South Africans did quite well in this match and they at least prevented Maclagan's men from crossing their line. The winning points came from a drop from the mark caught by W. G. Mitchell who, according to contemporary reports, "made a fair catch a yard from the '25' flag and dropped a goal, the ball striking the bar and bouncing over".

Barry Heatlie, who played in this match, just failed to tackle Mitchell as he took the ball, and he always remembered how the England full-back calmly assured his captain "It's all right, Bill, I'll drop a goal," before doing just that.

The British team also won the third and final test at Newlands, with H. H. Castens this time as the referee, but again the South Africans showed further signs that they had blossoming talent. The visitors could only win 4-0, after tries by Aston and Maclagan with Rotherham converting one, and for long spells they were forced on the defence by "fast and furious play".

Alf Richards (with Ben Duff certainly the most accomplished all-round player in South Africa at the time) captained the side and, like Castens, he was also later to play cricket for this country. His brother, Dicky, in fact played cricket for South Africa as early as the 1888/1889 season.

Alfred Renfrew Richards was born in Grahamstown in 1868 and died at the age of only 36, but in his short life he made a valuable contribution to rugby and cricket in South Africa. He played in all three tests against Maclagan's men, captained South Africa in the first test ever to be played at Newlands and in the 1895/96 season he earned international cricket colours against Lord Hawke's touring side.

Richards was described as South Africa's "mainstay" in the final test in 1891, "working indefatigably, he spoiled the English chances of success time after time....he had splendid dodgy runs and put in long punts", a reporter wrote after the game.

One more match remained for the tourists, a semi-official fixture against Stellenbosch, before they returned home. Their tour had been a tremendous success. They had scored 89 tries, 50 of them converted, four dropgoals, two goals dropped from a mark, one goal placed from a mark, six penalties and one goal dropped from a penalty for a total of 224 points. Against that formidable total South Africa could only offer the solitary point scored by Charlie (Hasie) Versfeld in the first match of the tour.

Our tally would have looked a little better had it not been for the sheer physical strength of Bill Maclagan. Jimmy Anderson, playing for Transvaal, was already over the line, when Maclagan picked him up and carried him, ball and all, back into the field of play. Something similar happened to Marthinus Daneel, the father of George, the famous Springbok loose-forward of nearly 40 years later, who also crossed for Stellenbosch only to be caught by Maclagan and dispossessed in what was then known as a "maul in goal". The laws of the time stipulated that other players of either side were not allowed to interfere in such a situation, which was considered a man-to-man clash.

The tour gave South African rugby a big boost towards the maturity it was to reach so soon and both Maclagan and his vice-captain Johnny Hammond (who later became such a good friend of South African sport) predicted a glorious future for the game before they departed on the *Garth Castle* from Cape Town on September 9, 1891. A farewell dance given to the team was one of the social highlights of the year. Bill Maclagan's wife, who was in South Africa at the time, attended, resplendent on the arm of her famous husband.

At least one member of the side was to anticipate the major problems touring teams of the future were to encounter in South Africa. "Hard grounds and hospitality", Paul Clauss, who played so brilliantly on the tour mused in an article written some years afterwards. "Too many dinners, dances, smokers? Certainly no modern team would dare to indulge in so many festivities, which often lasted far into the night"

W. E. Maclagan's touring team of 1891. They scored 89 tries with "Hasie" Versfeld the only South African to cross their line.

THE PIONEERS

A taste of victory

The "Thatched Tavern", just off Cape Town's Greenmarket Square, was a gathering place for distinguished citizens back in 1896 and it was there that the members of the South African Rugby Board met to discuss final arrangements for the arrival of the second British touring team.

Mr. W. V. Simkins presided and he was able to announce that Johnny Hammond, vice-captain under Bill Maclagan of the pioneering 1891 side, would be on the *Tartar*, due to dock on Wednesday July 8, with a team which would include players from England and Ireland only.

The ship steamed in too late that night for the passengers to disembark and a large group of enthusiasts and officials too eager to wait, promptly chartered the tug *Enterprise* and sailed out to meet the ocean liner. They boarded the boat and spent the night, enjoying breakfast with the ship's captain, his officers and the team before the whole lot streamed down the gangplank to head a procession all the way to the Royal Hotel where the British players were again to be quartered.

By that time word of mouth had already notified the whole of Cape Town that the men to watch were Tommy Crean, a tall Irish forward who was the fastest player in the side and who on the voyage had won every kind of game that could possibly be played on a ship's deck, and Louis Magee, also Irish and a stocky half-back.

Hammond, by now a veteran who left most of the on-the-field leadership to Crean, immediatcly took the team to Newlands to, as one newspaperman put it, "tune their breathing organs and to get rid of the softness resulting from their confinement on board ship" A large crowd turned up for the practice and they soon saw that, to quote the journalist again, "there were many bellows to mend after every fast burst".

Hammond and "Baby" Hancock, even heavier than in 1891, were the only members of the side who had been here before, but Cuthbert Mullins, a South African studying at Oxford, was obviously also familiar with local conditions. The team was full of interesting players. Walter Carey, the Oxford forward, in later years became the Bishop of Bloemfontein and it was he who coined the Barbarians motto that "Rugby Football is a game for gentlemen in all classes, but never for a bad sportsman in any class". Larry Q. Bulger, the Irish wing, laboured under the odd nick-name of "Fat Cupid" and two of the forwards, Crean and Robert Johnston, were both to be awarded the Victoria Cross, Britain's highest award for bravery in action, during the South African War only a few years after the tour.

Tommy Crean was far and away

John F. Hammond, the vice-captain in Maclagan's pioneering team, led the second touring side to visit South Africa in 1896.

Tommy Crean, a great player and a "lovable Irishman" was the outstanding member of Hammond's team.

the star of the team. Tall and beautifully proportioned, he was described in several reports as "exceedingly handsome" and was officially timed to have done the hundred yards in just over 10 seconds. Reminiscing about the tour many years later, Bishop Carey wrote about him: "He was the most Irish, the most inconsequent, the most gallant, the most lovable personality one could imagine, and he made the centre of the whole tour. Tommy subsequently won the Victoria Cross at Elandslaagte.

"The story told is that when with the First Imperial Light Horse Brigade, whilst attacking the Boer forces, something hit him and bowled him over. Momentarily dazed, he yelled: *'By......I'm kilt entoirely!'* However, he got up and found he was not dead, though badly wounded. But the insult had roused his Irish blood, and with a wild yell he led the bayonet charge and thus received the supreme award for his bravery".

The British players, picturesquely described by the *Cape Times* as "all lengthy specimens of manhood", were taken in landaus to Newlands for the opening match of the tour against Cape Town Clubs, where more than 5 000 spectators had already paid about £600 to see the game.

Barney Barnato, the little Londoner whose spectacular career on the Rand had by then made him a world famous millionaire, was in the crowd with "his face lit up with expectation of witnessing a rattling good mill", according to one newspaper report.

Barnato was not to be disappointed. It was a thrilling game, the touring team winning 14-9 with most of the second half played in gathering dusk. The kickoff was at 4.15 which was a little late for mid-winter on a field with the Table Mountain range towering over it. Both teams scored two tries (worth three points each by then), but J. F. Byrne made the difference with two penalties and a conversion.

The newspapers were ecstatic over Crean's performance. They described at length his "perfection of dribbling, such telling rushes combined with an honest share in the shoulder work and a great ability to keep his feet" but there was general disappointment over the standard of backplay. It was felt that the tourists had good forwards, but that they could teach South Africans nothing new about halfback and threequarter play.

After the match the usual round of social activities occupied the players. They attended a smoking concert which must have been an occasion to remember. A. D. Clinch, the powerful Dublin forward, sang *"Halligan's Aunt"*, which could well have been an "inimitable performance" as someone reported afterwards, and his teammate A. F. Todd weighed in with what was described as "tasteful renditions" of *"Sally in Our Alley"* and *"Lazily, dreamily"*, the big hit songs of the day.

A team composed of players from Cape Town's suburban clubs gave the tourists a stubborn argument before losing 0-8 in a match marked by Barry Heatlie's "ponderous kicks" and H. H. Castens' controversial performance as the referee. Several players were injured and the first signs were there that it was not going to be a tour quite as incident-free as the one of 1891.

The touring team's relaxed attitude to training took its toll when in their third match in five days, they were held to a scoreless draw by a Western Province team in which J. H. (Biddy) Anderson gave an outstanding performance. The game was rough and the crowd once booed Walter Carey for being too robust.

Considering the visitors' activities before the match, it is surprising that they were not beaten. At an official lunch at Groote Schuur, the Prime Minister's residence, Crean's only instruction was that no player should have "more than four tumblers of champagne"! In a return match later in the tour the British team, steering clear this time of champagne for lunch, took full revenge.

The British forwards, realising that their backs were not particularly good, perfected a technique of swinging the scrum after an initial heave as the ball was put in, and this manoeuvre gained them all the possession they required. They kept the ball mainly among the forwards and as they also had a way of pulling their opponents into their ranks and virtually holding them captive as the scrum swung, or "screwed", their tactics proved to be very effective.

Once they left Cape Town the long journeys by train and coach and the "gravel tracks" they had to play on in up-country centres like Kimberley and Johannesburg, caused injuries and many problems. The trip between

Left: Barry Heatlie, a fine forward and a magnificent leader. He captained the first South African team ever to win a test match.

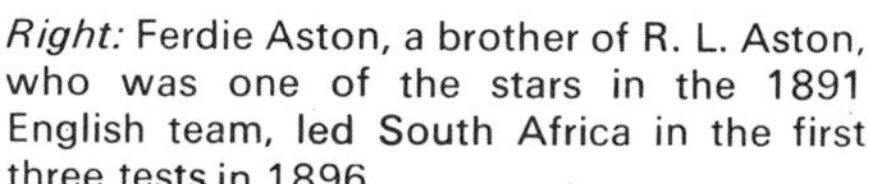

Right: Ferdie Aston, a brother of R. L. Aston, who was one of the stars in the 1891 English team, led South Africa in the first three tests in 1896.

Grahamstown and King William's Town took two days by Cape cart with the players doing more pushing than riding due to the poor roads. They had to sleep five in a bed at the only hotel at the halfway stage and it was reported that all the travellers following the route immediately after them had to go hungry as the tourists had eaten all the available food!

It was not long after the Jameson Raid and an atmosphere of uneasiness hung over Johannesburg and Pretoria. The team did attend a session of the Volksraad and saw Paul Kruger and they were also allowed to visit Sampson and Davis, two of the jailed "Reformers" in prison.

In Queenstown their arrival broke a drought that had threatened to ruin the farming community, but there were staunch rugby fans who said that the rain could have stayed away another day without causing much more damage.

Wherever they went the British team discovered that the opposition had become strong and confident. In Cape Town they had encountered players like Tommy Hepburn, J. H. Anderson, Percy Jones, "Patats" Cloete, "Fairy" Heatlie. In Kimberley they met the likes of T. A. Samuels and A. W. (Bertie) Powell. In the Transvaal Ferdie Aston, a brother of the England centre who was so brilliant on the 1891 tour, George St. Leger Devenish and Alf Larard impressed them deeply. The red-haired Larard, a dour and relentless competitor, they learnt to respect more than anybody else in South Africa and the bearded "Patats" Cloete of Villagers and Western Province was another opponent they feared.

Before their match against Transvaal, the visitors were warned that the Pirates wing, Jack Orr, was a murderous tackler and had been primed to put a few of them in hospital. Whether this rumour was true could never be proved because Orr was so badly injured in the first couple of minutes of the match that he had to be carried off.

Forward power enabled the British team to beat South Africa 8-0 in the first international match in Port Elizabeth. Crean and his pack dominated the first half in particular and only the superb defensive work of the halves F. R. Myburgh and F. H. Guthrie, saved South Africa on several occasions. Aston, who captained the local team, Anderson and Jones counter-attacked well from the few opportunities to come their way, but the critics roasted the South African forwards and Barry Heatlie, soon to be a national hero, was called "worse than useless" by one irate scribe.

The second test in Johannesburg on August 22 brought South Africa's rugby to another milestone when, for the first time, we managed to score points in an international match.

South Africa lost the match 8-17, but the score was not a fair reflection of the play. The British forwards did not have their usual complete control over affairs and only Hancock and Crean really outshone their opponents. It was only J. F. Byrne's place-kicking that gave the tourists their winning edge.

Ferdie Aston was the South African captain for the match and there had to be a last-minute change when wing F. Maxwell, of Transvaal, had to withdraw because of injury. It was decided to replace him with T. A. (Theo) Samuels. the Griqualand West

Above: George St. Leger Devenish, one of the best players in South Africa in 1896 and later to serve the game for many years as a national selector.

Left: T. A. (Theo) Samuels, of Griqualand West, scored South Africa's first two test tries. And he was only a last-minute replacement!

fullback. Such is fate; Maxwell today is forgotten while Samuels will always have a special place in South African sports history.

The British team led 5-0 at half-time after Crean had sent Todd over for Byrne to convert and it was the irrepressible Crean again who made it 10-0 with a converted try shortly after the resumption. Hancock then used his great strength and weight to bullock his way through for an unconverted try, but with the score 13-0, the South Africans suddenly became inspired.

Toski Smith managed to kick the ball forward and Charles Devenish followed up quickly to snap it up and pass to Aston. The South African captain ran hard for the line before passing to Forbes who whipped the ball to Samuels, the Kimberley man taking it while going at a cracking pace. This is how the *Cape Times* correspondent described what happened after that:

"Samuels, flashing up, received the pass and swerving through the threequarters, raced over grandly; tumultuous cheering, hats and sticks flying, greeting this great success of the celebrated fullback."

David (Davie) Cope, the Transvaal fullback destined to die only two years later in a tragic train crash at Mostert's Hoek, near Matjiesfontein, missed the conversion, but he was to get another chance at aiming for the posts not long afterwards.

It was certainly a great day for Samuels. The first man to score points for South Africa he was also to get the second try. This, according to a contemporary report was how it came:

"Another brilliant passing movement initiated by George St. Leger Devenish and participated in by Aston, was ended by the latter, after drawing his opponents' threequarters, passing out to Samuels who received the leather at top speed and easily got over for his second try, the applause being deafening and renewed when Cope this time converted".

And so Theo Samuels got the first two tries ever to be scored by South Africa and David Cope became the first player to succeed with a kick.

With the score suddenly 13-8 South Africa seemed to have a chance to make more history, but Charles Devenish had to be helped off with a knee injury and the local forwards faded. With a minute to go, Mackie made it 17-8 with a marvellous dropgoal.

A pigeon shooting competition was held in Kimberley before the third international and Ireland's J. T. Magee took the honours—and the stakes—by not missing a single shot. The tourists would more than likely have preferred to settle the test with shotguns rather than on the rock-hard Kimberley field, "that wretched pavement" they so detested. Some of them by then had acquired a knack to make their tackles in such a way that they were likely to fall on top of their opponents, but it was an "inexact science" at best and most of them nursed festering wounds long after they had said a gleeful farewell to Kimberley's dusty patch of earth "with nary a blade of grass", as a player later poetically referred to it.

The test was played at a blistering pace with South Africa again making history by for the first time holding the lead at half-time in an international. This time it was Percy Twentyman Jones, the Western Province centre and years later to become Judge President of the Cape, who

Right: When Davie Cope converted Samuels' second try in the second test in Johannesburg in 1896, he became the first South African to succeed with a kick in an international match.

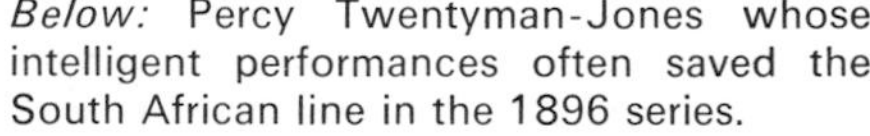

Below: Percy Twentyman-Jones whose intelligent performances often saved the South African line in the 1896 series.

sniped through for a try after A. M. Beswick and W. Cotty had driven the breach. Jones also took the conversion kick, but he made an awful hash of it.

After the resumption Britain had slightly the better of the battle and Byrne who played brilliantly converted a try by Mackie and then snapped over a swift drop in the final seconds of the match to give his team a 9-3 victory.

Percy Jones spent some time in Grahamstown after his feat in becoming only the second South African to score a test try, and he was persuaded to play for the town club. According to the press reports at the time he scored 16 points out of 19 (three tries and a dropgoal) in his first match in the Eastern Cape and then stayed on for one more game to help Albany to win the local league competition before returning to Cape Town again to turn out for Old Diocesans. Imagine the scramble for "guest Springboks" if the relaxed attitude of 80 years ago still existed!

Barry Heatlie Heatlie (that is correct, no hyphen!) was appointed to captain South Africa in the fourth and final test to be played at Newlands on September 5 and the gods had decreed that this broad-shouldered product of Diocesan College should be the first man to lead South Africa to an international victory.

Heatlie was born at Glen Heatlie, in the district of Worcester, on April 25, 1872, one of nine brothers who were all good athletes and sportsmen. And yet he did not play rugby at Diocesan College until he was 17 years old. He captained Bishops for four seasons and was still at the College when he was selected for Western Province at the age of 18, and for South Africa while in his 20th year. In 1894 when he first captained Western Province, Heatlie was still at Bishops and this is a record that will surely stand for ever. Altogether he represented Western Province in 41 matches and he was never on the losing side in 26 Currie Cup matches. After leaving college, he was briefly associated with Gardens before joining Villagers until 1905 when he ran into personal troubles and departed for the Argentine.

In South America, Heatlie joined a huge sugar company of which he was general manager by the time of his retirement in 1924. He had much to do with the establishment of rugby around Buenos Aires and was an active player until he broke three ribs at the age of 49. Heatlie returned to South Africa in 1925 and never lost his love for the game that made him famous. In April 1951 Heatlie was on his way to an Old Diocesan dinner when he was struck down by a car. He never fully recovered from his injuries and died on August 19 of the same year. He is buried in the Plumstead cemetery.

Known as "Ox" and "Fairy" to his contemporaries, Heatlie was a big, robust forward and an intelligent, inspiring leader. He suffered very little nonsense from his opponents and it is on record how that impeccable gentleman Paul Roos, playing with Heatlie, on one occasion jerked his head out of a scrum after an altercation, to reprimand his teammate: "Heatlie, you mean fellow!", Roos said, in sorrow rather than anger.

When Heatlie was given the captaincy of the South Africans for the final test in 1896, he decided to supply his team with jerseys from the Old Diocesan Club. It was a happy coincidence that the jerseys were green and that South Africa therefore won her first international wearing what was to become the national colours. (The full story of the evolution of the South African rugby uniform will be told in a later chapter.)

Again the South African team had to make a last-minute change in their side. J. J. Wessels was injured and Herman van Broekhuizen replaced him.

There was tremendous interest in the match with many women also attending. This is how a reporter described the scene at Newlands: "The bright costumes of the ladies and some remarkably fine specimens of the milliner's art, gave quite a brilliant appearance to that part of the football ground from which the fair sex, who were enthusiastic witnesses of the game, watched the final struggle of the tour".

There was a strong wind blowing across the field, favouring neither team, when Heatlie kicked off with the sun in his face. From the first blast of referee Alf Richards' whistle it was obvious that the South African forwards were no longer to be trifled with. Powerful dribbling rushes kept Britain on the defence and Richards was making them very unhappy by watching their scrummaging tactics closely.

Midway through the first half Larard, Aston, Anderson and Hepburn combined beautifully in a sweeping movement that took the South Africans deep into British territory. Byrne took the ball from the lineout, but was immediately brought down and Anderson took the ball from his hands and ran clear with only fullback Meares to beat. Like the intelligent player he was, Anderson allowed Meares to collar him before he passed to Larard who had an open field to score under the posts. Hepburn converted and South Africa led 5-0. The British team objected violently that it was illegal for Anderson to have taken the ball from Byrne in the manner which he did, but Alf Richards had made up his mind and the try was allowed.

Both teams attacked strongly in the second half and the posts on both ends of the field were peppered with abortive dropgoals and penalties. The crowd became more and more excited as the possibility of a South African victory loomed and the spectators were beside themselves with joy when the whistle went and South Africa had won an international match for the first time.

Controversy over Anderson's action which led to Larard's try unfortunately soured the taste of victory. Admitting that the British team had set the precedent with their "violent dispossessing", the *Cape Times* rugby critic launched a bitter tirade against Biddy Anderson: "It was a pity that the match should have been decided by what was after all a piece of sharp practice. A player less inclined than Anderson to take every advantage he can get whether lawful or unlawful, would have left Byrne in charge of the ball and allowed a scrum to be formed over the place where he was held".

The writer added however that the South Africans had deserved to win, anyway. "It was not a case of a well-whipped team snatching a lucky victory," he wrote. "It was apparent from the first ten minutes that the Englishmen had met their match".

Alf Richards said afterwards that the British appeal only came after Anderson was already on his way and that he could not have upheld it at that late stage.

The controversy did not bother the wildly excited supporters who gathered in large numbers outside the dressing rooms, shouting for their heroes. When Heatlie and his team finally appeared he, Percy Jones, Alf Larard and Theo Samuels were carried around the field in triumph.

The newspaper reporter who described the scene for the *Cape Times* readers then went on to add: "It was some time before the exhausted players could make their way to the station".

From that it would appear as if

Right: Alf Larard, who scored the winning try in South Africa's first test triumph.

Below left: J. H. ("Biddy") Anderson, central figure in a controversial incident in the test at Newlands in 1896.

Below right: Tommy Hepburn, one of the heroes in a great victory. He converted Larard's try and thus helped to give Heatlie's team a 5–0 victory.

Barry Heatlie and his 14 heroes had to rely on public transport to get home after their historic triumph.

I prefer to believe that it was a special train, meant for them alone. They certainly deserved nothing less.

Teachers taught

Japie Krige, one of the eight sons of a Dutch Reformed Church minister, was the finest centre three-quarter of his era and certainly the first South African rugby player to capture the national imagination.

Extremely quick off the mark, Krige was also extraordinarily agile and he could weave and dodge his way through the toughest defence. At the height of his powers, he was supremely individualistic and very difficult to combine with, but the astute A. F. Markötter, his coach at Stellenbosch, solved this problem by building the rest of the backline around the little genius, instead of attempting to curb him into conformity.

Small and blond with the innocent face of a boy not yet in his teens, Krige was an easy man to underestimate. He was quiet and somewhat introverted but on the field of play he was an autocrat who refused to suffer fools gladly, if at all. Even the feared Markötter could not intimidate him and on the few occasions that the irascible Mr. Mark gave him a tongue lashing, Japie sulkily withdrew from the practice until the coach would show in some way or other that he was sorry about his outburst.

Markötter, who never did play for South Africa because of a knee injury sustained in a cricket match, discovered and forged too many Springboks during his long career for anyone to deny claims that he was possibly the greatest rugby authority of his time, nevertheless had a soft spot for the temperamental "Witkoppie", as he called him. During Krige's early years at Stellenbosch it irked Markötter that he could not find a wing fast enough to keep up with the centre whenever he slipped through on one of his bewildering breaks.

He tried out a variety of partners for Krige, but no-one could quite manage to be on the spot when needed. Players brilliant in their own rights had to suffer the humiliation of having to take up their positions in front of Krige and even then they lacked the pace to be there for the final pass after he had ripped the defence apart.

Like Richard III offering his kingdom for a horse, Mr. Mark would wander around the rugby fields of Stellenbosch looking for a suitable partner for his little genius. One afternoon he was again bemoaning his fate when Dietlof Mare, himself later to become a member of the 1906 touring team to Britain happened to be within earshot.

"All I need is someone with real speed and courage. For the rest he can be the biggest fool in the world!", Mr. Mark was grumbling in his usual gruff manner.

Mare then suddenly remembered his room-mate, an athlete who only the previous year had beaten Japie Krige at a track meeting. Considering that Krige once came a close second to Reggie Walker, later to win an Olympic Gold Medal over 100 yards, this could not have been a mean feat.

"Mark, I think I've got the answer for you," Mare chipped in. "His name is Bob Loubser."

Loubser, short and stocky, was summoned to the ground immediately and from the moment he saw him Markötter knew that his search was over. Not only was Loubser incredibly fast, but he was a "born footballer", the highest accolade Markötter ever cared to bestow on anyone.

He prepared Loubser himself for his role as Krige's shadow and the two students developed quickly into a superb centre-wing combination, soon to be the best in the world.

At last Krige had someone he could really rely on. "Come, Bob!", he would command as he set off on a dodging, ducking path through the defence knowing that Loubser would be there when needed. Between them they scored dozens of brilliant tries and Loubser rapidly developed to the stage where he was every bit as dangerous on the attack as his quicksilver partner.

Krige remained a law unto himself throughout his career. Although he did become less of an individualist as he grew older he never in his life joined the common herd, so to speak. On rugby tours he was content to spend his time reading the Wild West novels so popular in those days

Japie Krige

Paul Roos. Painting by Neville Lewis.

A. F. Markotter. Painting by Neville Lewis.

and he seldom bothered to share in the shenanigans which are so much part of a rugby player's life.

Anecdotes abound to illustrate his magnificence during a career that spanned the decade 1896-1906. Some of the stories are no doubt apochryphal, but there is more than enough in the official records to make it easy to understand why the late Japie Krige has not been forgotten in spite of the fact that more than 70 years have passed since he packed away his boots.

He was only 17 when he gained his provincial colours and it is a remarkable fact that he never played in a losing match for Western Province. More often than not it was only Japie's genius that stood between his team and defeat. The Currie Cup final against Transvaal in 1906, for instance.

In the last few minutes of the match with no score on the board, the Transvaal fullback failed with a long touchkick. Krige caught the ball well into his own half and with the usual cry of "Come, Bob!" he started running. But this time, instead of going straight, he cut sharply infield, away from his wing.

He drew the Transvaal defence with him and then stopped suddenly in his tracks and streaked back towards the touchline—and the waiting Loubser. The Transvaal defenders had now been stretched to near-breaking point and not many remained in the path of the two flying Maties. With an exchange of beautifully-timed passes they progressed to within sight of the tryline. A long pass infield then gave the Western Province captain John Pritchard the decisive try.

Opponents eventually did not really know who to watch the more closely, Japie or Bob. In a club match at Newlands in 1902, Villagers decided that Loubser was really the more dangerous of the two and they concentrated all their efforts on the wing. Krige with that sixth sense unique to all great sports performers, realised this instantly and he took full advantage to score five tries of his own.

Both were obvious choices for the South African teams against Mark Morrison's touring team from Britain in 1903 and they were duly invited to play in the first test in Johannesburg. Krige accepted, but Loubser, then in his 20th year, declined on the advice of his future father-in-law.

Krige was far from happy with his first taste of international rugby. The South African half-backs, "Uncle" Dobbin and Jack Powell, were both from Griqualand West and used to a pattern that did not allow much scope for their threequarters.

One cannot dismiss Dobbin with undue haste as he was soon to prove himself to be one of the best, if not the best, halfbacks in the world.

Frederick James Dobbin, nicknamed "Uncle" for no reason that anyone ever bothered to record, was born in Bethulie in 1879, but he grew up in Kimberley.

He was a short, immensely powerful player in an era when half-backs still alternated between what we now know as the specialised positions of scrum- and flyhalf. He formed a splendid partnership with his provincial teammate Jackie Powell and between them they evolved an economical, cautious, style which was described by a contemporary critic as "cramping threequarter play".

On the 1906 tour of the United Kingdom, Dobbin had as his fellow-link the tall, well-built Dirk Cloete

A rare photograph of Bob Loubser in action. Here he is on his way to scoring for the University of Stellenbosch in a club match against Hamiltons at Newlands.

Johannes A. (Bob) Loubser, a brilliant wing made even more dangerous by his uncanny ability to dovetail with the genius of Japie Krige.

Jackson, a product of Diocesan College in Cape Town, and under his good influence he learnt to use his backs more freely. The result of this change of attitude was that Dobbin quickly earned the reputation of being the best halfback in the world. Jackson, known as "Mary" and also for no reason that I could discover, seemed to generally adopt what we now know as the flyhalf role more often than Dobbin, who preferred to work closer to his forwards. Both are described in newspaper reports of the time as "men of quiet and unassuming demeanors".

The Dobbin of the first test against Morrison's British tourists in Johannesburg in 1903, the third team from the U.K. to tour South Africa, was too much of an individualist for Japie Krige's liking however. The little centre from Stellenbosch was given no attacking opportunities to speak of and the 10-all draw rather flattered South Africa, who faded badly in the second half. The game was distinguished by a superb try by R. T. Skrimshire, a centre from Newport, Wales, who did almost exactly what Hansie Brewis was to do for the

Dr. Arthur Frew, an international player from Scotland, who captained South Africa in the first test against Mark Morrison's 1903 team from Britain.

Springboks against the All Blacks 46 years later. He received a pass, feinted to drop a goal and noticing the South Africans hesitate, he suddenly put on a burst of electrifying speed to score.

The highlight for South Africa came from Jimmy Sinclair, a Transvaal forward who incidentally was the first South African ever to score a century in a match against a touring cricket team (Lord Hawke's 1899 tourists) and who eventually totalled more than 1 000 runs and took 63 wickets in 25 tests. The tall Sinclair is still recognised as one of the greatest hitters the game of cricket has known and in his one and only rugby test he also certainly made his mark when he dribbled the ball for a full 40 yards through a maze of defenders. For the record, South Africa's tries were scored by Dobbin and Frew.

Krige, never one to allow himself to be trifled with, bluntly refused to play in the second test at Kimberley because, as he explained it to friends, "Powell and Dobbin won't let me see the ball". The veteran Springbok forward Barry Heatlie also had to withdraw so as to be in Cape Town for the birth of his second son. Another "casualty" was the Springbok captain Dr. Arthur Frew, a former Scottish international who handed over the leadership to Jackie Powell. The result of the test was another draw and this time neither side could notch a point.

The third international match, at Newlands on September 12, 1903, stands out as one of the real mileposts in the history of South African rugby. Barry Heatlie, a rugby giant if ever there was one, was brought back to captain the side and the Western Province Rugby Union who as the host province had the responsibility of nominating the players, promptly appointed him, Percy Jones and Biddy Anderson as the selectors. All three were from the same school, Bishops, and members of the same club, Villagers, which was a remarkable vote of confidence in the integrity of the three individuals concerned.

They promptly replaced Dobbin and Powell with Tommy Hobson, from the Hamiltons club, and Hugh Ferris, a former Ireland international

Jackie Powell, a strong-willed halfback from Kimberley who took over the leadership from Frew for the second test.

Mark Morrison, captain of the 1903 British touring team in South Africa.

Paul Roos and A. F. Markotter flanked by the legendary "Thin Red Line". *From left to right:* Japie Krige, Bob Loubser, Roos, Markotter, H. A. (Boy) de Villiers and Anton Stegmann.

then playing for Transvaal, thereby making sure that Japie Krige would be happy. Bob Loubser and Paddy Carolin joined Krige at centre. The first choice as Japie's partner was actually Sid Ashley who had done well in the second test, but he unfortunately injured himself when he got off a tram a few days before the match and his international career came to an abrupt halt.

But, most important of all from a historical point of view, was the fact this game saw the adoption of green as the South African rugby colours. As in 1896 when he captained his country in her first-ever international rugby victory, Heatlie again opted for the Diocesan Old Boys jerseys. This club had by then ceased to exist, but the outfitters had some stocks left and Heatlie therefore presented his team with these green jerseys with white collars, and black shorts. There were no socks available, but he had no difficulty in obtaining the consent of the Villagers Club for the South African team to wear their scarlet stockings. Resplendent in these outfits, Heatlie's team played brilliant rugby in atrocious conditions to win the test 8-0 and in the process giving South Africa an international "rubber" for the first time.

Probably influenced by the fact that Heatlie's Bishops colours had been worn in South Africa's two biggest triumphs up till then, the South African Rugby Board, according to their minutes dated September 12, 1906 settled on them as the official national colours.

When Paul Roos led the first-ever Springboks to Britain shortly afterwards his players wore green jerseys with white collars, a badge showing a jumping Springbok on the left breast, black shorts and dark blue stockings with two white stripes around the calf. Each player also received a green cap with gold trimmings and a Springbok badge.

This was to be the Springbok "uniform" until 1937 when the shorts became white, the collar the colour of old gold and the socks green. Against the Lions in 1938, the South Africans briefly reverted to black shorts, but finally permanently settled for white in 1949.

Jimmy Sinclair is best remembered as a big-hitting international batsman but he also played well in his only test appearance as a South African rugby forward.

R. T. Skrimshire, who scored a scintillating try for Britain against South Africa in the first test in 1903.

F. J, ("Uncle") Dobbin, who made his debut in 1903 and went on to become one of the best players of all time.

THE PIONEERS

The first Springboks

Standing on the touchline next to his bowler hatted father, 10-year-old Paul Roos saw W. E. Maclagen's rugby missionaries beat Stellenbosch in the final match of their 1891 tour.

Up till then young Paul's sporting activities had been confined to watching his father on the cricket field, wearing the inevitable bowler and, as he would so fondly recall in later years, often dropping both hat and ball when going for a catch.

Now a new world opened for him; the world of rugby football. He was to excel as a player and later as an administrator and would become a very special source of inspiration to more than one generation of young South Africans destined to make their mark in all spheres of life; not just on the field of play.

But above all, to Paul Roos belongs the unique distinction of having led the first South African rugby team on a tour overseas and it was he who told reporters that his players should be called "De Springbokken", a happy choice soon to be shortened to "Springbokke" or "Springboks". Paul Roos, therefore, was the spiritual father of all those who were to represent South Africa on the rugby field for the past 70 years, as he will be of all those who will earn that honour for all time to come. Destiny could not have given us a more solid foundation on which to build a tradition.

He was a forward, big and strong enough for his era, but rather small and light by today's standards. He had superb qualities of leadership however and his impeccable character and innate charm earned him the respect and affection of his players as well as his opponents.

To the end of his days he maintained that a man's motto should be "Let the stumbling blocks be your stepping stones" and in his own life he added to that utter devotion to duty and principles.

In those days all Currie Cup matches took place at a centralised tournament and in 1904 this was due to be played in East London. Roos felt that he could not spare so much time from his duties as a schoolmaster and declined the invitation to join the Western Province team.

When "Fairy" Heatlie, captaining the Western Province team, realised the strength of the Griqualand West and Transvaal teams he urgently wired Jan Hofmeyr, the famous statesman and newspaper editor of the Cape Colony, to persuade Roos to change his mind. Hofmeyr, the well-loved "Onze Jan". did not feel up to the task and he passed the buck to the Stellenbosch University authorities. A Professor Malherbe called Roos into his study, showed him the telegram and asked him if he would reconsider.

"I cannot go because I have my duties here," Roos informed him staunchly.

"It appears to me that your team also require you and that is also a duty," the professor sparred back.

Check-mated and no doubt wanting to play anyway, Roos pointed out that his going to East London would entail travelling on no less than two Sundays and would therefore not really be in line with his strong religious beliefs.

"We can serve God on the train, too," the professor countered and Roos, knowing when he was beaten, ran off to pack his bags. There is a happy ending to the story, Roos played a major role in beating both Griquas and Transvaal and Western Province brought home the Currie Cup.

His reluctance to travel on a Sunday was genuine and he avoided it whenever he could. When he was a schoolmaster in Pietersburg for a brief period, he cycled 70 miles to Pretoria every Saturday to play rugby. Immediately after the game he would start the arduous journey homewards to make sure that he would not desecrate the Sabbath for the sake of personal enjoyment.

As a teacher he was a strict disciplinarian who never spared the rod, but those who knew him remember him for his fierce interest in the welfare, material and spiritual, present and future, of each and every one of his pupils. It is a fact that he once on hearing that one of his former pupils preferred the bright lights to his studies at Stellenbosch, marched into Wilgenhof hostel with his cane and gave the erring student four of the best.

He was appallingly absent-minded, invariably late for everything and to have been a passenger in a car driven by him was according to one who did have the doubtful pleasure, "tantamount to a peep into the Valley of Death"! It was said that he held all records for speeding between Stellenbosch and surrounding towns. He never hesitated to lend his car to a student, but always with this advice: "Now look, my boy, you have just as much a right to be on the road as any other driver, but just be careful of trains!"

He was constitutionally unable to arrive for any appointment on time and this used to drive his teammates to distraction. People and their problems mattered far more to him than did clocks or watches. Once when captain of Stellenbosch, his team had already gathered at the station for the trip to Cape Town where they were to play at Newlands and still there was no sign of Polla, as he was usually called. Finally it was time for the train to depart, but fortunately the station master was a keen rugby fan and he gave instructions to the machinist to wait. Another 15 minutes ticked by with everybody growing more frantic with every passing second. Just when it looked as if even the co-operative station master had run out of patience, Roos came cycling up at a furious pace. Hurling his bike against the waitingroom wall, he rushed into the compartment to join his team, sagged back into the seat and panted "Wow! Just made it in time, eh!"

Near the end of his life Roos entered the political arena, but his one and only election campaign was conducted with so much sincerity, humanity and humour, that his popularity never suffered and this during a period in our history when bitterness was rife and the political divisions sharp.

As a backbencher in Parliament, he was a most impressive sight; big and powerful in his conservative suit with a stiff and formal wing collar, his hair thick and grey and his drooping soup-strainer moustache a bristling symbol of his individuality. At first the other Members delighted in teasing the old Springbok and headmaster, but he had too much natural dignity and commonsense to rise to the obvious bait and soon he was listened to in silence.

It is rather indicative of the man's character that his last speech in Parliament dealt with helping the underprivileged. Political correspondents who knew him well wrote at the time that the speech was not

Preceding pages: The first Springboks in action. Anton Stegmann cuts through the Glamorgan defence at Cardiff Arms Park in 1906 and he has Boy de Villiers in support on his left. Coming up at the back is Paul Roos and the South Africans on his inside are, from left to right, Klondyke Raaff, Cocky Brooks and "Uncle" Dobbin.

delivered in his usual flambouyant style, that the big, dark eyes so startling under the bushy eyebrows were, as usual, in eloquent support of his words but that his emphasising gesticulations were conspicuously missing. Only a few hours after completing his appeal for better housing for the poor, Paul Roos was dead.

This then was the man chosen in 1906 to lead the first South African rugby team to go overseas — to the United Kingdom, the birthplace of the game. Roos did not take part in the Currie Cup tournament that year and since these matches doubled as trials, he never did expect to make the side. National selectors J. H. Crosby, C. V. Becker, J. D. Heddon, A. Solomon, C. J. van Renen and C. Waymouth included him in the team nevertheless although they did not appoint him as the captain. This was a choice they left to the team. In other words, Roos became captain because the team voted for him and H. W. (Paddy) Carolin was honoured with the vice-captaincy in the same democratic manner.

John Cecil Carden, a Scot by birth, but a South African since the age of 17, was appointed as team manager and there is no doubt that "Daddy" (as he became known) made a very solid contribution to the success of the tour.

Carden was a good sprinter who also once held the high jump championship of the Cape Colony and as a rugby player he represented Eastern Province. His 75-yard-run against Transvaal in a Currie Cup match in 1899 must count among the great individual feats in the history of the competition. In a subsequent match against Griqualand West an extra back was played just to keep an eye on the dangerous Carden and there is evidence that this ploy eventually led to the four three-quarter system in South Africa.

Roos faced a colourful collection of characters when he addressed them after his election as captain in the now demolished Grand Hotel in Cape Town on the eve of departure on the *S.S. Gascon.*

"As a teacher I am within the law if I cane my lads" rumbled Polla in his deep voice, "but the law will not allow me to cane you. Therefore I can only lead willing men. We are not English-speaking or Afrikaans-speaking, but a band of happy South Africans." Surely these sentiments carry as much weight today as they did 71 years ago.

Harold W. (Paddy) Carolin, his vice-captain, was a magnificent all-round sportsman who won the Jameson Cup as Victor Ludorum for four years running while at Cape Town's Diocesan College. He also captained his school in cricket as well as rugby and he was often on the fringe of selection to the Springbok cricket teams of his time. From all accounts he was a good bowler and an attacking left-hand batsman. After leaving school he joined Villagers, a club he captained at the time of his selection for the touring party, and later in his career he and another great Springbok of a slightly later era, Fred Luyt, helped to establish Moorreesburg as a rugby force in the Boland.

Carolin was selected as a half-back and here some explanation is called for. In those early days flyhalf and scrumhalf positions were interchangeable and covered by the over-all definition of half-back. As with the forward positions it was very much a matter of who got there first when it came to fulfilling the various functions.

It is obvious from all sources that the 1906 South African team had extremely talented half-backs. Apart from Carolin, there were also Frederick James (Uncle) Dobbin, whom many overseas critics afterwards regarded as the best player in this position in the world, and the almost equally adept Dirk Cloete Jackson, known to all as "Mary".

The team was probably even better endowed with threequarters which included the legendary "Thin Red Line" from Stellenbosch — Johannes Alexander (Bob) Loubser, Jacob Daniel (Japie) Krige, Henry Alexander (Boy) de Villiers and Antonie Christopher Stegmann.

Unfortunately this combination, so devastating for Stellenbosch and Western Province in club and provincial rugby, had only one opportunity of playing together in an international match. Fate decreed this to be the disastrous test against Scotland, where the elements conspired to make slick threequarter attacks impossible.

Krige, outplayed the legendary Welshman Gwyn Nicholls, on the one and only occasion they were in opposition, and then and there eliminated all lingering doubts that he was indeed the best centre of his time. Both Krige and Nicholls, by the way, were past their best when they met.

Loubser, with 24 brilliant tries in 21 tour games (three in the four official tests) also confirmed his greatness while Anton Stegmann with 18 tries in only 16 matches, showed that he was not far behind his more illustrious teammates. Boy de Villiers, later to earn the nickname "Bekkies" as an auctioneer and the University of Cape Town rugby coach, was the perfect centre partner for the mercurial Krige; intelligently dovetailing with genius requires another and perhaps even more special kind of brilliance.

Paul Roos, captain of the first South African team to undertake an overseas tour. He told reporters to call his men "Springbokken".

Bob Loubser, who like several of the members of the 1906 Springbok team to Britain, shaved off his moustache during the boat trip.

Japie Krige, already past his best, but still better than anyone Britain had to offer in the winter of 1906.

Dietlof Mare, a versatile member of Roos' team who also wrote the first book on rugby in Afrikaans.

Krige and Loubser must have enjoyed almost unbelievable popularity in Cape Town when at the peak of their careers. The Cape's Malay population who so quickly took the game to their hearts and became knowledgeable if always emotional supporters, really loved them. I once had the opportunity of listening to an old gramophone record on which someone called W. Versfeld, who could have been a member of the famous rugby family, poked gentle fun at a Malay fan's turbulent afternoon watching "Bob and Sjapie" playing at Newlands.

It ends in a crescendo of excitement and an altercation with a fellow spectator who obviously backed the other team:

"*Loep, Bob, loep!*," the Matie supporter shouted in his inimitable Cape Afrikaans. "*Pass vir Sjapie! Moenie kick nie, Sjapie, moenie kick nie! Hardloep Sjapie, hardloep lat 'it bars, Sjapie! Toe nou! Toe nou! TOE NOUUU!*"

Delirious with happiness over his hero's try, he then turns to his complaining fellow spectator and with lofty indignation puts him in his place:

"*Ek jou ga-kick? Jy sta' dan agter my. Ek jou gabyt? Moenie laf wees nie. Sir, I am not hungry and even if I had been, I am not a cannibal!*"

I am afraid it defies translation and must remain an in-joke for South Africans alone!

Dietlof Siegfriedt Maré was another often forgotten personality in that 1906 team. Selected as a half-back, he played in nine matches as a forward and only three times behind the scrum! In the end-of-tour match against France he scored 22 points on his own which, had this been an official test, would still have been a South African record, shared since 1975 by Gerald Bosch. Maré is also the first Afrikaans-speaking South African to write a book on rugby. His "*Hints on Rugby Football*" was published more than 70 years ago.

And then, of course, there was Arthur Frederick W. Marsberg, born in the tiny and bitterly cold village of Sterkstroom in 1883 and destined to become one of the first in a long line of great players to fill the fullback position for South Africa.

Tall and angular in build, Marsberg was a natural athlete who was playing in grown-up company in Kimberley by the time he was 15 years old. He then spent a short time in Johannesburg with a theatrical company, but unfortunately it cannot be determined in what sort of capacity. Looking at his lean and hungry face on the yellowing photographs, it is possible that he could have been a fine Cassius or perhaps even a Hamlet.

On his return to Kimberley Marsberg played himself into the 1906 touring team as a wing and full back understudy for Arthur Burmeister. On the tour Burmeister broke a rib and Marsberg took over. With his fearless defence and speed on the counter-attack he promptly established himself as the best fullback in the world.

Altogether 10 members of the 1906 contingent were Maties and of them only Dietlof Maré (then playing for Transvaal) was not a current member of the club. The other Maties in the side were Roos, Daniel (Koei) Brink, Henry Daneel, Pietie le Roux and Stevie Joubert, who at the time was studying in Holland and joined the team in England. Joubert was originally selected but could not accept because of his studies. Ironically enough, Burmeister was the man chosen to replace him. When Burmeister was injured, Joubert was prevailed upon to play after all.

Shortly before the departure of the touring party, they were split into two sides and each in turn played the Rest of Western Province at Newlands. They were beaten both times!

Even back in 1906 touring rugby players were a mischievous lot and the good ship *Gascon* must have developed a few extra creaks and squeaks on the way over with 30 lively young men aboard. One evening not long before the boat was due to arrive at Southampton, a couple of players celebrated a little more thoroughly than usual and in the process hurled all the deck chairs overboard. All but one, that is, and this one they placed in a conspicuous position and labelled it "J. C. Carden". The caper cost the tour management a fair amount of cash, but "Daddy" Carden's main objection was the obvious attempt to saddle him with the blame!

The team officially became "Springboks" shortly after their arrival in England and the London newspapers wasted no time in assigning their most imaginative reporters to satisfy public curiosity in the little band of cheerful, handsome and healthy "Colonials" from Darkest Africa. The result was some of the most bizarre articles ever to be written about rugby players from any country.

The team battle cry of "Igamaliyo" was interpreted as something the Springboks shout back home at the

Eight outstanding members of the 1906/07 Springbok team to Britain. *Top row, left to right:* F. J. Dobbin, D. C. Jackson and J. W. E. Raaff. *Left:* W. S. Morkel. *Right:* A. F. W. Marsberg. *Bottom row, left to right:* H. W. Carolin, A. C. Stegmann and H. A. de Villiers.

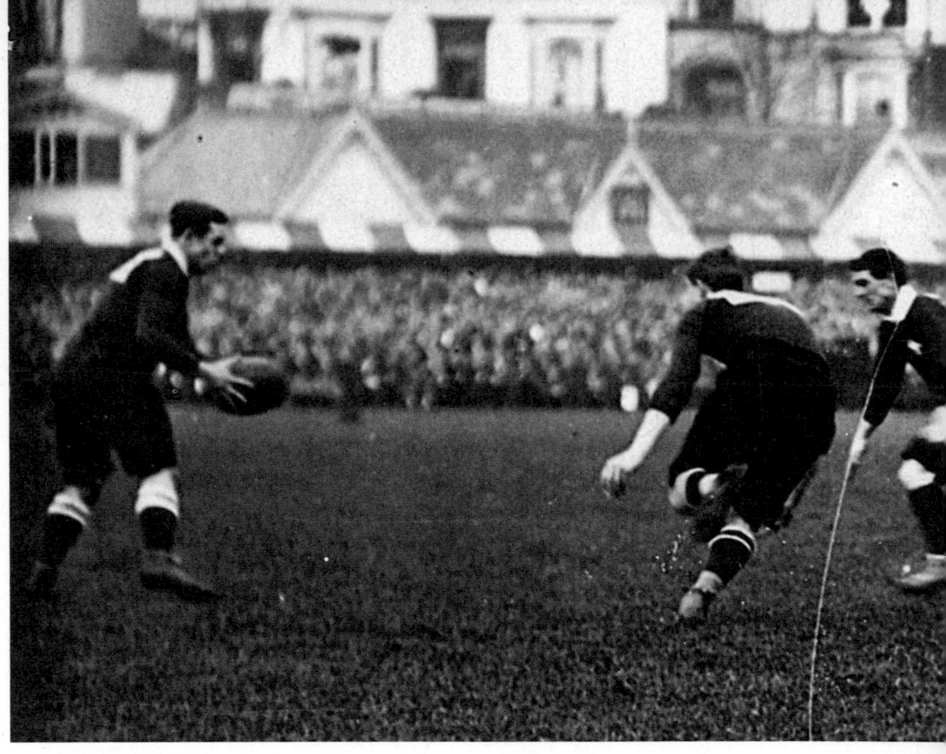

Right: "Uncle" Dobbin receives the ball from "Mary" Jackson after the Springboks had won a scrum against Wales at St. Helen's, Swansea, in 1906. Arthur Marsberg is the Springbok with his back to the camera but soon after this picture was taken early in the match, he switched from wing to fullback. Henry Daneel (with scrum-cap) and "Bingo" Burger already have their heads out of the scrum and the Welsh player coming up on defence is scrumhalf R. M. Owen.

exact moment they drive an assegai into a foe's heart and a perfectly innocent visit to the London Zoo gave another reporter the opportunity to portray the Springboks as a most naive lot who stood transfixed and open-mouthed as they watched a couple of seals fighting over a herring.

The Springboks quickly learnt to poke fun at the gullible reporters and there is the story of Paddy Carolin telling the general manager of British Railways that he did not think Eerste River station was quite as big as Clapham Junction!

One reporter gave the following account of Springbok activities in the early morning:

"After Mr. Carden had read the leading articles in the *Daily Mail* to the team at their hotel yesterday morning, followed by a refreshing shower and a Zulu hymn, the broad-shouldered fellows issued forth for a trip to the Old Kent Road. On their arrival, something like a demonstration took place near the Bermondsey Arms. The big-lunged Roos sang a verse of the famous song "Knocked 'em in the Old Kent Road" with a slight Dutch accent but in perfect tune and the crowd took up the chorus with verve"!

The Springboks liked using the well known and innocent Afrikaans expletive "allemagtig' and, no doubt with the aid of a tongue-in-cheek South African, one newspaper solemnly interpreted this as a "Zulu war cry frequently heard in the Karoo desert and other parts of Central Africa"!

On the actual field of play the first of the Springboks to really capture the popular fancy was the Griqualand West fullback A. F. W. Marsberg, who proved absolutely fearless in the face of the dribbling forward rushes which was such a feature of the game in the United Kingdom at the time.

The Australian A. G. Hales, a best-selling novelist at the time, really took the Springboks to his heart and he covered most of their games on the tour. He had a flowery, but most colourful style and he really poured it on thick whenever he wrote about Arthur Marsberg. This is what he told his readers after one match:

"I have to get back to Marsberg, for he made himself pretty near football famous this day. Once, when his goal was in danger, he went for the ball in a lightning-like rush, snapped it up and was off like a wild steer into the bush. He fairly flew for a few yards and then they came at him. He put all his great strength into the task and went through them or over them like wind through a wheatfield.... One got the shoulder, another the outstretched arm and hand; round this one he dodged like a Johannesburg debtor doubling around corners; over the next he bounded, making straight for the English goal line as a wilful woman for the divorce court. 'Stop him!' yelled the crowd again. They might as well have yelled to a politician to practice what he preaches or a lawyer not to lie. It was a splendid rush and stamped the player as a crackerjack in any company in any country".

On another occasion he had this to say about the whole team:

"The New Zealanders always took themselves pretty seriously, but up-to-date Africa seems to look on it all as a ripping joke. But when something rouses them, or the fit takes them, they can play like Dooley's dog after a liver-and-bacon breakfast...."

In Wales where a no-frills man of courage is always appreciated, Marsberg was a particularly big hero, but it was the quicksilver "Uncle" Dobbin who really fired the imagination of the rugby lovers in England. One writer was even moved to poetry and he wrote, in part:

"With pace and dash
like lightning flash,
See him through tacklers weaving
His way — it lies
to brilliant tries,
The luckless loons deceiving.
Oh, five-feet six
of guile and tricks! —
Eleven-stone-three most gritty.
We've few like you to work the pack,
or start a movement of attack,
In Britain — more's the pity!"

With a magnificent set of backs and lively, though smallish forwards, the Springboks played excellent rugby leading up to the first of the four tests —against Scotland. They were considered firm favourites to beat the Scots, but heavy rain and bitter cold weather gave the home team just the sort of conditions they wanted.

Hampden Park, Glasgow, was already water-logged on the morning of the match and another deluge a few hours before kick-off had the Scottish team rubbing their hands and saying "*gran' weether for the drooning of the Boks*". And this is exactly what happened. The bigger home forwards knew all about playing with a heavy

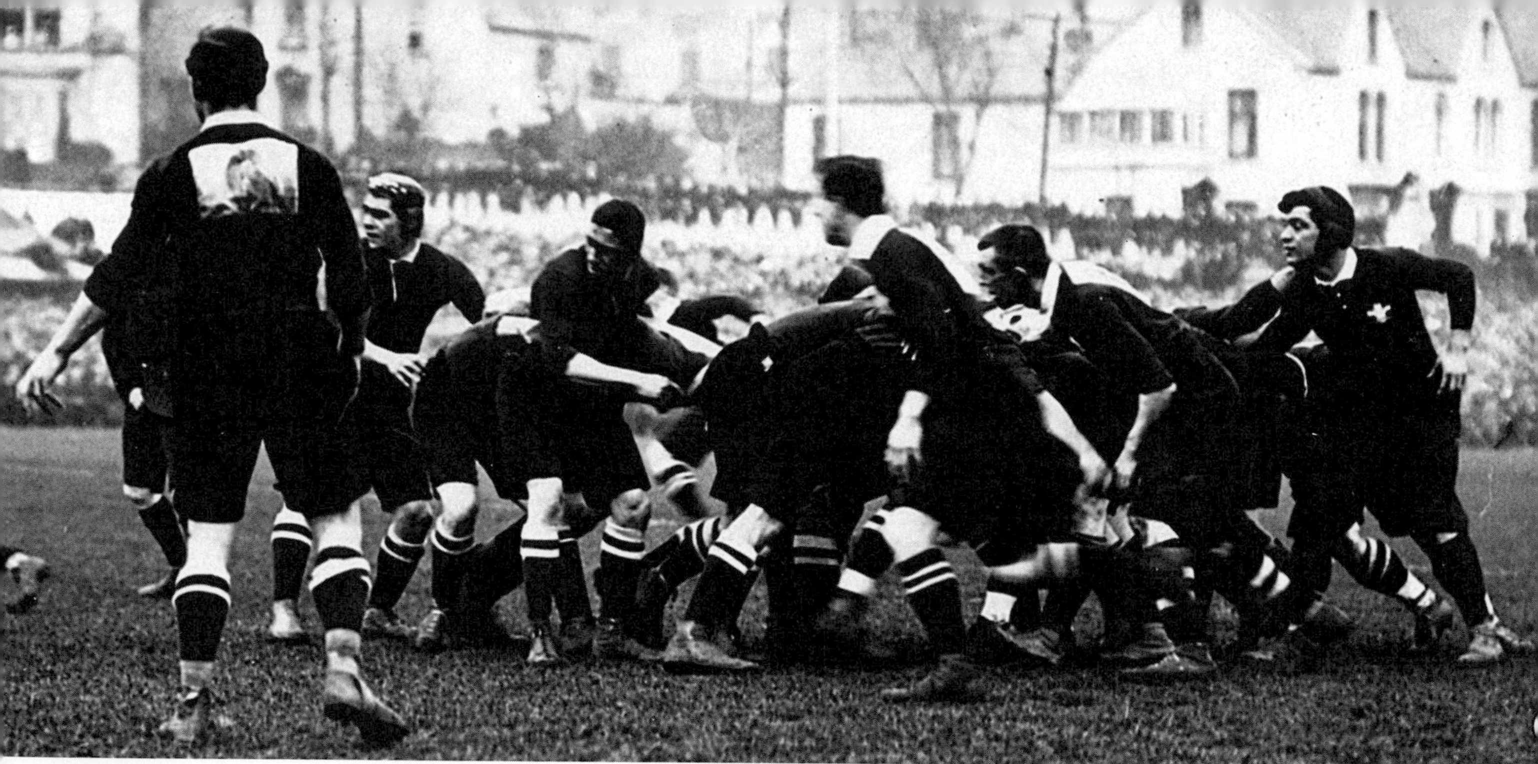

Above: Paul Roos, holding the ball, leads his team in a practice during the tour. *From left to right are:* Bill Neill, Klondike Raaff, Cocky Brooks and Bert Reid.

Right: Springboks in action on foreign soil for the first time. Duggie Morkel has just taken the ball in a lineout against East Midlands at Northampton, the first match of the 1906/07 tour. Sommy Morkel is just behind Duggie and the two Springboks turning around to help are "Koei" Brink and Paul Roos.

Sound handling was one of the reasons why the 1906 Springboks left Britain with a wonderful reputation for playing attractive rugby. Here Sommy Morkel, Paddy Carolin and Duggie Morkel brush up on their passing during training.

Arthur Burmeister and "Mary" Jackson look on as Pietie le Roux prepares for a punt during a practice session on the 1906 tour.

wet ball in mud and sludge and it was a case of "Feet, Scotland, feet!" from the first whistle to the last. While the visitors were trying to handle the treacherous ball and in the process, "working hands and arms like deaf mutes signalling for a fire escape", as the ever-present Hales described it, the Scots launched one dribbling rush atfer the other.

Marsberg was badly injured after a typically brave effort to stop such a charge and carried off the field unconscious. Dietlof Maré had two broken fingers and Brink a damaged ankle after other attempts to stem the tide and eventually it was nothing short of a miracle that South Africa did not lose by a bigger margin than 6-0.

The test against Ireland at Balmoral, Belfast, was played under much better conditions and must have been one of the most exciting international matches in rugby history. The Springboks led 12-3 at half-time and seemed set to score an easy victory, but then a splendid try by wing Basil McLear led an Irish revival and in the end the tourists had to be content with a narrow 15-12 win.

The scoring began with a penalty by Steve Joubert and then Bob Loubser, that truly great wing, beat two forwards, as well as Maclear, his opposite number, and G. J. Henebrey, the fullback, with a wonderful swerving run for a try to remember. Within minutes he went over again after Japie Krige, like the Mannetjies Roux of more than 60 years later, had taken advantage of an Irish mistake. Krige himself scored the next try when he again grabbed a fumbled pass and cork-screwed his way through the defence.

In the second half it was all Ireland. First Parke scored a penalty goal and then came Maclear's amazing effort. He scooped up a ball deep in his own half, stumbled and, off-balance, somehow managed to flounder past several defenders. Then, suddenly, he was at full pace with Bob Loubser sprinting after him. For once Loubser was up against a man almost as fast as he was and Maclear's head-start was too much even for him. The only man who could stop the flying Maclear was Stevie Joubert, but a terrific hand-off left the Matie sprawling in his wake. Almost immediately afterwards, Ireland drew level when they wheeled the scrum and Sugars went over after an irresistable dribbling charge.

Midst heart-stopping excitement, the Springboks swept back into the attack and wing Anton Stegmann sped all along the touchline for the winning points. There was some controversy over this as "Klondike" Raaff, the South African touchjudge, in his delight had hurled his flag skywards and for a moment it looked as if Stegmann had stepped out. But those were the days when even spectators knew how to accept defeat and the Springbok victory was generously applauded, to quote from a contemporary report.

Then came the big one, the test against Wales. To beat Wales on their own ground was then and always will be one of the toughest jobs any team can tackle. And it was a good Welsh team, that year, with men like Percy Bush and Dicky Owen at halfback, the immortal Gwyn Nicholls persuaded to wear the red jersey just once more and R. T. Gabe at centre, and Teddy Morgan and J. L. Williams on the wing. In front of them this talented array had a typical Welsh pack of forwards; strong, fiery and cunning.

Extra spice was added by the prospect of a duel between Nicholls and Krige, both then contenders for the title of the world's best centre.

The game took place at Swansea before more than 45 000 Welshmen, singing lustily those wonderfully lilting Welsh songs like *"Land of my Fathers"* and *"Sospan Foch"*. A small gathering of South Africans, mainly students from Edinburgh and London, fought a losing battle with brave renditions of *"Sarie Marais"* and other Afrikaans ditties.

The Springboks had other problems to contend with too. Stegmann and Le Roux were out because of injury and Marsberg had been selected to play on the wing with Joubert at fullback. Well, this was the original plan anyway. In that age of individualism you could not tell a man like Marsberg what to do and it is on record that soon after the game started he simply took up the fullback position and Stevie had no choice but to go on the wing.

But the Springboks also had a secret weapon they were about to try out on the Welshmen. Earlier in the tour, against Glamorgan and Newport, they had been badly beaten in the scrums because Wales, before any other rugby-playing nation had by then discovered the value of the loosehead. The Springboks were quick to learn and in the test for the first time, "Mary" Jackson was to use his throw-in only on the side where his pack had the loose head. To make matters worse for Wales, the Springboks did not hesitate to pack 4-3-1 whenever it was their opponents' throw-in thereby giving themselves the advantage, whatever happened!

With the Welsh forwards beaten at their own game, the Springbok backs had a good opportunity to emphasise their superiority. Krige outplayed Nicholls on the day. Dobbin, De Villiers, Marsberg, Loubser, and Jackson all proved to be better than their illustrious opposite numbers and Raaff was the star of the pack.

John W. E. Raaff, as a schoolboy in Kimberley, had refused to wear shorts because he was ashamed of his spindly legs. This prompted his friends to suspect that he feared cold weather and by a rather convoluted process of association, he was given the nickname "Klondike". It stuck to him for the rest of his life.

Again it was A. G. Hales who gave the most colourful description of the match.

This is what he wrote about "Klondike" Raaff:

"He sent the Welshmen headlong to grass; he spun them around like so many teetotums. He caught them in their stride and helped them onward a yard or two, until they thought they were flying machines whizzing around on the whiskers of the world.. when they charged him he filled his lungs with air and met the rush, and they bounced from the shock as a he-goat bounces when he butts at a kopje. They brought him to earth now and again, but when this happened he was always up and off in a moment, whilst the men who tackled him limped as if they had been stopping trains...."

And this is how he described the highlights of the match:

"The Welshmen were determined to feed their old champion Nicholls; but either De Villiers or Krige was eternally in the way. Krige was watching the champion as a brood hen watches a weasel and his speed was too great for the Welsh wonder... then Morgan came into evidence. He made a bold and dashing run, beating first one man and then another until nothing lay between him and the coveted try — but Marsberg.

"The Celtic crowd shrieked out wild cheers as their man strode boldly onward. Marsberg did not appear to be the least bit disturbed as Morgan came sweeping down on him.... Fixing his eye on his man, the great African player strode steadily to meet him as he came. Marsberg looked wonderfully slow in comparison with the fine runner who was making a bee line for the spot that would give him the long looked for try.... Suddenly Marsberg spread out his long, lean arms; he dropped his chin on his chest and shot forward like a South Sea Islander diving from a schooner's bows....One long brown hand closed on Morgan's breast bone, the other on the point of his shoulder. And then with a mighty heave Morgan was sent headlong to earth, and with a cry that rang to the cloud-clapped skies, the Welshmen mourned their idol's fall....

"A little later Dobbin made the Celts wonder who had told them that their men were the trickiest players alive," the novelist continued. "At this stage in fact Dobbin and Jackson were as full of tricks as a Zoo full of monkeys with Caruso's pet thrown in....South Africa came away with a wet sail....Loubser sent to Krige; the latter threw out to De Villiers who in masterly fashion drew the defence, and whipping the ball to Joubert, gave that artist a clear field, and he was over the line like a nigger into a neighbour's mealie patch.

"Fired by this success, in spite of a failure to convert, the Springboks were down on the Celtic stronghold

in a moment. Joubert especially put in some fine work. He went through the enemy's line like a rat through a drain pipe, and could not be captured. But it was Loubser who got over the Welsh line, scudding like a hunted hare. Half time showed two tries to nil, and Wales was beaten. They played pluckily in the second half, but their wonderful system that had carried them so often to victory had broken down badly. . . . The fight became hot and the tackling very hard, and then Raaff went over the Celts' line for the third time. Joubert converted and scoring for the day ceased. When the fateful whistle sounded 40 000 Celts walked away in gloomy silence, wondering what in the name of all the saints was going to happen to 'The Land of Our Fathers'. As a general rule they sing this and wonder what is going to happen to the other folk"

Thus the description by the famous novelist of the Springboks' finest all-round performance of the tour. The Welshmen themselves said afterwards that Marsberg and Dobbin were the best players in their respective positions in the world. But Japie Krige, Boy de Villiers and Mary Jackson were also consistently brilliant throughout the match. It was, incidentally, to be the legendary Japie's last test match. He had to undergo an appendicitis operation shortly afterwards and did not play in any of the remaining matches of the tour.

The final test, against England at Crystal Palace, was played in appalling conditions and ended in a hard-fought but unspectacular draw. It was a game for forwards only, played in mud and slush and the threequarters "shivered like stray dogs at a street corner", to quote from one of the after-match reports. Once Marsberg went down to stop a forward rush and when he rose, a reporter wrote, "he looked like a garden plot up for auction"!

The Springboks' try was scored by Billy Millar after Jackett, the English fullback, had fumbled a kick from Marsberg and it is back to A. G. Hales for an inimitable description of the score:

"It came out of a wild mix-up," Hales wrote. "First one man and then another got the ball, ran a yard and flopped face downwards, where each in turn was walked on, sat on, flopped on by friend and foe."

After half-time England equalised through a grand individualistic try by Freddie Brooks, a Rhodesian who actually competed in the 1906 Currie Cup competition, but could not be selected for South Africa because of the residential rule.

The Springboks were severely handicapped by an injury to Sommy Morkel in the second half and it was generally agreed that, but for this, the touring team would have won.

In the final match of the tour the Springboks were thrashed 17-0 by an inspired Cardiff team on a sopping wet field and in a howling gale. The South Africans just could not adjust themselves to the conditions and they were outplayed in all facets. Krige was not there to keep a watchful eye on Gwynn Nicholls who shrewdly guided his team and even Marsberg, for once, did not tackle with the deadly ferocity that made him a household name in Britain in their winter of 1906-7.

The great adventure was over. Paul Roos and his team had established South Africa in the international rugby arena, the foundation was laid for future generations of Springboks to build on.

Before their departure for home, the South Africans asked the rugby authorities for permission to play one match in France. This turned out to be a strange affair. The Springboks beat a scratch side 55-6 (with Dietlof Maré notching 22 on his own) and scoring 13 tries. The game offered more humour than excitement with the Frenchmen often politely applauding their opponents.

At the banquet afterwards Paul Roos was at his schoolmasterly best when he admonished the Frenchmen for not trying hard enough and giving them a motto in the process:

"Remember in rugby it is a matter of all for the team, not each one for himself."

South African rugby owes Paul Roos a very big debt, but it would appear as if France should remember him too.

Above:

Stevie Joubert moves in to pick up a loose ball in the test against Wales.

Below:

A final war cry as the first-ever Springboks say goodbye to England.

The 'cripple' who became captain

South African rugby history is studded with examples of players conquering adversity and handicaps to play for their country. William Alexander (Billy) Millar is the only one, however, who had to overcome the effects of a serious war wound before he could even begin his rugby career.

Born at Bedford in the Eastern Cape on November 6, 1883, Millar was introduced to the game at the South African College School, but at the age of 17 his restless spirit made him exchange the rugby ball for the rifle when the South African War broke out late in 1899. He joined a cycle corps whose job it was presumably to deliver dispatches, but Billy was soon involved in heavy fighting. He received a severe wound in the left shoulder and after many months in hospital was discharged with a medical certificate declaring that he would probably never again have the full use of his left arm and could also be an invalid for the rest of his life.

He obtained a job with the Railway Department, but found that he had such constant pain that he could hardly do the work. A doctor advised him to get as much exercise as possible and he immediately took up long distance walking, mountaineering and boxing with an almost fanatical dedication. It must have been largely a case of the mind overruling the matter because in spite of almost instant success in every sport he tackled, Millar never really did recover fully from his wound.

A civil service job had little appeal for Millar, a man of action if ever there was one. He went on prospecting expeditions to Rhodesia and South West Africa before returning to Cape Town where he once again concentrated on boxing.

Professional fighters like Jack Valentine and Jack Lalor coached him and according to the available records he never lost a bout in a fairly long and active career as an amateur heavyweight. As champion of the Western Province, Billy sparred regularly against first-class visiting professionals in his weight division, but he never did consider fighting for anything more but fun.

Walking was a popular form of competitive athletics in those days and between 1903 and 1906 he won races over distances varying between two and 50 miles. In 1903 he also began playing rugby again, gaining his Western Province colours in 1906. In between he found time to play tennis, golf and cricket. As a golfer he was quite outstanding, with a handicap of three, but on the tennis court and the cricket field he revealed more exuberance and enthusiasm than talent.

It was rugby that suited his temperament best and he was considered a certain selection for Paul Roos' 1906 touring team to the United Kingdom, particularly after a series of outstanding performances in that year's Currie Cup tournament which served as trials for the tour. Astonishingly, he was not selected, but got his place anyway when Bertie Mosenthal had to withdraw. Millar, one of the youngest players in the team, proved to be an unqualified success and it was he who scored a vital try in the drawn test against England.

Millar captained the invincible Western Province teams in the years following his return from the history-making tour with Paul Roos and by the time Tom Smyth brought the fourth touring side over from England in 1910, he was an obvious choice to lead the Springboks.

Dr. Smyth's team was not a great side, but among the members were some outstanding individualists and from them further lessons were learnt to make the South Africans the unbeatable players they were soon to become. During this tour the duties of the forwards became more defined; especially that it must be their main function to obtain clean possession for the backs to exploit. It was also

William Alexander (Billy) Millar was so seriously wounded in the South African War that doctors thought that he would be an invalid for the rest of his life. But he recovered to lead the Springboks.

becoming more obvious that the two half-back positions should be filled by specialists and the traditional interchanging between the two became less frequent.

In J. P. (Ponty) Jones the British team had a brilliant centre and Stanley Williams was a fullback who could hold his own in any company. Harry Jarman, Phil Waller, W. (Billy) Tyrrell, R. Stevenson and J. Webb were outstanding forwards and in Charles Henry (Cherry) Pillman the tourists had a true rugby genius of his era.

Then only 20 years old, the black-haired, tall and slender Pillman was the game's first real loose-forward. He could handle the ball as surely as any threequarter, could kick brilliantly and to add to it all he was fast and had an instinctive flair for doing the right thing at the right time. In later years Pillman became a distinguished and highly respectable member of the London Stock Exchange, but back in 1910 he was the scourge of the Springbok threequarters; the man who really laid the foundations for the roving forward style of play adopted eagerly by the South Africans and eventually perfected by Hennie Muller, four decades later.

Phil Waller also had a lesson to teach us as he specialised in hooking the ball from the scrums, opening Springbok eyes to another valuable facet of the game. Waller, incidentally, stayed on in South Africa after the tour and was a member of the South African Heavy Artillery when he was killed in France in World War I.

Harry Jarman, one of the stars of the tour, also died a hero's death some years later. Jarman, a Welsh coal-miner, was at work one day when he spotted an uncoupled truck speeding towards a group of playing children. Without hesitation he threw himself in front of it and succeeded in derailing and overturning the truck before it could hit the children. In the process Jarman received appalling injuries and in the words of a contemporary report, "he died a slow and painful death".

A new generation of brilliant young players blended with a sprinkling of veterans to make Springbok rugby particularly strong at the time. W. H. (Boy) Morkel and D. F. T. (Duggie) Morkel carried on the remarkable tradition started in 1903 when Andrew became the first of no less than 10 members of this family to earn Springbok colours in the next 25 years. Freddie and Richard Luyt also appeared on the scene and C. H. L. ("Hudie" also known as "Cocky") Hahn had a brief spell of glory as a hard-running wing. Richard Luyt, consummately clever, had a perfect centre partner in Dirkie de Villiers (a Cambridge "Blue") while Freddie Luyt, as outstanding as his brother, was partnered at half-back in the first test by the experienced "Uncle" Dobbin, but combined with his Western Province teammate Clive van Ryneveld (whose son many years later played rugby for England and captained South Africa at cricket) in the final two international matches of the tour.

Gideon Roos, younger brother of Paul, and P. A. Marsberg, younger brother of A. F. W., gained their Springbok colours in 1910 and the selection of Harry Walker for all three tests would have added significance when his brother Alf played for South Africa in 1921 and 1924 and Alf's son Harry Newton gained his colours 43 years later.

Billy Millar would almost certainly have captained the Springboks in the first test in Johannesburg, but he could not obtain leave from his job and the honour went to Duggie Morkel, a balding giant who must be regarded as the first in a long line of superb Springbok placekickers.

Transvaal's "Hudie" Hahn made an outstanding international debut in the test (one Johannesburg newspaper headlined its report of the match "Our Magnificent Hahn") and his powerful running and the incisiveness of Freddie Luyt, Dirkie de Villiers' clever work at centre and a real skipper's game by Duggie Morkel

Left: Outstanding personalities of the 1910 series between Tom Smyth's British touring team and the Springboks. Top left is "Cherry" Pillman, the versatile England forward. Below him is Harry Jarman, who died a hero's death in an accident a few years after the tour. Jarman was one of the best forwards in the pack. Second from the bottom is the hard-running Transvaal wing "Hudie" Hahn and on the left is Richard Luyt, a centre threequarter from the Western Province who has had few peers before or since.

managed to tip the scales 14-10 in favour of the Springboks.

Millar took over the captaincy for the second test in Port Elizabeth and again the Springboks started off well with a try by wing Wally Mills, beautifully engineered between Dick Luyt, in Springbok colours for the first time, and De Villiers. But in the second half, the amazing Pillman, playing at flyhalf of all places, took over completely.

One report described Pillman as "playing a game invented by himself". Although officially down to play at half-back, Pillman actually bobbed up from centre to wing to fullback, wherever the need arose and he also led one forward rush after the other! His tackling demoralized the Springboks and he initiated both of his team's tries, one with a perfectly-placed tactical kick, and he also put over a difficult conversion.

As Billy Millar himself wrote years later: "My memories of this game are all dwarfed by Pillman's brilliance. I confidently assert that if ever a man can have been said to have won an international match through his own unorthodox and lone-handed efforts it can be said of the inspired black-haired Pillman I played against on the Crusaders' ground on August 27, 1910. . . ."

With the series poised at one win each, the third test at Newlands in 1910 created more public interest than any other rugby match up to then and for the first time reports in the old newspapers refer to the "perpetual Newlands roar".

Smyth's team lost their star fullback Stanley Williams within the first ten minutes and they never really stood much of a chance after that set-back. Fred Luyt was in scintillating form and with Van Ryneveld and his forwards giving him more than enough possession, he launched one attack after the other. Here must have been a magnificent player with razor-sharp reflexes and a keen rugby brain. He opened up the defence for the first Springbok try, for instance, by feinting as if to pass to his backs and then suddenly streaking through a gap before switching direction again towards his forwards and sending Gideon Roos over for Duggie Morkel to convert with a beautiful kick from a difficult angle. This match, incidentally, saw the international debut of Boy Morkel, regarded by many old-timers as the finest all-round forward the world has known.

The highlight of the match was undoubtedly a try scored by Percy Allport, the Springbok fullback in the last two tests of this series. Allport, who played centre as often as fullback for Villagers and Western Province, caught the ball from an abortive kick somewhere near the halfway line. He was about to boot for touch when he realised that he had half of the British pack on top of him. He dodged and swerved past them and suddenly saw that he had a clear field ahead. With a terrific burst of speed he just managed to beat the covering three-quarters to fling himself over the line. It was to be 45 years before Roy Dryburgh emulated Allport's feat when in 1955 and also at Newlands, he became only the second Springbok fullback in history to score a try in a test.

In reports of this test the first evidence can be found that tempers also flared in those days. This is how Millar described it:

"Then in the excitement of the moment, and when blood was rather heated from the virile nature of the play, a few of us lost our heads. Punishment had to be exacted, and a penalty goal was added to Britain's debit balance. . . ."

The kick failed, but Britain did get a consolation try by Jack Spoors, following a break by Jones, late in the second half. By that time the Springboks were already in an unassailable position, however, and the final score was 21-5. Spoors, incidentally, scored a try in each of the three tests, the only player so far to have notched a try in each test of a series against South Africa. No Springbok has yet achieved this feat.

Right: Four brilliant Springboks who made their mark in the 1910 series against Tom Smyth's British team. *Top* is Freddie Luyt, Richard's brother who shone at half-back. Below him is Dirkie de Villiers, who formed such an effective combination with Richard Luyt at centre and second from the bottom is Clive van Ryneveld, Richard Luyt's half-back partner in the last two tests. At the bottom on the right is Percy Allport, one of only two Springbok fullbacks ever to have scored a try in a test.

Duggie Morkel, a member of South African rugby's most famous family and the first great Springbok placekicker.

Family affair

For some reason never disclosed the national selectors whose job it was to pick the members of the second Springbok touring team to Britain and France in 1912 did not want Billy Millar as their captain.

They felt that he should be in the team, but strongly recommended that he should not be appointed as the captain. The South African Rugby Board disagreed and they over-ruled the selectors. It proved to be a wise decision as Millar's team won all the tests and were beaten only thrice, by Newport; London Counties and Swansea. They thoroughly avenged the 1906 defeat against Scotland and beat Ireland 38-0, an international record which was to stand until 1951 when the Springboks scored a 44-0 victory over Scotland.

The 1912-13 Springboks were in fact a very powerful combination. The forwards were heavier and better on the whole than their 1906 predecessors and the backs proved to be a lot more competent than originally expected.

"Uncle" Dobbin, playing in his fourth successive test series, was as full of tricks as ever and Jan Stegmann, E. E. (Boetie) McHardy, Wally Mills, Jackie Morkel and Richard and Freddie Luyt were always consistent and often brilliant.

The team was almost a family affair. Richard, Freddie and John Luyt were brothers and so were Gerhard and Jackie Morkel. Boy Morkel was their first cousin and Duggie Morkel was also related. Jan Stegmann was a brother of the 1906 Springbok Anton, Willie Krige was a brother of the legendary Japie and Wally Mills and Louis Louw, one of the best of the forwards on the tour, were first cousins.

Altogether 10 members of the Morkel family of Somerset West gained Springbok colours between 1903 and 1928; a feat unlikely ever to be beaten or even equalled. There were four Morkels in the 1912/13 team and this seems to be an opportune moment to digress and to take a closer look at a family who played such a major role in early South African rugby history.

The South African origin of the family dates back to 1691 when Philip Morkel arrived at the Cape as a gunner on board the "*Oosterstyn*". He and his brother Wilhelm (Willem) had joined the Dutch East India Company after leaving Hamburg at the insistence of their father who did not want his sons to be conscripted into German military service.

Philip and Willem decided to settle in the Cape, then still little more than a half-way station for the Dutch merchant ships on their way to and from the East. Willem never married, but Philip's second marriage produced the four children from whom sprang rugby's most famous clan. For several generations the Morkels, who married mainly into the Myburgh family, remained clustered around Somerset West and they prospered on now historic farms like "Onverwacht", "Rome", "Broadland", "Morning Star" and "Oatlands". They were the recognised leaders of their community and history mentions that even the mysterious Lady Anne Barnard once spent a night at "Onverwacht" and at the time of the first British occupation in 1795, the same farm served as temporary headquarters for a commando of farmers who were trying to defend the settlement against the invaders.

Near the end of the 19th century several members of the family moved to the then recently discovered gold fields of the Witwatersrand and it is recorded how Paul Andrew Morkel won four prizes for riding and wrestling on bareback horses at a meeting of the Wanderers Gymkhana Club. His opponent in the finals was the future mining magnate and financier Abe Bailey. According to a contemporary newspaper report the 22-year-old Morkel was the winner after a "heroic struggle".

Other members of the family who preferred the excitement of mushrooming Johannesburg to gracious living at Somerset West were Carolus Frederick, whose son Philip eventually founded the wellknown firm which still carries his name, and Michiel

Jurgens Morkel who was less fortunate. A burgher in a Boer commando, he was killed in a skirmish with British troops near the Tugela River in Natal during the South African War.

The intense interest in rugby seemed to have originated on the farm "Rome" where the Morkel boys laid out their own field and played their bare-footed games against all comers. The Somerset West Rugby Club almost certainly developed around this nucleus of enthusiasts, but for many years the only organised games were played after Cape cart journeys to the surrounding districts like Caledon, Stellenbosch and The Strand. Nicolaas Morkel was the first captain when the club finally became affiliated to the Western Province Rugby Union in 1904. A year earlier Andrew Morkel had already become the first Morkel to represent South Africa when he played in the first test against Mark Morrison's touring team from Britain.

He also gained his place in the first Springbok team to Britain and this time he was joined by the brothers William Somerset (Sommy) and Douglas.

D. F. T. (Duggie) Morkel was a matchwinning kicker and altogether a splendid forward. Born in 1886, he learned the rudiments of the game in Kimberley, but soon moved to Johannesburg where, at the age of 17, he played for a Witwatersrand team against the 1903 British side. From 1906 until 1913 Duggie Morkel played in nine tests and he must count among the most spectacular kickers ever to wear the Springbok jersey.

In 1910 W. H. Morkel appeared on the scene. Better known as "Boy", he was considered by internationally-known authorities as the best all-round forward of his time. Boy was born in Somerset West in 1886, but he played for Diggers in Johannesburg at the start of his career before returning to the Cape where he became captain of Western Province. In later years he farmed in the district of Potchefstroom from where he was recalled to join Theo Pienaar's 1921 touring team to New Zealand. He was then 35 years old and yet he led the Springboks in all three tests.

In the 1912 team to Britain the Morkels were represented by Duggie, Boy, Jackie, a powerful centre, and his brother Gerhard who was to become the first player to be labelled "the prince of fullbacks", a tag used so often since that it has become a rugby cliche.

Pieter Gerhard Morkel was born at Somerset West on October 15, 1888 and in spite of his instinctive talent, no player ever worked harder to perfect his game. As a youngster he was hardly ever without a tennis ball in his hands and this probably contributed much to the safe catching for which he was to be renowned throughout his long career.

Even as an established player, he regularly organised little bands of schoolboys to pepper him with kicks during long hours on the practice field. He also acquired the knack of screwing the ball off his boot to follow a curved route before swinging out, thereby ensuring that he gained the maximum ground even when he had to kick only a few feet in from touch. His dropkicks were legendary and here again it was as the result of long practice. His positional play was perfect making up for a definite lack of speed on the run and enabling him to play outstanding international rugby when already 33 years old.

Gerhard Morkel was also blessed with the perfect temperament for sport at the highest level and perhaps this was because there was no place on earth he would rather have been than on a rugby field. He had the great player's intuitive ability to sum up a situation in a glance and he himself often claimed that he hardly ever looked at the posts when dropping for goal; he simply sensed where they were.

He first played for Somerset West when only 16 years old, although it was by chance rather than design that he got into the senior team at such an early age. He happened to be on the station when the team, about to depart for Caledon, discovered that they were one man short. A quick whip-around raised enough money for his trainfare and he turned in such a brilliant performance that he became a regular member of the team.

Henry, Royal and Harry Morkel only gained their Springbok colours after World War I and all three were members of the 1921 team to New Zealand when there were altogether five Morkels in the touring party. At school Henry gave no indication that he would follow in the Morkel tradition; he was described as clumsy and soft. Once he was moved from the pack to the wing, however, he quickly established himself. Fast and powerful, he had an extremely high knee action and it was positively dangerous to tackle him from the front. It usually took more than one defender to stop him.

Royal Morkel, born on March 22 1896, was massive for his era at 6 ft 2 and more than 230 lbs. His contemporaries always used to insist that it was his great fondness for fish and chips that made Royal so big and strong. Apparently he enjoyed matches at Newlands, in particular, because afterwards he would go to "Joe's

W. H. ("Boy") Morkel, a magnificent forward.

Gerhard Morkel, remarkable full-back.

Jackie Morkel, powerful threequarter.

A contemporary cartoonist's conception of Jan Stegmann, the Springbok wing who scored three tries against Ireland in Dublin in 1912. Below is a picture taken of Stegmann a few years ago. At the time of writing the 90-year-old Dr. Stegmann is South Africa's oldest living Springbok.

E. E. ("Boetie") McHardy, the Free State wing who also notched three tries against Ireland in the same test as Stegmann, as seen by the same artist. McHardy, in fact, completed his hat-trick before his team-mate. Below is a photograph of McHardy as he looked a few years before his death in Bloemfontein.

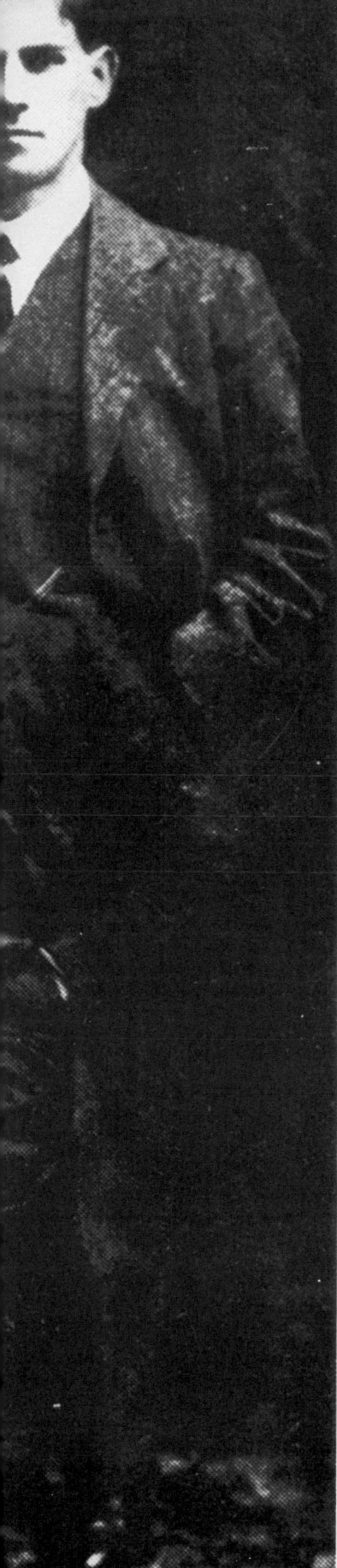

Cafe" in Salt River where huge quantities of his idea of a delicacy were available for a few pennies. After such a feast he liked nothing better than a couple of bottles of ginger beer. As a forward, Royal Morkel was a human steamroller, almost unstoppable when in sight of his opponents' goal-line.

The last of the Morkels to wear the Springbok jersey was "P.K." who played on the wing in the fourth test against Maurice Brownlie's All Blacks in 1928. All the Morkels were also interested in other sports and Royal was a particularly good swimmer and boxer while Denys, who did not reach international status as a rugby player, did gain Springbok colours as a cricketer. All of them were good cricketers, in fact, and no slouches on the tennis court either.

I have mentioned only those members of the family who represented South Africa, but their impact on our sport can probably be best underlined if it is pointed out that in the years just before World War I there were no less than 22 Morkels playing senior rugby in all parts of the country. This so impressed Sir Abe Bailey that he was actually in the process of arranging a tour to England for a rugby team consisting only of Morkels when the war broke out and ruined his plans.

The three Luyt brothers in Millar's side also deserve a special niche in Springbok rugby history. Freddie Luyt was a brilliant half-back, Richard as good at centre while John who was not quite up to the high standard of his brothers, was nevertheless a good forward. He later on wrote extensively on the game and travelled with the 1921 Springboks to New Zealand as a special press correspondent.

Frederick Pieter Luyt was the youngest of the brothers. Born at Ceres on February 26, 1888, he was already an outstanding rugby player and cricketer when he went to Stellenbosch where he concentrated on the fullback position. He was at Stellenbosch for only one season before transferring to the old South African College, now the University of Cape Town. While qualifying as an attorney he represented the university at both rugby and cricket and by 1910 when he played against Tommy Smyth's visiting British team in all three internationals, he was generally regarded as easily the best halfback in the country. He dovetailed particularly well with Clive van Ryneveld and his brother Richard and it is recorded that these three formed the best match-winning combination of their day.

Freddie Luyt also frequently played cricket for Western Province as a batsman-wicketkeeper, but rugby was his first love. In the newspaper reports of his time Freddie Luyt was often described as a "sports idealist". Even in the heat of international competition, he never forgot his manners or the principles of fair play.

At the same time he was an extremely clever player who brought a new dimension to the functions of a flyhalf, a position he preferred before the era of specialisation, by designing various attacking ploys with his threequarters. Luyt's career was cut short by a bad knee injury and at the end of the tour to Britain he retired to practice law in partnership with the 1906 Springbok Paddy Carolin in Moorreesburg where the two did much to establish rugby in the Boland areas. He also became a fine golfer after his retirement from the more robust games.

Freddie Luyt's older brother Dick was ranked by his contemporaries as a centre as good as Japie Krige and, surely, at that time there could not have been higher praise. He was nowhere near as spectacular as Krige, but he had the same uncanny ability to create openings for his teammates.

Richard Robins Luyt was born on April 16, 1886 on the same Ceres farm as his brother, but he stayed at Stellenbosch for several years before joining Fred at the South African College. While at Stellenbosch he played mainly as a fullback, but it was as a halfback that he was distinctly unlucky not to make Paul Roos' team in 1906. In that year, however, he finally switched to his proper position as a centre threequarter and after that there was no holding him. Dick Luyt was an outstanding attacker, but it would seem as if he was also South Africa's first hard-tackling centre. Reports of games he played in invariably refer to his "rapid bottling up" of opponents.

He was obviously also the best cricketer in the Luyt family and was

The Luyt brothers, three of whom made a substantial contribution to the game in South Africa. From left to right, are John and Freddie, G. J., who was a good all-round sportsman but who never attained international status, and Richard.

described as a "magnificent wicket-keeper, a splendid batsman and a dangerous googlie bowler". He narrowly missed selection as a Springbok cricketer. In later years when he lived in Worcester, he ironically enough became a national cricket selector and at an advanced age he continued to play club cricket often completing a season with an average of 80 or higher. He was interested in all games and in addition to being a fine competitive swimmer, he also excelled in golf and billiards.

Millar's team started their tour with six successive victories before they made the fatal mistake of underestimating Newport. For this match the Springboks should have selected their test side, but instead they ignored the well-meant warnings of their hosts, and paid the penalty. One Springbok who did come out of the defeat with an enhanced reputation was Richard Luyt, who beat the Newport defence with a scintillating break to send Duggie Morkel over for the South Africans' only score.

The Springboks only had themselves to blame for this defeat as they had already barely survived a match against Llanelly a week before and should have recognised the enormous strength and vigour of all Welsh teams. Only the individual brilliance of Jackie Morkel enabled them to beat Llanelly. It was the big Somerset West centre who drew the defence in a tangle for Alex van der Hoff's early try which Jackie also converted. Almost immediately afterwards Llanelly got an unconverted try and the Springboks could only draw further ahead after the interval when Morkel ripped through all on his own for a try he failed to convert. This set-back stung the Llanelly forwards into furious action and the game became a real war of attrition.

Billy Millar years afterwards described the match in his own inimitable way:

"I took the touch flag on this occasion and believe me that wonderful Welsh crowd — probably the finest judges of football — gave me a roasting whenever I was on what is commonly known as the popular side. At length a rather hoarse voice shouted to me clearly above the din: 'What do you think of Llanelly now?' Rather foolishly I shouted back: 'Play the whole damn lot for Wales!' ....I now became the favourite of the crowd, instead of being barracked, I was applauded for everything I did. As a matter of fact, when Jackie Morkel, who really won the game for us off his own bat, scored the second try, the crowd encroached on to the field of play and I was forced to hit one fervent Welsh objector over the head with my flag stick. My drastic treatment immediately met with whole-hearted approval, for now I could do nothing wrong!"

Millar never forgot the amazing scenes when Hiams, a Llanelly forward, dropped a goal a few minutes before the end to bring the Welsh team to within one point of the Springbok score.

"A huge crowd swarmed onto the field, shouldered Hiams and proceeded to march round the field with him, singing "*Sospan Foch*" ("The little saucepan"). Gil Evans, the referee, blew his whistle continuously, but he had perforce to await the pleasure of those wonderful Welsh enthusiasts."

The Springboks held out to win 8-7 and Millar was subsequently formally presented with a saucepan, a hole punched in its bottom, which according to Welsh rugby tradition in those days had been perched on the crossbar throughout the match. In the early years of rugby and including at the time of this tour, the Cornishmen had a somewhat similar tradition. They used to have a pasty tied to the crossbar during a match.

After the Newport defeat, Millar and manager Max Honnet never again suffered from over-confidence. In fact they approached the next match, against a powerful London combination, as if it was a test and the team was only selected after hours of discussion. It was their first encounter with Adrian Stoop, the flyhalf who was to English rugby then what Bennie Osler was to be for Springbok rugby a generation later. Stoop was an autocratic tactician, with a scientific approach well ahead of his time. The story is told of how he once tried to introduce a complicated system of signals based on numbers to be shouted by him at scrums and line-outs. One of his centres simply could not get the hang of it and on one occasion was not in position for the pass after Stoop had shouted: "Three-four-five-seven!" or whatever it might have been. Stoop glared at the offender who shrugged and said: "Sorry, Adrian, the number was engaged!"

The London match was played in a quagmire and it was Dick Luyt who once again guided the Springboks to victory, creating the openings for two wonderful tries by the Free State wing Boetie McHardy, one of which was converted by Duggie Morkel. Both teams were reduced to 14 men in the second half with the Springboks losing Wally Mills with a pulled leg muscle. The London forwards were on top after half-time and Stoop was a constant threat, but he was invariably let down by his three-quarters who, strangely enough, failed to adapt as well as the South Africans to the terrible weather conditions.

Nevertheless it was often only Gerhard Morkel, magnificent at full-back, who stood between the Springboks and defeat. A reporter wrote afterwards that Morkel had "gained for him a niche in the gallery of the world's greatest fullbacks" and Millar described his performance many years later as "daring to the point of recklessness".

After four consecutive breaks by Stoop had broken down in the face of great tackling, Douglas Morkel and Dick Luyt collided with a sickening thud and Morkel was so badly injured that he had to be carried off.

"Uncle" Dobbin is about to pass the ball to Freddie Luyt as Duggie Morkel looks on. This historic photograph was taken during the second match between Billy Millar's Springboks and London. The South Africans lost 8–10 but Luyt and Dobbin were in brilliant form.

With only 13 men left, the Springboks faltered and Stoop again drove an opening and this time Cherry Pillman, the English hero of the 1910 series, scored. Inspired by the example of Gerhard Morkel, Millar's men then staged a tremendous fight-back and as one critic put it, "actually had the impudence to open the game". From a scrum, that shrewd old campaigner Dobbin feinted towards the blindside and then hurled a long pass to Jackie Morkel on the open side who dropped a beautiful goal. Although London got another try before the final whistle after an all-out forward attack, they could not make up the leeway and the Springboks squeezed home 12-8.

Strangely enough, in a second encounter against London six matches later, the Springboks lost 8-10 on a fine, firm surface which should have suited them perfectly. This match was memorable for the fact that a penalty try was awarded against the Springboks: still the only time in our history that this has happened.

A. O. Jones, the referee and a former England cricket captain, took the drastic decision after a long kick-ahead had sent the ball rolling over the South African goalline. The London loose forward W. S. D. Craven was chasing after it when the referee ruled that Gerhard Morkel had obstructed him with his elbow.

It was a bad day generally for the Springboks. Mills and Millar were both injured and virtually passengers and the backs, even Dick Luyt, were right off form. Jan Stegmann, in spite of defending well, was particularly unhappy and did not look like the player who got four tries in the match against Glamorgan and who was to do so well in the tests later on the tour. Millett, the London fullback was the hero of the match and his desperate tackles after breaks by Dobbin and Fred Luyt, saved certain tries. Playing for London was W. J. A. (Dave) Davies, one of the greatest flyhalves in rugby history. Davies made his test debut against Millar's Springboks and went on to play for England for 11 years.

One of the major missions of Millar's team was to avenge the 1906 defeat by Scotland. Their chances of doing so were not regarded as being particularly good, mainly because their performances up to that stage of the tour were rather erratic.

Millar was injured and could not play in the test and "Uncle" Dobbin, a survivor of the 1906 defeat in the mud, took over the captaincy. This time the raw Scottish elements did not come to the home team's aid; the weather was fine and the ground reasonably firm when the two teams trotted onto Inverleith, Edinburgh, accompanied by a band of pipers. In the vast crowd were about 200 South Africans who were studying at various universities in Britain and who had organised themselves into a small but very noisy task force of supporters. Millar who spent the match chewing his nails on the main stand, said afterwards that these students sang well-known Afrikaans folk songs with such gusto that they often drowned the vocal support from the thousands of home team supporters. Not that Scotland's backers had much to shout about as the Springboks were in control from the first whistle to the last.

The forwards were in particularly good form. Scotland, in those days, relied heavily on dribbling charges, but the Springboks countered this by falling on the ball and then quickly forming a loose scrum to regain possession. The plan was to beat Scotland up front before bringing the backs into the picture and it worked a lot quicker than the South Africans ever dared to hope for. Scotland obviously had the same strategy and when they suddenly found that their forwards could not take charge, they seemed too surprised to be able to think of an alternative.

The Springboks occasionally tried a backline movement, but with W. M. Dickson, a South African studying at Oxford, saving time and again they decided to hold the threequarters in reserve until their opponents had been thoroughly softened up. It was a pattern foreign to Springbok teams of those days and it had Scotland

really puzzled. In fact, the subdue-and-penetrate philosophy which was to become so ingrained in South African rugby was probably born that afternoon of November 23, 1912. It is a strategy that can obviously only work if backed up by a powerful pack and Duggie Morkel that day was certainly leading an unstoppable line-up.

Just before half-time Jackie Morkel put a left-footed kick across the field towards the corner flag and right wing Boetie McHardy set off in hot pursuit. For once Dickson made a mistake. Instead of keeping his eye on the ball he glanced at the burly Free Stater steaming down on him and in an instant McHardy had whipped it away from him to crash over the line with, as Millar invariably described it in the many articles he was eventually to write about this great triumph, "his legs and arm flying". I take it that the old Springbok captain was being a stickler for accuracy and that he referred to the arm in the singular because McHardy's other arm presumably was occupied in keeping the ball under control.

During the interval Dobbin gave instructions that the backs were now ready to do their share and the second half was to prove sheer hell for Scotland. Quick and smooth handling gave McHardy a chance to knock several opponents flying as he streaked to the corner flag. A desperate tackle not only stopped him from scoring, but, according to contemporary reports, hurled him into the lap of a lady spectator. This could not have been a pleasant experience for the lady of whose subsequent fate the journalists failed to inform us. McHardy was 6 ft 2 inches tall and while the official records had him down for 180 lbs he always insisted that he actually weighed just over 200 lbs at the time of the tour.

Minutes later the Springboks struck again and this time the move was so slick that not even the fiercest tackling could prevent a try. Freddie Luyt started it from the flyhalf position and the ball was handled twice by several players before Jan Stegmann scored in an easy position for Gerhard Morkel to convert. Another brilliant movement followed in which the passing between the backs and the forwards was so fast that by the time Dick Luyt got the ball at centre, the defence was already hopelessly outflanked and Stegmann galloped through a wide gap to notch his second try.

A brief fight-back by Scotland gave Gerhard Morkel a chance to bring friends and foes to their feet with a rivetting tackle on wing W. R. Sutherland, but it was just a dying effort on the part of the beaten but brave Scots team. Now all they could do was to defend dourly and for the last few minutes of what must have been a truly marvellous game, I quote Millar again:

"It was irresistible football", he reminisced about it later. "We belching forth fierce and scientific raids, and Scotland meeting the attack without bending. There were two movements by our backs and forwards combined, when the ball went right across the ground and back, and not a weak link in the defence was discernible. Then we delivered a pounding forward rush — it was like a volcano and we carried everything before us, including Dickson, the fullback, who, however, held on to the ball to go to earth with six stalwart Springboks on top of him.

"Right on top of our game, our backs were handling the ball in a way which defied the Scots. Once again

Left
The match against Swansea was played on a sopping St. Helen's field and at half-time the Springboks took advantage of the many puddles to wash some of the mud off their hands and faces. The South Africans were beaten 0–3.

the ball crossed the whole line to Stegmann on the right. The winger gave an inside pass, and away went the ball to McHardy on the left. The Free Stater found the way blocked — he could not get through. But Dobbin was lying handy, so "Mac" threw the ball to the little halfback. "Uncle" put in a short snappy sprint, side-stepped an opponent — an old trick of his — and then cross-kicked. It was a dainty touch. Douglas Morkel, ever watchful, came through, snapped up the ball and sent out to Boy Morkel. Away went the Somerset West skipper in his 25 yards dash for the line, to crown one of the most brilliant movements ever witnessed. The ball, in this movement, passed three times across the field, and no one player at any time was tackled in possession!"

West of Scotland was humbled 38-3 only a few days later with McHardy scoring a hat-trick as a harbinger of what he and Jan Stegmann had in store for Ireland in the second test of the tour at Dublin on November 30, 1912.

The hopelessly outclassed Irishmen gave the Springboks the opportunity to establish records it took 40 years and longer to better or equal and the total of 10 tries is still the most ever to be scored by South Africa in an official test. Stegmann and McHardy both got hat-tricks and the feat of two Springboks getting three tries each in the same test has also not yet been equalled.

Jan, younger brother of the 1906 Springbok Anton Stegmann was a big, exceptionally strong runner, who scored five tries in the five tests he played for South Africa. Johannes Augustus (Jan) Stegmann was born at Bedford, Cape, on June 21, 1887, the ninth child of a family of 13. Although he played most of his rugby for Stellenbosch and Western Province, Stegmann was actually a member of Johannesburg's Diggers Club when he gained his Springbok colours in 1912. He retired from rugby after the tour to study dentistry at the University of Edinburgh. He subsequently represented Scotland as a hurdler against Wales, England and Ireland.

Both Anton and Jan always insisted that their brother Ebbie was actually the best player in the family, but a knee injury handicapped his career.

At the time of writing Dr. Jan Stegmann, 90 years old, is South Africa's oldest living Springbok.

McHardy, like Stegmann was tall, powerful and a wonderful athlete. He was the first Springbok ever to score a hat-trick in a test and he totalled an amazing six tries in the five tests he played in an international career brought to a halt by World War I.

Evelyn Edgar McHardy, known throughout the 70 years of his life as "Boetie", was born on June 11, 1890 in Bloemfontein and he was an outstanding athlete at Grey College. Some of his track and field records stood for many years and while doing his matric in 1910, Boetie also won Free State provincial championships over 100, 220 and 440 yards. A year later he represented Free State at the South African athletics championships in Cape Town and in that same year he also made his rugby debut for his province. It is interesting to note that McHardy somehow found the time to play first division hockey as well and that he also took part in soccer when he was a teenager.

McHardy holds another distinction in that he was the first Free Stater ever to score a try against Western Province and it is also a little-known fact that he represented his province from 1911 until 1924! In later years he also served as a provincial coach and selector.

That famous day in Dublin, McHardy was 22 years old, brimful of confidence, and a member of a team which, viewed in retrospect, had few if any weaknesses. The weather was cold, but frost had made the ground hard but firm, the sort of conditions the mobile Springboks relished.

Except for a few sporadic attempts early in the match it was just not a day for the Irish. Gerhard Morkel and Richard Luyt halted an early Irish rush with beautiful defensive work and from the next onslaught from the home team, who were in their traditional green after the Springboks had sportingly agreed to wear white jerseys, South Africa launched a counter attack that just about broke the spirit of their opponents. The Irish forwards were dribbling furiously towards the Springbok line when Fred Luyt, with breathtaking timing, scooped the ball off an opponent's boot and whipped a lightning pass to Dobbin. The veteran Springbok halfback passed to Jackie Morkel deep in his own half, then it was on to Dick Luyt and finally safely into the hands of Jan Stegmann.

Stegmann jerked himself past his opposite number, beat another defender and left the fullback standing to score after a magnificent 55-yard run. Not long afterwards McHardy received the ball three times in fairly quick succession and on each occasion he scored. The first of his three tries was a really splendid effort as it came after a 50-yard sprint in which the fullback, who tried to tackle him, was sent cartwheeling as he bounced off the big Springbok's muscular body. The half-time score was 12-0.

The second half was a nightmare for the Irish supporters. "All Ireland won here yesterday was the toss", one reporter wrote later and another described the Springbok attacks as "the most impudent" he had ever seen. Stegmann added two more tries to his tally to also notch a hat-trick, Jackie Morkel got two tries and forwards J. A. J. (Joe) Francis and Billy Millar got one each. Freddie Luyt succeeded with one conversion and Gerhard Morkel with three.

David McDonigal, a well known referee who settled in Cape Town in later years, saw the Lansdowne slaughter as a boy and he gave a most amusing if not always strictly correct, description of what it was like to be Irish that day.

"How optimistic we were!", he

wrote. "Did we not remember that Paul Roos and his male beauty chorus had only just succeeded in beating us in 1906? And were we not given to understand that the 1906 Springboks were better than the 1912 variety? And had we not got the great Dickey Lloyd, the nippy Harry Read, the elusive Jeb Minch and the untiring Billy Burgess? What was there to be afraid of?

"Alas, what vain optimism. Ireland won the toss — it was the only thing we won that afternoon — and South Africa kicked off. The ball was fumbled and went into touch near our '25'. From the lineout there was a scrum. I distinctly saw the ball heeled cleanly into the hands of the waiting half, and the next thing I saw was a gentleman called Stegmann taking long strides up to the touch-line and scoring behind the posts. He was a Springbok sprightly springing, or, as they say in Ireland, 'Away he went, leppin' like a hare'. That was only the beginning and I think it best to draw a veil over the rest of that awful day. I well remember a remark passed by a friend of mine from far-away Kerry. The Springboks had rattled up some 20 points and Ireland were kicking off for the umpteenth time. During that moment of waiting, my friend exclaimed: '*Dearly beloved brethren, let us join in singing God Save Oireland, for it's destroyed we are, entoirely!*'

"When we were walking away from the ground I happened to say 'Well, anyhow, it was a glorious exhibition of rugby.'

"My friend replied: '*Bedad, me bhoy, that wasn't rugby at all. At laste, if it was, heaven alone knows what we've been playing these past years!*' "

A cartoon published in a Dublin newspaper the day after the game showed Billy Millar eating 38 pieces of shamrock while Dickie Lloyd, drawn as a sad-looking Irish terrier, is sitting up, begging for a piece. The caption read: "And so the poor dog got none!"

Cardiff Arms Park was so waterlogged for the test against Wales that the Springboks fully expected to lose. But not even the Welshmen could come to terms with blinding rain and gale strength wind which tortured players alike throughout the game. The imperturbable Duggie Morkel somehow steered a penalty over the crossbar early in the match and after that it was mainly a matter of, as Millar described it, "heavy tackling, battering, slashing — in fact a cheery mill".

Gerhard Morkel and Boetie McHardy distinguished themselves with tremendous work on the defence, but with the players slithering and sliding all over the place in the pelting rain, proper rugby was out of the question. Wales had a wonderful opportunity of levelling the score when they received a penalty virtually in front of the posts in the second half, but to the utter despair of thousands of drenched supporters, centre F. W. Birt, reputed to be the best placekicker in Wales at the time, sliced the ball so badly that Stegmann caught it on the corner flag!

It must have been a fantastic match for Free State's Boetie McHardy. Reports of the game describe at least three occasions where he saved the Springboks with his alert cover defence and on reading this, one cannot help but see a strong similarity between him and the Jannie Engelbrecht of nearly 50 years later. Like Engelbrecht, McHardy used his exceptional speed and intuitive positioning to act as an extra fullback.

In the final 10 minutes of the match McHardy very nearly crowned his remarkable performance with two tries. The first time he followed up his own punt only to lose the slippery ball as he dived over the line and on the second occasion he was stopped with literally inches to go. In the end it was Duggie Morkel's penalty that made all the difference, just as Keith Oxlee's one swung the scales South Africa's way 48 years later on the same field and under equally atrocious conditions.

The Springboks then, as now, enjoyed their rugby in Wales; hard and uncompromising, but with a genuinely warm spirit of hospitality afterwards. The remarkable enthusiasm of the crowds thrilled Billy Millar's men although Joe Francis, for one, had reason to be sympathetic towards the problems of the brave fellows who were prepared to act as referees in Wales in those days. In the match against Neath, Francis was standing around minding his own business during a stoppage for injury. His one mistake was that he was near the referee, a not very popular one with the crowd. Suddenly a clod of earth intended for the official sailed from the crowd and hit Francis solidly on the ear. Apparently Francis could swear with particular fluency and he spent a full minute loudly vowing vengeance.

The match against Cardiff, who beat the 1906 Springboks, must have been the most exciting of the tour. It was a fine, sunny day and the South Africans should have won without too much trouble, but in R. F. Williams Cardiff had a fullback who could tackle a demon. A small chap who had lost the thumb and two fingers of one hand, he time and again tackled the dangerous Stegmann in full cry — a remarkable performance as Stegmann in addition to his speed, had a difficult high-kneed action. All the Springboks were unanimous that they had never seen a better tackler and for Stegmann, who rarely in his life failed to beat a fullback in a man-to-man situation, it must have been a most frustrating experience. McHardy also did not have a good day; with the line open in front of him he once slipped and fell for no apparent reason.

The Springboks eventually won 7-6 after a dropgoal by Jackie Morkel and a penalty by Duggie Morkel, a man who always seemed to kick best when the pressure was on. The penalty, given against Williams for obstruction should, under the advantage rule, not have been given as both Morkel and Stegmann were in position to score a try. Instead of that, it was up to Morkel to bang over a penalty from virtually the halfway line. This he did and another 1906 defeat was avenged.

The test against England will always be remembered for the superb try by the England centre Ronnie Poulton. From an orthodox threequarter movement, Poulton suddenly cut sharply inside before swerving his way right through the Springbok team to score under the posts. Incredibly, the conversion kick was fluffed. Not long afterwards the great England player very nearly succeeded with a similar break, but McHardy's blistering speed on the cover defence stopped him a yard from the line. Typical work by Dick Luyt enabled Jackie Morkel to score the equalising try and two fine penalty goals from a long way out by that valuable forward Duggie Morkel sealed England's fate and gave the 1912/13 Springboks a clean sweep of the four tests. There is a tragic footnote to this match. Both Jackie Morkel and Poulton were killed in battle during World War I. Poulton, incidentally, changed his name to Poulton Palmer in April, 1914, after his uncle, the Rt. Hon. G. W. Palmer had died, leaving him a fortune.

Duggie Morkel's awesome kicking impressed the Twickenham crowd almost as much as brilliant tries by Poulton and Jackie Morkel.

After the second penalty sailed over the crossbar from near the halfway line, a cockney spectator was heard to remark to his chum:

"Say, 'Erb, they'll 'ave to lengthen this 'ere ground if that bloke's goin' to stick 'round 'ere!"

The tour ended with a test against France at Bordeaux and although the Springboks won 38-5, veterans of the 1906 tour could note a marked improvement in French rugby.

The French pack turned in a lively performance, but their backs were woefully weak. McHardy scored two tries and Duggie Morkel tallied 13 points on his own, including a massive dropped penalty from near the halfway line and two tries.

The kick came after the referee had given the Springboks a penalty Billy Millar did not really want to accept as he thought the decision was unfair. He instructed Morkel to give the French fullback a high-up-and-under with plenty of time to gather and clear. Morkel, however, preferred to take a pot at goal and it is said that even the French players applauded when the ball sailed high over the crossbar.

And so Billy Millar's Springboks ended their tour on a triumphant note. They played exciting rugby, behaved impeccably and built further on the foundation laid so solidly by Paul Roos six years earlier.

As for Billy Millar, he was still not ready to settle down to the quiet life. When World War I broke out, he immediately joined the action. Once again, he was severely wounded, but with typical resilience fought back to recover his health. Virtually one-armed, he returned to civilian life to become a better-than-average golfer and as a referee he took the whistle in two of the four tests against Cove-Smith's touring team in South Africa in 1924.

Cardiff Arms Park was a sea of mud and water when Wales and the Springboks met in 1912. Here Duggie Morkel is photographed in the act of kicking the decisive penalty which gave his team victory.

Steel meets steel

Theo Pienaar was already past his best but he was considered the man best qualified to lead the first Springbok team to tour New Zealand.

The Great War of 1914/18 was the only reason why the first clash between world rugby's lustiest infants, New Zealand and South Africa, did not take place until 1921; more than a decade and a half after both had made their first successful tours to Britain.

We got some experience of All Blacks rugby when a team selected from New Zealand's Armed Forces paid us a brief visit in 1919 and by winning 10 out of 14 matches with one drawn, they caused serious pondering among the locals over how difficult it must be to take on a fully representative side from the two little islands way down under.

The opportunity to find out came at last in 1921, when New Zealand invited the Springboks for a full-scale tour. And since they would be in the vicinity anyway, the South Africans were also asked to play a few matches in Australia where the game was then still in the fledgling stage and almost entirely confined to New South Wales.

National selectors Bill Schreiner, A. F. Markotter, James Leck (a gentleman almost as irritable as Mr. Mark and who, as a referee, once gave Springbok and Western Province captain Billy Millar his marching orders in a Currie Cup match), S. A. Townsend and C. V. Becker, although they did their best, found there was rather general dissatisfaction with the team they selected to do battle with the mighty All Blacks. In retrospect, this lack of confidence is inexplicable as the team was studded with players whose names are now bywords in the history of South African rugby.

Theodorus Barend Pienaar, born on November 25, 1888, and thus already in his 33rd year, was given the captaincy, although it was obvious to all that he was past his best and unlikely to earn a place in the test teams. But Theo Pienaar had undoubted leadership qualities and the selectors' decision was certainly based on a desire to give H. C. Bennett, the tour manager, some mature assistance.

Pienaar, one of eight sons born to a Dutch Reformed Church minister at Somerset West, was a good forward in his day and a member of Boy Morkel's 1914 Western Province team, for many years considered to be the finest provincial combination ever to be assembled in this country. He later often captained Western Province and had an instinctive knack of handling a band of boisterous players.

William Henry (Boy) Morkel, long established as one of the mightiest forwards in the world, was appointed the vice-captain and at 35, he was even older than Pienaar. There were four other Morkels in the side, full-back Gerhard, wing Henry and the two brothers Harry and Royal, who were both forwards. Gerhard, one of the heroes of the 1912/13 team in Britain and France, was then 33 years old, but such a master of positional play that his marked slowness was hardly a handicap. It is a fact that he was never, even when at his peak, fast on his feet.

The selection of Boy Morkel was really an indication of how independently selectors could act in those days. Morkel was then farming in the Western Transvaal and playing only the occasional match. When the selectors called on him he, in the tradition of the Roman general Cincinnatus, left his plough because his country needed him more than his farm did.

The tour also marked the appearance on the international scene of Phil Mostert, destined to become one of the finest forwards ever to wear the Springbok jersey, but before we focus on this rugby giant, there are a few other interesting members of the 1921 side who deserve special mention.

The tall, strongly-built wing, Attie van Heerden, was born on March 10, 1898, one of the two sons of a Dutch Reformed Church minister, and both he and his brother Nico followed in their father's footsteps and played for the University of Stellenbosch. Attie was also an outstanding sprinter and he represented South Africa at the Olympic Games in Antwerp in 1920 before he joined the exclusive brotherhood of double Springboks a year later. Van Heerden, rather surprisingly, left for England after the tour to play professionally for the rugby league club, Wigan.

Frank Whitmore Mellish was a double international with a difference. In the European rugby season just before he gained his Springbok colours, Mellish represented England against Scotland, Ireland, Wales and France. A tough bustling forward, Frank Mellish was born at Rondebosch in 1897 and learnt his rugby at Wynberg Boys High, Rondebosch Boys High and the South African College School. As a teenager he joined the Cape Town Highlanders and fought in what was then known as German South West Africa during World War I. He later joined the South African Heavy Artillery in France and won a commission and the Military Cross during the bloody battles near the end of the war. Mellish, who attained the rank of Colonel in World War II, was to play for South Africa in six tests, but it would not be an injustice to say that his most lasting contribution to South

W. H. Morkel, better known as "Boy", was recalled to duty from his Western Transvaal farm and this mighty forward captained the Springboks in all three tests against the All Blacks.

Phil Mostert, in action for his club, Somerset West. Strong and intelligent, Mostert was one of the finest all-round forwards in South African rugby history.

Die Burger

African rugby was the magnificent job he did as manager of the marvellous Springbok touring team to Britain and France in 1951-52.

The 1921 team also included Billy Sendin, a Griqualand West centre-threequarter who, at 132 lbs, is still the lightest player ever to represent South Africa. There have been many arguments over Sendin's weight over the years. He once admitted that acting on the advice of Jimmy Leck, one of the 1921 national selectors, he had told the authorities that his weight was 150 lbs! Leck knew that his colleagues were on the look-out for heavy backs for New Zealand's wet conditions and that they would never have considered Sendin had they known how little he really weighed.

L. B. Siedle, another member of the team at 5ft 9½ and 168 lbs, must be the smallest forward ever to wear the Springbok jersey. Siedle, incidentally, was injured in the first match and he did not play again on the tour.

The years to come would also give significance to the selection of Alf Walker, Nic du Plessis and Phil Mostert. Walker, the brother of the 1910 Springbok Henry Walker, lived to see his son, Harry Newton, earn his own green and gold jersey against Australia in 1953 while Mostert's nephew was Jan Lotz, one of the most outstanding members of the 1937 Springbok team to tour New Zealand. Nic du Plessis' nephew, Felix, captained South Africa against the All Blacks 28 years later, while Felix's son, Morne, earned the same honour in 1975 against France and a year later against the All Blacks.

But the greatest player to emerge from the 1921 tour was undoubtedly Phillipus Jacobus Mostert. He was born in Krugersdorp on October 30 1898, but his widowed mother shortly afterwards moved to Somerset West where his instinctive rugby talent had the opportunity of blossoming in one of the strongest club sides in the country.

Phil Mostert had the solid build of the ideal forward, but he was also remarkably fast and he could kick and handle with the aplomb of a top-class flyhalf. In fact, he is still the only Springbok ever to have dropped a goal from a mark in a test match (against Maurice Brownlie's All Blacks at Ellis Park in 1928) and he often did the most unpredictable things on the field. That dropkicking genius Bennie Osler, who always regarded Mostert as the best player he ever saw in any position, used to enjoy telling how Phil, in an interprovincial match, once refused to pass him the ball in an ideal situation for a pot at goal. Mostert, instead, took the kick himself and succeeded! As the ball sailed over the crossbar, this most charming of men turned to the gaping Osler and grinned: "You see, Bennie? You thought you're the only man who could do this sort of thing, eh?"

Superlatively fit, Mostert could maintain a cracking pace for the full duration of a match and at the start of his career his exuberance often tempted him into some aimless running around. Again it was the genius of Markotter who guided him on the right track. Mark knocked this particular habit out of young Mostert with a single sarcastic remark. "Mostert, you're a first-class player," the Matie coach told him one day, "but somebody should put a saddle and reins on you!" Mostert got the message and he quickly developed into a remarkably intelligent forward. A very tough man physically, Mostert believed in playing the game cleanly and his method of retaliation was to smile at his opponent, crack a joke, and then to squeeze the very life out of him with legitimately-used strength. He had a very nimble brain with a refined aptitude for all forms of gamesmanship; something which is really part of all sport and must not be confused with cheating.

Danie Craven tells the story of how Mostert once tackled a Stellenbosch player from a blatantly off-side position when he realised a try could not be stopped. He then proceeded to put up such an excellent act of having accidentally stumbled into the path of the attacking Matie, that the referee awarded a scrum instead of a penalty try or, at the very least, a penalty. Craven immediately reproached him about this, but Mostert took all the wind out of his sails by replying: "Daantjie, these little things will happen. You fellows are going to win, anyway!"

For many years there was a strong belief among fans and even some players that Mostert actually carried a black glove in a pocket of his shorts which he would use for "hooking" the ball with his hand. This was one story this invariably calm and relaxed Springbok denied vehemently.

"We must have had blind referees all over the place if they could not see the difference between a hand, covered in a black glove or not, and a rugby boot," he once told me. "I did enjoy making a few jokes on the field, but they were always harmless and never affected the result of a game."

But he never denied one of the best of the many stories told about him. During the 1931 trials Mostert once kicked the ball too hard in a dribbling rush and Gerry Brand had all the time in the world to save the situation. The national selectors happened to be sitting on the touchline and, while the drop-out was being taken, Phil took the opportunity of loudly berating his fellow forwards for having done such a stupid thing. It is doubtful whether he fooled the selectors, even more doubtful whether he intended fooling them, but there can be no doubt at all that he gave everybody around a good laugh. He was booked for the tour to Britain long before the trials took place, anyway.

Mostert always had a particularly high regard for his fellow forwards on the 1921 tour. He considered Theuns Kruger ("as good as any specialist in every position in the pack"), Mervyn Ellis ("the finest and fastest loose-forward I ever saw") Tank van Rooyen, Nic du Plessis, Alf Walker, Frank Mellish and Boy Morkel, although then past his best, as players who would have more than held their own in any era of Springbok rugby history.

Pienaar and his men set out for the big adventure on the *S.S. Aeneas* and after 17 days on the high seas they docked in Adelaide harbour for the Australian part of the tour.

For the first match against the Springboks, an unofficial fixture, the small rugby community of Victoria had to actually advertise for players in order to raise a full team and it is hardly surprising that the South

Frank Mellish earned the distinction of having played for both England and South Africa. Photographed here in his World War I uniform, Mellish was awarded the Military Cross in World War I and attained the rank of colonel in World War II.

Africans romped home 51-0 without exactly over-exerting themselves. The three consecutive matches against New South Wales were also won, but the opposition was a lot more fierce.

In the first match against New South Wales, Attie van Heerden's flashing speed carried him to five tries, a Springbok record until Roy Dryburgh notched six tries against Queensland in 1956. In one of the matches Gerhard Morkel's deadly crashtackling so annoyed a section of the crowd that he afterwards had to be smuggled back to his hotel with the aid of his Australian opponents. Although a veteran of 33, he was to play first league club rugby for another 10 years. Morkel was still a tremendous player; plain murder against opponents who did not know with what bullet-like force he could launch his tackles from the slight crouch he used to adopt as an attacker sped towards him.

Undefeated at the end of the Australian leg of the tour, the Springboks nevertheless were not in a happy mood when they boarded the *S.S. Mararoa* for the big stuff against New Zealand. No less than eight members of the team had been injured in the five matches in Australia, including L. B. ("Jack") Siedle whose knee injury would spell the end of his playing days, skipper Theo Pienaar with severe concussion and Gerhard Morkel with a dislocated elbow from which it took him several weeks to recover.

Then, as now, New Zealanders loved their rugby and the Springboks were stunned at the warmth of their reception, with cheering crowds, pipers and brass bands meeting and following them wherever they went.

Sas de Kock, the Springbok flyhalf, broke his ankle against Wangunui in the first game on New Zealand soil and was out for practically the rest of the tour. There was enough reserve strength in the touring party, however, for them not to worry unduly over the fact that their call for replacements had fallen on deaf ears and they managed to get through the tough provincial fixtures with only one defeat (4-6 to Canterbury) and one draw (0-0 against Taranaki).

In these matches the Springboks encountered two opponents who deserve some special mention. Playing at centre for Wellington against them was a "Reverend Paul Markham" who was reported to have been a monk whose real name was Father Paul Kane.

In the Hawke's Bay/Povery Bay side they met a solid young lock

Gerhard Morkel had reached the veteran stage by the time the Springboks first clashed with the All Blacks. And yet this legendary fullback played brilliantly in all three tests.

The hospitality in New Zealand was wonderful and Pienaar's Springboks did not lack entertainment off the field. Here Tank van Rooyen, Harry Morkel, Mervyn Ellis and Gerhard Morkel show their catch after a fishing trip.

The Springbok line-up just before the start of the first-ever test against the All Blacks
From left to right: Theo Pienaar, Boy Morkel, Gerhard Morkel, Mannetjies Michau, Wally Clarkson, C. du P. Meyer, Frank Mellish, Baby Michau, Harry Morkel, Henry Morkel, Phil Mostert, Hugo Scholtz, Attie van Heerden, Alf Walker, Teuns Kruger, W. H. Townsend.

forward called Thomas Heeney, who was later to gain considerable fame as a heavyweight boxer. Seven years after playing against the Springboks, Tom Heeney challenged champion Gene Tunney for the world heavyweight championship. Nick-named "The Hard Rock from Down Under", Heeney was knocked out after a brave battle against one of the greatest of all heavyweight champions.

The first-ever test match between the Springboks and the All Blacks took place at Carisbrook, Dunedin, on Saturday, August 13, 1921 beginning one of the keenest rivalries in sport.

With Theo Pienaar injured, the South Africans were led by Boy Morkel while George Aitken was in charge of the All Blacks. Aitken was a centre threequarter described by contemporary newspaper reports as someone who "understood the art of making gaps for his wings". Morkel retained the captaincy for all three tests, but Aitken took some of the blame for the defeat in the second test and had to make way for Teddy Roberts. The chopping of a captain after defeat was something to be not exactly uncommon in all future series between the Springboks and the All Blacks, and a practice not peculiar to the New Zealanders only.

In the words of Hugo (Tokkie) Scholtz, who played in that historic first test between the two countries, both teams were "too scared to open up for the first 25 minutes".

Then the Springboks suddenly shook off their bad case of nerves and Attie van Heerden, showing the pace that made him an Olympic sprinter, slashed through for a try next to the posts. Gerhard Morkel converted and the half-time score was 5-0.

In the second half the All Blacks woke up with a vengeance and for the first time the Springboks got a taste of the fury of a thoroughly aroused New Zealand pack. With loose forward "Moke" Belliss playing like a man gone berserk, the All Blacks ran the South Africans off their feet to score three tries; two converted by young Mark Nicholls who was still to play such a major role in one of the epic future battles between the two countries. One of the tries was notched by the rampant Belliss while wings Percy Storey and Jack Steel got one each to give New Zealand a convincing 13-5 victory.

Steel's try must have been something to see. New Zealand were pinned back deep in their own half when the ball was thrown haphazardly in Steel's direction. It went over his shoulder, but he flung up an arm and somehow managed to clamp it between his shoulder blades. With the ball held in this extremely akward position, he squeezed past the defence and was in the clear and running as hard as he could while frantically trying to get a more manageable grasp on it. A few yards from the Springbok goal-line he at last had the ball in his hands to score what must have been a remarkable try.

More than 40 000 people paid more than £4 000 to see the second test at Eden Park, Auckland. On a hard, dry surface the Springboks, forwards in particular, played much better than in the first international. "Tank" van Rooyen, a muscular Transvaler who hardly ever made his provincial team because he was considered "too dumb", but whose latent talent was immediately spotted by the omniscient Markotter, was perhaps the best of a brilliant pack. Van Rooyen turned professional shortly after the tour to play Rugby League for Wigan in England — a great loss to Springbok rugby.

It was he who initiated the South Africans' only try when he picked up the loose ball after a fine break by the balding C. Meyer, who was playing at flyhalf, although originally selected as a centre or wing. Van Rooyen passed to Mannetjies Michau who ran well before giving to Wally Clarkson whose perfectly-timed pass enabled Billy Sendin, the little Griqualand West centre, to go over in a good position for Gerhard Morkel to convert. The All Blacks equalized quickly enough when McLean scored after some good work between Roberts, Nicholls, Badeley, Aitken and the ever-present Belliss. Nicholls converted with a rather lucky kick, the ball hitting the far upright and rebounding over the cross-bar.

With the score level, the two teams really flew into the fray but according to contemporary reports the match stayed clean but "rather untidy". After half-time came the most memorable moment of the match. The All Blacks forwards started a dribbling rush, but the ball was kicked too far ahead and Gerhard Morkel picked it up near the half-way line and a few feet from touch. He ran infield a few steps and then, as one of the reporters wrote afterwards "he let go with the right foot, the ball sailing fairly and squarely between the goalposts and high up over the centre".

The magnificent kick so thrilled the sporting crowd that, so the legend goes, a few uninhibited souls actually ran on to the field and offered the Springbok fullback a drink. Morkel solemnly lifted the glass in a toast to the crowd and took a few sips, again strictly according to unofficial reports.

The huge crowd did, in fact, get rather out of hand in the tense second half. Springbok wing Bill Zeller, who was one of the out-standing players of the day, was in the clear once after a strong run when he found himself surrounded by so many spectators that he mistakenly thought that he had run into touch. He duly stopped and gave the ball to an opponent for a line-out only to discover to his horror that he was still very much in the playing area!

And so the Springboks won 9-5 to keep the series in the balance, but for at least one of them there was already a prize to take home. The Auckland rugby authorities presented Gerhard Morkel with a gold medal to commemorate his outstanding performance and, more particularly, that drop goal that won the match for his team.

E. E. Hughes, one of the New Zealand forwards in this test, actually first represented the All Blacks in 1907! He then turned professional but regained his amateur status eventually. He was certainly over 40 years old when he played against Pienaar's team, and he and Les Saxby, who represented England against the 1931/32 Springboks when already in his 40's, must be the oldest players ever to have played test rugby.

The third and deciding test was played at Athletic Park, Wellington in pouring rain and with a gale-strength wind which really made it impossible for either team to play constructive rugby. It is hardly surprising that neither side could score any points, but it was nevertheless a tense and exciting match.

Both fullbacks, C. N. Kingstone of New Zealand and Gerhard Morkel, were magnificent and the two packs "laboured mightily in the mud". Morkel in the final test of his career, did not put a foot wrong and years later Phil Mostert recounted how he and his teammates would time and again hear the sound as the wet and heavy ball slapped into his hands followed by an even louder thud as his powerful boot would thump it into touch a split-second later. "It was raining so heavily that we could hardly see one another," Mostert remembered. "Gerhard was like a ghostly shadow somewhere at the back of us and he saved us from defeat, that's for sure".

New Zealand came closest to scoring a try in the match when Keith Siddells, on the wing, dived on a loose ball behind the goal-line, but Mr. A. E. Neilson, the referee, ruled that he did not get his hands to the ball. As

Left: Gerhard Morkel converts a try by Attie van Heerden in the first test against the All Blacks in 1921. On the right is Boy Morkel.

Above: Attie van Heerden, a tall and extremely fast wing from University of Stellenbosch, splashes towards a loose ball. Van Heerden, who also represented South Africa at the 1920 Olympic Games as a sprinter, scored the first-ever try between the Springboks and the All Blacks in the first test of the 1921 series.

recently as 1967, Siddells was quoted in a newspaper report as saying that Mr. Neilson was "a little too fair" to the Springboks on that rain-swept afternoon. The Springboks also had their hard-luck story. Phil Mostert, who played a storming game, once lost the slippery ball even in the act of diving over the New Zealand goal-line.

The final whistle blew with no score on the board and the first test series between the Springboks and the All Blacks had ended with honours even.

Theo Pienaar and his men were never given full credit for what they achieved on the first tour of New Zealand. Injuries hit the side so hard that they rarely had more than 24 players to draw from and why their request for two replacements was not only ignored by the rugby authorities, but actually ridiculed by some of the newspaper critics, is impossible to understand. Even after the return of the team, South Africans seemed reluctant to give them their due. No wonder Theo Pienaar was compelled to write in an article published shortly afterwards:

"True, we may not have done much that was sensational, but let me stress this point, there is neither time nor place for the sensational in New Zealand football". Over the years a succession of Springbok teams have learnt through bitter experience that a world of wisdom was locked up in Pienaar's statement.

The New Zealanders were much more kind to their visitors. They labelled them the "greatest defensive team" they had ever seen, pointing out that only 13 tries were scored against the Springboks in their 19 matches. What was praise in the land of the Kiwi was perverted into criticism in South Africa where, as Pienaar said even before the tour began, "the public had a sad lack of loyalty to their own chosen gladiators".

"The Springboks were sent to attack, not to defend", some critics claimed and for them Pienaar had an answer the truth of which we were to learn in the years to come:

"Go out there yourselves and fight a New Zealand team on its own soil," he said. "A team that is filled with consciousness of its own prowess and flushed with great achievements of the past. And if you do not eat humble pie on your return, well — I shall!"

His words are still valid after 55 years of relentless rivalry. And what he said about New Zealand rugby, the All Blacks subsequently found to be as true of the game in South Africa.

2 / THE GOLDEN ERA

Mr Mark's choice

Pieter Kuyper Albertyn, known throughout his life as Pierre or "P.K.", would probably never have played for South Africa had it not been for a homeopath's treatment and the determination of A. F. Markotter that such instinctive talent should not go to waste.

It would obviously be unfair not to mention his own perseverance in conquering what was considered to be a crippling injury and his courage in risking further injury. But it was "professor" Clifford Severn, the nature cure specialist, who proved the original medical diagnosis incorrect and it was Markotter who refused to forget his former protege.

Albertyn was a brilliant left-wing at the University of Stellenbosch; so outstanding that Markotter ranked him with Japie Krige and Bob Loubser as one of the three greatest players he ever saw. "The world beaters", he used to call them. Albertyn was tall and strong and he could hold his own with top athletes over the sprint distances, but he could also sidestep with bewildering ease and guiding all that natural ability was a subtle rugby brain.

It was Paul Roos who first talked young Pierre's reluctant mother into allowing the boy to play when he was still a pupil at Stellenbosch Boys High. The old Springbok captain was principal of this school which was eventually to carry his name. Albertyn showed instant promise and at the age of 17 he was playing senior rugby and leaving such renowned tacklers as Gerhard Morkel sprawled in his wake after dazzling sidesteps.

Early in the 1919 season, playing for Stellenbosch against Villagers at Newlands, he scored no less than six tries in the first 15 minutes of the match. At half-time Markotter, who always had a soft spot for Villagers, a club he once belonged to, instructed his surprised Maties to keep the ball among the forwards for the rest of the match. His excuse was that he wanted them to practice wheeling the scrum, but all the players knew and accepted that he did not want Villagers to suffer any further humiliation. His orders were followed so meticulously that Stellenbosch added only one more try in the second half and Albertyn did not get any more chances to add to his already amazing tally.

Not long afterwards Albertyn was selected for Western Province Universities to play against a New Zealand Imperial Services team then on a 14-match tour of South Africa. It was to be just another step up the ladder to Springbok colours, but it was in this game that he suffered the injury that should really have ended his career.

Slipping between two defenders, he was heavily tackled from both sides and one of the New Zealanders came down with his full weight on the young wing's akwardly-angled leg. The impact tore all the ligaments in his knee and there was so much internal bleeding that the leg actually turned black later that night. Doctors told him never to play rugby again, adding that he would be fortunate not to be crippled for life.

Clifford Severn, one of the best-known nature cure exponents in South Africa in those days, took a personal interest in the 22-year-old student's predicament. With massage and other treatment, he managed to get the knee back into some sort of working order and a special guard made from crepe bandage, rubber bands and elastic was designed for further protection. Amazingly enough, Albertyn was able to play again after only six weeks of treatment and he celebrated his return by scoring five tries against Somerset West; leaving Gerhard Morkel helpless on more than one occasion with a sidestep the veteran Springbok fullback simply could not solve.

But Albertyn realised nevertheless that he would never again be quite the player he used to be and with typical level-headedness he decided to adapt his game to his new handicap. He accepted that his days as a wing were over because he could not risk being tackled in full flight and he also felt that he no longer had the speed so essential in this position. Albertyn played several matches as an extra back as Stellenbosch could afford to

P. K. Albertyn, the 1924 Springbok captain, and A. F. Markotter, who never lost faith in his protege. Four years before he gained international colours, doctors advised Albertyn to retire rather than risk further injury.

go on the field with only seven forwards, but he found that he could no longer turn or change direction suddenly without feeling discomfort and his career was certainly in the balance when, at the end of that season, he left for Guy's Hospital to study dentistry.

The softer grounds in England did not put quite such a strain on his weak leg and he played some of the most enjoyable rugby of his life for this famous hospital. He even represented the Barbarians, but refused an invitation to play in the England trials.

When he returned to South Africa three years later, Albertyn regarded himself as virtually retired although he was then only 26 years old. He opened a practice at George and played in matches for the town club without a thought of attempting anything more ambitious.

But A. F. Markotter had not forgotten him. His mind was made up that Albertyn would be one of the Springbok centres against R. Cove-Smith's 1924 British touring team, regardless of what the other selectors might think. Albertyn was not selected for the first trials and there was general consensus that the team for the first test would come from a nucleus of 17 players whose names were announced afterwards. Albertyn's name was not on the list but in the meantime the determined Markotter had asked somebody whose opinion he valued to take a look at Albertyn's form in club matches. He received an encouraging reply and acting in his usual unilateral way, he simply ordered Albertyn to report for a trials match to be played in Durban.

A youthful Bennie Osler, wearing the Springbok jersey for the first time, is photographed a few days before making his international debut.

This game was actually regarded by most as just a practice run for the probable Springbok side. When Albertyn arrived in Durban, Mr. Mark gave him only one instruction: "Don't go and make a bloody fool of yourself!" Albertyn proceeded to do nothing foolish and that night to the astonishment of just about everybody, it was announced that he was to be South Africa's new rugby captain.

Bad luck dogged Ronald Cove-Smith's 1924 British team almost from the moment the names of the members of the touring party were announced. Several had to withdraw for various reasons and injuries presented a problem from the first practice when the one fullback, W. F. Gaisford, was eliminated for the rest of the tour and the other fullback, T. E. Holliday suffered the same fate in the first match. Fortunately the No. I. choice for this position, Dan Drysdale, survived. W. A. Cunningham, an Irish international then resident in Johannesburg, was invited to join the side and he actually played in the third test and also scored a try. Halfway through the tour H. J. Davies, a Welsh centre, was sent over as a replacement and he also twice made appearances at fullback.

There had to be constant juggling throughout the tour to field a full team and the versatile Tom Voyce, for instance, played a few matches as a wing or a fullback. Jamie Clinch and Stanley Harris, forward and wing respectively, also had to fill in whenever the sorely-tried Drysdale needed a rest. Drysdale, incidentally, was one of the best players in the team although he did miss an easy penalty kick which could have given the "Lions", as they were beginning to be called, their only test victory.

J. D. Clinch, whose father A. D. Clinch was a member of Hammond's 1896 team, was also outstanding and so was Voyce, who by accident or design was switched from centre to the pack during the England trials for the tour and nevertheless managed to earn his place.

There were several interesting players in the touring team, with the selection of some gaining added significance in later years. Herbert Waddell, the Scottish flyhalf, is the father of Gordon Waddell who also toured South Africa with the Lions many years later and who is now a member of our Parliament. A. F. Blakiston, the Blackheath and England forward, eventually became Sir Arthur Blakiston after inheriting his father's baronetcy and Stanley Harris was not only a good wing, but also a quite remarkable all-rounder. He was actually playing club rugby for Pirates, in Johannesburg, when he was chosen to join Cove-Smith's touring party.

Harris, who had played rugby for Transvaal as far back as 1914, had declined an invitation to represent England as an athlete at the 1920 Olympic Games in order to concentrate on rugby and he had also once progressed to the finals in the world ballroom dancing championships!

He spent most of his life in South Africa and in 1921 the amazing Harris won the South African amateur light-heavyweight boxing championship in his spare time so to speak and as a tennis player, he represented South Africa in a Davis Cup tournament! And that is still not the end of the sporting feats achieved by the late Colonel Stanley Harris C.B.E. He also won the All-England mixed doubles tennis title and played polo for England.

In World War I Harris was badly wounded as a gunnery officer in France and Flanders and it was while recuperating that he took up dancing. As a prisoner in World War II this amazing man survived a spell of working on the "Rail of Death" in Siam and he retained his sprightly interest in all sport until his death in Cape Town in 1973.

In South African rugby history, 1924 must be remembered as the year in which Bennie Osler made his international debut. For almost a decade he was destined to dominate the scene as readers will see in the next few chapters.

Albertyn led the Springbok team with calm confidence and as a centre he played with sound judgement, often creating gaps for his wings and scoring a try in the second test. Bennie Osler always insisted that in spite of his bad knee, Albertyn played well enough in that series for him to rate him among the best centres he ever saw. Osler was also deeply impressed by Albertyn's leadership qualities, remembering in particular how Albertyn patted him on the shoulder after he had stabbed over the first dropgoal of his test career, and said: "Now I know why the Maties are so scared of you!" Albertyn, of course, was overseas when Osler first made his name for the University of Cape Town, so often at the expense of Stellenbosch, and he up till then had only heard of the young matchwinner's deadly boot.

Highlights of the first test was

Osler's dropgoal at a crucial stage of the game and a positively brilliant break by Albertyn's centre partner Wally Clarkson, which led to a try by Hans Aucamp on the wing. It also spelt tragedy for Clarkson because he tore a muscle so badly in making the try possible that he was a passenger for the rest of the match and never again played for his country.

The Springbok pack was outstanding because this was the era of men like Teuns Kruger, Phil Mostert, Jack van Druten, Frank Mellish, Nic du Plessis and Mervyn Ellis, to name only a few, and it was rare for South Africa to have problems up front. For the second test the selectors gave Osler his favourite scrumhalf partner, Pally Truter, in the place of "Champion" Myburgh who worked the scrum in the first international. This was probably the reason why the Springboks functioned so smoothly that they won 17-0. The British team was plagued by every misfortune and even their best player, Drysdale, was badly injured in the final few minutes after having played with great courage and skill.

The third test was a disaster for both teams. For some unaccountable reason the selectors dropped Truter in favour of Dauncey Devine, a Transvaal scrumhalf with whom Osler simply could not combine. Phil Mostert was out of the game because of injury and the Springboks just could not find their feet. It was a windy, miserable day in Port Elizabeth and Cove-Smith's men were desperately unlucky not to have won it. With the scores level at 3-all, Drysdale missed a penalty from in front of the Springbok posts and the match ended in a draw everybody tried to forget as soon as possible.

Truter and Phil Mostert were both back for the final test at Newlands and although played on a wet and muddy surface, this was an exciting, enterprising, game which the Springboks won 16-9 after Kenny Starke, on the left wing, had scored 10 of the points.

Starke, who had been quietly efficient in the first three tests, turned in an inspired performance. Early in the match he dropped a superb goal from an acute angle and later he cut through twice for tries the defence had no hope of preventing. The Springbok backs hardly put a foot wrong under Albertyn's shrewd guidance and Phil Mostert led a pack of forwards that earned full marks from such authorities as Paul Roos, Billy Millar and Theo Pienaar in after-

Ronald Cove-Smith, who led the ill-fated 1924 Lions with dogged determination.

Mervyn Ellis, an outstanding Springbok forward in the early 1920s.

Stanley Harris, a member of the 1924 Lions team who also played Davis Cup tennis for South Africa.

Teuns Kruger, undoubtedly one of the best forwards in Springbok history.

Above: Action in the final test of the 1924 series at Newlands. A Lions defender is collared by Alf Walker as he is about to kick.

Kenny Starke, Springbok hero of the fourth test against the 1924 Lions. He scored two tries and dropped a goal for a personal tally of 10 points.

T. Blyth Clayton

Below: Tommy Voyce, a versatile member of Cove-Smith's team. Invited to the British trials as a centre, he was selected as a forward but played in several different positions on the tour.

match interviews. Mostert was particularly outstanding, but so, also, was Teuns Kruger until he was hurt mid-way through the first half. For the rest of the game the Springboks had to make do with only seven forwards, but they not only survived, but stayed on top throughout.

The Springbok superiority was never seriously in doubt throughout the series, but Cove-Smith and his men earned everyone's respect for the cheerful way in which they stuck to their guns in the face of misfortune.

Luck was never on their side. It is hardly surprising that Cove-Smith, just before the departure of the team, presented Albertyn with their mascot, a toy dog called Bonzo.

They could not have had much affection for Bonzo. He was the one member of the side who never pulled his weight.

Albertyn continued to play on and off for several more seasons and it is no secret that Markotter would have liked to have had him in the Springbok team against the All Blacks in 1928. He did play in the trials, but in an interview with sportswriter A. C. Parker many years later, he said: "On the Monday I played badly; on the Tuesday I was worse and on the Wednesday I was terrible!"

Two years later he retired finally from the game, more than 10 years after he had been told that he might be crippled for life.

SOUTH AFRICA WIN THE FIRS TEST MATCH

NEW ZEALA OUTPLAYED

IN MAGNIFICENT

At Durb scored a magnificent victory, beating
w Zealand,
Of these
4, while S
There w

description of t which are desc e, states:

s round of ap ce Brownlie as he o the field, but it w nou ne reception Phil Mosterc and his men received as they cantered on to the field clad in the famous green jerseys and black shorts.

The All Blacks gave their Maori war cry, to be followed by the Springboks and their war cry.

The All Blacks lost the toss and M. Brownlie kicked towards the town end. Tindall fielded the ball, but failed to find touch, and Lindsay booted out near the ten yards' line.

From the line-out the All Blacks immediately set the backs in motion, and Johnson lifting the ball over the Springboks' heads, his forwards carried play dangerously close to South Africa's lines, dismal groans from the crowd indicating the anxiety of those few moments as Strang steadied himself for a drop. He was immediately set upon, however, and from a loose scrum De Villiers whipped the ball out to Bennie Osler, who kicked up field, relieving the tension.

GRENSIDE SAVES.

Lindsay was caught in possession, and the South African forwards swarming over him retransferred play into the All Blacks' territory. Here South Africa won a scrum, but De Villiers's pass to B. Osler was mulled. Dr. van Druten saved the situation by a good touch-kick. Play settled down amongst the forwards, being hard and fast until the Springboks swung the scrum on the All Blacks' "25," and with the ball at their feet set out for their opponents' line. The crowd jumped to their feet as the bal was carried over, but Grenside, reali ing the danger, dashed across the nick of time touched d

South Africa had won th scrums, and well-placed t by B. Osler kept New Zeala in in their own territory un relieved with a good line kick a result of a penalty for a scrum fringement. A further penalty sen South Africa back to midfield. The Springboks were taking the scrums at this stage in preference to the line-outs, but a third penalty against South Africa (this time for off-side) resulted in a line-out near the Springboks' "25."

S. Osl

A mark by Sta his kicking a finder, which s scuttling back t the line-out, ho broke through ground by me rush.

Play no een the half and Spring-bok gro was still taking f the line-outs. en packing in th , scrummed 3—4— exploting the wheel

Th re pressing home ever heir forwards in par a magnificent game an r opponents largely or e.

our penalties had been against South Africa, the ders seemed to be incap- king off the determined attack of the home team, Johnson on two occasions palpably failing to take an easy pass from Dalley. Play once more settled down in midfield until New Zealand attempted a back-line movement. Carleton, however, was beautifully tackled by Duffy

J. Slater.

while in possession the ball, and Slater, nipping up the ball which rolled loose, endeavoured to find touch down the field. Lindsay, however, fielded and also tried to find touch, but failed, and Tindall, who was deceived by the bounce of the ball, just cleared in time with a good line kick.

Another penalty against the Spring boks saw Lindsay attempt a place-kick, from a yard over the half-way line, his kick, though a good one, falling short, and Van Druten found touch near the half-way. From a line-out and the resultant loose scrum, the ball was whipped out to the South Africans' backs. S. Osler punted high to gather again and send Slater away on a magnificent dash down the line. But Lindsay stood the test and with a good tackle grassed South Africa's wing near the line.

There were thrills galore at this stage, and the crowd rose to its feet when Osler again put his backs in motion. S. Osler slipped through the defence, and when Scrimshaw stopped his progress he passed to Prinsloo, who was, however, grassed by Grenside as the result of a magnificent low tackle.

BENNIE OSLER SCORES.

South Africa had almost drawn first blood as the result of these two movements; but, not disheartened by failure, they continued to hammer at New Zealand's great defence. With the very next movement, however, their efforts were crowned with success when what everyone had been waiting for came.

Bennie Osler, after steadying himself on the All Blacks' "25," sent the ball flying high over the posts with a magnificent drop-kick.

A lead for South Africa of four points to nil was signalled by the referee amid indescribable scenes of enthusiasm all round the packed field.

Up to this point South Africa had won 15 scrums to New Zealand's six. Right from the kick-off South Africa immediately returned to the attack, and New Zealand had to defend with all their might in their own territory. When the All Blacks secured a penalty on their own 25, and Johnson, instead of finding touch, punted into S. Osler's hands, the crowd were delighted at his audacity in attempting to drop a goal from over the half-way line. It was an excellent effort and well worth the attempt, the ball just dropping short of the cross-bar.

ROBILLIARD NEARLY OVER.

By wheeling every scrum the Sprin boks continued New Zeala heavily, dan se to th The f rds on casion scra d over, but ck-out from "25" was orde by Mr. Neser was controll the game in admirable m ner. From kick-off New Z land once m found por relief, worki way down the field, mai bling rushes, which John with a good blind-side m touch-finder. From the li liard, jumping high i dashed through an op tackled by Tindall wit line.

A. C. Robilliard.

In the forward a New Zeal

, and tested defence which, despite vigorous slaughts, did not yield. The tack was hard and keen, and a player sooner touched the ball than he grassed in no gentle manner.

Gradually the South Africans gained the lost territory and, he by a free kick, retransferred play midway, where frequent tou lowed down the play.

Half-time arrived with no fur score, South Africa leading by points to nil.

Half-time:

South Africa	4 pts.
New Zealand	0 pts.

B. OSLER SCORES AGAIN.

Duffy, who had a shaking up, the field during half-time, and did resume after the interval, Pret taking his place at centre. In diately from the kick-off South A returned to the attack, and fro loose scrum after the line-out in corner of the "25" B. Osler repe his ealier performance by again d ping a magnificent goal withi minute of the resumption, g South Africa a more than useful of eight points.

Spurred on by this set-back, Zealand furiously attacked from kick-off, carrying play into Sprin territory, where Van Druten reli with a magnificent 50-yard touch. the result of a free-kick play s settled in the tourists' half, w Stewart fielded a high kick, but on to the ball too long, and a kick was awarded to South Afric Osler attempting a penalty which, however, fell short.

Scrimshaw fielded and punted u field, but Hazlett being offsi scrum was awarded close to th Blacks' line.

INCREASED TO ELEVEN

In a tight scrum M. Brownlie off-side and, from near the c of the 25. B. Osler with uncann curacy sent a beautiful place soaring high over the posts t crease the South African lea eleven points. B. Osler up to had been responsible for all points, his kicking being magni whether peppering the All B posts or relieving pressure on hi by means of long touch-finding.

From the kick-off, New Ze attacked heavily, but the Sprin were now in winning mood and not to be held. Gaining the b

Autocratic genius

When the *"Euripides"* steamed into Durban harbour in mid-May 1928 and Maurice Brownlie led ashore the first fully-fledged team of All Blacks to come to South Africa, the large number of officials and supporters gathered to welcome them suddenly felt their hearts sinking.

"I have never seen men of such magnificent physique," 'Long George' Devenish, one of the national selectors, remarked to a colleague and when a little group began singing "*I want to be a Springbok till I die*", they sounded more like prophets of doom than Springbok supporters.

Even back in New Zealand the experts were unanimous that an exceptionally fine team had been picked to be the first All Blacks to visit South Africa and some went so far as to claim that they were potentially a better combination than the 1924 "Invincibles" which had swept unbeaten through the United Kingdom and France.

For some inexplicable reason South African rugby authorities and fans were in a state of nerves anyway. There was a feeling that the general standard had dropped since the rather lacklustre series against Cove-Smith's team four years earlier and reports of New Zealand's prowess certainly helped to create an air of apprehension. And when the All Blacks finally arrived and looked the part to boot, South Africans were only too ready to hail them as supermen. "A team of muffled giants", one newspaper report trumpeted, referring to the thick scarves they wore on arrival, and another paper regarded it as newsworthy to point out that some of the backs were actually smaller than the forwards.

The All Blacks lost their invincible tag very quickly, however, because their antiquated scrummaging technique could not hold any well-drilled 3-4-1 South African formation. They also took a long time to come to terms with our less-pointed ball and they blundered in not realising until it was too late that in Mark Nicholls, their vice-captain, they had the one man who could have turned the tide in their favour.

Since the two countries had first clashed seven years earlier, South African rugby had developed a new pattern built around powerful and intelligent forwards and a fair-haired, freckle-faced, stocky and slightly bow-legged genius called Bennie Osler.

Osler was a master of the art of kicking and he backed it up with a shrewd, analytical, mind. No player before him or since, for that matter, could spot a weakness quicker or exploit it more mercilessly. A dominating personality, he played the game to win and to him this meant making fewer mistakes than his opponents.

Osler believed in using his threequarters only when the time was ripe and he was the sole judge of that. His immaculate touchkicking, invariably to the side nearest to his forwards, was a boon to any hard-working pack and his tactical punting, cross-kicks and grubberkicks, could crack the most organised defence. In those days a dropgoal counted four points and Osler won many games by putting them over from the most acute angles and, more often than not, with only a split-second in which to do it. But this most talented of players could also break a line with devastating effect when he spotted a gap and he handled and passed with swift precision.

He played in 17 tests for South Africa between 1924 and 1933 and completely dominated the era with his controversial brilliance. Controversial he certainly was, because not everybody agreed with his heavy reliance on tactical kicking. Many thought that he was stifling the development of good threequarters, but even his severest critics had to admit he was a supreme matchwinner.

Benjamin Louwrens Osler was born at Aliwal North on November 23, 1901 and as a youngster at Western Province Preparatory School, later at Rondebosch Boys High and finally at Kingswood College, Grahamstown,

Bennie Osler, most feared Springbok of his time.

he showed extraordinary potential as a rugby player and to a lesser extent, as a cricketer. He studied law at the University of Cape Town between 1920 and 1925 and it was in this period, so he always insisted, that he played the best rugby of his career.

This was before he had become the most famous player in the country and therefore the automatic target for all his opponents. The newspaper reports of the time confirm that he was then a daring, attacking, flyhalf who liked to run the ball. At the age of 20, Osler made his debut for Western Province as a centre three-quarter, but he soon became his provincial team's flyhalf and in 1924 played in the first of what was to be an unbroken run of 17 tests.

Osler's value as a player can perhaps best be proved by the fact that South Africa never lost an international series with him in the pivotal position, Western Province kept the Currie Cup throughout the period he regularly played for them, and University of Cape Town, Hamiltons and Villagers won the Grand Challenge competition in that order as he moved from one club to the other.

Osler perfected his skill through regular practice and he insisted to his dying day that his younger brother Stanley, or "Sharkie" as he liked to call him, was a more natural and better player than he ever was. Markotter, that doyen of rugby authorities, agreed on this point, but always qualified his statement by saying: "If I wanted to play rugby, I would select Stanley. If I wanted to win, I would play Bennie".

Of all the matches Osler won off his own bat, he remembered with the most enjoyment the one when he scored a last-minute dropgoal to snatch victory for Kingswood over Grey High School.

He also always had a particular fondness and respect for the University of Stellenbosch (where his only daughter in later years took her B.Comm degree) and he preferred reminiscing about the keen intervarsity matches between the Ikeys and the Maties to talking about dour international battles.

An intervarsity he remembered with particular pleasure was his final one in 1925 when U.C.T. fought back from a 0-7 deficit to win 14-7. It was in this match that Osler dropped two long-range goals and there was always the inevitable chuckle in his voice whenever he recounted how he heard Markotter shout at his players from the touchline: "Don't wait, you fools! Run him down!" when they seemed to hesitate as he shaped for the second kick.

Osler was an autocrat on the field and he was quite capable of giving erring players, particularly scrumhalves, a tongue-lashing. He preferred his UCT and 1924 Springbok partner Pally Truter to all the scrumhalves he played with, but also had the highest praise for Pierre de Villiers and Danie Craven. Craven, eventually to become the best-known personality in world rugby, has often admitted that his respect for Osler bordered on awe and there is no doubt that he must have been a difficult man to combine with.

Osler's influence had spread throughout South Africa by the time the All Blacks arrived here in 1928 and almost invariably they encountered kicking flyhalves working with varying degrees of efficiency off a strong forward platform. Their biggest problem throughout the tour, however, was to try and cope with the South Africans' expert scrummaging methods.

It is an unfortunate co-incidence that the 1928 All Blacks like their successors of nearly 50 years later also happened to be in Cape Town at the time of civil unrest. Their first two matches were to be at Newlands and after their arrival in Cape Town, where thousands thronged the station to welcome them, they were caught in riots which erupted with the hoisting of the newly adopted Union flag. Several members of the team, as were Bryan Williams and a few other All Blacks in 1976, were close enough to the flare-ups to have a moment or two of real anxiety. In fact, one of Brownlie's team took a strange souvenir back home with him; a brick which was hurled through the windscreen of a car and which had hit him on the shoulder.

In only their second match of the tour, the All Blacks suffered their first defeat when they met a powerful team selected from the various Cape Town clubs and which included players like Bennie and Stanley Osler, Jackie

Top left: Maurice Brownlie, captain of the 1928 All Blacks, meets General J. C. Smuts, shortly after the team's arrival in Cape Town.

Left: B. A. Grenside, the All Blacks left-wing, puts in a good run against Cape Town Clubs in the second match of the 1928 tour at Newlands. But the New Zealanders were beaten 3–7.

Right: Bennie Osler and his younger brother Stanley, who also gained Springbok colours in 1928. Stanley (on the left) was regarded by many as an even more talented player than his famous brother but his career was cut short by injury.

Akkersdyk

Tindall, Phil Mostert, J. C. van der Westhuizen, George Daneel and T. G. Osler; in fact a side not far short of international strength.

On their first visit to the Cape they took advantage of visiting the "Constantia vineyards where Jock van Niekerk, a crack South African wing, makes excellent wine", to quote from the interesting book Mark Nicholls wrote afterwards. They also went to Stellenbosch and this is what Nicholls had to say about that particular experience:

"It is here at Stellenbosch that A. F. Markotter ('Mark'), that directing genius of Springbok rugby, teaches the young South Africans all that he knows. There is a story of 'Mark' at which all South Africans laughed. A hundred yards champion of the Union, who was asked to represent his country at the Olympic Games, was playing his first match at Stellenbosch at wing three-quarter. He was told to run hard to the fullback whenever he got the ball. On one occasion when the fullback was right out of position, and the wing had a clear run in, he charged across the paddock, into the arms of the bewildered fullback, who was bowled over. 'Mark', waving his famous walking stick frantically, rushed up to the threequarter to know the reason why.

" 'You told me to run to the fullback every time I got the ball," said the wing. 'Oh my God, what a magnificent fool!' said the desperate Markotter as he walked slowly to the sideline shaking his head."

The Springbok selectors (of whom Markotter was one) got on very well with Brownlie's team and spent many hours in their company. "Mr. Mark" fancied himself as a snooker player, but it is on record that Mark Nicholls beat him in two out of three in an unofficial "test series". Bill Schreiner, who was a keen and knowledgeable angler, took every opportunity to discuss the world famous streams around Rotorua in New Zealand with the visitors, a fisherman's paradise he always wanted to visit but never did.

There is a strong affinity between New Zealanders and South Africans and the 1928 All Blacks enjoyed their tour as much as their hosts loved having them here. They must have been a particularly nice bunch of fellows off the field because nowhere in all the thousands of words written about the tour can one find one line where they complained about the fact that they were given some of their toughest opponents within the first couple of weeks of the tour, with long zigzagging train trips thrown in for good measure.

Nine of their players were out of commission through sickness or injury at various stages of the tour, six of them for five-week stretches, but these misfortunes were never used as excuses.

The tour produced a fair share of rough play but was free of the kind of "blown-up incident" we have so much of in modern international rugby; perhaps because there were only five newspapermen travelling with the team in contrast with the vast army of highly competitive correspondents who flock along these days!

The New Zealand forward Ian Finlayson was sent off the field for hitting an opponent in the match against Transvaal, but, as F. M. Howard, (the late F. M. Honoré) reported afterwards:

"He was far from being the worst offender on the field. I had my field glasses focussed on the play at the time of the incident, which took place right in front of the grandstand, and I saw every detail of what occurred. It is only fair to state on behalf of Finlayson, not as an excuse, but to situate the facts quite clearly, that his blow was an act of retaliation. . . ."

According to the report, the referee, Mr. J. G. Finlay, was told by the All Black forward afterwards that he "fully deserved his punishment" and that he knew the moment he had hit his opponent that he was "due to take a walk".

The Transvaal player Finlayson punched was Manie Geere, a powerful forward who won his Springbok colours three years later. Geere, who, with Teuns Kruger was the outstanding forward on the field when Transvaal beat the All Blacks 6-0 that day, received a stern warning from the referee later in the match and also came close to being sent off.

Brownlie's men were a cheerful lot though, who did not share the Spring-

Mark Nicholls, vice-captain of the 1928 All Blacks whose brilliance was recognised too late by his team management.

Blyth Clayton

Live broadcasts of rugby did more than anything else to make the "wireless" popular in South Africa. Here Archie Shacksnovis, the first of the great commentators, describes the action at Newlands in 1928.

bok superstition that players who sing on the way to a match, stand a good chance of losing. They quickly learnt the tune and some of the words of "*Sarie Marais*" and added it to a repertoire that otherwise seemed limited to "*Charmaine*", "*Old McDonald had a farm*" and "*The N.Z. boys are happy*".

After losing two of their first four matches, the All Blacks scored four successive wins leading up to the first test at the old Kingsmead ground, Durban, on June 30, 1928. There was tremendous interest in the game. The Springboks and the All Blacks were all square after the 1921 series and subsequently the All Blacks had their undefeated tour of Britain. As far as the average rugby follower was concerned, the match was for the championship of the world.

There was a tremendous public outcry afterwards when the match was not broadcast "live" by the then privately-owned radio network. They explained that the post office authorities had refused them telephone wire facilities and newspaper editors taking up the cudgels on behalf of their disgruntled readers, launched violent attacks in all directions.

Only a few years earlier Cape Town's "wireless station", as it was called in those days, had been the first in the world to give a live broadcast of a rugby match and listeners had come to expect this service as a matter of routine. Many people had bought and installed wireless sets for the sole purpose of listening to the live broadcasts of the tests against the All Blacks by that pioneer of commentators Archie Shacksnovis, and the disappointment was great indeed.

In a leading article *The Cape Argus* stated its editorial view in the firmest terms:

"Looked at in its widest sense, this love of the game is emphatically for the national good. There is in our land today no more potent leveller of racial and class barriers than rugby. It is giving both races and all classes a common interest; it is providing them with a congenial topic; it is truly fostering a national pride, and a healthy pride at that; and it is rapidly leading to a better understanding. Nothing but good can result from the broadcast of test matches...."

The agitation brought happy results. The final three tests were all broadcast.

The historic first test between the Springboks and the All Blacks on South African soil was recorded in literally thousands of words published in every newspaper in the country and overnight Bennie Osler became a national hero.

This is how he himself described to me what had become known as "Osler's match", many years later when we collaborated on his biography:

"We were quite confident beforehand, mainly because we knew that the All Blacks could not hold us in the scrums with their outmoded 2-3-2 formation, but as usual the butterflies started fluttering inside me as the day of the match drew nearer. I was always terribly nervous before any big match and before my test debut against the British team in 1924, I just about drove Mr. Mark to distraction when I virtually went into a state of shock on the morning of the match and could only make croaking sounds in reply to his questions!

"Kingsmead was packed with the biggest crowd ever to attend a sporting event in Durban up to that time. People came from all parts of South Africa and Rhodesia and by 6.30 on the morning of the match, the queues were already forming outside the ground.

"The weather was bad. Rain was threatening and a freezing, gusty, wind whipped through the stadium when we arrived to sit through a curtain-raiser between Michaelhouse and Technical High School. I remember how I tried to calm my nerves by singing a popular song of the day under my breath....'*I might as well be, where the Mountains of Mourne sweep down to the sea....*'

"Then followed a farcical affair between a team called 'The All Brokes' and another motley team whose name I cannot recall. All I can remember of the few minutes I saw of this was that one of the members of the 'All Brokes' side, broke his ankle.

"I suffered the usual pangs of the

Phil Mostert and Pierre de Villiers, two of the greatest names in Springbok history. Mostert led the Springboks in all four tests against Brownlie's All Blacks and De Villiers made his debut as Osler's scrumhalf partner.

Bennie Osler is the epitome of pace and purpose as he evades a defender and is about to place the Springboks on the attack in the first test in 1928, a match he completely dominated.

Above: Phil Mostert leads his Springboks in a rendition of their 'war cry" before the start of the first test in Durban.

Below: Springbok wing Jack Slater takes the ball above his head in this picture taken during the Durban test. Slater scored South Africa's only try in the match which the Springboks won 17–0. Fourteen of the points were contributed by Osler, who scored with two dropped goals and two penalties.

damned in the dressingroom although it was not quite as bad as four years earlier when I waited in the same room to trot out for my first international.

"Finally Phil Mostert, our captain, led us out onto the field where Maurice Brownlie and his All Blacks were already waiting. We stood in single file as the All Blacks danced the "*Haka*" and then we replied with our own war cry of those days, a mixture of bad Zulu and gibberish, if I remember correctly. The good thing about those war cries was that it allowed you to blow off a bit of steam.

"At last the referee, Boet Neser, could start the game and as usual my nervousness magically disappeared. The All Blacks had to defend the Umgeni end and as I glanced up at the sky I saw the clouds breaking and the sun coming through. We'll have the sun in our eyes this half, flashed through my mind and then Brownlie himself kicked off; too deep and our fullback Jackie Tindall, one of the best and most versatile players of my era, caught it safely and banged it into touch.

"We were forced on the defensive at the start and for a while things looked bleak. The All Blacks missed three penalties in a row and then gradually our magnificent forwards began to assert themselves and I could drive our opponents back by using the touchline. I don't think I've ever seen a more relaxed and supremely confident Springbok pack than the one old Phil commanded that afternoon. I am not telling you a word of a lie, they kept chattering to each other throughout the match! Pierre de Villiers, my little scrumhalf

Above: Gerry Brand, destined to become a legend in his own life-time, entered the international arena in 1928. This rare picture shows him in action at a very early stage in his career.

Below: With Maurice Brownlie a split-second too late, Dauncey Devine gets his pass away in the second test at Ellis Park. The All Blacks won 7–6.

partner from Paarl, was also in great form and he was getting his passes to me in spite of the attentions of his lively opposite number, Dalley.

"About 20 minutes into the first half we struck with a threequarter movement and Jack Slater, on the wing, had my brother Stanley unmarked next to him when he, for some reason, neglected to pass and ran slap into the arms of the All Blacks fullback, Lindsay. We were nicely on top and I, for one, quickly forgave Jack his lapse. Then disaster struck when Bernard Duffy, Stanley's fellow-centre, was badly concussed in a tackle and both Phil and I knew that he could never see out the game. From virtually the next scrum Pierre dodged Scrimshaw, who was acting as the All Blacks' so-called 'rover' that day, and passed the ball to me. I was pretty hemmed in by the defence, but instead of smothering me as quickly as they could, the defence hesitated, the biggest crime you can commit in test rugby. I dropped for goal and we were leading 4-0 at half-time."

Above: S. P. van Wyk was one of the few stars in the lethargic Springbok team who lost the second test to the All Blacks. Here he hands off R. G. McWilliams.

"We had to make do with 14 players throughout the second spell as poor Duffy simply could not be allowed to risk further injury. Phil decided at half-time to take Nick Pretorius out of the pack and we were still discussing our bad luck when Mr. Mark walked up to us.

" 'What are you going to do now, Osler?', he asked me in his usual abrupt manner.

"Startled, I stuttered: 'I don't know, Mr. Mark. I'm not the captain. Phil is.'

"But Phil did not have an answer either and Mr. Mark just glared at us as the seconds ticked away. We simply had to think, which was Mr. Mark's way of doing things.

"Finally I said: 'From some of the scrums in the middle of the field I'll use Stanley on the blindside. But the rest of the time I feel I must use the touchline as long as Phil and the forwards can stay on top.'

"Mr. Mark nodded. 'That's it', he said and walked away.

"Soon after the resumption I dropped my second goal and about three minutes later one of their forwards, Johnson, late-tackled me after I had punted ahead and Neser gave a penalty where the ball had landed, an uncommon thing for referees to do in those days. I was a bit shaken from the knock, but it was an easy kick and we were now leading 11-0. Pretorius was doing well among the backs and with such a useful lead, I began to use my threequarters more freely, Stanley, who was never again to play for South

Below: George Daneel has just scored the Springboks' third try in their 11–6 victory over the All Blacks in Port Elizabeth.

Africa because of injury, twice nearly went over and Phil also just failed to get a try after another break by my brother.

"In between I managed to add another penalty to our score and it was then that I again tried the plan to use Stanley on the blindside. He streaked right through and gave to Prinsloo on the wing, who dropped the ball as he went over the line! A few minutes later we tried again, except that this time I made the initial break myself. I slipped the ball to Jack Slater about 10 yards from the goalline. Jack was a burly and determined wing and he ploughed through to score. I gave the difficult conversion to Jackie Tindall, who could not get it over.

"It was only in the dressingroom later that I found out that my 14 points was a record individual contribution in a test, a record that was to stand for 21 years until Okey Geffin bettered it with five penalties against the 1949 All Blacks. Frankly, and this is not false modesty, the victory belonged to Phil Mostert and his forwards. I might have scored the points, but they did the work."

The public and the press went hysterical over Osler's performance. One report read:

"Bennie Osler was the murderer! His second dropgoal within a minute after the resumption, and his penalty goal a few minutes later, quenched the fire in the hearts of the New Zealanders. No team can stand that kind of thing. . . ."

Now the Springboks were the ones hailed as the supermen of rugby and the trouble was that some of them must have believed what they read in the newspapers. Less than a month after being beaten 17-0 in Durban, the All Blacks won the second test in Johannesburg 7-6 before what was then a record crowd of 38 000 which included such dignitaries as the Prime Minister, General J. B. M. Hertzog. With the best tickets in the stadium priced at £2.2.0 (a massive sum in those days), it was hardly surprising that the gate receipts put the Transvaal Rugby Union well on its way to becoming the wealthiest amateur sporting body in the world.

The injured Stanley Osler and Bernard Duffy were replaced by J. A. R. Dobie and J. C. van der Westhuizen, and Gerry Brand and N. S. ("Jacko") Tod were the new wings. The selection of Brand, soon to become one of the most respected players in South Africa, caused quite an upset, of all places in the Western Province where he was not then highly regarded. The rugby correspondent of the *Cape Times* was particularly scathing and he must have regretted his article for many years to come as Brand, both as a wing and later as a fullback, gave one magnificent performance after the other.

The selectors did make one big blunder, though, by, for no real reason whatsoever, dropping Pierre de Villiers and giving Bennie Osler Transvaal's Dauncey Devine as his scrumhalf. Devine had played well for Transvaal against the All Blacks and the selectors thought that he should get a chance.

The unwarranted tampering with a match-winning combination and an overdose of self-confidence proved the Springbok's undoing. Devine, whose passing was erratic, and Osler could not strike up an understanding and the centres also could not find their feet. In addition to all their other problems, Tod, the one new Springbok wing, was badly injured after only a few minutes.

Yet, the Springboks led in the scoring for most of the match after Phil Mostert had dropped a miraculous goal from a mark, caught after a drop-out, and Osler had succeeded with a penalty. Until late in the match the All Blacks had only a penalty by Lindsay to show for all their excellent efforts. Then W. A. Strang dropped a beautiful goal to give them a one-point lead and the Springboks, who played in a most desultory fashion, could not make up the leeway. In this period of desperate attack, Gerry Brand served notice of many wonderful efforts to come, when he hit the upright with a dropgoal described afterwards as one of the highlights of the match in spite of the fact that it failed.

Charlie Lambe, a Transvaal rugby official and also a freelance writer, said afterwards: "Like bad investors, the Springboks speculated on a very narrow margin — sat on their lead, but sat too long. Strang's sensational goal in the last 15 minutes of the match robbed South Africa both of their slight advantage and of their contentment of the state of affairs. The South Africans had their opportunities but frittered them away through sheer lack of enterprise. . . . No excuses can be made for Devine's weak exhibition, but Osler himself did not come out of the fray with an enhanced reputation. . . . Both fullbacks played well, though Lindsay was the more impressive, even though he has no left foot. . . . There was little

fault to find with any of the New Zealand backs, even though only the scrumhalf, Dalley, was outstanding. Of the South African backs, apart from fullback Tindall who was in fine form, Van der Westhuizen was easily the best. Brand was also most convincing, both on attack and defence. . . ."

As far as the Springboks were concerned the All Blacks' forwards were the real heroes of the day. They were learning to cope with the South African scrummaging technique and often pushed the Springboks clean off the ball.

"In the second half the Springbok forwards were smitten hip and thigh," New Zealand journalist Graham Beamish wrote for the folks at home. "They took command to display craft, pace and precision, which

Cay's Photo Service

Above: Maurice Brownlie leads his All Blacks onto the field for the final test at Newlands, the famous "Umbrella Test".

Cay's Photo Service

Left: Flocks of photographers, amateur and professional, were already part of the rugby scene in 1928. Here they await the appearance of the two teams for the Newlands test. African Mirror's newsreel cameraman is on the right, ready to record the event for the cinema screen.

surprised the most fervent New Zealand followers and sent them into ecstacies of joy. . . ."

Phil Mostert agreed. In an after-match interview he said bluntly: "It was their forwards who carried the day".

The selectors did a good job for the third and crucial test in Port Elizabeth on August 18. Pierre de Villiers came back into the side and Manus de Jongh, on the wing, and Willie Rousseau, at centre, were new caps. Other newcomers were M. M. (Boy) Louw who was to serve South Africa so well for a full decade, and the props, John Oliver, of Transvaal, and A. F. du Toit, of Western Province. Eleven members of the Springbok team were from the Western Province, including the entire back line, three from Transvaal and one from Natal. It was also to be the first test in which the Springboks were to wear white shorts; the only reason being to make it easier for Mr. V. H. Neser who refereed all four tests, to distinguish between the two teams.

This time it was a record crowd for Port Elizabeth and to their great delight a far more purposeful South African team led 5-0 after only five minutes.

A bad pass under pressure had bounced off fullback Lindsay's shoulder and Phil Nel, the sole Natal representative, was over in a flash. Osler converted from a difficult position.

It became a pretty robust struggle between the forwards after that with Boy Louw showing that he was not the kind to be intimidated. Fine work by Finlayson at a lineout, a few yards from the Springbok line, enabled Stewart to dive over for a try, but Lindsay's kick bounced away after hitting the post. Manus de Jongh then had his nose broken and Nick Pretorius had to substitute for him for a few minutes. On his return to the field, De Jongh, broken nose and all, scored a beautiful try after Jack van Druten, Bennie Osler, Rousseau and Van der Westhuizen had forced the gap.

Osler missed the conversion and with Grenside adding another unconverted try, the half-time score was 8-6 in favour of the Springboks. The second half was a titanic struggle with splendid touchkicking the deciding factor. He nursed his pack carefully, but also never missed an opportunity to use his backs. It was the most exciting match of the series

Left: P. K. Morkel and Willie Rousseau make doubly sure that this All Black does not get away.

Right: Mark Nicholls was the hero of the All Blacks' 13–5 victory over the Springboks in the final test on a rain-swept Newlands. He scored two penalties and a dropgoal but this picture shows him missing the conversion of Swain's try.

as first one team and then the other narrowly missed scoring chances until finally, after a concerted attack, George Daneel went over for a try with Osler's kick just shaving the upright.

With the score 11-6 to the Springboks and time about up, Lilburne, Hazlett and Swain launched a terrific attack which stretched the Springbok defence to breaking point. A final pass gave Grenside a clear run to the goalline, but Brand and Van der Westhuizen, both showing tremendous pace, caught up with the galloping wing and crashtackled him on the corner flag. Neser blew the final whistle immediately afterwards.

Phil Mostert summed it up for all thirty players when he told an interviewer in the dressingroom: "This was one of the hardest games in which I have ever participated. Right up to the last minute no one could be sure of the result."

In the last match before the final test, Western Province, virtually a Springbok team, handed the All Blacks their fifth defeat of the tour after yet another brilliant display by Pierre de Villiers and Bennie Osler, in conjunction with a pack led by Phil Mostert. P. K. Morkel scored a try with the dazzling double sidestep which earned him Springbok colours for the last test and Osler added a dropgoal and a penalty against an unconverted try by Dalley for Western Province to win 10-3. Osler actually put over two drops, but referee Alec van der Horst ruled that in his first effort the ball had touched the All Black, Harvey, and refused to award the four points.

With the unlucky Jock van Niekerk, one of the great wings in our rugby history, selected for the one and only test of his career and P. K. Morkel having earned his place after his fine showing for Western Province, there were only two changes, both on the wing, in the Springbok team for the final test.

The All Blacks made a far more significant change for what was for them a do-or-die match. They brought in Mark Nicholls at flyhalf and it was due almost entirely to this gifted player, who scored 10 points with two penalties and a dropgoal, that New Zealand managed to win the test and so to draw the series.

Nicholls and the inspired All Black forwards did to the Springboks almost exactly what Osler and his pack did to them in the first test. The match which took place before 23 000 drenched spectators at Newlands on September 1, 1928 was instantly named the "Umbrella Test" as it rained almost continuously throughout. The Springboks simply could not cope with the conditions, but it is doubtful whether any team could have beaten the All Blacks that afternoon. As Mark Nicholls said afterwards: "It was the day for the good, honest and strong forward — the man who could push, scrum, dribble and possess 'devil' and to this we owed our success."

He was too modest a man to add that for all his forwards' wonderful display, New Zealand would still have lost had it not been for his remarkable ability to boot that soggy and shapeless ball over the crossbar.

South Africa did not concede their first defeat at Newlands for 37 years without an almighty struggle, but on the day the All Blacks deserved their victory. The game was often rough and at least two All Blacks received serious lectures from Mr. Neser, but the Springboks were no angels either.

The All Blacks had finally learnt to hold their own in the scrums and in all other facets of play they held the upper hand. J. C. van der Westhuizen scored South Africa's try, converted by Osler, while Swain scored a try for the All Blacks with Nicholls adding his two penalties and a superb dropgoal.

Although there was still an unofficial match against Combined Universities to follow (arranged only because of a delay in the departure of the *Ceramic*), the All Blacks tour of South Africa was over and again the spoils were evenly divided.

It remained for skipper Maurice Brownlie to sum it all up when he said in his parting speech:

"In all our matches we have found South Africans most worthy foemen, and we shall carry away with us most pleasant recollections of the many hard matches we have enjoyed."

Mud and glory

A youthful Danie Craven is on his toes at scrumhalf as Phil Mostert and Fanie Louw battle for the ball in a lineout during the match against Midland Counties at Leicester in 1931. The Springbok behind Louw is Ferdie Bergh.

The third Springbok visit to Britain in the Northern Hemisphere rugby season of 1931/32 was South Africa's most successful overseas tour since we entered the international arena in 1891. All four tests were won, the Springboks were defeated on only one occasion and twice held to a draw.

And yet, history has passed a rather harsh judgement on the team. Under the captaincy of Bennie Osler, then past his best and as he himself said with his usual frankness, playing the worst rugby of his career, the side received a reputation for having been preoccupied with winning and having relied on stodgy and over-cautious methods to achieve their success.

In the last few years of his life I often discussed this controversial tour with Osler and it was his firm belief that a more free and easy approach would have been disastrous.

"We played to our strength and we would have been foolish to adopt any other approach," he explained. "We had a magnificent pack of forwards, outstanding scrumhalves in Craven and De Villiers and a matchwinning fullback in Gerry Brand. Our best wing, Jock van Niekerk, was injured right at the beginning of the tour, several of our other attacking three-quarters were also handicapped by injury and our steadiest centre, my vice-captain J. C. van der Westhuizen, as well as the other senior players, were in general agreement with my tactics on the heavy grounds we invariably encountered in Britain."

The Springboks played according to the same pattern they had employed against the 1928 All Blacks and which was one based on forward supremacy and Osler's tactical kicking. Against Australia, a year later, Osler bowed to public opinion and changed the tried and tested approach with disastrous consequences for the Springboks, proving in the process that he knew what he was doing all along.

The 1931/32 Springboks were selected following a week of gruelling trials at Newlands and Markotter's remarkable ability to spot hidden talent was again much in evidence.

Andre McDonald, for instance, was a centre in the Stellenbosch second team and a mediocre one at best, when Mr. Mark at a practice one afternoon ordered him to buy a scrumcap.

McDonald did as he was told, but when he turned up the next day with it he was horrified when the short-tempered coach told him to join the forwards as an eighthman. McDonald seemed to lack the physical qualities of a forward and after only a few minutes up front he had to be helped off the field. But Markotter was far from repentant. He forced McDonald to stay at No. 8 and almost without knowing how it happened, the young theological student was outstanding in his new position; good enough to gain his place in the touring side. George Daneel, who played scrumhalf in the lower teams while at Cape Town University, was also plucked from obscurity by Mr. Mark when he made him an eighthman at Stellenbosch. He also became a member of the 1931 touring team.

And then there was Jimmy White, a product of Queens College, Queenstown, who played for Border as a centre, flyhalf and fullback, but impressed his own province so little that they did not even nominate him for the trials. Fortunately, Markotter had seen him in action and it was at his insistence that the national selectors invited White to Cape Town. He also made the team and developed into one of the finest crash-tacklers ever to play centre for South Africa.

The Cape Times published this cartoon by Wyndham Robinson on the morning Bennie Osler and his team departed on the third Springbok tour of Britain.

Ferdie Bergh was messing around in the lower teams at Stellenbosch University when Markotter noticed his massive but symmetrical build and soon he was an outstanding forward in the first team and went on to play 17 tests for the Springboks and, with seven tries, was South Africa's leading try-scorer for more than 25 years. Bergh was already an established player by the time of the 1931 trials, but the tour was to be his first taste of international rugby.

Danie Craven was perhaps Markotter's "masterpiece". He came to Stellenbosch from the little Free State town of Lindley and as an under-19 scrumhalf, ended his first season for the Maties by playing in the fourth team. The next year he was down to play in the second team in a practice against the senior side, when Markotter suddenly thundered: "Craven, where are you? Go first team!"

His first senior club match was a disaster. Playing against a Hamiltons team studded with names like Bennie Osler, Gerry Brand, Jack Tindall and S. P. van Wyk, the Maties received a hiding and Craven was convinced that he would be dropped.

But it did not happen although Craven swears that he played match after match with the axe poised over his head. A few days before that year's intervarsity against University of Cape Town, the first four teams were addressed by Markotter. His first words were: "Where's Craven?" And then he launched an absolute torrent of words at the squirming young scrumhalf.

"You play rugby like a sheep," Markotter continued. "Talk to your forwards during a game, instead of standing around with a mouth full of teeth. How do you expect them to know what's going on, if you don't tell them?"

Craven was stunned at the tirade and then came the extra sentence that made everything bearable.

"Remember, Craven" the coach added in a softer tone. "I only shout at players whom I like".

It was to be the first of many such harsh lectures and each one contained at least one pearl of rugby wisdom which helped Craven on the way to becoming one of the greatest players of all time and eventually to earn international recognition as an administrator. Oubaas Mark gave us many Springboks, but in giving us Craven he supplied us with perhaps the only man who could have steered South African rugby through the turbulent years of trouble and change the old coach could never have suspected were lying ahead for the game he loved so much.

At the age of 20 and without any experience of provincial rugby, Craven was invited to the Newlands trials. Drenched with a bucket of water in a student prank, he picked up a bad dose of flu before the trials, but he played against Oubaas Mark's instructions. Near the end of the week, however, he did well enough to slip into the touring party as Pierre de

Cay's Photo Service

The captains of four Springbok touring teams photographed together just before the 1931 side's departure. *Left to right:* Paul Roos (1906), Billy Millar (1912), Theo Pienaar (1921 and also manager of the 1931 team) and Bennie Osler.

Villiers' understudy.

It is a sad fact that Craven's selection was accepted with comparative equanimity throughout the country except in his home province where one Bloemfontein newspaper made such acid comments that the youngster's ever-loyal father promptly cancelled his subscription of many years standing!

The team was actually a good blend of experience and youthful enthusiasm. Jackie Tindall and Phil Mostert were the veterans with the 33-year-old Somerset West forward embarking on his fourth international series and Tindall, like his 29-year-old skipper Osler, wearing Springbok colours for the third time. Gerry Brand, J. C. van der Westhuizen, Pierre de Villiers, Boy Louw, Phil Nel, Jock van Niekerk and George Daneel had all been blooded against the 1928 All Blacks and were players with exceptional ability.

The tour was to establish Gerry Brand, in particular, as one of the legendary figures in Springbok annals.

Gerhard Hamilton Brand was born in Cape Town on October 8, 1906, and he grew up in a family where rugby was a major interest. It was his grandfather, in fact, who suggested that his second christian name should be Hamilton, in honour of the Hamilton Rugby Club. It is rather fitting that Brand played for this club throughout his serious career.

Although Bennie Osler and other authorities often expressed the view that Brand was an even better wing than fullback it was for his performances in the last line of defence that he will always be remembered. He had a wonderful sense of anticipation and his fielding was immaculate, his tackling deadly. Although he was not particularly powerfully built, his timing was so perfect and his speed so great, that he was one of the most feared tacklers of his era. It was rare for him to miss his man and veteran sportswriter Maxwell Price was once moved to write: "On the field Brand was always a silent, mystic figure, whose presence on the opposing side always seemed to have an engulfing effect on the attackers. He would draw the player with the ball to his tackle like a human magnet. . . ."

Brand had an instinctive flair for the game, but nevertheless perfected his kicking with hours and hours of practice. He was a left-footer, but could kick equally well with his right. His natural rhythm, such a vital factor for success at the highest level of sport, was a gift of nature, but it was sheer hard work that helped him to develop an exquisitely-timed screw-kick with which he could kick touches of enormous length and as a place- and dropkicker he has had few equals.

Brand was painfully shy as a youngster and even at the height of his fame when he was the most-discussed player in South Africa since the heyday of Bennie Osler, he did not do much talking. Old-timers will tell you that Gerry Brand was always one

Three great fullbacks together. *From the left:* Arthur Marsberg (1906), Jackie Tindall (1924–1931) and Gerhard Morkel (1912–1921). Tindall nearly lost his life on the 1931/32 tour.

Jackie Tindall, regarded by Bennie Osler as the best fullback of his era.

of the neatest players on the field, his hair slicked back and everything clean from the collar of his jersey to the tips of his boots. After tackling an opponent he would, to quote Maxwell Price again, "trip back to position, quite unnecessarily dusting his white shorts which seldom were soiled in a game of rugby."

South Africa has produced many world-class fullbacks over the past 86 years and only a fool would try and point to one player as being the best of them; it is after all impossible for anyone to have seen them all in action. It is sufficient to say that in his era Gerry Brand had no peers.

The Springboks left for Britain on the *Windsor Castle* and the team manager, Theo Pienaar, gave them a serious lecture on the responsibilities of representing their country on an overseas tour. The team was supposed to keep fit in the ship's gymnasium, but only the younger players bothered much about this instruction. Handling practices also came to an abrupt stop after three brand-new balls had been lost over-board and it was in a vain attempt to stop one that Jock van Niekerk, that most unfortunate of all Springboks, hurt the knee which was to ruin the tour for him and to end his career.

The tour started off rather badly with the Springboks erratic in their first match and losing the Transvaal wing Floors Venter with a broken nose in the process. They failed to score a single try and dropgoals by Van der Westhuizen and Osler and a penalty apiece from Osler and Brand, gave them their 14-3 win. Four tries in the next match, against powerful Newport, made their critics a bit more wary, but they were still being regarded as well below the standard of previous Springbok touring teams.

Maurice Zimerman, the muscular Western Province wing, scored his first try against Newport and showed the hard-running, bullocking, style which made him such a success on the tour.

Zimerman scored many tries from kicks to the cornerflag by Osler, always spurred on by his captain's shout "Run, Zimmie, run!", and the instruction became something of a team joke. It is said that Zimerman on one occasion after just having returned from a long run and hearing the order again, panted in reply: "Run yourself, dammit!"

The third match of the tour, against Swansea, must rate among the roughest and dirtiest a Springbok team has ever played in. The crowd of Welsh coalminers hurled anything they could lay their hands on at the players and a stone once whistled between Craven and Boy Louw, missing them narrowly. According to Craven, both teams were guilty of dirty tactics and at one stage George Daneel, a Dutch Reformed Church Minister, pulled his head out of a scrum and in exasperation said:

"Look, kick if you must, punch if you must, but please stop the swearing!"

The Springboks eventually won 10-3, but the spectators were in such an ugly mood that the players had to be kept behind a locked door in the dressingroom until things had simmered down a bit. By the time the two teams met again at the official banquet the Welshmen were as hospitable as only these wonderful people can be, although several players on both sides were nursing the scars of battle.

Osler, who did not play that afternoon, and Theo Pienaar were very upset, however, and in a team talk Pienaar threatened that the next Springbok to make himself guilty of dirty play would be summarily sent back home.

In the next match, against Abertillery and Cross Keys, trouble flared again and at first the Springboks, mindful of their manager's warning, did not retaliate, but they could endure only so much, and this game also deteriorated into a brawl. This time the Springboks were not really to be blamed and Pienaar decided not to carry out his threat.

The match against Combined London, the team's first appearance at tradition-rich Twickenham, followed and for once everything clicked.

Maurice Zimerman scored two typical storming tries, the burly Nic Bierman, got two and Osler and Brand, playing on the leftwing, also went over. But Gerry Brand, promptly nicknamed "Firebrand" by an appreciative crowd, was the hero of the match. He converted all six tries with beautifully-judged kicks. It was an excellent victory for the Springboks but they had to pay dearly for it as Geoff Gray suffered a cracked collarbone and Bennie Osler had a rib fractured.

Cape Town's Malay community always loved Osler whom they called "Baas Bennie" or "Mr. King", and before the team's departure an old Imam, or priest, brought him some stuff which looked like sand, and which he said would protect Bennie on the tour. Osler was sceptical about it all, but he naturally accepted the "gift" with good grace and had it stitched into a little bag which he carried in a pocket of his shorts. The first and only time he neglected to do so was at Twickenham the day a wild kick fractured his ribs.

While in London the Springboks were taken to St. James to meet the Prince of Wales and Dr. Craven tells the story of how, while they were waiting in the reception room, Fanie Louw discovered a cache of royal cigarettes which promptly disappeared into a multitude of pockets. After leaving the palace the Springboks

Pierre de Villiers

Geoff Gray

Fanie Louw

Maurice Zimerman

Boy Louw

Ferdie Bergh

Frankie Waring

Andre Macdonald

Phil Nel

George Daneel

made a big pantomime out of smoking the cigarettes the way they imagined Royalty would do, not realising that a newsreel cameraman was around. There was some general embarrassment when they saw their antics on the screen a few nights later!

In the next match, against Midland Counties, Jock van Niekerk made his first appearance of the tour and the first time he got the ball his weak knee packed up completely and he was never to play again.

With the injury list now ominously long, Theo Pienaar immediately cabled the South African Rugby Board, suggesting that D. O. Williams, an 18-year-old Villagers wing with outstanding potential, be sent over to help out. It was to be several weeks before the black-haired Dai, South Africa's youngest international player in history and destined to be a Springbok stalwart until World War II brought everything to a halt, could arrive because there was no such thing as air travel for passengers in those days. In fact, the Springboks must be among the first South Africans to ever receive airmail letters as this service was only started between South Africa and England at about the time they were in London.

In the match against Cambridge, Craven finally learnt to relax and to

Left: Bennie Osler, resplendent in the fashionable attire for men in 1931, goes out to inspect the pitch before the Springboks' match against Gloucester-Somerset at Bristol. His team won 16–5.

Right: The Springboks attend a race meeting at Newbury and from their expressions it does not look as if they backed Sandals, the 25/1 outsider which won the Autumn Cup, the feature race of the day. *From the left:* Bennie Osler, Theo Pienaar, H. Forrest and Maurice Zimerman.

combine smoothly with Osler who had by then fully recovered from his injury. Craven admits that at first he was too scared of incurring Osler's displeasure to play his natural game and he got on far better with Tiny Francis, Bennie's very able understudy on the tour. Craven, a much stronger man than Pierre de Villiers, was obviously a better bet on the heavy overseas fields and once he proved that he could dovetail with Osler, his place in the international matches was virtually assured.

The Springbok's only defeat of the tour came at Leicester against Midland Counties. They were hopelessly outplayed for most of the match and deep in the second half, found themselves trailing 6-24. With that powerful scrummager Fanie Louw injured and off the field, the future looked dark for the South Africans, but they hit back with a series of marvellous attacks, including four tries by the unstoppable Zimerman who on one occasion knocked five defenders off their feet as he ploughed for the line.

With the score 21-24 the Counties got an easy penalty, however, and it knocked the stuffing out of the Springboks' come-back. They finally lost 21-30 and the traditional Springbok head which up till then had played the role of a totem pole in the South African camp, was formally handed over to that great forward George Beamish, as captain of the first team to beat them.

The 30 points scored by Midland Counties in this match is still the most ever to be notched against a South African team, including test matches.

Barry Heatlie, one of the great pioneers of South African rugby who travelled with the team, had this to say about the match in an article written years later:

"Defeats are not national calamities. There is no need for a wave of depression to sweep the country, if a team should suffer defeat, such as was evidently the case here. When the 1931 team was beaten at Leicester, I received on that occasion a cable from a certain town which shall be nameless, reading: 'Send the team back home to come and plant potatoes'!

"A team may be greater in defeat than in victory. That defeat at Leicester meant more to the prestige and the sportsmanship of our team than all our victories. The way in which we took it made an indelible impression on all who saw it."

Bennie Osler, giving one of his best performances of the tour, restored the team's self-confidence by guiding them to an excellent victory over mighty Cardiff and Llanelly and Neath and Aberavon also had to bow the knee before the big crunch came against Wales.

Tests between the Springboks and Wales are like the battles against the All Blacks; they have a special significance, an added spice.

Danie Craven, in his biography "*Ek Speel vir Suid-Afrika*" published in 1949, has described better than anyone else what it was like before, during and after that famous match against Wales at St. Helens, Swansea, on December 5, 1931. Here are extracts from what he wrote:

"Uncle Theo had hardly finished reading out the names of the test team, when Pierre de Villiers came over to congratulate me. That there could be so much sportsmanship in any man, I could never forget.

"The Friday before the match it rained continuously. The many cables of congratulations made the tension even worse. You begin to wonder why you ever started to play rugby. There is a paralysis in your muscles and a slowness in your movements. Willpower seems to have disappeared. Your thoughts are centred around the game and there is fear that you might disappoint your team and your country. The night before the match

A tragic moment in South African rugby history. Jock van Niekerk, regarded by many as one of the best wings of all time, looks back wistfully as he is helped off the field after injuring his always suspect knee against Midland Counties. Van Niekerk never again wore the Springbok jersey.

you cannot sleep and nightmares interrupt what rest you do get. Once I actually fell out of the bed and after that I gave up trying to sleep. Andre McDonald was my room mate and was in exactly the same state.

"Breakfast tasted terrible and after the early lunch we slumped around the place, sighing and yawning although there was no sleepiness. A traffic constable with his siren screaming led our bus through the rain and milling crowds towards the stadium and we arrived just in time to go to the dressingroom and to start changing.

"In silence we selected our little corners, our emotions now closed to everything except the impending battle. We tried to warm up, but our actions felt like slow motion.

"Bennie calls us together. He has his one foot on a little bench and we are around him in a circle. 'Boys', he starts, 'we are all feeling a little scared. It is a feeling we all share. It is right that we feel like that, because the honour of our country is at stake.' At that moment the brass band blared out the first few notes of the Welsh anthem and the huge crowd began to sing, their voices rising to the heavens through the sheets of rain pouring on their heads. Bennie stopped speaking, and we are hardly breathing. We knew the anthem by then; it was played and sung before every match in Wales:

Land of my fathers, from where I first came,
Oh glory and honour to be thy fair name....

"Then it is over and Bennie is speaking again. I have never heard such a speech before. Silently we listen to every word. Every word gives us more strength and courage. Each sentence brings back the will to win. Now we are ready. Come what may, we will live, we will die for South Africa. Bennie's last words are: 'Remember, we will try to handle the ball. Let me have it. If we find that we can't handle the wet ball, I will tell you what to do.'

"We threw everything into the game from the start, but missed two quick tries through our own mistakes. Once the ball got lost between Zimerman and I, and my desperate grab actually sent it right into the hands of Boon, their fast left-wing. At that moment my whole life passed before my eyes and I could see how we have lost the game, and all my fault. The next moment I could kiss Gerry Brand as he bundled Boon into touch. By now Bennie had decided on a change of tactics. It is now up to the two of us to kick, every conceivable kind of kick as long as it goes towards the Welsh half of the field. Our forwards are up to press ahead as Bennie and I launched one kick after the other.

"The Welshmen were still trying to handle the slippery, heavy ball and doing it darn well too as most of their backs were actually wearing gloves with the finger parts cut away. There was one exception, Powell, their big and strong scrumhalf, whose passes to his flyhalf, Ralph, were wild.

"Bennie Osler changed his tactics again at this stage. Instructing our looseforwards George Daneel, Andre McDonald and Alfi van der Merwe, to chase the ball with everything they've got, he ordered our forwards to actually give Wales the ball from the scrums and the lineouts. But a high punt from Boon presented Wales with first blood when Zimerman slipped and a second kick sent the ball past Brand for Davies to score an unconverted try. Midway through the second half another one of Powell's wild passes missed Ralph and this time Osler himself was on the spot. The ball bounced in his hands and he instantly placed a short kick ahead for his forwards. Ferdie Bergh dribbled it further and then George Daneel shot through like a bullet to score the equalising try. Gerry's conversion missed and although we could feel that we were getting on top, we just could not get through for the winning points. With less than ten minutes to go, Phil Nel broke through from a lineout with the ball at his feet, He dribbled it through the sea of water as one defender after the other was beaten. Finally it was kicked past fullback Bassett and as Nel fell over him, Bergh tapped the ball over the line to score. Osler took the conversion himself and when he succeeded, we knew that we had won. Wales attacked furiously in the few remaining minutes, but our defence held".

Thus Danie Craven's description of one of the epic victories in Springbok history; beating Wales in their own backyard and under their own conditions will always be an achievement to point at with pride.

The match against Lancashire and Cheshire immediately following the test, was in many respects the most amazing of the tour. Although the Springboks won, no less than five of their players had to leave the field because of injury, leaving them with a scrum consisting of three forwards!

At one point, one of the Lancashire players suggested to his captain that it would be a good idea to take line-outs instead of scrums only to get an answer so typical from rugby in England in those days:

"There are only three of them left. It would be unfair to capitalise on their misfortune. We don't play rugby only to win, you know."

Such chivalry, I am afraid, no longer exists anywhere in international sport!

The test against Ireland was a lot easier than the one against Wales, but again the Springboks trailed at half-time. After the resumption, the forwards improved however and Craven and Osler got more room in which to move. Zimerman scored a typical try after a high punt from Osler had caught the Irish fullback in two minds and near the end of the match Osler broke around the blind-side and gave the ball to Frankie Waring with Zimerman next to him, and only the fullback to beat. Waring, for a reason known only to himself, cut inside instead of drawing the fullback and passing to Zimerman. He ran right into the arms of loose-forward Jamie Clinch, a veteran of the 1924 tour to South Africa, but somehow he managed to wriggle past for the winning try which Osler converted to make the final score 8-3.

The second match against London nearly brought tragedy when Jackie Tindall was seriously injured and his life was only saved after an emergency operation and a lengthy period in hospital during which he was desperately ill.

Then came the test against England. the most disappointing match of the tour. Ferdie Bergh scored an unconverted try and in the last thirty seconds of the game, Gerry Brand caught a poor clearing kick on the halfway line and right on touch. From this spot he calmly kicked a dropgoal, still considered to be the best to have been seen at Twickenham.

It is said that somebody afterwards went and measured the distance from where Brand kicked to the point where the ball landed after sailing between the uprights. The distance was found to be 85 yards. No wonder "Fire-brand" was the toast of Twickenham. His miracle kick was one of only three highlights in a dull match, won 7-0 by the Springboks. The only other

Gerry Brand, whose wonderful kicking made him the hero of Twickenham.

occasions the crowd had anything to shout over was when Bergh got his try after a fumble by Barr, the England fullback, and when Roger Spong, the home team's flyhalf, slipped through the entire Springbok defence and had what he thought was a clear field ahead of him. He reckoned without the exceptional speed of George Daneel, who flew across to cut him down with a magnificent tackle. The England test, incidentally, was the only international on the tour in which Craven did not play.

After the match the Springboks were invited to Buckingham Palace to meet George V and this occasion led to the most familiar anecdote in our rugby history. Apparently the players were lined up for the traditional introduction and handshake and to their surprise they discovered that the king had some sort of question or banter for each of them. When he got to Pierre de Villiers, looking smaller than ever as he was flanked by two huge forwards, he seemed amused and asked the little scrumhalf from Paarl which position he filled on the field. The story goes that De Villiers who normally had quite a deep voice for his size, suddenly lost it and squeaked: "Scrumhalf, Mr. King!"

The only thing that bothered the Springboks at this late stage of their tour was the news that Jackie Tindall was still in a critical condition in a London hospital. Osler and Pienaar were at his bedside and kept the team informed with regular telegrams. They had already decided that should their teammate die, no further matches would be played. Osler returned to the team just before the test against Scotland, the final match of the tour, with the news that there was a definite improvement in Tindall's condition and that he had expressed the special wish that they should not cancel the game.

There were more than 74 000 people packed around Murrayfield and once again the weather was appalling. The first half the Springboks played against a strong wind which drove sleet with terrific force into their faces.

Scotland scored first when their flyhalf H. Lind picked up and cut through after Osler had tried an interception, but the conversion was a total disaster. The home team nevertheless had the best of the first half and their dribbling rushes to the accompaniment of the chant "Feet, Scotland, feet!" from the crowd, caused the Springboks one nightmare after the other.

In the second half, the Springboks had the advantage of the wind, but it was so powerful that it never really helped either side. The Springbok forwards were gradually getting on top, however, and a strong run by Floors Venter took the touring team to within striking distance. Scotland hooked from the scrum, but they heeled too slowly and the pass between Logan and Lind went astray. Bennie Osler, who told me once that by that time he was a distinct shade of blue from the biting wind, somehow managed to swoop down on it and before the defence could recover he was over the line. To try and convert was a waste of time and Brand's effort never looked like going in the right direction.

Scotland fought back with everything they had and managed to drive the Springboks back to their own goalline from where Craven used the gale effectively to find touch not many yards from the Scottish line!

From the next scrum McDonald fooled the defence by breaking away quickly, but without the ball. The Scottish looseforwards charged down on him, leaving a gap which Craven took to score near the posts. Brand missed even this comparatively easy conversion as the wind blew the ball over in the fraction of a second before his boot hit it. But it did not really matter. The Springboks had won 6-3 and the tour had ended on a triumphant note.

Phil Mostert is brought down by a tackle in the test against England at Twickenham in 1932. There is not a single Springbok up in support but South Africa won 7–0.

The first Wallabies – and the dirtiest test

1933 was one of the strangest years in South African rugby history. Still flushed with the success of the tour to Britain and with a whole new crop of established young Springboks backed up by a strong sprinkling of vastly experienced veterans, they should have been more than prepared to deal with any challenge. But in the second test of the series against Australia that winter the Springboks suffered their biggest defeat up to that time and in the final international they were beaten again in a match that has often been described as the worst performance ever by a South African side.

It was Australia's first fully representative venture into the international rugby arena. Known until then as the Waratahs and with their players coming almost exclusively from New South Wales, the game had spread sufficiently to other states like Queensland and Victoria to acquire more of a national look about it. They were tabbed the Wallabies and under the captaincy of the New South Wales fullback Alec Ross, they came to South Africa for a full-length tour which was to include, for the first and last time, five test matches.

The Wallabies introduced a new concept of rugby to the South African public. Backed up by light and fast forwards, they played attacking rugby with an abandon we had never seen before. It was risky stuff, but the spectators loved it and the South African rugby authorities openly suggested that the Springboks should follow suit. Even though the Australians were beaten frequently in the matches leading up to the first international, the whole country was overcome with a fever of enthusiasm for the open game and there was insiduous but powerful pressure on the Springboks to discard the subdue-probe-and-penetrate pattern they had so successfully evolved over many years.

The Wallabies lost five of the nine matches played before the first test, but almost every team who met them left the field with a feeling that here was a team not to be dallied with. They were very quick to capitalise on mistakes and the best tactics against them would obviously be to dominate the tight phases to nulify their loose forwards and to be in complete control of possession.

Even with their captain Alec Ross out because of an appendicitis operation and the vice-captain and best scrumhalf S. J. Malcolm also injured, they were obviously in the process of perfecting their opportunistic style and the Springboks selected for the first test at Newlands were far from confident.

The team was selected after a week of trials matches played in the rain and the national selectors, Markotter, Schreiner, Devenish, Townsend and Gog Kriek, decided to play it safe and they included eleven members from Osler's 1931/32 touring party. The newcomers were Leon Barnard, a wing from South Western Districts who shone during the trials, Jack Gage, a Free State wing who had already represented Ireland, George D'Alton and Innes Lyndon ("Fronie") Froneman, really tight forwards from Western Province and Border respectively but selected as flankers.

Shortly before the test, Barnard developed an angry boil on his arm and he had to be replaced by Freddie Turner, then a youthful second division player but destined to become one of the big stars of Springbok rugby in the 1930's because of his versatility. Turner was flown down from Port Elizabeth for the test, probably the first Springbok to make use of a form of transport then still in its infancy and at 19 years and

The Cape Times

Above: Freddie Turner, a last-minute call to the team for the first test, made him the youngest player ever to represent South Africa in an international match.

Below: Danie Craven, not yet 23 years old but already considered by many to be the best scrumhalf in the world, scores the first try of the 1933 series after a typical break early in the first test at Newlands.

Alec Ross, captain of the first Australian team to visit South Africa.

$3\frac{1}{2}$ months certainly the youngest to have actually played in a test to this day. Barnard, incidentally, never got another chance.

The selectors decided to include the veteran Bennie Osler in the team, but, rather harshly, took the captaincy from him and gave it to Phil Nel, the Natal lock forward. Many years later Nel told with what mixed feelings he accepted the honour:

"There was, for me, a tinge of regret that Bennie Osler had been deposed after our victorious tour of Britain. I felt, on hearing the news, that in some ways an injustice had been done to him. I was sitting in the lounge of a Cape Town hotel after Bill Schreiner had pinned the names of the selected players on the notice board and I was quite frankly shocked to hear that I had been nominated as captain. Just then I was called to the telephone. It was Bennie to wish me good luck, to add his congratulations on my appointment and to promise me his full support and loyalty. To me this was as fine a sporting gesture as I ever came across. Bennie and I always remained the firmest of friends and I admired his strategic approach to the game tremendously."

The reason for Osler's demotion could only have been that the selectors were unhappy with the winning but sometimes unattractive rugby the team had played in Britain. Battle-hardened veterans they might have been, but it seems as if even the national selectors were being influenced by the press and public to adopt the newly-acclaimed Wallaby style.

The team refused to be influenced, however, and it was with typical forward domination that the Springboks won 17-3. A clever break by Craven brought the first try and at half-time the score was 6-0 after Brand had steered a penalty over the crossbar. After halftime Ferdie Bergh went over for two unconverted tries and Osler, whose tactical kicking often bewildered the Wallabies, slipped through for a try of his own, converted by Brand.

The final score indicated an easy victory as the Wallabies only had a penalty by flyhalf R. R. Biilmann to show for their efforts, but the Springboks, unlike the experts on the grandstand, knew only too well how often only a stroke of luck prevented the Wallabies from getting points. They knew that to change their tactics and approach would only serve to accommodate the Australians.

The game was rough at times and even this seemed to worry the rugby authorities who had the strangest desire to lean over backwards in favour of the visitors. The Springboks got most of the blame for the incidents and nobody seemed to realise that in "Wild Bill" Cerutti and Aubrey Hodgson the Wallabies had forwards who were certainly no angels.

To improve relations between the teams a banquet was arranged before the second test in Durban and, as Craven was to put it later, it had a good influence on the Springboks for that particular game, but not then, or later, on the Australians!

Phil Nel was injured in the first test and Osler took over the captaincy and was immediately subjected to a campaign from all sides to "play open rugby". The atmosphere for the test was all wrong; the Springboks were unmotivated and spent most of the time before the game enjoying themselves in the Durban surf. In addition the selectors had made some inexplicable changes to the combination which won the Newlands international, switching Turner from wing to centre and Waring from centre to wing for reasons known only to themselves. The young Turner had been extremely successful at Newlands and, in fact, so was Waring.

Osler, nearing the end of his illustrious career, was so sick and tired of the clamour for open rugby, which most people interpreted as a policy of never kicking, that he decided that just for once, he would allow

The Star

Danie Craven has the Australian defence in a tangle as he breaks powerfully in the third test at Ellis Park.

Springbok centre Frankie Waring about to score against Australia in the second test in Durban. But it was a bad day for South Africa.

himself to be dictated to. He knew only too well that the Springbok forwards, big and heavy men, needed nursing with judicious kicking and that they could never last the pace in 80 minutes of uninterrupted running, but, if that was what the public and the authorities wanted, then that was what they would get this time.

The result was a humiliating defeat with the Wallabies playing sensibly and kicking whenever necessary, winning 21-6. The Springboks were run ragged and except when Brand put over a penalty with a smooth dropkick and Waring scored a nice try, they seemed merely on the field for the sake of formality. Fullback J. C. Steggall, wing J. D. Kelaher (an outstanding player in any company), flyhalf Biilmann and forward Bill Cerutti looked like world champions against the flat-footed Springboks.

Australia's winning margin of 15 points was the biggest against the Springboks until 1965 when the All Blacks won 20-3 at Auckland.

The selectors did a far better job for the third test in Johannesburg bringing in Floors Venter on one wing and restoring Freddie Turner to the other, combining Jimmy White and Frankie Waring at centre and giving the forwards a little more pace with the inclusion of Fred Smollan and W. H. Clarke, both of whom had played well when Transvaal beat the Wallabies five days before the international. Phil Nel, recovered from his injury, took over the captaincy again from Osler.

This time there were no shenanigans. The Springboks played it their way and with excellent tries by Boy Louw and Turner, one converted by Brand, and a dropgoal by Osler to an unconverted try by Cowper, won a good match 12-3. This incidentally was the fourth and final dropgoal of Osler's international career, a record for a South African in tests until Hansie Brewis made his career total five in the test against Wales in 1951.

Craven became seriously ill after this test when he picked up a virulent skin infection from a masseur and, although he had practically recovered by the time of the fourth international in Port Elizabeth, he was not expected to play. On the Thursday before the match, however, both Turner and Venter were injured and Craven had to fill one of the centre positions with Waring and with Jimmy White and Gerry Brand in the wing positions while Border's Bunny Reid was brought in at fullback. Pierre de Villiers came back into the team as Osler's partner. It turned out to be a miserable match with the Wallabies concentrating so much on Osler that they forgot all about their 15-man pattern. The Springboks won 11-0 after tries by White and Fanie Louw, with Brand adding a penalty and Osler a conversion.

With victory in the series now assured, the selectors again made too many changes for the final international in Bloemfontein. The Wallabies had the services of their captain Alec Ross for the first time in the tests and generally they were far better motivated.

It has been said that the discipline in the Springbok camp before this match was shocking. There were far too many social events and even a champagne party until the small hours of the morning. If the rumours were true, then it is hardly surprising that they gave just about the worst performance in South African rugby history. They were so ponderous and disinterested that it was rather a reflection on the Wallabies that they did not win by a bigger score than 15-4.

In the second half, with both Phil Nel and Fanie Louw injured and off the field, the Australians also seemed to lose interest in the affair and both teams but particularly the Springboks, slunk back to their dressingrooms as thousands of disgruntled spectators trooped home. The only good thing to come out of this distressing match was that it brought home to the rugby authorities the fact that a test series should never consist of more than four tests.

It is a pity that the international career of the great Bennie Osler should have ended on such a dismal note. There was one consolation for the old master matchwinner, though. A week later, in the final match of the tour, the Wallabies were beaten at Newlands by a team combined from Western Province Town and Country clubs. The score was 4-0 and it was Bennie Osler, with a typical dropgoal, who scored the points.

Four years later Australia and South Africa tackled each other again when Phil Nel's mighty 1937 Springboks called around briefly before going on to their triumphant tour of New Zealand. This time it was a different story altogether.

In the first test on a soaking wet Oval Cricket Ground in Sydney, the Springboks played brilliantly although the final score was only 9-5. In many ways this was Jimmy White's match. White played opposite Cyril Towers, Australia's captain and star centre, and beforehand the Border Springbok was often told what a tough job he was in for. It was just the stuff to motivate him into giving a superb exhibition of crashtackling and poor Towers was drilled into the mud time and again. According to Craven, who played flyhalf in this test, White never stopped talking throughout the match; he wanted everybody to share his enjoyment.

An interesting sidelight to this match was the fact that a radio broadcaster brought a microphone on to the field at half-time and asked the Springboks if they had any messages for their teammate Ben du Toit, who had had a vertebra cracked in one of the early matches of the tour and was listening to the commentary from his hospital bed. The messages were in Afrikaans and unprintable in a South African publication!

The second international, on the same ground, was a vicious affair, considered by some to have been the dirtiest test of all time. In the second half in particular the referee, W. F. B. Kilner, of New South Wales, might as well have taken a seat on the stand for all the use he was.

The Springboks were badly hit by injuries before the match and really only had seven fit forwards at their disposal. In addition, they were tipped off that the Wallabies had a scheme to give the South African flyhalf a deliberate inside gap and then, with the aid of their exceptionally fast looseforwards, to cut him off from the backline they feared so much.

The Springboks decided to counter this by using the powerfully-built Craven at No. 8 with the idea that he would also act as extra flyhalf and so to further confuse the Australians. This decision, incidentally, meant that Craven would hold a record of having played in a different position in each of four consecutive tests.

The plan worked well from the outset and the Springboks had 26 points on the board at halftime. The first half was rough enough, but in the second half the Wallabies must have decided that their only hope lay in provoking their opponents into losing their cool. They succeeded only too well.

From the moment Pierre de Villiers was crumpled into unconsciousness with a blatant kick and had to be carried off the field by Boy Louw "like a father removing the body of his child from the scene of an accident", as one writer put it, the game became a bar-room brawl. Brave little Pierre returned after a while, but George van Reenen was hurt so badly that he could not resume. Fights broke out all over the place with the Springboks so incensed that they virtually forgot all about the ball and allowed the Wallabies to notch 11 points without reply.

Harry ("Kalfie") Martin and the Australian eighthman Aubrey Hodgson flew into each other on one occasion and stood exchanging punches like two boxers. More than 30 years after the incident, Martin, then the recently retired Chief of Staff in the South African Air Force, but only a lieutenant in his Springbok days, talked about that infamous incident.

"De Villiers was laid out completely. He was in a terrible state, his eyes were rolling and his tongue was hanging out. It really upset us and this is the only instance in my rugby career that I can recall being deliberately attacked and retaliating. Normally I never lost my temper on the field as I actually treated sport as an occasion for discipline."

Freddie Turner gapes with astonishment as Harry Martin and Aubrey Hodgson adopt fighting stances during the second test against Australia in 1937. It was one of the most vicious tests in Springbok history. Note the prostrate Australian in the background.

Hodgson, who was dubbed "Awesome Aub" by Australian sportswriters following a tremendous fight he had with that other rough man of Wallaby rugby "Wild Bill" Cerutti, in a club match, also much later gave his version of that violent clash with the Springboks in an interview with the Australian *Daily Mirror*. The interview, in part and as written by the reporter, read:

"One of the men marked by the Australians was the mighty Springbok halfback Pierre de Villers. Again Aub Hodgson was chosen to play the leading role. He did it this way.

"Winning the ball in a lineout, Hodgson would draw the ball to his chest, turn into the opposition and run forward. Then coming up to De Villiers he would gently hand him the ball. The next instant the little half would find himself in the centre of a ruck and at the Australians' mercy.

"It was during this game that Hodgson and the Springbok front-rower Harry Martin, stood right on the sideline and treated the 30 000 fans to an exhibition of moderately scientific boxing. Hodgson was charging down the line with the ball when Martin hurled himself forward with a fearsome tackle. The Australian breakaway was thrown off his feet, but on his way to the ground managed to get in a hard elbow blow to Martin's face.

"Then, as Hodgson scrambled to his feet, Martin bored in with a swift uppercut. The Australian shook his head and replied with a straight left and right. Hodgson ran the risk of being sent off but the referee was busy elsewhere, trying to break up the individual brawls that were developing all over the field".

Jimmy White, whose crushing tackles helped the Springboks to win the first test against Australia in 1937.

Even Craven lost his self control as the match degenerated further. And again Hodgson was the central figure. It came after De Villiers had returned on the field and Boy Louw had told Craven to stop the Australian No. 8 from getting to the little scrumhalf. In the tussle that followed Craven was kicked on the shin and, very angry, the Springbok instructed Dai Williams at the lineout to throw the ball directly at Hodgson. As Williams threw, Craven climbed into "Awesome Aub" but unfortunately Dai's throw-in did not get to the right man and the referee caught Craven in the act, so to speak.

While the referee was lecturing Craven and actually threatening to send him off the field, Hodgson jumped off the deck and kicked the Springbok three times on the shin! The referee decided that Craven was the original offender and the Wallabies got the penalty.

The next day the newspapers were full of photographs showing players kicking, punching and squaring up to each other. Both teams, but particularly the Springboks, were criticised and by the time they arrived in New Zealand they were sick of looking at pictures of the "Battle of Sydney Oval"

One picture showed Boy Louw in a boxing pose with his right hand cocked for a swing from way back. He had his own explanation for this one. "They're all wrong. I remember this incident very well. I didn't want to hit anyone. Somebody had jerked me out of a lineout and I was swinging my arms around to keep my balance!"

The 1937 Springboks learnt a lesson from the match after all. Realising that they had scored 26 points before halftime but nothing after they had lost their tempers and, in fact, that they had conceded 11 points instead, they never again lost their self control on that wonderful tour of 1937.

The greatest Springboks

The police had given up and traffic was being choked to a halt by the restless throng milling around in front of the Metropole Hotel in Long Street, Cape Town.

It was getting towards midnight on Saturday April 10, 1937 and inside the hotel more than a hundred of South Africa's finest rugby players were waiting to hear which of them would be among the lucky 29 chosen to undertake the second tour of Australia and New Zealand in Springbok history.

A week of trials matches had ended at Newlands that afternoon and the national selectors were now deliberating in the Civil Service Club while the players were dining at the hotel. W. R. (Bill) Schreiner, chairman of the selectors, had promised to announce the names of the touring party at the hotel and hundreds of rugby fans had gathered in the street to wait for the big news.

For most of the players the dinner was a fiendish form of torture. Percy Twentyman-Jones, a former international player himself and then Judge President of the Cape Province, was in charge of the affair and he did his best to soothe raw nerves with a witty speech. Those were the days before smoking was regarded as an invitation to an early death and one newspaper reporter described the scene as one of players huddled in their chairs "trimming their finger-nails with their teeth, gulping down stimulants to help to forget their anxiety, or strewing the carpets with cigarette ends as plentifully as autumn leaves. . . ."

At the Civil Service Club proceedings were certainly a lot more decorous but no less tense as five powerful personalities wrestled for consensus.

Bill Schreiner who became a national selector at the age of 26 while still an active player, was then in his 16th year as chairman (he retired in 1952 after 40 years of unselfish service to the game). With him on the panel he had A. F. Markotter, a man of emphatic views, unorthodox methods and an unerring eye for talent, George St. Leger Devenish who played for South Africa as far back as 1896, Frank Mellish who had the distinction of having represented both England and South Africa, and "Gubby" Barlow, also an outspoken man with years of experience.

Several players were obvious selections for the tour while Markotter with his usual supreme self confidence had several places "booked" for players in whom he had complete faith. Dr. Danie Craven recently revealed that Gerry Brand, Boy and Fanie Louw, Flappie Lochner and himself were notified well in advance that they would be making the tour. He also divulged for the first time that Mr. Mark actually told him before the trials that he would be captain of the 1937 team. For once, something must have gone wrong with Markotter's plans because Philip Nel, and not Craven, eventually received the skipper's job. There is some evidence of disagreement between the selectors that year and the South African Rugby Board because it is a fact that Schreiner and his panel did not approve of the appointment of Percy Day as manager and Alec de Villiers as assistant manager of the side.

Reading about the trials now, 40 years later, it is rather startling to discover that Dauncey Devine, a 1924 Springbok scrumhalf and one of the originators of the dive-pass perfected by Craven, actually took part in them. This means that Devine must surely have enjoyed one of the longest first-class careers in our rugby history.

Ben du Toit, then regarded as the best looseforward in South Africa, had been invited to the trials, but for some reason or other had decided to not make himself available for the tour. He came down from the Transvaal to watch the trials, however, and with the irascible "help" of Mr. Mark changed his mind and decided to play after all. The story is told that Du Toit was watching the trials from a seat in the stands when he felt a sudden urge to play. He then rushed to where the selectors were sitting and offered his services. The trials

Ben du Toit

Jan Lotz

Mauritz van den Berg

Johnny Bester

Louis Babrow

Right: Phil Nel, the farmer from Kranskop, in the district of Greytown, who became captain of the 1937 Springboks.

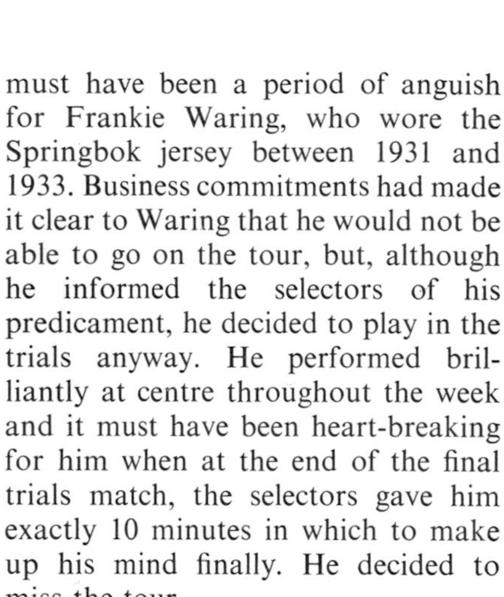

must have been a period of anguish for Frankie Waring, who wore the Springbok jersey between 1931 and 1933. Business commitments had made it clear to Waring that he would not be able to go on the tour, but, although he informed the selectors of his predicament, he decided to play in the trials anyway. He performed brilliantly at centre throughout the week and it must have been heart-breaking for him when at the end of the final trials match, the selectors gave him exactly 10 minutes in which to make up his mind finally. He decided to miss the tour.

As they debated in the Civil Service Club, the selectors must have had their biggest headaches over the centre and flyhalf positions. Jimmy White, an experienced international player and the deadliest tackler of his day, was badly off-form, Louis Babrow and "Koffie" Hofmeyr were also erratic and only the 19-year-old Johannes Lodewyk Augustinus Bester, known as "Johnny", of Western Province had played consistently well throughout the week. The selectors decided to take the risk and to pick all four — a decision they were never to regret.

Outstanding flyhalves were even scarcer at the trials. The newcomers performed in the shadow of the retired Bennie Osler and their weaknesses were easier to spot than their strengths. Finally Dirk van de Vyver and the virtually untried Tony Harris got the nod with the versatile Flappie Lochner selected as an utility back, but like the equally versatile Freddie Turner who was named as Gerry Brand's understudy at fullback, destined to make his mark elsewhere among the threequarters.

Agreement reached at last, the selectors went to the Metropole Hotel where "Uncle Bill" Schreiner like a Roman senator of old, took up position on the first-floor balcony to read out the team to the players, at the same time giving the crowd in the street the opportunity to hear the names.

Philip Nel, a 34-year-old farmer from Greytown, Natal, who began his international rugby career against Maurice Brownlie's All Blacks, was a rather surprising selection as captain. Nel had virtually retired after leading the Springboks to victory over the 1933 Wallabies and was enjoying himself playing carefree rugby for Natal under the captaincy of Ebbo Bastard. A man of great strength of character, he was highly respected in South African rugby however and captained the A-team throughout the week of trials matches. He himself thought that his age would militate against him, but the authorities had other ideas and Nel was to prove more than worthy of the confidence placed in his leadership.

Nel, the eldest son in a family of five, was born on a farm in the district of Kranskop, Natal, in 1902 and he saw his first game of rugby when he was already 15 years old and had just enrolled as a pupil at Maritzburg College. His parents refused him permission to play because a relative had developed cancer after breaking a hip in a rugby match. Young Phil kept on pestering them though and they finally relented. Tall and heavy for his age, Nel was quickly promoted from the fourth to the first team and while still at school he gained his provincial colours for Natal under the captaincy of Herby Taylor, one of this country's most famous cricketers who was also a fine flyhalf in

his younger days.

After he left school Nel continued to play rugby although it meant getting up in the small hours of a Saturday morning, riding 30 miles on horseback from his farm to Greytown and then clubbing together with a few other players to hire a taxi to get to Pietermaritzburg for a club match. After the game the same tedious process would have to be repeated.

Philip and his younger brother Maritz were invited to the national trials in 1928 and in one of the matches the selector and former Springbok captain Theo Pienaar took the whistle. During the match Pienaar collided with Maritz Nel and had to be taken to hospital. The younger Nel never did make the Springbok team, but Phil played in all four tests. In 1931 he was included in Bennie Osler's touring side to Britain where he again played in all the tests. He replaced Osler as Springbok captain in four of the five Tests against the touring Wallabies in 1933 and then, more or less accepting the fact that his international career was over and being heavily committed to his farming duties, Nel withdrew as Natal captain. He was playing such good rugby though that the selectors refused to discard him and so he was given the job of leading a side not many of the critics, professional or amateur, considered particularly strong.

Even Markotter had his doubts. "Phil, your forwards are good. I'm not so sure about your backs," he said to Nel after the announcement of the team.

In retrospect, the doubts seemed unwarranted. At fullback there was Gerry Brand, a rugby genius in every respect, and as an understudy he had Freddie Turner, who turned out to be one of the stars of the tour as a wing threequarter with a deceptive sidestep.

Dai Williams, tall and black-haired, is still rated as one of the best wings ever to play for South Africa, combining intelligence with pace and the ability to put a cross-kick exactly where he wanted it. Louis Babrow, aggressive and enterprising, combined well at centre with either White, whom the New Zealanders called "Jimmy-the-killer" because of his devastating tackles, or the cool and immaculate Flappie Lochner. Behind the scrum there was Danie Craven with a pass that travelled like a bullet, who could break like a rampaging forward and who was already then a master tactician and there was Pierre de Villiers, a veteran of many battles, but still well up to the standard that made him one of the best scrum-halves the game has known.

At fly-half Tony Harris revealed beautiful hands, a quick eye for an opening, and, above all, the rhythm and ball-sense to bring out the best in his talented threequarters.

Up front the 1937 Springboks were invincible. There were the brothers, Fanie and Boy Louw, Jan Lotz whom many still say is the best hooker ever to represent South Africa, the huge but mobile Ferdie Bergh, Mauritz van den Berg who overcame a physical disability with characteristic courage, the tenacious Lucas Strachan and the hard-working William Eberhard (Ebbo) Bastard whose death in a shooting incident some years later led to one of the most sensational trials of the 1940's. These are the immortal names in our rugby annals, but in fact, all 14 forwards in the side were players of exceptional ability.

1937

Left: Two of the greatest Springbok forwards of all time. Boy Louw, on the left, with his brother Fanie.

Above: The "Big Five" who controlled the destiny of the 1937 Springboks. *From the left:* Danie Craven, Gerry Brand, Lucas Strachan, Boy Louw and Phil Nel.

Matthys Michael (Boy) Louw, in particular, has become a legend in his own lifetime. A man of enormous physical strength, Louw also had an instinctive flair for the game and he understood the fundamentals down to the most minute detail. Near the end of his career as a player and especially in later years when he did (and is still doing) so much for rugby as a coach, selector and administrator, Louw became known as "The Old Master" and there can be no more apt nickname for this phenomenal player. Boy Louw was a hard, relentless, competitor who stood no nonsense from anyone, but it was his brain and not his brawn that earned him such a special place in our rugby history.

Boy Louw might just be the most colourful personality ever to have worn the Springbok jersey. Born on February 2, 1906 on a farm in the district of Wellington in the heart of the Boland, Boy was the fifth of 10 brothers and four sisters. One of his brothers died while still very young, but the other nine all played senior rugby. Boy and Fanie became Springboks and four of the other brothers progressed to interprovincial level.

Boy Louw took his rugby seriously and not even the dictatorial Bennie Osler ever tried to overrule him in a match. Danie Craven tells the story of how Osler once called for the ball from a scrum during the wet and windswept test against Scotland in 1932.

"Hold, and play with the forwards!", Louw countermanded his captain's order from the frontrow. But Osler again commanded Craven to pass. This time Louw whipped his head from the forming scrum and snorted:

"Nonsense with you, Bennie! We're keeping it up front!" In fact he used a word much stronger than "nonsense" and Osler saw no point in further argument.

On another occasion he told a captain: "You make the speeches, I'll lead the pack!" and that is the way it was.

Louw has often fought a losing battle with tongue twisters and his malapropisms have kept several generations of players amused. Some of the stories told about him are no doubt apochryphal, but it is a fact that he does sometimes produce a somewhat mixed-up version of what he really intended to say.

One of the most delightful anecdotes is the one Craven told recently of the time Boy and his pack were battling mightily in a match when Springbok centre Johnny Bester not only dropped hard-earned possession, but stood rooted on the spot and did not fall back to recover the situation. As Boy ran past Bester, he slapped him on the rump and reprimanded:

"Hey, do you think you have bought this ground of plot?"

Craven also vouches for the fact that it was indeed Boy who once looked at a sloppy lineout and said: "Why you stand so crooked? Can't you stand in a straight stripe?"

Louw took his rugby seriously and throughout his long international career which included 18 tests, he was invariably the man the half-backs and threequarters turned to whenever they were the victims of dirty tactics from the opposing forwards. Boy's retribution was always swift and merciless. Again to quote Danie Craven:

"In one of the matches in New Zealand in 1937 there was a forward wearing a number 12 jersey who kept on climbing in on the wrong side of the loose scrums, kicking and trampling whoever happened to be in the way. I dealt with him twice, but he persisted in his evil ways and each time Mauritz van den Berg would ask me who it was and I would answer that it was number 12 again. Finally it was all too much for Boy. 'What's wrong with you fellows today?', he asked of no-one in particular and at the next opportunity the offending number 12 came flying out of the loose scrum to land at my feet, one eye already coming up like a balloon. Then I heard Boy's voice: 'Mr. Ref, you can blow your whistle now, number 12 is off!' "

Louw like so many other members of that mighty 1937 pack were at the peak of their careers at the time of the tour and an older generation of New Zealanders insist to this day that Phil Nel's forwards were the best ever to visit their country. But when the team gathered in Durban in May that year to await departure on the *"Ulysses"* most South Africans were apprehensive about their prospects. Paul Roos travelled all the way from Cape Town to give them his blessing.

Above: An Australian photographer took this sequence of Gerry Brand at the Sydney Oval in 1937, showing how the famous Springbok fullback executed a dropkick.

Above: Danie Craven was one of the most popular members of a popular Springbok team. Here he makes friends with a Maori family in Rotorua.

Green & Hann

Below: With Pierre de Villiers behind him and Lucas Strachan and Jan Lotz providing a protective screen, Fanie Louw bursts away during the match against Canterbury.

His huge black moustache quivering with sincerity, Roos made his speech:

"We want the public and the men themselves to know that we are not sending the team over to become world champions. They must remember that they have been invited as guests rather than rivals. We hope that we shall learn mutually; you go over there as ambassadors of good sport and friendship. And my final words to you are that you keep yourselves in the pink of condition, because you have a duty to perform to your hosts who have invited you and secondly to your country which is sending you...."

But Paul Roos was not the best-known headmaster of his day for nothing and he ended his speech with a ringing instruction:

"Let the spirit be the spirit of the Charge of the Light Brigade! Theirs not to reason why, theirs but to do or die!

"The message I bring to you from the South African Rugby Board is that you should go forth, my boys, and win your spurs!"

The 1937 team was run by the players for the players and perhaps there is a valuable lesson to be learnt in this. Percy Day, the manager, had no say in the training or selection of the side, which was entirely the responsibility of a committee consisting of Philip Nel, Gerry Brand, Danie Craven, Boy Louw and Lucas Strachan. In fact, Day's functions were so limited that when he for reasons never officially explained, returned to South Africa before the end of the tour, it hardly seemed to cause any comment.

Once the ship left Durban, Nel set out to build the vital team spirit every touring side needs. One of the off-the-record agreements between the players was for example that should one of them become inebriated on occasions — and this can happen in the best of company — the rest must see to it that he is escorted to his room and ensure that he is safe and not in danger of disgracing himself in public.

Nel, being thoroughly bilingual, also made it his job to have private chats to each of the players and in many respects this was the most democratically-run Springbok team in history. At the team talks all the players were allowed to voice their opinions and the backs and three-quarters made it clear from the start that they would not tolerate a stodgy approach. Everybody had faith in the forwards and the backs felt confident that they would be able to make the most of their opportunities.

One of the major problems on board the *Ulysses* was finding a method to keep fit. There was only one rugby ball on the ship and it was soon sent bobbing along the Indian Ocean waves by an unwise pass. After that mishap the players had to do the best they could with a medicine ball from the gymnasium which might have developed a few stronger wrists, but certainly could not have helped

Above: With Nel injured, Craven had to lead the Springboks in the first test of the series. Here he and Ron King are bringing their teams on to the field. The Springboks following Craven are Ferdie Bergh and Jan Lotz.

Below: Johnny Dick scores the All Blacks' try in the first test.

Right: C. B. Jennings' tackle sends All Black wing Cobden flying into the air in the hard-fought first test match.

C. P. S. Boyer

much to promote swift handling.

The team was also sharply divided on the kind of exercises required. One school of thought backed Lucas Strachan, a detective-sergeant, who believed that the players should spend an hour or two a day hopping and running around the deck. Others preferred to follow Harry Martin, then an instructor in the South African Air Force, who advocated a system designed for the building of muscles. The tour committee allowed the players to choose for themselves which one of the "schools" to follow. John E. (Jack) Sacks, sports editor of the *Rand Daily Mail* and *Sunday Times* who meticulously recorded the tour in his now rarely-found book *"South Africa's Greatest Springboks"*, wrote that the players soon settled for short, sharp sprints and trots rather than calisthenics.

Philip Nel's 1937 Springboks provided one of the most glorious chapters in South African rugby history. In fact, there is ample evidence to support the frequent claim that this was indeed the greatest team ever to wear the Green and Gold.

On the tour of just under four months, they played 28 matches, including two unofficial fixtures, in Australia and New Zealand, were beaten only twice, and scored 855 points to 180. Both internationals in Australia were won and the series against the All Blacks went 2-1 to the Springboks — still the one and only time in the 56-year-old rivalry between the two countries that a rubber had been won by the touring side. To crown it all, the Springboks played the attractive, balanced rugby they had promised to produce.

The Springboks were a happy blend of experience and youthful enterprise. Skipper Philip Nel, at 34, was the oldest man in the side, with Gerry Brand, Boy Louw and Pierre de Villiers the only other players to have reached the 30 mark. Yet, no fewer than eleven members of the team, had extensive international experience. Nel, Brand, Boy Louw and De Villiers had played against the 1928 All Blacks.

The Springboks started the New Zealand leg of the tour after winning both tests against Australia, but losing 17-6 to New South Wales, in a match played in mud and rain. This defeat was given an exaggerated importance by the New Zealand critics, who confidently predicted that Auckland, Taranaki, Wellington, Canterbury, Southland, Otago and Hawke's Bay would be too strong for the tourists. As for the tests, there was no doubt in any New Zealand mind that the All Blacks would win.

The New Zealanders were adamant that the series would decide the rugby championship of the world and the Springboks were treated like visiting royalty.

Danie Craven was a particular favourite of the crowds and the press. Reports of his revolutionary dive pass preceded him and the photographers always on the lookout for an angle, singled him out for special attention. When it was discovered that, on top of everything else, the 26-year-old M.A. graduate was also most articulate, Craven was given no rest. He was flooded with requests to address societies, schools and universities and, since he was once a theological student, he even had to deliver several sermons.

The Springboks beat Auckland 19-5 in the first match of the tour, but nevertheless found their opponents strong and accomplished spoilers. From the lessons learnt in this match the Springboks evolved the tactics which were to prove so successful. It was mainly to concentrate on firm and solid scrummaging, thereby forcing the opposing forwards to stay in the scrum and leaving the Springbok backs free to cope with their opposite numbers on a man-for-man basis. Since there was the option between scrums and line-outs in those days, the plan worked like a charm.

Waikato (combining with King Country and Thames Valley) were the next to fall, and in this match Gerry Brand finally struck the top form which had eluded him on the Australian part of the tour.

Up till then, this legendary fullback was playing so badly that the tour selectors were beginning to look

Flappie Lochner rips through a gap in the decisive third test against the All Blacks in 1937. Freddie Turner is in support and New Zealand wing Jack Sullivan tries desperately to cover.

elsewhere for the approaching tests. But against the Waikato combination, in pelting rain and on a muddy field, Brand was flawless.

No-one could stop the Springbok victory march and Taranaki was beaten 17-3, Manawatu 39-3 and Wellington 29-0 before the first test in Wellington.

For days before the big match it rained steadily and the field was in a shocking state. The poor conditions moved the Springboks to decide on kicking tactics and for this purpose the tour committee decided to play Craven at fly-half. Craven and Nel were against the switch, both preferring to give Harris a chance, but they were outvoted. In fact, Craven was asked to leave the meeting while the matter was under discussion.

This was the match that led to a superstition most older Springboks believe in to this day — there must be no singing or facetiousness in the dressing room before a big game. The Boks' big victories over the strong provincial sides had given them a little too much confidence and in the dressing room they sang and joked as if victory was already theirs.

In fact, Craven was so worried about the light-hearted approach of the players that before the teams trotted out, he told Philip Nel that the Springboks were going to lose. Gerry Brand was injured and so was Boy Louw, while skipper Nel, was left out of the side which meant that the Springboks were without three of their most experienced players.

The All Blacks, inspired by a wildly-cheering crowd, had the bit between their teeth from the start. The mud and rain proved too much for the Springboks, who were outplayed and never looked like a winning combination; even after a brilliant unconverted try by Dai Williams had enabled them to catch up with the All Blacks who were off to a flying start with an early penalty by flyhalf Dave Trevathan.

At half-time the All Blacks were in the lead again after another fine penalty kick by Trevathan, and after the resumption it was soon obvious that everything was over bar the shouting.

A brilliant back-line movement between Dalton, Hooper and Sullivan ripped the Bok defence to shreds for

winger Dick to score, and not long afterwards it was Trevathan again with a fine drop goal. It was reported afterwards that even the referee L. E. Macassey, like Trevathan an Otago man, jumped with joy when the ball sailed over the crossbar.

This setback finally seemed to jerk the Springboks out of their lethargy and centre Jimmy White, feared mainly for his crash tackling, snapped over a drop goal from nowhere. All other attempts to shake off the All Blacks stranglehold failed, however, and the Boks were beaten 13-7. It was a major triumph for the New Zealand forwards in particular, but selection blunders by the Springboks contributed heavily to their own downfall.

Nursing their wounds and taking stock of their mistakes, the Springboks went on from there to whip Nelson, Golden Bay-Motueka and Marlborough 22-0, and followed up with wins over Canterbury (23-8), West Coast Buller (31-6), and South Canterbury (43-6) before going off to Christchurch for the second and decisive test.

This time there was no false confidence. The test players were only too painfully aware of the task awaiting them. The New Zealand newspapers were freely predicting another convincing win for their team, and there was even a note of pity for the poor visitors in some of the reports.

In his book "*Ek speel vir Suid-Afrika*" Danie Craven admits that the Springboks definitely expected the worst in this match. Their nerves were stretched to breaking point by the time they ran on to the field before 45 000 roaring spectators.

But when the first whistle went all the pent-up tension found sudden and violent release and the All Blacks were swept into their own half. For several minutes the Springboks launched attack after attack, with the All Blacks defence only just managing to hold.

And then followed the sort of sheer misfortune which would certainly have broken the spirit of a lesser team than the 1937 Springboks.

They were on the attack when the All Blacks centre Jack Sullivan intercepted between Tony Harris and Louis Babrow and rushed through for an unconverted try. That was shock number one. Shock number two came only minutes later when he did exactly the same thing; but this time he kicked far over Brand's head to beat Dai Williams in a desperate race for the ball to score his second unconverted try.

The Springboks were reeling and from then until half-time it appeared to be only a matter of time before the All Blacks would add more points to their 6-0 lead.

Yet somehow, in those few short minutes of rest, the embattled South Africans found the inspiration for a second-half fight back which must rank with the most glorious in our rugby history.

Early in the second half Boy Louw, who was playing a magnificent game, was injured and for the rest of the match he was not aware of what he was doing. A head injury can trigger the strangest reactions and in the

Tony Harris was an outstanding success in the 1937 Springbok team. Here the little flyhalf slips past two opponents in the third test.

mighty Boy's case it was a never-ending fit of the giggles. Like a silly schoolgirl, he ran around the field giggling and demanding to know from all and sundry what exactly was going on.

In exasperation Craven told him to stop the All Blacks forward Dalton from breaking through the line-outs. At the very next line-out, Boy, still giggling, sidled up gleefully to Dalton and, although the ball was nowhere near the bewildered New Zealander, flew into him with all his strength. Dalton disappeared under a welter of flying fists and feet, but fortunately the referee was following the ball and did not see the semi-conscious Springbok's literal execution of his vice-captain's orders.

"Is that what you wanted me to do, Daantjie?" Louw panted as he finally caught up with Craven again and for most of the rest of the match he continued his aimless running and even more aimless laughing. Phil Nel even had to pack in his place in the frontrow while Louw did the best he could in whatever position he could find.

"It may be funny now, but it wasn't funny then", Craven said years later, "The seconds were ticking away and we just could not break through the All Blacks defence and with a stalwart like Boy incapacitated, our future looked grim indeed."

But slowly and surely the Springbok machine accelerated into higher gear and the pressure grew stronger and stronger. Then, from a scrum in the All Blacks twenty-five, Craven whipped the ball to White on the blind side who passed quickly to Freddie Turner on the left wing. Turner deftly sidestepped his way around one defender, handed off Dick and with a quick change of direction sped over the line for a try under the posts. Gerry Brand made no mistake with the conversion and the Springboks trailed by only one point.

But bad luck was still hounding the Springboks, With Boy Louw already dazed, they lost their second forward when the hard-working Ebbo Bastard was knocked into a state of semi-consciousness. He refused to go off the field but charged from scrum to loose scrum and back again, sobbing wildly and forcing Nel to make more emergency changes in his pack.

It was at this point that Boy Louw had a rare moment of lucidity. He actually caught a crucial mark and put the Springboks on the attack with a magnificent touch kick. Babrow almost got through after a quick heel, and from the ensuing scrum Craven was tackled illegally. The penalty was given on the halfway line and at a sharp angle. "Well, its up to you now, Gerry!", Nel remarked as he gave the slender Springbok fullback the ball for one of the most vital kicks of his career.

The crowd was silent as Brand, with tantalising care, placed the ball and prepared for the kick. A few seconds later they sat stunned as the ball rose and rose and then settled, like an arrow in flight, on its path to the crossbar. In the pavilion, the non-playing Springboks became almost hysterical with delight and Howard Watt jumped about so much in his glee that he sprained his ankle!

Two points ahead and with only a few minutes to go, the Springboks refused to sit on their slender lead. From the kick-off, Lucas Strachan jerked himself into a gap and kicked ahead for the ever-alert Freddie Turner, who jumped high off the ground to take it in full stride before passing to Jimmy White. White forced a huge hole in the demoralised defence before passing inside towards Babrow, but it was the half-dazed Ebbo Bastard who bobbed up between them and instinctively held on to the ball to dive over the line. To make absolutely sure of the result the ice-cool Gerry Brand converted with yet another magnificent kick and the Springboks had won the second test 13-6. As they left the field, Boy Louw collapsed and had to be helped off.

Back in their dressing room, the South Africans and their few supporters were almost delirious with delight. The test players were embraced and kissed, and the story is told that Pat Lyster went even further in his ecstacy. Running up to Louis Babrow, he shouted: "Hit me, Louis! Hit me under the chin!" Babrow took him at his word and plonked him on the jaw with a blow which stretched him out unconscious!

A New Zealander watching all this came over and dared Babrow to try the same with him "Why should I?" Babrow asked. "Because I give you the right to try, " the New Zealander answered.

Prompted by the other players, the powerfully-built Springbok centre said: "OK, are you ready?" and then let rip with his right. The New Zealander followed Lyster into the land of dreams.

This unfortunate fellow was not the only All Blacks supporter to be stunned after the match. They simply could not believe that their mighty team had been so decisively beaten after looking like winners all the way in the first half.

As for the triumphant Boks, they moved on to beat Southland (30-17) Otago (47-7), Hawke's Bay (21-12) and Poverty Bay — Bay of Plenty — East Coast (33-3) before it was time again to tackle the now deadly determined All Blacks in the third, final and decisive test of the tour. And if the All Blacks were determined, their loyal supporters were supremely confident. One even offered to bet his farm on the result.

The Springboks, while not quite as keyed-up as they were for that remarkable second test, were again in a perfect frame of mind to throw everything into the fray. They had several new plans ready, including one tactical move in which they hoped to use the exaggerated respect the All Blacks had developed for Craven's spectacular dive pass....

There were 55 000 people packed around the Auckland rugby field, Eden Park, when Philip Nel and Ron King led their teams on to the field for the battle to decide the "world rugby crown", as the newspapers labelled it. The Springboks were fielding the same side that so gloriously won the second test except that the injured White was replaced by flaxen-haired Flappie Lochner.

The Springboks had decided to pin a great deal of their hopes on their acknowledged scrummaging supremacy. They exercised their option to select scrums instead of line-outs at every opportunity and this perhaps more than anything else, drove the nails into the All Blacks coffin.

The first four scrums of the match all went to the Springboks and from the fifth they suddenly struck. Not a second wasted between Craven and Harris and there was Flappie Lochner pinning his ears back and sailing through the gap between Hooper and Mitchell. He drew the fullback beautifully to send Babrow over for a try Brand could not convert, but which gave the Springboks an early 3-0 lead.

After both Brand and Trevathan had missed penalties with a ball both agreed had something wrong with it, Babrow, playing brilliantly, slipped through the defence with a devastating break and Ferdie Bergh collected his perfect cross-kick to dive over near the posts. This one Brand could not miss and the Springboks led 8-0 as

the crowd gaped in disbelief.

There was nothing wrong with New Zealand's fighting spirit, however, and after a good penalty goal by Trevathan, it was the local team who did all the attacking for the last 15 minutes before half time.

Shortly after the resumption, Craven and Harris, both in tremendous form, decided to introduce some unorthodox tactics into the game. At a scrum, Craven, making sure that his opponents would notice, kept waving Harris further away from him. Harris eventually moved to a position virtually in the middle of the field and Trevathan, the All Blacks fly half, misled by the publicity about the distance Craven was supposed to be able to throw a ball with his dive pass, moved into position directly opposite him. This led to a huge gap being opened in the All Blacks line.

Jan Lotz hooked clean and fast, and when Craven picked up the ball Freddie Turner, who had streaked in from the blind side, virtually took it from his hands. Turner ran through the midfield gap and right up to fullback Taylor before he passed to Lochner who sent Babrow over in the corner for his second try. Brand failed to convert but there is no doubt that it was this sudden, magnificently-executed try that knocked all the wind out of the All Blacks.

From another scrum in the middle of the field that great wing, Dai Williams, was brought into the attack and there was no stopping him as he beat two defenders in a superb run to the corner flag. The conversion hit the upright, but it did not really matter any more with the score standing at 14-3 and the Springboks in full control. But the game was not over yet; the South Africans were ready to pile on more agony. Freddie Turner got another chance to run and he also went over in the corner for an unconverted try after Strachan had given him a long pass from a loose scrum.

Shortly afterwards the All Blacks got some consolation in the form of a penalty from Trevathan, but when the final whistle shrilled, the Springboks had won 17-6, five tries (one converted) to two penalties.

And so the 1937 Springboks returned to South Africa as champions of the rugby world — a title they were to hold for nearly twenty years.

On the boat returning home, Philip Nel formally announced his retirement from rugby by throwing his boots into the sea. He had no further need for them because like Alexander the Great, he had no more worlds left to conquer.

Above: Craven's bullet-like dive-pass was a nightmare to the All Blacks. Their exaggerated respect for it gave the Springboks a chance to use it as a tactical ploy.

Left: Springbok wing Dai Williams catches an opponent on the wrong foot in the third test.

Right: The Springboks scored five tries in their magnificent 17–6 victory over the All Blacks in the third test, the match which clinched the series. Here Dai Williams is about to dot down just inside the corner flag after beating New Zealand's fullback J. M. Taylor, seen somersaulting over the touchline. Lochner and Harris are the Springboks nearest to Williams.

Title retained

Danie Craven, Springbok captain against Sam Walker's 1938 Lions, is supported by Ebbo Bastard and Lucas Strachan as he breaks around the scrum in this scene from the third test at Newlands.

The Cape Times

The year: 1938. The scene: A packed Ellis Park, South Africa's biggest stadium. Not an inch of space left. Hours before the game the Transvaal rugby authorities have decided to abandon the gates and thousands more have streamed in, jamming themselves together on the ramps and spilling onto the field, right up to the touchline.

Now the match is on.

For nearly 80 minutes there has been one continuous roar from the crowd as the Springboks and the Lions thrust and counter in the sort of rugby test most of us can only hope to see once or twice in a lifetime.

David Owen ("Dai") Williams, a picture of power, pace and grace, has slipped around his opponent to flash over near the corner flag.

Now there is silence as Gerry Brand prepares to take the conversion. In those days the rules stipulated that a teammate had to place the ball for the kicker when a conversion was to be attempted. With the spot a foot in from the touchline there is simply no room for Danie Craven to prostrate himself for the placing of the ball and there is also no way in which Brand can take his run-up for the kick.

The spectators do their best; they heave and struggle back until some space has been cleared. Craven is about to go down when he notices hundreds of burning cigarette stubs and these have to be cleared away before he can ease himself down to hold the ball.

He glances up and notices that Brand has had to cut his usual run-up by several steps, that he is standing as far back as he can between the widespread legs of a woman spectator, trying vainly to maintain her modesty as well as give the Springbok fullback an extra inch in which to manouevre. Craven cannot help smiling. "Gerry," he remarks to his old teammate, "I'll buy you a farm in Eloff Street if you get this one over."

"Watch me," Brand grins back and from that truncated run he slams his left boot into the ball to lift it high over the crossbar. The final whistle is blown and the Springboks have won the first test 26-12.

We will return later to this tremendous game, rated by Danie Craven as second only to the Murrayfield Massacre of 1951 for sheer Springbok brilliance.

Let us start at the beginning of the 1938 tour by Sam Walker and his Lions, the last international rugby to be played by South Africa before World War II.

Walker, a 26-year-old Belfast Irishman, brought out a most powerful combination with only six of the members not having played international rugby before, and it was only the second time that we were visited by a team truly representative of the British Isles. It was also a happy incident-free tour with the Lions having as their South African manager that great old Springbok of yesteryear, Richard Luyt.

After a hesitant start, they really found their feet and played attractive winning rugby; as bright as the 1933 Wallabies any day, but more constructive and certainly a lot cleaner.

The Springboks, of course, were riding the crest of the wave after the glorious tour of New Zealand. The nucleus of that tremendous team was available and the national selectors were so confident that for once no national trials were even considered. A number of players were invited, however, to attend a one-day session at the Old Wanderers ground in Johannesburg.

Three weeks before the first test the Lions had beaten Northern Transvaal, a new-born union destined to have a wonderful future and already then a powerful factor in our rugby. Northerns had Springboks Ferdie Bergh, Roger Sherriff, Nic Bierman, Harry Martin and Lucas Strachan among their forwards and Danie Craven and J. A. Broodryk behind the scrum and yet the tourists won 20-12. More ominous than the score was the fact that the visitors looked completely at home with the now established 3-4-1 scrum formation and their threequarters outclassed the Northern Transvaal line.

Craven who had moved to Pretoria after resigning as a teacher at St. Andrews, Grahamstown, in order to become director of physical education for the South African Defence Force, suffered a bad cut over the eye in this match. He turned up at the Wanderers with the rest of the players, but did not get a place in any of the trials teams. Mr. Markotter only reluctantly allowed him to change.

A disconsolate Craven was sitting on the touchline among some spectators and they kept on shouting for him to get onto the field and finally Markotter relented.

"Go on, pass the ball a few times, but don't allow yourself to be kicked to pieces," Markotter instructed the man who was to remain his particular protege no matter how far he would wander from Stellenbosch.

Within minutes Craven stopped a forward rush by falling on the ball and the terrible-tempered Mr. Mark almost exploded with anger. Hurling abuse at all and sundry, but particularly at Craven, he rushed him off the field with an order to go for a run on another nearby ground. Craven now knew that he was a certainty for the first test team and all possible doubts about this disappeared when Gerry Brand, Ben du Toit and Tony Harris joined him a little later after all three had first earned the "Oubaas' " wrath for taking risks.

When the team was announced it was obvious that the selectors had wisely opted for the men who had done so well in Australia and New Zealand the previous season. The only newcomer in the side was Piet de Wet, the Western Province centre, who filled the place of Louis Babrow who was then furthering his medical career at Guy's Hospital, London. The selectors certainly did strange things in those days and newspapers were a lot less inquisitive and adamant

Left: The first test against the Lions at Ellis Park in 1938 produced several of the most amazing kicks in rugby history. Here Springbok fullback Gerry Brand succeeds with a conversion as referee At Horak watches. Craven is the player on the deck.

Right: It is that man Brand again. A rare photo showing the famous Springbok fullback using his potent left-boot to punt into touch.

than they are now. In the published statement giving the names of the Springboks no mention was made about the captaincy!

On his way from Pretoria to Johannesburg on the Friday before the test Craven bought a newspaper and to his astonishment saw that he had been appointed captain with Boy Louw as his understudy.

The only preparation the team had was a long get-together on the night before the test where Craven and Louw outlined a few plans. The players knew each other so well that nothing more was really needed. That night they also received a telegram from the South African Rugby Board which can only be regarded as a most thoughtless gesture. The telegram warned the Springboks that dirty play would not be tolerated and that any player who ignored this warning would never again represent South Africa. It was absolutely uncalled for and these men who had done so much for their country's sports prestige, were justifiably upset. There was also a decision that the Springboks would again be wearing black shorts, and not the white they wore against the All Blacks.

A touring team usually has a slight advantage over the home side in that they have had more opportunities of polishing their combinations, but with the Springboks having played together so often the previous year, they had no problems and swung into top gear almost from the start.

The match was played at a terrific pace with one movement following the other and both sides opening up from all angles.

The Lions led for a few minutes after a penalty from slap in front of the Springbok posts, but Gerry Brand soon equalized when the referee, Mr. At Horak, spotted an infringement and presented the South Africans with almost as easy a penalty. Not long afterwards the Springboks erred again just inside the Lions' half and the crowd laughed derisively when Vivian Jenkins, their Welsh fullback, indicated that he was going to kick for goal. But Jenkins, in later years probably the world's best-known rugby writer, knew exactly what he was doing and there was a split-second of stunned silence before a burst of cheering hailed the first of the many astonishing kicks which were to make this match so memorable.

The set-back did not bother the Springboks in the slightest and they sailed into the attack to drive the Lions deep into their own territory. Craven, realising that it was time to do something out of the ordinary, decided to repeat the ruse that worked so well in the final test against the All Blacks in 1937.

He waved Tony Harris further and further away from the scrum and the Lion's flyhalf Jeff Reynolds saw it as a plan to break through on the blindside. He ran up to his forwards and warned them to be on the alert for such a move. Nothing could have suited the Springboks better. When Jan Lotz hooked, Freddie Turner cut in from the blindside wing to take the ball from Craven's pass. Once Turner had driven the breach he sent a perfect pass to Flappie Lochner who waited for the right moment before giving to D. O. Williams for a beautiful try, converted by Brand.

The Springboks led 8-6, but only briefly as Jenkins again kicked a penalty from near the half-way line. The lead switched hands minutes later when Fanie Louw, almost as good a forward as his brother, barged over after clever work between Craven and

Ben du Toit. Brand made the half-time score 13-9 in favour of the Springboks.

After the resumption the Springboks gave their delighted supporters a chance to see the sort of rugby which won them the world championship the year before.

The inspiration came from Gerry Brand who kicked a penalty dropgoal from a distance and an angle even he thought was impossible. The Springboks were given a penalty a few yards from touch and several yards into the South African half of the field. When Craven threw him the ball, Brand looked at him enquiringly. Craven pointed to the posts, but Brand shook his head and said: "No ways, Daantjie. I can never get the distance." But Craven had remembered seeing Brand succeed with two kicks from even further out in a club match at coast level and he was adamant that the fullback could do it in the rarified Rand atmosphere.

Brand shrugged his shoulders, flipped the ball around once or twice, glanced at the posts, and then swung his left foot with perfect timing and all the dynamic power that lurked in that trim body of his. The ball cleared the crossbar with room to spare. It was not the most vital kick Brand had ever put over for the Springboks, but with the possible exception of the one at Twickenham six years earlier, certainly the most spectacular and the crowd roared their approval.

The kick broke the spirit of the opposition and Tony Harris, an attacking flyhalf of the highest class, attempted his only break of the match and sniped through without a finger being laid on him. Brand, the man with iced water for blood, placed the conversion without any problems and although Jenkins helped his side with another penalty, the match had been won and lost. The Springboks used their threequarters time and again and in what was to be the final movement of the day, Dai Williams scored again in the corner for Brand to convert under the remarkable conditions described at the beginning of this chapter.

Nobody could have known it then, but this was to be Gerry Brand's last test. He was injured on the Thursday before the next test and could not play in the final two internationals. World War II then intervened and by the time it was over and top-level sport could be resumed, the serious playing days of Gerhard Hamilton Brand were over. It was fitting indeed that his career was destined to end in such a blaze of glory.

With Brand out, the selectors sensibly made only a slight reshuffle for the second test in Port Elizabeth. Turner, that versatile genius, went to fullback and Johnny Bester replaced him on the wing. Up front John Apsey, of Western Province, took over from Ebbo Bastard.

Craven has always referred to this match as the "tropical test". The temperature was in the 90's and it is really a miracle that the players managed to survive what must have been an ordeal. There was a great deal of furious activity at the start, but long before half-time both sets of forwards were dragging themselves around the field. At halftime most of the players simply dropped where they were and could not raise the energy to walk to the touchline for some refreshment.

The heatwave had been on for several days and Craven had realised that the team who could hit first, both at the start of the match and again immediately after the resumption, would almost certainly win.

This the Springboks had managed to do. Ben du Toit and Flappie Lochner scored outstanding tries in the first half and Turner converted both.

Early in the second half Craven broke on the blindside and Jannie Bester went over for an unconverted try to push the Springbok lead to 13-0. By that time the two weary teams were almost taking turns to rest and the backs, more often than the gasping forwards, were doing most of the work. Two successive penalties by Turner made it 19-0 with very little left for play. Strangely enough, the Lions seemed to endure the heat better than the South Africans and they then came back strongly with Reynolds, who later settled in South Africa, breaking brilliantly to send Laurie Duff through for an unconverted try. The Springbok forwards were stumbling around in a heat-induced daze when the final whistle blew and most of them hardly cared that they had won the match and retained the rubber.

The players were so tired afterwards that most of them went straight to bed.

The last test, at Newlands, once again produced sparkling rugby with the Lions showing the remarkable resilience for which they are justly famous.

On the boat trip from Port Elizabeth to Cape Town, Mr. Markotter was asked to select the Lions team he would like to see in the last test. He wrote the names on a piece of paper and handed it to Sam Walker. According to legend, the Lions followed Mr. Mark's advice to the letter and it is, of course, history how they won the Newlands international against all the odds.

Actually the team was something of a scratch affair because injury had depleted their ranks to the point where they had to make do with whoever happened to be fit and available. Jimmy Giles, a scrumhalf, was at centre and Bob Graves, a hooker, had to pack in the frontrow. Laurie Duff, an outstanding lock, was switched to flank and Charlie Grieve was at fullback, a position he had also filled in the second test as Jenkins, who proved so valuable at Ellis Park, had been injured.

Knowing that the rubber was safe, the Springboks found it difficult to get themselves in a proper frame of mind for a test match. They were put up in a quiet out-of-town hotel, but complained so bitterly about this that Craven had to ask the Rugby Board for them to be moved to one nearer the city. At first the Rugby Board refused and there was actually talk of the players refusing to play, unless their demand was met! This gives an indication of the kind of mood they were in.

Craven and Boy Louw did their best, but they could not motivate the team which with Bastard back again, consisted almost entirely of very experienced test players.

A strong wind was blowing on the day of the match, but Craven was assured by Johnny Robeck, who had been the caretaker at Newlands for many years, that it was bound to drop completely by half-time. So, when the Springbok captain won the toss for the third time running with the "lucky" gold 10/- coin given to him before the series by the then Mayor of Johannesburg, he decided to play with the wind in the first half, something he would normally not have done. When the wind did not drop at half-time the Springboks had it in their faces for the whole of the second half, a tremendous psychological disadvantage, if nothing else.

The Lions got an early unconverted try by Jones but the Springboks replied soon enough when Freddie Turner went over after a pin-point crosskick by Dai Williams. Turner injured his ankle in the movement, but managed to convert. Incidentally Turner's try brought South Africa's points total to 500 in exactly 50 tests.

A lightning interception by Johnny Bester gave the South Africans another unexpected bonus and they were leading 10-3 after Turner had again succeeded with the kick. Jan Lotz made it 13-3 before half-time and at this stage it looked as if Craven and Louw's premonitions of doom were wrong.

But after half-time, with the stronger-than-ever wind helping, the Lions came back with tremendous fury. The Springboks by now also had a lot of problems with injuries: fullback Georgie Smith had a bad finger, Turner was limping and so was Piet de Wet. The Lions forwards were getting on top gradually and a converted try by Dancer, followed by a penalty by McKibbin, brought them to within two points of the Springboks' score. Then Bob Alexander, an Irish forward who later died in the war, added another try and the Lions were in the lead by one point. A penalty from Turner nosed the Springboks ahead again, but Charlie Grieve forced the lead to change hands once more with a dropkick which might not have been allowed had the Springboks not sportingly indicated to the referee, Nick Pretorius, that it was over, the last four point drop to have been scored in South Africa.

Above: Freddie Turner, who took over the kicking role in the last two tests of the series after Brand had been injured, shows impeccable style as he steers the ball over the cross-bar. The player on the ground is Flappie Lochner.

Below: Carrying the team mascot and followed by the massive Boy Louw, Danie Craven leads the Springboks onto the field for the third test at Newlands. **The Cape Times**

Laurie Duff then came hammering through for his team's fourth try and with the score 16-21, the South Africans were reeling to defeat.

A scrum, and the referee informed the two teams that it would be the last of the match. The Springboks hooked, Craven broke around the blindside and passed to Johnny Bester. The young centre drew fullback Grieve beautifully and D. O. Williams was in full stride as he took the ball. He was over the line and behind the posts for what everybody, including the Lions, thought was the goal that would draw the match.

But it was not to be. The referee ruled that the pass between Bester and Williams had been forward and he blew the whistle to end the match.

A brief moment of disappointment and then the Springboks carried Sam Walker off the field. Vivian Jenkins wrote years later that seeing Walker on the shoulders of his defeated opponents, was perhaps the real highlight of a series to remember.

It was to be the end of all international rugby for a whole generation of Springboks. World War II broke out within a year after Walker and his team had returned home and by the time it was over and organized sport could be resumed, players who were youngsters in 1938, had lost the best years of their lives. It meant that Tony Harris had his career ended at the age of 22, Freddie Turner at 24, Flappie Lochner at 24, D. O. Williams at 24, Danie Craven at 27, Ebbo Bastard at 26, Ben du Toit at 25 and Jan Lotz at 27. Fanie Louw, a wonderful forward in the prime of his life, collapsed and died a year later after captaining Transvaal in a match against Western Province at Ellis Park.

All Blacks white-washed

It was Adolph Hitler's birthday and as a special treat the commandant of the sprawling prisoner of war camp at Thorn, Poland, granted everybody an extra hour in bed on that fresh early-spring morning of April 20, 1944.

The Führer's birthday could not have been better timed as far as the South African and New Zealand inmates of the camp were concerned. They needed that extra bit of rest because the first rugby trials matches were scheduled to be played later in the day. For some time the main topic of conversation in the rows and rows of dismal bungalows had been a proposed "test series" between the rugby world's two keenest rivals and preparations for the big crunch were about to go into full swing.

Bill Payn, the 1924 Springbok forward, was the main organiser and he and Peter Pienaar, son of the 1921 Springbok captain Theo Pienaar, and Billy Millar jnr., son of the 1912 South African captain, very quickly discovered that there was more than enough talent available among their fellow prisoners.

The senior medical officer in the camp had given permission for the games to be played, but he added a warning that he would soon put a stop to the activities if "any player walks into hospital with a broken neck".

A field was marked off with yellow clay lines on the vast sandy parade ground and with Army boots considered too lethal for a match between "All Blacks" and "Springboks", the players played with bare feet, in socks and with here and there a particularly fortunate one in tattered tackies.

One of the most enthusiastic players among the South Africans was a burly Jewish boy born 22 years before, less than a good touch kick's distance away from the Ellis Park rugby ground, the stadium where he once saw Gerry Brand in action and promptly acquired a healthy dose of hero worship.

His fellow-prisoners knew him as "Ox" Geffin and his raw strength and accurate bare-footed kicking, made him one of the stars in the many rough-and-ready matches to follow; merciless affairs which might have reminded the ancient forests surrounding the camp of the brutal executions that terminated the religious riots that once made Thorn Europe's main trouble spot 220 years before.

Geffin learnt a lot in those matches and it could well be, as has often been written, that he practiced his placekicking on the mass grave in which thousands of Nazi-executed Poles were buried, but the truth is that he was already a promising member of Johannesburg Pirates by the time he donned the khaki uniform. It was at the Pirates club that Freddie Turner, the great Springbok of the 1930's, first spotted his potential and it was Turner who gave him his first practical lessons in the art of placekicking. Geffin was fortunate that he encountered a coach as intelligent as Turner, whose own style was completely different from the one the youngster used. Turner used to lift the ball very high while Geffin's kicks had a low trajectory. Instead of trying to change the boy's style, Turner merely helped him to make the most of it. As an under-19 player Geffin once succeeded with 12 out of 13 conversions and he was obviously already on his way to bigger things when the war intervened.

When the hostilities finally ceased and he could resume his rugby career "Ox" became "Okey" (nobody really knows how or why) and he was soon a regular frontranker in the powerful Transvaal pack under Jan Lotz in the late 1940's. It is an interesting fact that Geffin must be the only Springbok never to have an official Christian name. Everybody accepted it to be Aaron but on his birth certificate there was nothing but a blank space until he had it rectified years later. Okey has always had his own explanation for this. "When my father went to register my birth and they asked him for my Christian names he must have said: 'He's a Jewish boy! He's got no Christian names!' And

The sight the 1949 All Blacks hated. Okey Geffin, wearing Transvaal colours, kicks for goal.

years later it cost me R30 to make it official that I am Aaron Okey Geffin!"

But whether he was "Ox", "Okey" or "Aaron", this bull-necked Transvaler, with Hennie Muller and Hannes Brewis, filled the leading roles in the first post-war test series when the Springboks had to defend their rugby crown against the All Blacks.

Originally the All Blacks were supposed to visit us in 1947, but they kept on asking for postponements and it was not until May 1949 that the *Tamaroa* finally delivered Fred Allen and his long-awaited team to our shores. They had made sure that they were well prepared to avenge the rubber defeat in 1937. Several members of the side had had some experience of international rugby, a rare and invaluable asset in the years immediately following the war.

It was a team with an immensely powerful pack of forwards. Johnny Simpson, Has Catley, and Kevin Skinner formed one of the best front-rows in rugby history. Simpson was as solid as the proverbial rock, but he added to this a smouldering truculence on the field that made him one of the most fearsome forwards of his day. Catley, who knew more tricks than a circus clown and was not called "the problem child of New Zealand rugby" for nothing, believed that the end always justifies the means when it comes to either hooking the ball or preventing his opponents from getting it. Skinner, then only 20 years old, was almost as strong and rough as Simpson and he was a lot more mobile. The newsreel sequence of Hansie Brewis' amazing try in the second test at Ellis Park bears striking testimony to the speed this New Zealand tighthead prop could generate in an emergency. When Brewis flashed over the line, Skinner was the only New Zealand forward anywhere near the scene.

Lauchie Grant was a magnificent lineout forward and C. C. (Charlie) Willocks and Lester Harvey were also outstanding locks. P. J. B. (Pat) Crowley, Peter Johnstone and J. R. (Jack) McNab were fiery loose-forwards. In spite of an injury to Morrie Goddard and K. E. (Keith) Gudsell, the All Blacks also had excellent threequarters. Fred Allen had a dazzling sidestep, Ron Elvidge was a strong, courageous centre, Graham ("Red") Delamore was a master of the inside break and Bill Meates, Eric Boggs and Peter ("Sammy") Henderson were good, aggressive wings. Henderson, an Empire Games sprinter, was particularly dangerous and also splendid as a cover-defender.

In Bob Scott, the All Blacks had the world's best fullback of his time. His placekicking on the tour was abysmal, but as a player it is doubtful whether the balding Scott made a single mistake in the 17 matches he played in South Africa. Scott had poliomyelitis as a child, but it left him with no permanent disabilities and he could dodge his way out of the tightest corners.

The team's weakness was at scrum-half where both Bill Conrad and Larry Savage were split-seconds too slow in serving a flyhalf like Jim Kearney, who was not particularly fast off the mark. This opened the way for the Springboks, guided by their coach and national selector Danie Craven, to use Hennie Muller to nullify all their opponent's efforts to mount constructive attacks.

There is no doubt that at his peak Hennie Muller was the fastest forward ever to wear the Springbok jersey. In addition, he could tackle with frightening ferocity and he was a complete master of all the basics of the game. He was also always superbly fit and if ever a player had the "killer instinct" it was this lean, almost gaunt, Springbok so aptly named "Die Windhond" ("The Greyhound") by Craven.

As a member of the mighty Transvaal pack of the time, Muller used to rove around the field with a mainly attacking brief from his captain, Jan Lotz, but Craven decided to turn him into a one-man demolition squad to seek and destroy the All Black halves and threequarters. The instant the ball left the scrum or the lineout, Muller would swoop down on the flyhalf and if he should by some miracle or other manage to get the ball to the centres, Muller's exceptional pace would enable him to arrive virtually simultaneously with the ball. The All Blacks, but mainly their camp followers, screamed long and loud over what they labelled Muller's spoiling tactics, but there was nothing illegal about it and they were just unfortunate that Hendrik Scholtz Vosloo Muller was born in Witbank, Transvaal, and not in Whangarei, North Island.

Muller's defensive-offensive function soon expanded as it became clear that the All Blacks were developing a complex about him. He was often used as a decoy and once that death-defying crashtackler Ryk van Schoor had been added to the Springbok line-up, Muller, of course, had the additional pleasure of frequently picking up a loose ball dropped from the limp fingers of an All Black centre who had just been flattened.

"I would unhesitatingly say that Hennie Muller was the greatest loose-forward I have ever seen." Bob Scott wrote in his biography, published some time after the tour. "He was the complete player and he, more than anybody, Geffin and Hannes Brewis included, determined the result of the tests. To start with, he had great speed; he was very nearly as fast as our Peter Henderson, who was an Empire Games sprinter. His hands were good, he could kick well, he was as alert as a hungry hawk and he could last out a test match on a hard ground and a warm day without visible difficulty. And to top everything, he was completely fearless and quite ruthless. . . ."

Hannes Brewis, a slender, dark and restless Pretoria policeman, was the third trumpcard in Craven's hand. Brewis was as near as could be the perfect flyhalf for modern international rugby. He could handle and kick beautifully and his brain and reflexes were quicker than those of any player I, personally, have ever seen. Brewis had the ability to sum up a situation in the wink of an eye and his value to the Springbok team can be best underlined by pointing to the fact that they won every one of the ten tests he played in during his career.

The Springboks' biggest handicap for the series was their total lack of international experience while the All Blacks, again, made the mistake of over-preparing for the tour. Selected the season before their departure, they spent two weeks training at Hermanus before the tour started and it seemed at times as if many of their players went stale far too early in the tour.

The South African selectors, Craven, Bill Schreiner, Frank Mellish, Bill Zeller and Jack Kipling, organised a week of trial matches in Pretoria shortly after the tourists' arrival, trials that Hennie Muller very nearly missed.

Left: Bob Scott, doing some barefooted practising, was the greatest fullback of his time, but his placekicking was erratic.

Right: Hennie Muller, the relentless "Windhond" of South African rugby, made life miserable for Fred Allen's All Blacks. This picture shows Muller at his incomparable best.

Die Burger

Muller had so badly injured his knee the previous season that he had to spend three months in hospital and a further six weeks hobbling around with his leg in plaster. When he could discard his crutches, he slowly, but with indomitable determination, rebuilt the shrivelled muscles in his leg. He used to cycle to and from work, 12 miles a day, and run up and down the E.R.P.M. mine-dumps every morning until he felt ready to accept the invitation to the trials. For the rest of his career Muller wore a kneeguard although he was the first to admit that it was for the sense of security it gave him, nothing else.

At the end of the trials the selectors named 32 players as being "possibles" for the first test and, ironically enough, the name of Brewis was not on the list. In the meantime the All Blacks had had mixed fortunes in the early half of their tour, but succeeded in ruining the reputations of several fancied candidates for the first Springbok test team in the process. When they beat Western Province on the Saturday before the first test they actually forced the national selectors to change a team they had already selected. Chum Ochse, Dennis Fry and Otto van Niekerk, three Western Province players who had been in the side, were then dropped. Fry and Ochse later on did get their Springbok colours, but the unfortunate Van Niekerk, a truly great wing then in the veteran stage, never got his chance.

Felix du Plessis, a Transvaal lock forward who had been a navigator in the South African Air Force during the war, was finally appointed captain of a team of Springboks, all of whom had had no experience of international rugby. Du Plessis was a nephew of Nic du Plessis, the 1921-24 Springbok, and 30 years old. He was born at Steynsburg in the Free State and had started his provincial career for Northern Transvaal just before the war began. While in the S.A.A.F., Du Plessis played for South African Forces against their New Zealand counterparts in Rome and at the time of his selection for the test, was considered the best lineout specialist in the country.

A man of imposing presence and natural dignity, Du Plessis did much to keep his jittery team of "greenhorns" from breaking down completely in the dressingroom at Newlands. Boy Louw looked in briefly and in his usual brusque way managed to raise a few pale smiles, but generally this was a bunch of Springboks who resembled condemned men rather than an international team. Brewis told me later that when he ran on to the field he was so bewildered that he ran into the flag on the halfway line.

In retrospect, the Springboks settled down remarkably quickly. Jack van der Schyff, the young Griqualand West fullback with the booming boot, kicked some magnificent touches although he did fail with an early penalty, and Tjol Lategan, the quiet Matie student who was so soon to become a national hero, was only just stopped after a typically subtle break past Allen. But in the 14th minute of the match Bob Scott placed a penalty for the All Blacks and after that the Springboks seemed to lose their impetus. A poor clearance by Van der Schyff was charged down by Sammy Henderson and, with the try converted by Scott, the All Blacks led 8-0.

The tall Van der Schyff, willowy Floris Duvenage (then past his best, but a brilliant player in his day), Brewis and Okey Geffin were the acknowledged placekickers in the team. Van der Schyff got the first two chances, but fluffed them and

Above left: Felix du Plessis leads his untried team of Springboks onto the Newlands turf for the first test of the 1949 series. Following on his heels are Floris Duvenage, Hoppy van Jaarsveld, Okey Geffin and Jack van der Schyff.

The Cape Times

Above: Okey Geffin turns away after succeeding with one of the five penalty goals he placed to win the first test for his team.

Die Huisgenoot

when Savage was caught with his hands in the scrum about 30 yards from his own posts, the ball just happened to land virtually at Geffin's feet and Du Plessis nodded.

Placing the ball in the oblong hole he had dug with his left boot, with the laces down and a little mound of earth and grass to cushion the front, he stepped back five or six yards, his chin resting on his chest and his eyes always on the ball. Running up, he struck the ball just below the centre and the follow-through was so complete that his right boot ended up virtually in line with his head. Throughout his career Geffin never followed the flight of the ball until after his follow-through had brought his boot in line with his vision. He believed that this was the secret of timing and accuracy.

With the score 8-3, things looked a little rosier but just before half-time the All Blacks added another three points when Kearney lifted over an excellent dropgoal.

The second half belonged to Okey Geffin as he methodically kicked the Springboks to victory with four successive penalties. The referee, Eddie Hofmeyr, a former Western Province crosscountry champion, was violently criticised afterwards for some of his decisions. In an article in the South African "*Rugby News*" recently, he gave his reasons for penalising the All Blacks and giving Okey Geffin the chance to kick himself into rugby immortality.

"In the first half I gave a penalty against Savage for hands in the scrum. In the second half the Springboks got another penalty for off-sides by Grant in the line-out. Then followed three penalties in the last 15 minutes for obstruction by Eric Boggs, Morrie Goddard and again by Boggs. In each case it followed diagonal kicks by Hansie Brewis, which were chased by Cecil Moss.

"In the first case Moss was prevented from getting to the ball when Boggs ran between him and the ball, and Scott fielded. The second one was almost identical, but it was Goddard who interfered.

"In the third case Boggs was again the culprit, but Moss nearly got to the ball before Scott, and I had to consider the possibility of a penalty try. However, I could see Peter Henderson, then the New Zealand sprint champion, coming across in cover defence and he would doubtless have prevented a try. After the match

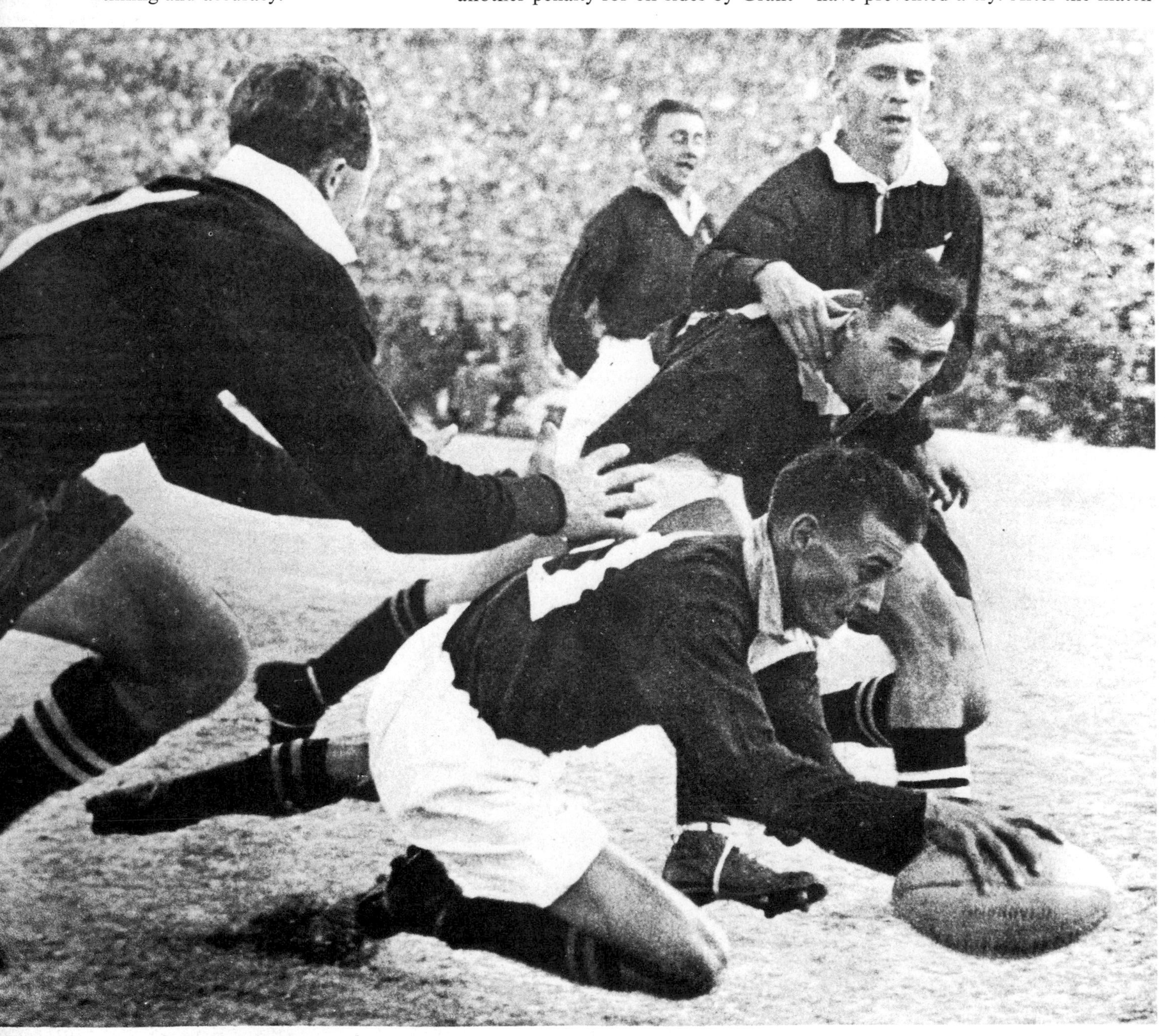

Boggs wanted to hit me, but other All Blacks stopped him. Dr. Danie Craven, manager of the Springboks, and Mr. Sport Pienaar, then president of the South African Rugby Board, were of the opinion that I should have awarded the Springboks a penalty try. Fred Allen, on the other hand, told me afterwards that if I had awarded a penalty try he would have taken the All Blacks off the field."

Geffin's five successive penalties not only brought the Springboks a rather lucky victory, but also enabled the burly frontranker to break the individual test scoring record of 14 points held by Bennie Osler since 1928 and equalled by Gerry Brand in 1938.

It is not too much to say that South Africa's rugby honour was at stake when the Springboks trotted onto Ellis Park for the second test on August 13, 1949. More than 70 000 spectators circled the ground and most of them did not know what to hope for. There was little real confidence in Felix du Plessis' side, twelve of whom had been members of the team which looked so unconvincing at Newlands.

Although Bob Scott again gave the All Blacks an early lead with a penalty, the Springboks were a lot more purposeful from the start and thinking back now to what was the first test I had ever seen, I can remember the unbelievable feeling of exhilaration when Fonnie du Toit and Hansie Brewis, Ryk van Schoor and Tjol Lategan, two legendary combinations together for the first time in international rugby, began to run with a safe, sure rhythm, and Hennie Muller popped up here, there and everywhere. Two giants of South African rugby made their debuts that clear, sunny afternoon, Chris Koch and Salty du Rand, and long and honourably they were to serve their country.

Geffin soon levelled the scores with his sixth successive penalty goal against the All Blacks and then came one of the most marvellous tries in rugby history.

Left: Hansie Brewis about to score one of the finest tries in Springbok history. Cecil Moss is up to help and Bob Scott (left) and Bill Meates are too late to do anything about it. Ryk van Schoor is in the background.

Pat Smith

Right: Hannes Brewis, the best flyhalf of his era. The Springboks had him as a pivot in 10 successive tests and won all of them.

C. J. Siebert

There was a scrum near the grand stand touchline and deep into All Blacks territory. Jorrie Jordaan hooked and the ball flashed into Hansie Brewis' hands. For a split second it looked as if he would drop for goal and the All Blacks thought so too. A battalion of defenders charged down on Brewis, but in the wink of an eye he changed his mind and streaked around the blindside with his opponents caught off balance and going the wrong way.

He was now very near the goalline, but again his way was blocked. The quickest brain in rugby was working with computer-like efficiency and he feinted as if to kick towards the corner flag. The All Blacks hesitated for a fatal instant and suddenly Brewis was off again like a rocket.

A few yards from the line he was threatened once more and this time Brewis dummied to the inside, fooled yet another defender, and then he straightened out and went over with Scott too late to do more than just brush his shoulder.

The more than 70 000 spectators went raving mad, most of us who were there were hoarse for days afterwards. Of all the great moments in sport that I have seen since, from Newlands to Madison Square Garden, there has never been anything that could approach those fleeting seconds just after 12 minutes after four o'clock on the afternoon of August 13, 1949 when Hansie Brewis gave back to the Springboks their self respect.

Geffin missed the conversion, the first time he had failed so far, but it did not really matter as the Springboks with Hennie Muller criss-crossing the field on defence and attack, were playing inspired rugby. In the second half Chris Koch and Salty du Rand followed by Du Plessis, Jordaan and Louis Strydom, charged through the All Blacks ranks as if they did not exist. It was Du Rand who got the ball back to Fonnie du Toit and from him into the safe hands of Brewis. The flyhalf wasted no time before passing and with Hennie Muller taking the ball, the All Black centres were in a quandary. Tjol Lategan slipped through the gap as only he could and as Bob Scott put it years later: "All I could do was whistle 'Goodbye, it's been good to know you' as he beat me on the inside."

Kearney halted the rampant South Africans briefly with a mighty left-footed dropgoal, but not long afterwards Brewis showed that he could do the same with the right boot. The All Blacks made a last desperate onslaught but Hennie Muller and Jack van der Schyff combined to stop the danger and shortly afterwards the referee, Ralph Burmeister, ended it all with a final blast on his whistle with the score 12-6 and the series already safe for South Africa.

The third test in Durban, two weeks later, is best forgotten. Both

Below: Ryk van Schoor and Tjol Lategan joined forces in the second test of the 1949 series to form a legendary partnership as centres for the Springbok team.

Die Huisgenoot

teams played without fire and apart from another three penalties by the infallible Geffin, the abiding memory of the test is one of collapsing scrums and leaden-footed forwards. Three of the Springboks, Du Plessis with a sore neck, Bubbles Koch with a heavy cold, and Salty du Rand with a troublesome shoulder, were below form. After a good try by Morrie Goddard, the All Blacks seemed petrified by the spectre of Geffin and although the match clinched the series for the Springboks, it was a miserable afternoon for both sides.

But it did leave the Springboks poised to make a clean sweep in a home series for the first time in our rugby history and with the All Blacks desperate to avoid being whitewashed, the final test in Port Elizabeth had a special significance.

With an eye to the future, the national selectors decided to replace Felix du Plessis with Willem Barnard and to hand the captaincy to Basil Kenyon, who had led Border so well against the touring team. Border beat the All Blacks 9-0, still New Zealand's biggest defeat against a provincial team in South Africa. In a second match between the two teams the result was a 6-all draw. Piet Malan, a bustling, balding ,Transvaal flanker came in for the injured Du Rand and "Carrots" Geraghty got his one and only test cap. Kenyon replaced Bubbles Koch on the flank, who moved to lock in place of Flip Geel.

It was a match packed with thrills. Early in the first half Fonnie du Toit intercepted and with a long way to go to an open line, was overhauled from behind by Henderson and Meates. On another occasion Brewis broke cleanly and flipped the ball to Hennie Muller who ran like the wind with Sammy Henderson coming across from the other side to cut him off. The two bodies collided in mid-air as Muller dived for the line and the referee, Mr. Burmeister, who was on the spot, ruled that the "Windhond" did not get the try.

In the process Muller was badly concussed and he played the rest of the match without being able to focus properly. Tries by Johnstone and Elvidge and a conversion from Scott, gave the All Blacks their eight points, but it was not good enough. An inevitable penalty by Geffin, a try by Fonnie du Toit converted by Geffin and a soaring dropgoal by Brewis made the Springbok tally eleven and a sad bunch of All Blacks trooped off the Crusaders field.

In the dressingroom Bob Scott burst into tears, convinced that it was his poor placekicking which had let his team down. It was a black day in New Zealand rugby history, but fate had already decreed that revenge, almost as total as their humiliation was then, would be only a few short years away.

Jack van der Schyff

Bubbles Koch

Cecil Moss

Louis Strydom

Jorrie Jordaan

Buks Marais

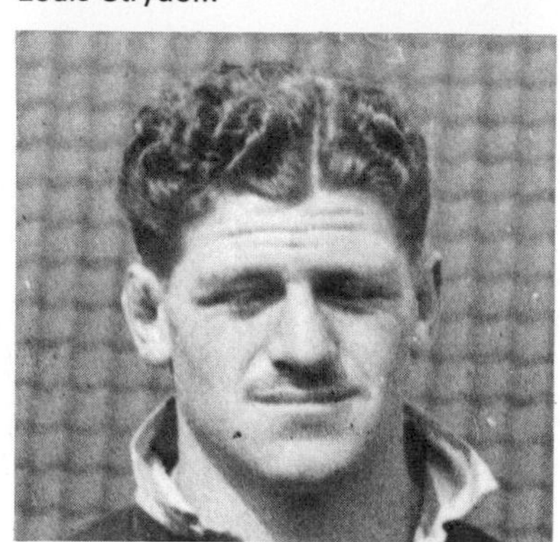

Salty du Rand

Chris Koch

Fonnie du Toit

A team to remember

Prince Philip, the Duke of Edinburgh, meets the 1951/52 Springboks before the start of the test against England at Twickenham. Here Hennie Muller, who took over the captaincy from the injured Basil Kenyon, introduces him to Stephen Fry as manager Frank Mellish *(far left)* looks on. Other Springboks on the picture are, *from the left:* William Delport, Salty du Rand, Ernst Dinkelmann, Jaap Bekker.

They were the heroes of my youth and I am grateful to them for never letting me down. Even when they were beaten, and it happened only once, they made my suffering easier to bear by behaving in the way I, in my innocence, expected all heroes to behave in adversity.

From the most uncomfortable angles at Ellis Park and Loftus Versfeld, I had seen some of them play and there were carefully-clipped newspaper and magazine photographs of each and every one in my scrap-books. I eagerly strained to hear their names as Paul Bothma described mighty deeds in places with strange sounding names over a radio that always seemed to start crackling at the most critical times.

In later years I was fortunate to meet many of them in person, to interview them, even to report on some of them playing Test rugby in the autumn of their careers. A few of them I can today count among my friends.

And, although a quarter of a century has since passed, the 1951-52 Springboks who toured the United Kingdom and France still epitomise to me all that is best in rugby, on the field and off it.

The bare statistics of their tour can be dismissed with a glance: 31 matches played in Britain and France, 30 victories, one defeat, 562 points for, 167 against. An on-the-field record that is only a fraction short of perfection, studded by magnificent performances they still talk about from Cardiff to Toulouse, Twickenham to Paris, and crowned by that incredible 44-0 massacre of Scotland at Murrayfield.

But the real triumph of this tour cannot be found in the record books and there is only a hint of it in what was written afterwards by the sports-writers who accompanied the Springboks. The nearest an outsider can get to the real truth is to be there when a few of the members of that team are together and sharing the memories not even the passage of time can dim.

Only then can you begin to understand why this was such a great team; why there is a special place reserved for it in our rugby annals.

It was a team with a heart; warm, human and not afraid to show genuine sentiment. Could there in all our sports history have been a more touching scene than the team's visit to Basil Kenyon in his hospital room in London on Christmas morning, 1951?

The Springbok captain was recovering from an operation that saved his sight after an eye injury suffered at Pontypool early in the tour. But he knew, and his team knew, that he would never be able to play again.

Team manager Frank Mellish, coach Danie Craven and 29 players filed into his room, ranged themselves around the bed and sang the time-honoured carol *Silent Night* to their captain. Basie Viviers who usually reserved his rich baritone for more robust renditions, led the singing and when it was over, young Johnny Buchler read the prayers. Of all the honours Kenyon garnered during his career the memory of this spontaneous tribute is sure to mean most to him when he one day retires to that little farm on the Tsitsikama Coast.

This kind of warmth was a general characteristic of the team and not confined to their contact with each other. The Springboks mixed freely with their hosts, their camp followers, British rugby fans and even with their opponents. They never clustered together in exclusive little huddles at those interminable parties and dinners, but, in a most natural and sincere way, made conversation with whoever happened to be around.

The British public responded by going out of their way to be hospitable and I understand that not one Springbok returned to South Africa without some gift or souvenir from a particularly grateful fan.

Chum Ochse, Hansie Brewis and Hansie Oelofse will never be able to forget, for example, the old lady from North Berwick. She really "adopted" Ochse, whose shy but highly intelligent personality she found so appealing that she called him "Johnny" in honour of a son she always wanted but never had. It was she who invited Ochse, Brewis and Oelofse to spend a day sightseeing in Edinburgh and at the end of it presented each with a Scottish woollen rug and also a camera for the Western Province wing, her particular favourite.

The Springboks did everything they could not to disappoint their hosts: with men like Mellish, Craven, Kenyon and Hennie Muller in control it could not have been otherwise.

Dr. Craven will never forget how the Springboks returned to their hotel in Belfast one night after seeing Mario Lanza in "*The Great Caruso*" and then settled down for the usual cup of tea before bed. At that point an Irish international player walked in and told them that an advertisement had appeared in the newspapers

Basil Kenyon, captain of the fourth Springbok team to tour the United Kingdom. After suffering an eye injury, Kenyon had to delegate on-the-field leadership to Hennie Muller. Dr. Danie Craven has often said that Kenyon was the greatest of all Springbok captains.

saying that the Springboks would attend a certain dance, and that the people there were waiting for their arrival. In actual fact the Springboks knew nothing about the affair, but, rather than disappoint somebody, they wearily dragged themselves off to the dance. They arrived there at about midnight and such was the hospitality that they only left at half-past five in the morning!

"I had the boys on the practice field a few hours later, but after five minutes we all gave up and returned to our rooms," Dr. Craven remembers.

It was this same big-heartedness that motivated the Springboks to accept an ordinary camp follower like Worcester businessman Morrie Lazarus as a sort of extra assistant

Above: On their arrival in London in September 1951 available members of the team co-operated with a press photographer for this informal group shot. *Standing, left to right:* Basie van Wyk, Danie Craven, Stephen Fry, Jaap Bekker, Jaap Wessels, Tjol Lategan, Ernst Dinkelmann, Hansie Oelofse, Jan Pickard, Ben Myburgh, Willem Barnard, Frans van der Ryst, Salty du Rand, Okey Geffin, Gert Dannhauser, Johnny Buchler. *Kneeling, from the left:* Fonnie du Toit, Buks Marais, Hansie Brewis, Basil Kenyon, Ryk van Schoor, Des Sinclair, Jakkals Keevy, Dennis Fry, Paul Johnstone.

Left: Salty du Rand and Chris Koch sample blackberries during the team's stay in Bournemouth. **The Cape Times**

Bottom left: Stephen Fry and Jan Pickard lend "assistance" to Chum Ochse as they prepare for one of the many formal occasions on the tour.

Bottom: Hennie Muller, for once not quite sure what to do with a ball in his hands.

Bottom right: Springboks and friends take a last look at Cape Town from the top of Table Mountain before their departure. Players in front are: Chum Ochse, Ernst Dinkelmann and Chris Koch. On the far left is Martin Saunders, Tjol Lategan and Willem Delport (partly obscured). Crouching at the back is Jaap Bekker.

Above: Chris Koch, Jakkals Keevy and Buks Marais try to look like Londoners as they doff their bowlers.

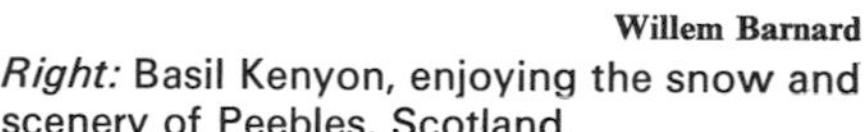

Willem Barnard

Right: Basil Kenyon, enjoying the snow and scenery of Peebles, Scotland.

Below: One of the biggest successes in a brilliant team was Paul Johnstone, a versatile wing from the University of Cape Town.

Right: Chum Ochse scored miraculous tries to give his team victory over Cardiff and Wales. Here he dives over in the corner after clever work by Hansie Brewis against Cardiff.

luggage master when they realized how lonely Morrie was (This was long before the days when chartered flights enabled hundreds of South Africans to follow their team around in a foreign country).

Dave Lewis, an Englishman who was the official baggage master, learnt to love his protegés so much that when the time came to say goodbye, he disappeared quietly, sending a note to explain that he would have broken down and wept had he stayed to shake hands with every member of the team.

The loyalty between the players was amazingly strong and there is no better example than Ernst Dinkle-mann (a doctor by profession) nursing Salty du Rand before the test against Wales and then declaring him fit for the game although he knew that he would be the one to get Du Rand's place in the team should the then Rhodesian lock not be well enough to play. In fact, he was unselfish to a fault because Du Rand had not fully recovered from the attack of flu when he received the go-ahead from Dinkelmann.

And after the Springboks had beaten Cardiff with a last-minute combination of the genius of Brewis and the alertness of Ochse, Basie Viviers, who was the touchjudge, actually burst out crying from sheer joy.

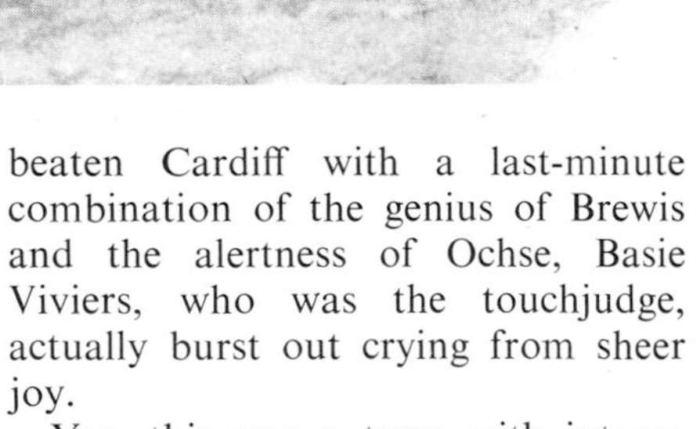

Yes, this was a team with intense emotions, but they had the necessary maturity to balance it. In retrospect, they all seemed so "grown-up", without any prima donnas as far as I can discover, and each player so fully aware of his responsibility to his team and his country.

This, in spite of (or perhaps because of) the fact that few touring sides from this country has ever had more players with a liking for mischief. Salty du Rand, Ryk van Schoor, Hennie Muller (who took over the captaincy with such distinction after Kenyon's injury), Ben Myburgh (whose highly cultured English accent was a source of never-ending delight to his teammates), Basie Viviers, Basie van Wyk and Des Sinclair (who only had to wear his "innocent look" to be borselled for something he had either done or intended to do) were always alert to any opportunity to play a prank and Mellish and Craven were not exempt as targets.

It was a team who believed in singing and laughter. Apart from powerful Gert Dannhauser who could deliver the old Irish ballad *Galway Bay* with some considerable feeling and expertise and Basie Viviers, most of the others had to compensate with sheer volume and enthusiasm for a lack of a real musical talent.

Okey Geffin's stirring *Jio Lelle Mama* was always a big favourite with the team and the irrepressible Ryk van Schoor had a remarkable repertoire of self-composed songs, which he fortunately only sang on special occasions.

The words of one have been saved for posterity. It went something like this:

"*Maak oop die garage se deur,*
Maak oop die garage se deur
Dat pa kan in reverse. . . . !"

Mellish and Craven paid their charges the supreme compliment of treating them like adults because they behaved accordingly. There was no one waiting in hotel lobbies to jot down the names of players who reached the hotel a little after curfew time and very often it was the

late "Uncle Frank" himself who started the fun on his guitar.

Other players, by nature more quiet, also contributed in their own ways to the general happiness that gave this team such an unique team spirit. A player, for example, like that enormously strong but always polite frontranker Jaap Bekker who had his own version of a threat he once heard a cowboy hero utter on the screen.

"I blows you up!", Jaap used to say darkly to all and sundry and eventually he bought some firecrackers to give his threat a little more effect. Once in a room on the first floor, Jaap was being kept awake by noisy revellers just under his window. He opened the window, shouted his usual "I blows you up!" and hurled down a "bomb". He had peace for the rest of the night.

Paul Johnstone, one of the outstanding successes of the tour, will always be remembered for his decision in the match against Munster that it was high time somebody went to the assistance of Bekker who was receiving a pummelling from an opponent who was confusing boxing with rugby. Slenderly-built Paul was all for climbing in when lock forward Willem Barnard gently pushed him away from the scrum saying: "Wait a minute, Paultjie. This is a place for us big fellows". But for the rest of the tour Johnstone was known as "The Killer of Munster".

The 1951-52 Springboks never started any rough stuff — all their opponents subsequently vouched for that — but heaven help any team who did not keep things clean. Eventually their reputation as hard but fair players spread throughout the British Isles and even to France and they hardly ever had problems with punch-or-boot-happy opponents.

It was never any secret that the team did have a small group of "shock troops" who could, if necessary, take over, but their services were rarely needed.

One of the most enduring legends of the tour was the one of Basie van Wyk, the Witch Doctor. It all started when the magnificent bald-headed flanker from Transvaal had trouble with a toe-nail that was injured and took an uncommonly long time to work itself off.

The sight of the big, tough, forward limping along in slippers was just too inviting for the rest of the team and while preparing at Porthcawl for the forthcoming test against Wales, a whole gang of players overpowered him and ripped off the nail. Van Wyk, after that, used the nail and some pebbles he had picked off the beach, to "throw the bones" whenever the team had some minor problem — like who were the culprits who tied everybody's pyjamas into knots! He invariably found himself to be innocent, that's for sure.

Basie later received some real "bones" from South Africa for the job, but as far as most of the players can remember his toe-nail continued to play a major role in his acts of "divination".

There can be no doubt that the tour management (and that included Muller, Kenyon, and Fonnie du Toit, who took over the vice-captaincy when Muller effectively became captain) actively encouraged the light-hearted off-the-field approach to prevent the players from going stale on such a long assignment. But when it came to the actual playing side of

Topsport

Hennie Muller leads the Springboks onto Murrayfield for the test against Scotland. They won 44–0 still the biggest victory in the history of test rugby. Following Muller are Okey Geffin, Chris Koch, Salty du Rand and Ernst Dinkelmann.

things, few teams have ever approached their task with more dedication.

Craven, whenever he felt it necessary, gave them training sessions so tough that it sometimes left the fittest players in a state of collapse. One such practice, on the St. Paul's School field in London, will never be forgotten by any member of that team.

"I swear some of us will turn pale whenever you suddenly whisper 'St. Paul's' to them," Ryk van Schoor once told me.

A close watch was also kept on their eating, drinking and smoking habits. In those days smoking was not yet the dirty word it is to today's athletes and many of the players were addicted to the habit. Hansie Brewis (that genius of a flyhalf who always insisted anyway that he played his best rugby when not quite fit!) was one and Gert Dannhauser (whom the French rugby writers liked to call the "*homme de fer*" or "Man of Iron"), was another. So, for that matter was Frank Mellish, who used to cut down his pre-breakfast intake to six cigarettes as a special concession on the mornings of a test!

Buks Marais, a born rugby player who never quite realized his full potential, was the member of the team whose big appetite caused him the most trouble. He and Chris Koch were also the champion biltong eaters, but no amount of food consumption seemed to affect Koch, who played fantastic rugby on this tour and earned himself the nickname of "*Sledge Mawr*" (Celtic for "Sledgehammer") from an admiring Welsh public.

The Springbok threequarters took some time to settle down on the heavier fields in Britain but once they discovered the inside gap, the machine broke down only once — when London Counties beat them.

In a few other matches the machine sometimes faltered occasionally, but always recovered in time to win.

The main strengths of the team lay in their powerful, but mobile, pack and outstanding half-backs in Fonnie du Toit and Hansie Brewis. Second-string scrumhalf Hansie Oelofse was often bothered by injury, but Brewis throughout the tour had a deputy in Dennis Fry who probably in any other post-World War II era, would have been South Africa's No. 1 test flyhalf.

Ryk van Schoor, famous for his murderous tackling, and Tjol Lategan, a subtle attacker, were the obvious centre-pair and Chum Ochse who, as Dr. Craven puts it, was better at scoring difficult tries than easy ones, and the versatile Paul Johnstone were brilliant wings. At full-back, the quiet, deeply religious and totally confident Johnny Buchler played as well as any one who ever wore a green-and-gold jersey in this position.

The Springbok frontrow trio of Bekker, Willem Delport and Koch are still considered to be possibly the best in our history and the loose-forward combination of Stephen Fry, Basie van Wyk and Hennie Muller might just have been equalled but certainly never bettered. On the whole tour the Springboks enountered only two players who could conceivably have forced their way into the South African test team — lock Roy John and centre Bleddyn Williams, both from Wales.

It was a tour of many highlights; veritable Everests in our rugby history.

One was the match against Cardiff, on October 20, 1951. Glance at the statistics of this match and you marvel that the Springboks ever managed to win. They lost the scrums 18-26, the lineouts 15-18 and there were 15 penalties against them with nine in their favour.

With 12 minutes to go the Springboks were still trailing by one point and were only then beginning to master the Cardiff forwards and, more specifically, understand the interpretations of referee H. Joynson. In the last minute of the match there was a lineout on the right-hand side of Cardiff Arms Park and the referee informed skipper Muller that it would probably be the last of the match. "Get me the ball, whatever happens," fly-half Brewis told his leader.

The Boks duly won the ball and it went quickly to scrumhalf Hansie Oelofse who gave Brewis a perfect pass. Brewis, in the meantime, had signalled that he would kick for the left-hand corner flag and this he did with such accuracy that Ochse could beat Trott to the touchdown with about a metre to spare.

And, of course, there was Scotland at Murrayfield on November 24, 1951. For once the weather was really kind. The field was firm and there was even a little sunshine. "On a day like this we can beat any team by double figures," Muller predicted beforehand but not even he could have expected a winning margin of 44 points.

The Springboks were in total control and with backs and forwards combining perfectly in one sweeping movement after the other, often from their own goalline, they scored nine tries, a dropgoal and seven conversions.

Deep in the second half, Hennie Muller felt so sorry for his battered opponents that he actually told Angus Cameron, the young Scottish captain, to try and keep his forwards together a bit more effectively. It was the sort

of sportsmanship you could have expected from that team and the Scots reciprocated by showing their admiration when they carried Muller off the field after the final whistle.

For the record, here are the scorers in that historic match: tries by Chris Koch (2), Salty du Rand, Willem Delport, Basie van Wyk, Hennie Muller, Ernst Dinkelmann, Ryk van Schoor and Tjol Lategan. Add to that a drop from Brewis and seven conversions from Okey Geffin.

Against Ireland on December 9, 1951. Seven minutes after the kickoff, Ryk van Schoor was carried off the field, unconscious, after mistiming a tackle on the powerfully-built Browne. The Springbok machine was not working on all cylinders and at half-time the score was 3-5 in Ireland's favour.

Meanwhile there was even more drama in the dressingroom where three doctors decided that Van Schoor was too badly concussed to return to the field. Van Schoor insisted that he must and finally a worried Frank Mellish, after asking Ryk a few questions to determine whether he had some idea of where he was, accepted the responsibility for the stocky Springbok's return to action.

His courage seemed to inspire the Springboks. First Muller and Brewis combined to send Ochse over in the corner and then Brewis, ending once and for all the myth that Jackie Kyle was the world's best flyhalf of the era, stabbed over a superb dropgoal. Then followed a try by Basie van Wyk and with that Ireland's hopes of victory crumbled to ashes.

The final try of the match will be remembered as long as the game of rugby is played. An attack from the Boks was stopped; from the loose scrum the ball reached the dazed Van Schoor. Through instinct rather than intent he beat his man on the inside, stumbled, cut inside past several other defenders and then with an incredible final sidestep again to the inside, he left the fullback grasping vainly to score the greatest try of his illustrious career. Immediately after the match Van Schoor had to go to bed where he stayed for 48 hours.

The test against Wales, another titanic battle with Johnny Buchler in

Above: Chum Ochse beats Gerwyn Williams and Ken Jones to score the only try for South Africa against Wales at Cardiff Arms Park in 1951.

Below: Tjol Lategan shows his wounds to an unimpressed Ryk van Schoor and Chris Koch. Three of the greatest Springboks of all time together in the dressingroom after a match on the 1951/52 tour.

Die Huisgenoot

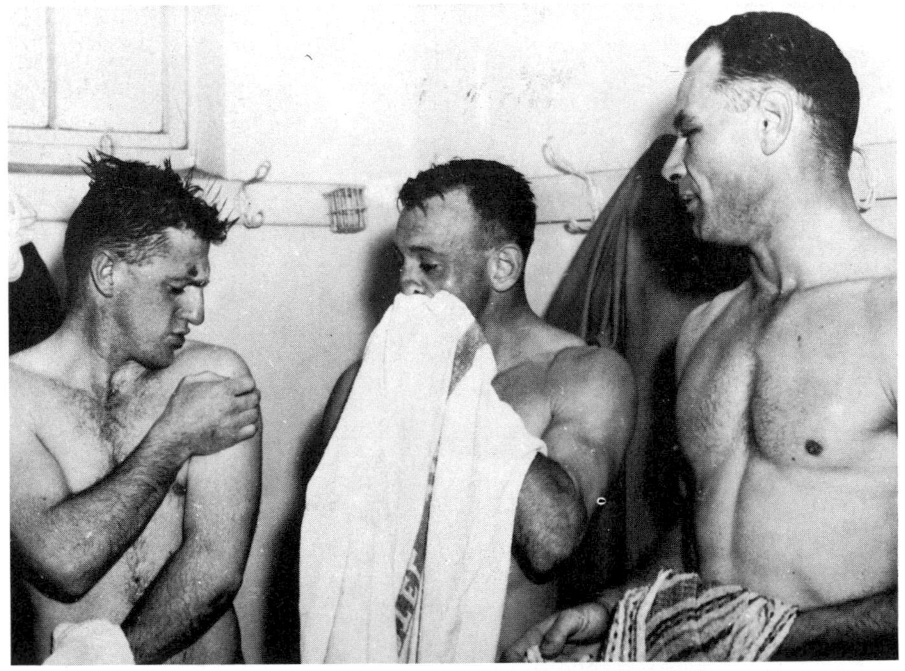

splendid form as the soon-to-be-famous Cliff Morgan wasted the hard-won possession gained for him by his forwards, particularly the mighty Roy John who completely outplayed a sick Salty du Rand in the lineouts. In a vain attempt to foil the fast-breaking Springbok loose forwards and the ruthless defence of the centres, Morgan and his threequarters confined themselves to grubberkicks and Buchler easily dealt with these, driving the Welshmen back time and again.

Starved of possession, the Springbok backs had only two real opportunities to strike. The first time Brewis broke just far enough to draw Bleddyn Williams before passing to Lategan who flipped the ball high over Van Schoor and straight into the hands of Chum Ochse. The little wing with the baggy pants scurried through and over in the corner with three defenders on his back, beating Olympic sprinter Ken Jones in the process.

The second chance came when the Welsh looseforwards hesitated ever so slightly to tackle Brewis. This was all the "Old Sarge" needed and in the wink of an eye his dropped goal had added another three points to the Springbok total. The Boks won 6-3, but without Johnny Buchler, the cover defence of Van Wyk, Fry and Muller and the attacking genius of Brewis and Ochse, they would certainly have been defeated.

England was beaten 8-3 through a typical try by Fonnie du Toit and a conversion and a penalty from Hennie Muller who proved his remarkable versatility by using himself as the placekicker. It was, from all aspects, the dullest of the tests played on the tour.

The test against France, won 25-3, produced a final try which was a fitting climax to a tour that will stand for all time to come as a testimonial to Springbok rugby at its best. Let Dr. Danie Craven describe it:

"There was a scrum near our twenty-five. We hooked and the ball flashed from Du Toit to Brewis, Lategan, Van Schoor and Ochse. Chum was half-way round his man when he passed inside to Van Schoor who gave to the forwards. With short, snappy passes they gained ground before passing to the backs, with everything happening so fast that Ochse was not yet back in position by the time it again came his way. But Johnstone had shot across to take the pass and he in turn fed the forwards on his inside. They carried on with another passing movement and then back again to the threequarters, all the way down the line to Ochse who lifted a short cross-kick for Basie van Wyk, surrounded by Springboks, to pick up and dive over.

"How often that ball was handled, nobody will ever know. But what we do know for sure is that Johnny Buchler is the only player who did not feature in the movement and that some players handled the ball five times and others three times!"

Yes, they were giants, those members of the 1951-52 Springbok touring side. South Africa can never forget them or the example they set on and off the field of play.

25 years later . . .

Members of the magnificent 1951/52 held a re-union in Johannesburg in 1976 and freelance journalist Koos van der Merwe was there to take these photographs of three famous partnerships, 25 years after they had worn the green jersey on the fields of Britain and France. Below, left, are Fonnie du Toit and Hansie Brewis, a half-back combination in eight successive test victories. On the right below are lock-forwards Ernst Dinkelmann and Salty du Rand and, at the bottom of the page, the loose-forward trio of Stephen Fry, Hennie Muller and Basie van Wyk. A few months after this picture was taken Muller died after a heart attack.

Die Huisgenoot

3/ FALTERING CHAMPIONS

You cannot win them all

Like a man behind the wheel of a stately Rolls Royce envying the swashbuckler careering through the traffic on his flashy red scooter, South African rugby fans — and authorities — have always been almost irrationally fascinated by the Australian style and approach to the game.

We fell for it in 1933 and again in 1953, although both times we snapped out of it before it was too late.

It is really a strange phenomenon, this desire on our part to beat the Wallabies by playing it their way. Part of it, I am sure, has to do with the fact that they often look so easy to beat, a fatal error to begin with, and, almost as important, their touring teams are usually run by affable men who have no difficulty in charming hordes of South African rugby writers into espousing the cause of "open rugby".

The strength of the 1953 Wallabies, like that of their predecessors of 20 years earlier, was exceptional pace, up front and behind the scrum. Their only hope therefore lay in running the Springboks off their feet and capitalising on every mistake. The odds were a lot more in their favour whenever the Springboks forgot where their own strength lay. The Aussies have a natural aptitude for the psychology of sport and their so-called commitment to open rugby was hardly in evidence in 1963 when they visited South Africa with a pack of solid forwards for a change and outstanding half-backs in Ken Catchpole and Phil Hawthorne.

But, back to John Solomon and his 1953 Wallabies. Probably the best player in the side was Eddie Stapleton, a tall and heavy 21-year-old wing from New South Wales; a splendid runner who never panicked and always seemed to do the right thing. Garth Jones, a flame-haired, thin-as-a-reed Queenslander had blazing speed on the leftwing and his famous try in the Newlands test assured him of a special niche in our rugby history, but he was not as good an allround player as Stapleton.

John Solomon was far-and-away the best centre in the touring party, quick-thinking and a sophisticated tactician. He was also an excellent captain who, like his team manager Wylie Breckenridge, was always charming and tactful throughout the three months and six days that the tour lasted. The Wallabies had great hopes for Jimmy Phipps as Solomon's partner, but after his first encounter with Ryk van Schoor he was never again a threat to the Springboks. The Wallabies should have dropped him, and not Solomon, to make place for the solid Herb Barker in the final test.

Barker was bothered with injuries throughout the tour and his safe placekicking was often missed. Morrie Tate and Johnny Bosler were mediocre halves, but the slightly-built Cyril Burke and the veteran Spanner Brown formed a good combination. Keith Cross, Norman Hughes and Brian Johnson, three quick, intelligent loose-forwards, were the real king-pins of the team. They had a deep respect for Hennie Muller, the Springbok captain, and his style so intrigued them that they often cornered him at after-match functions and asked him for advice! Muller, such a murderous competitor on the field, but a true gentleman off it, freely assisted them whenever he could. He told me once that by the time the tour had ended, Johnson was as good an eighthman as anyone he had played against.

The tight forwards were adequate, no more than that, with Tony Miller (who played for Australia for 16 years), and Alan Cameron easily the best. Nic Shehadie, Solomon's vice-captain, had the misfortune of having to pack against the mighty Jaap Bekker and he took a merciless pounding in the third test in particular.

The Wallabies wore green jerseys that year and the South Africans, as a gesture of hospitality, settled for white jerseys in the tests.

Solomon's men opened their tour with a surprising defeat against Natal with Roy McLean, at flyhalf, dropping the winning goal. Only a few months earlier it was the same McLean, a brilliant attacking batsman, who had slammed the Australian cricket team

John Solomon, a good captain and an excellent player, led the unpredictable 1953 Wallabies. Here he trots onto Newlands with his vice-captain, Nic Shehadie just behind him.

into defeat in a thrilling test in Melbourne.

Leading up to the first test they were also beaten by Free State (with Basie Viviers collecting 16 points on his own), Transvaal, Griquas and Northern Transvaal and in one of their three consecutive matches against Rhodesia they were held to a draw. Their best performance was a narrow win over Western Province who threw the game away with shocking mistakes. Whether they lost or won though, the Wallabies flung the ball around with the proverbial gay abandon and soon there was a tremendous campaign for their opponents to follow suit.

Wylie Breckenridge was subtly putting across his message in after-match speeches, calling for less kicking and more passing movements, imploring the referees to be less whistle-happy and making everybody feel a little guilty because they were beating the Wallabies.

I remember talking to George van Reenen, the 1937 Springbok forward, one afternoon while listening to the applause following one of Breckenridge's passionate appeals. Van Reenen was, frankly, livid.

"We're doing it again," he snorted, "we're falling for all this talk about open rugby. It's going to be 1933 all over again and you mark my words, we're in for a shock!"

The Springbok team for the first test at Ellis Park was selected entirely from members of the team who visited Britain and France in 1951/52 and Hennie Muller, after a struggle to regain something of his old form at the age of 31, was given the captaincy.

After eight successive and successful tests with Hansie Brewis, Fonnie du Toit, an outstanding little scrumhalf who throughout his career regarded the serving and protection of his flyhalf as his main responsibility, had to make way for the more dynamic Hansie Oelofse. Injuries frequently interrupted Oelofse's career, but at his best he was a match-winner on his own; certainly there was no-one remotely approaching his all-round ability in 1953.

The first signs of the effects of the propaganda campaign could already be seen in this test. The game was often loose and without purpose, but in between there were flashes of brilliance from the Springboks. Practically in the first minute of the match, Ryk van Schoor nailed Phipps on the halfway line with a tackle that made the chalk and dry grass fly and the forwards and backs combined smoothly and often. From one such movement Buks Marais went over for a try he converted himself. The Boland wing, who far too seldom fully realised his enormous potential as a player, also put over a penalty just before half-time after Oelofse had worked beautifully with his forwards before Du Rand was sent over. Against all this the outclassed Wallabies could only show a penalty by Tom Sweeney.

In the second half Hansie Oelofse broke again and this time he needed no help from anybody. Then Johnny Buchler, as quietly efficient as ever, dropped a lovely penalty goal. Another crushing tackle by Van Schoor gave the Springboks their next try. As the ball popped loose, Tjol Lategan was on the spot to snatch it up and weave his way through. Shortly before the end Van Schoor slipped through a gap with Stephen Fry, Basie van Wyk and Hennie Muller up in support. It was Muller who finally outstripped the shattered defence for a try near the posts.

The Springboks won 25-3, scored five excellent tries and kept the ball in play as much as possible, Brewis often passing when his sound rugby brain actually dictated that he should have kicked. But no-one is more fervent than a recent convert and the clamouring for "open rugby" continued, with several former Springboks who should have known better, joining in the appeals for "less kicking". It must have been a confused bunch of Springboks who read the newspaper reports the next morning.

Hansie Brewis was axed for the Newlands international. He was already well in his thirties and a jaw injury suffered in the match between Northern Transvaal and the Australians, was worrying him. A year later Brewis was still good enough to beat Western Province practically off his own bat, but he was never again to be considered for a Springbok team.

His place was taken by Ian Kirkpatrick, a lanky youngster who had played well for Griquas against the tourists and he was the only newcomer in the team. In later years Kirkpatrick became a regular Springbok centre, but his debut at flyhalf was a most unhappy one. He was jeered everytime he kicked by a section of the crowd who did not know what they wanted and afterwards he was saddled with much of the blame for South Africa's first defeat in 11 tests.

It cannot be denied that the Springboks were a little over confident for the second test. They had beaten the Wallabies without difficulty in the first encounter and on the Tuesday before the second international, Combined Southern Universities had made the Wallabies look like leaden-footed third-raters. The Springboks were well on top in the first half and there were ominous signs that they were rather too relaxed after the resumption.

It is my theory however that the Springboks lost mainly because they had been subtly brainwashed into playing a game that was basically not sound. In the second half John Solomon went off the field briefly after an injury and when he returned, he roved among his threequarters, looking sorry for himself and leaving Brian Johnson on the right wing and Eddie Stapleton at centre.

This left Hennie Muller with the option whether to keep his pack intact and control possession completely or also to put a forward among the backs. He decided to keep his forwards together and was criticised severely for this later when Solomon suddenly came to life to help give Garth Jones the winning try. Yet Muller's plan would have worked had the Springboks confined themselves to driving against that depleted and already beaten Australian pack. Instead Oelofse, renowned for his ability to play back to his forwards, kept on passing to his backs.

Muller admitted often in later years that he knew that every member of his team wanted to "show up" the crowd and the critics by keeping the ball in play as much as possible.

But it would be churlish to make too many apologies and to degrade what was one of the finest fight-backs in modern rugby history.

Tries by Du Rand, Chum Ochse and Chris Koch, one converted by Buks Marais, to an unconverted try by Stapleton, gave the Springboks a lead of 11-3 at half-time. Within minutes of the re-start Basie van Wyk made it 14-3 after a lightning break by Oelofse and it really looked as if the Wallabies might as well surrender. Instead they fought back and Cross was awarded a try after some untidy play. It was converted by Colbert and shortly afterwards Solomon and Phipps reverse-passed smoothly after a loose ball had been picked up. Brown took the movement further and as he was about to be tackled by Muller, he timed a perfect pass to Brian Johnson. It was a try right in the corner, but Stapleton converted

with the kind of kick that wins matches.

With the lead whittled down to one point the Springboks woke up and launched a series of attacks. Chris Koch and Basie van Wyk missed tries by losing the ball in the act of diving for the line and Marais could not take full advantage of an overlap created by Lategan. To make matters worse, Marais and Buchler took turns to miss two fairly easy penalties.

In the first minute of injury time the Wallabies got their winning points from an unforgettable try. Once again it came from a loose ball, some ten yards from their own goal-line. Brown immediately started a movement and when Solomon came into the lineup to pass to Stapleton, the Springboks were in trouble. The big wing ran up to the 10-yard line before giving his partner Garth Jones a pass so perfect that the lanky Queenslander could take it without any slackening of his pace. Johnny Buchler, the Springbok fullback, made the mistake of not trying to force Jones infield where Muller, in full chase, might have had a chance of getting him in his sights.

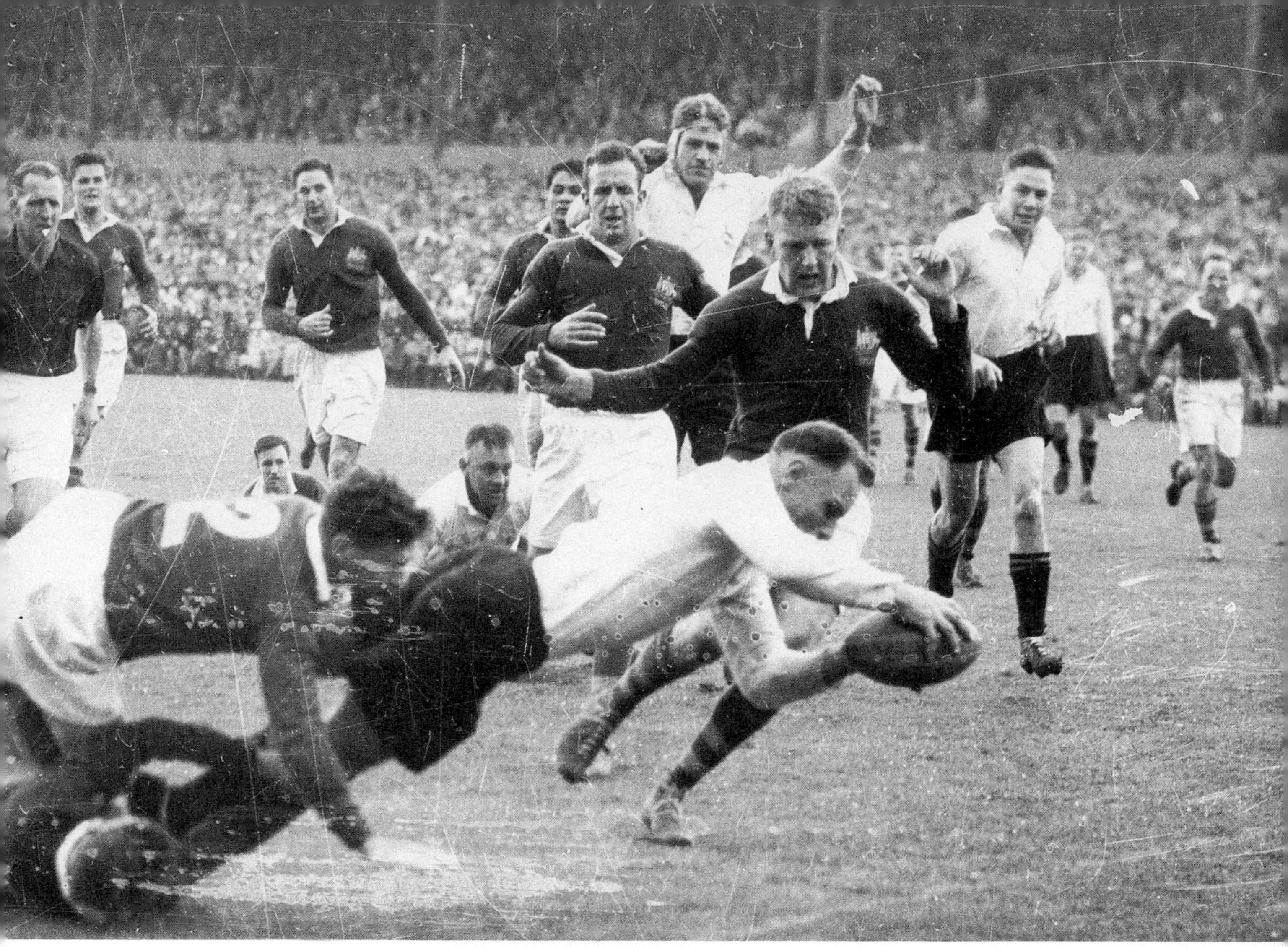

Above: An outstanding action picture shows Chris Koch ploughing his way over the line to score for the white-jersied Springboks in the second test at Newlands. On the left is Basie van Wyk and Saltie du Rand and Willem Delport are in the background.

The Cape Times

Right: Garth Jones, the Australian wing whose thrilling try in the second test at Newlands cost the Springboks the match but provided one of the most dramatic moments in rugby history.

Above: Johnny Buchler, the young fullback whose calm competence meant so much to the Springboks in the nine tests played between 1951 and 1953.

Instead Jones found himself with a long but clear run to the Springbok line, feeling, as he put it afterwards, "Muller's breath on my neck every inch of the way!"

All along the railway stand side of Newlands the two ran, Muller just too far behind to risk a desperate dive-tackle. Muller was then well past his best, nearly 10 years older than the wing, but he kept pounding after the flying Australian, the gap neither closing nor widening. Finally Jones crossed the line and collapsed behind the posts, completely exhausted. Muller pulled up a few feet behind him, shoulders hunched and knowing for the first time in his test career what defeat tasted like.

The 14-18 disaster was just the medicine the Springboks, the selectors and a large section of the press and public needed. Chris Koch, Chum Ochse, Buks Marais, Ernst Dinkelmann and Ian Kirkpatrick were left out for the third test. Jan Pickard, not nick-named "Jan Bull" for nothing, got his first test "cap" in place of his 1951-52 teammate Dinkelmann while Koch was, as it soon proved to be, temporarily displaced by Harry Newton Walker, whose father Alf had played for South Africa in 1921/24. Steve Hoffman, a player who was to fritter away his great talent, and Dolf Bekker, the younger brother of Jaap, were the new wings. Most significant was the selection of Transvaal's Natie Rens as the flyhalf. Rens was built like Brewis and he played like Brewis. He did not have Hansie's superb judgement and quickness, but he was an outstanding kicker with both feet, had good hands and, above all, the perfect big-match temperament. Known to his Transvaal teammates as "Bokspeen", this wiry dairy farmer was one of the best place-and drop-kickers of his day and the tougher the situation, the better he was likely to play. The season before the Australian visit, Rens was the main factor behind Transvaal's success in retaining the Currie Cup, including the clinching of the final against Boland with a dropgoal in the last minute.

A further change was made to the team a few days before the test when Tjol Lategan, after ten successive internationals as Ryk van Schoor's partner, had to withdraw because of an injured shoulder. His place was taken by Daantjie Rossouw, a young Matie who had done well for Southern Universities against the Wallabies.

Some time before the third test Hennie Muller visited Dr. Danie Craven at Stellenbosch. He was being

Hansie Oelofse and Natie Rens formed a highly-efficient half-back combination to help the Springboks save the series.

Die Burger

Jan Pickard, here in deep thought with the "Old Master" Boy Louw, added strength and fire to the Springbok pack after the Newlands defeat.

blamed heavily for the Newlands debacle and this sensitive and deeply emotional man was close to a nervous collapse. Muller was never to forget Craven's encouragement and willingness to share with him whatever blame there was. During their chat they also agreed that the Springboks would no longer allow themselves to be influenced. The Kingsmead test would be played according to the traditional South African pattern.

With solid scrummaging, good lineout work and sensible use of possession, the Springboks won 18-8 and the Wallabies were never really in the picture. The spectators, probably chastened by what had happened at Newlands, cheered rather than jeered Rens's long touchfinders and they understood and appreciated the tactics from the first whistle. Once the Wallabies had been properly softened up, the Springboks scored some of the finest tries of the series, at least one the sort of effort the Wallabies would have been proud of. It came from a lineout with Dolf Bekker throwing to Jan Pickard who, as quickly, whipped the ball back to the wing who went over in the corner before the Australians really knew what it was all about. Rens made the difficult conversion look easy and the half-time score was 10-0 including another converted try, scored by Rossouw who beat several defenders in a darting solo run after Hennie Muller had started a movement. Ryk van Schoor's deadly tackles provided Stephen Fry, Basie van Wyk and Muller with plenty of loose balls from which to attack and early in the second half it was from such a movement that Jaap Bekker eventually received and steamrollered through for Rens to convert. Dolf and Jaap Bekker are still the only two Springbok brothers to each score a try in the same test.

A penalty dropgoal from Solomon followed, a neat piece of work from this fine player, but then Oelofse, one of the best breaking scrumhalves we have ever produced, slipped through once again. Fry was up to give Van Wyk, his bald head shining under the Natal sun, a try which Rens, for once, could not convert.

With the score 18-3 the match was won and lost and even the Springboks must have felt like cheering when the Wallabies, showing their typical never-say-die opportunism, got the final try. It came after Burke had picked up a careless pass before giving to Keith Cross who ran practically the length of the field to score. Van Schoor, the only Springbok in a position to chase Cross, gave up after a few strides and smiled at Hennie Muller.

"Wow, that guy Jones can move, eh Hennie?" he remarked.

"What do you mean Jones?" Muller replied. "That's Keith Cross!"

"What!" Van Schoor exclaimed. "A forward too fast for me? Man, I'm out of the next test, that's for sure!"

Ochse and Koch, at the expense of Hoffman and Walker, returned to the team for the fourth test against the Wallabies who could now, at best, only share the series. Hoffman never again played for the Springboks, but Newton Walker was in the touring team to New Zealand three years later.

The Port Elizabeth test was not much of a game. The Springbok forwards took over gradually but thoroughly and in the second half had complete control. The Wallabies on the other hand, had decided on spoiling tactics this time; their backs lined up very shallow and they tried to counter Van Schoor's murderous tackling by kicking grubbers with monotonous regularity. Not very cleverly placed either, and Johnny Buchler had no problems in coping with them. The Wallabies were still in there with a hope at halftime after Stapleton had scored an unconverted try and Herb Barker two penalty goals, but their efforts

Ryk van Schoor, whose deadly tackling made him one of the most feared Springboks of all time, in a characteristic pose. He ended his test career against the 1953 Wallabies.
Die Huisgenoot

The Springboks have won the third test and an exhausted Hennie Muller is being warmly congratulated by John Solomon. Jaap Bekker, a front-ranker of legendary strength, moves up for a handshake and on the left, patting him on the shoulder, is Nic Shehadie. Muller's face is lined with fatigue and at the end of the final test of this series he announced his retirement from international rugby.

Pat Smith

were nullified by Natie Rens with two penalties and a dropgoal of his own.

In the second half the Springboks battered their brave opponents who could do little more than defend, and this they did very well. Chris Koch, a frontrow forward who could run like a wing threequarter, got the first try after Oelofse had once again combined well with Van Wyk and Fry. Then Oelofse, brilliant in this match, punted ahead and scored from his own kick and Rens, who never put a foot wrong, hit the target with both conversion kicks. In the last few minutes Buchler coolly collected a poor clearance from one of the Australians and lifted over a dropgoal to make the final score 22-9. The series, in the balance while the Springboks flirted with a style that did not suit them, was well and truly won after all.

It was to be the final test for a whole host of great Springboks who had reached the end of their playing days. Ryk van Schoor and Tjol Lategan, Chum Ochse and Willem Delport never again played for South Africa and injury was to virtually hound Oelofse into retirement. Why Natie Rens, who made no mistakes and scored 19 points in only two tests, was never again considered by the national selectors nobody knows. He and the Western Province flyhalf Len Rodriques, who never did get his Springbok colours, would certainly have been worth their weight in gold to the embattled Springboks in New Zealand less than three years later.

It was also the last test for Hennie Muller whose extreme exhaustion after each of the four internationals was known to be a source of worry to Dr. Craven. The "Greyhound of the Veld", as his great opponent Bob Scott once described him, listened to the advice of the man who had been with him in triumph and defeat and so one of the most illustrious Springboks in rugby history came to the end of the trail.

Lions roar

Their mascot was an outsize toy lion called Elmer and bagpipes and a shillelagh formed part of the luggage, all solemnly marked "team equipment" to save the individual owners any possible penalty for exceeding the weight limit imposed on each member of the first British team to travel to and in South Africa by air.

Robin Thompson's 1955 Lions were also the first team from the United Kingdom to show South Africa the new uniform they had adopted only five years before; the now famous red jersey with the rose of England, the thistle of Scotland, the shamrock of Ireland and the three feathers of Wales combined in a shield-shaped badge on the left breast.

Back in the days of the "missionary tours" to the colonies before the turn of the century, the British rugby teams wore red and white striped jerseys with navy blue knickerbockers, as their pants which could never have been mistaken for shorts, were called then. In the 1920's they changed to dark blue jerseys, white shorts and red stockings, annoying the Irish members more than somewhat by giving them no recogniton whatsoever. The All Blacks were not happy either; they considered the dark blue too close to their own revered black! The ruffled feelings from all quarters were finally smoothed in 1950 when the Lions, a nickname they had received in South Africa on their 1924 tour, decided to change to red tops with the combined badge, white shorts and blue stockings with green turnovers as an extra concession to the Irish who had been slighted for so long.

But the 1955 Lions had more than a new uniform to offer. Their tour record was the best of any team to visit South Africa since Johnny Hammond and his men rumbled triumphantly around the Cape Colony, Natal and the two Boer Republics on slow stagecoaches and even slower trains, 59 years earlier. They drew the four-test series and lost only three other matches with one drawn out of 24. Far more important, they played splendid rugby and it is probably not unfair to claim that they still rate as the most generally-liked rugby tourists ever to visit South Africa.

They radiated charm from the moment they stepped off the aircraft after the long and tiring flight from London and gave the large number of fans and newspapermen waiting for them, a spontaneous "concert". Bathed in the floodlights of the newsreel cameramen, Cliff Morgan, the little flyhalf from the Rhondda Valley, led the team in one song after the other and it must have been close to half-an-hour before the cheering crowd would let them tumble into the waiting buses to leave for their hotel.

This was to be the pattern for the tour. They always had time for their public, even near the end of what was a most strenuous tour, and they seemed to take a genuine delight in entertaining whoever was in earshot with impromptu "acts" and singing.

Cliff Morgan usually conducted the "choir" and he and Tony O'Reilly were both pianists of no mean skill. Cecil Pedlow and Pat Quinn were no strangers to the drums and cymbals respectively, and Tom Reid, a tall Irishman, whom the team for some reason or other called "Colonel", was a sentimental troubadour in the Basie Viviers and Gert Dannhauser mould.

With 10 Welshmen in the party and with Gareth Griffiths joining the team later to make the contingent even stronger, the communal singing was never less than good and often close to professional standard and their phonetic rendition of *Sarie Marais* is a memory to treasure. Danny Davies, a former captain of Cardiff, who was the assistant manager and by far the oldest member of the touring party had a particular fondness for giving voice to *"Is you from Dixie?"* and this very early on in the tour earned him the nickname of "Massa Dan".

He was not the only one in the team to acquire a label of some idiosyncracy or other. Bryn Meredith was called "Beetle" because of his puckered brow whenever he had something on his mind, while Ernie Michie, burdened with the formidable names Ernest Stutely, was known to his teammates as "Fourteen", not only because that was his tour number, but more particularly because they enjoyed hearing him pronounce it in his Aberdeen accent.

Michie did not play in any one of the tests, but, kilted and suitably dignified for the occasion, he always led the way on to the field with his bagpipes wailing. His practices on this musical instrument always had to be preceded by a careful soundproofing of his hotel room and one of the crises of the tour came when he discovered that our dry Highveld atmosphere had caused the thing to spring a "leak", so to speak. Urgent appeals to local Caledonian societies soon had it back in good working condition.

But Robin Henderson Thompson, a soft-spoken but strong-willed Ulsterman, did not bring his team to South Africa for high jinks alone and they took the game seriously indeed without, with the noticeable exception of the third test, ever adopting a dour approach.

The team was packed with talent, but looking back now after more than 20 years there were five absolutely superb players in the side who added the touch of genius. They were the two England centres Phil Davies and Jeff Butterfield, Tony O'Reilly, the Irish right wing, Cliff Morgan, the flyhalf from Wales, and Bryn Meredith, also from the Welsh valleys who was a hooker of the highest class, but was also an extra loose forward. Other members of the team often gave inspired performances, flanker Jim Greenwood to mention only one, but it was the "Big Five" who threatened Springbok supremacy.

Of the five it was Cliff Morgan who really captured the imagination in South Africa, even more so than the big and handsome teenager Tony O'Reilly, who invariably seemed to be surrounded by a bevy of gaping girls. It can be said that Clifford Isaac Morgan was by the end of the tour second only to Tom van Vollenhoven as the paying public's favourite player.

The Lions started off their tour with a loss to Western Transvaal when, as in all of their defeats until they departed some three months later, their forwards failed to get enough clean possession to their dangerous backs.

Eastern Province, guided and driven by that shrewd and powerful frontranker Amos du Plooy, capitalised on this weakness to tumble them 20-0

Cliff Morgan, the Welsh flyhalf in the 1955 Lions team and one of the most brilliant players ever to visit South Africa, is collared by Springbok wing Theunis Briers in the exciting first test of the series at Ellis Park. Morgan's outstanding performance was one of the main reasons why the Lions won this match.

on the only other occasion they faltered in the 12 matches leading up to the first test in Johannesburg. By this time former Springboks like Tony Harris and Freddie Turner were warning that the Springboks were up against a far from ordinary team and Danie Craven the Springbok coach and national selector, made no bones about the fact that he regarded the Lions as the most dangerous combination yet to visit South Africa.

When they massacred Transvaal 36-13, scoring seven tries in the process, the situation appeared to be desperate. Many people regarded it as a foregone conclusion that the Springboks would be beaten and Danie Craven was even advised by well-meaning friends and relatives not to have anything to do with the preparation of the Springbok team as he would place his reputation in jeopardy!

The selectors decided to give Stephen Perry Fry, the flaxen-haired Western Province flanker and 1951/52 veteran, the formidable task of leading South Africa against the Lions. There must have been occasions during the series when this quiet but highly sophisticated man, wondered whether it was all worthwhile as he became the target of a venomous campaign from an ill-bred section of the South African public.

Fry immediately called on Craven to advise him and throughout that thrilling series these two suffered and rejoiced together. Both got more criticism than credit and Fry even received threatening letters at one stage of the tour when it looked as if the Springboks would be toppled from the throne. It was disgraceful treatment of one of our great Springboks and it could be the reason why Fry, who has all the qualifications for administrative office, has made his retirement from the game so utterly final.

The team for the first test was selected after extensive trials and a Junior Springbok tour, and it marked the debut of several players who became household names in the years to follow. Men like Theunis Briers, the young Paarl farmer who scored five tries in the series, a record for a Springbok on our own fields, and Karel Thomas (Tom) van Vollenhoven, Johan Claassen, a future captain and one of the finest lock-forwards in rugby history, and Daan Retief, a black-haired former Northern Transvaal wing who was converted into an eighthman and was one of South Africa's best forwards of his era.

Jack van der Schyff whose prodigious punting could never be forgotten by anyone who ever saw it, returned to the team after not having been considered by the national selectors for nearly six years, a period during which he, among other things, made a living as a crocodile hunter in what is now known as Zambia. The selection of Josias (Sias) Swart, on the left-wing, also established a new record as he was the first Springbok from South West Africa, while scrum-half Tommy Gentles at 5 ft 3 is still the shortest player to have represented South Africa.

The interest in this test was unbelievable. There was a flourishing black market, people paid the most ridiculous prices for tickets and eventually the biggest crowd ever to see a rugby international (estimates varied between 90,000 and 100,000) crammed into Ellis Park for the match.

On the way to the ground the bus with the Springboks was held up outside a church as a bridal couple was just coming out. Several of the Springboks began serenading them and even posed for photographs with the newly-weds. This was a sure sign to Danie Craven and, among others, an old war-horse like Salty du Rand, that the Springboks were not properly motivated.

"I first saw signs of it while the Springboks were having their early lunch," Dr. Craven said later. "Some of the younger ones were far too concerned with other matters and also ate too much. Stephen Fry spoke to them then about their attitude but when they were also late for the bus's departure and after that debacle outside the church, I had my doubts whether we would be able to make it. You must be keyed-up for a big occasion and this belief among old Springboks that a team that sings before a test, is destined to weep afterwards, is not just a silly superstition."

The Lions, on the other hand, were in a determined mood and an official who came to the Press Box after a peep into their dressingroom, told me before the start of the match that the scene in there was like "a gathering of professional mourners".

The crowd, so huge that there was something frightening about it, saw a match to remember. Perhaps those who have called it the most thrilling test of all time are right. There was exhilarating rugby from both sides and the result was in the balance until the final few seconds.

Cecil Pedlow, a young wing from County Armagh in Ireland, whose one weakness was poor fielding of a high ball because of bad eyesight aggravated by the strong South African sun, got the first points, but the try really belonged to Jeff Butterfield. The brilliant Yorkshireman, a centre threequarter in the classic tradition, broke beautifully after his partner, the powerfully-built Phil Davies, had nosed into a gap between Des Sinclair and Tom van Vollenhoven in the midfield.

Davies threw a rather careless pass to Butterfield who scooped the ball towards him with one arm and then drew the defence before sending Pedlow over.

Two excellent penalties in succession by Van der Schyff took the Springboks in the lead; lovely kicks most people forgot in the wave of unfair recrimination which was to follow. An outstanding joint effort between Tommy Gentles and Stephen Fry,

Left: Stephen Fry, a picture of determination, led South Africa in all four tests against the 1955 Lions.

Right: Tom van Vollenhoven, one of the fastest and best wings in rugby history, had a shaky start to his test career but by the end of the series he was a national hero.

Below: Theunis Briers, a farmer from the district of Paarl, scored five tries in the four tests. Briers had pace and power and the Lions respected him as much as they did Van Vollenhoven.

then gave Briers a chance to pound away on a typical run, his inside swerve foxing Morgan. Van der Schyff converted, making the score 11-3.

In swift retaliation, Morgan drove a big gap in the Springbok defence and when Davies passed to Butterfield he had O'Reilly on his outside. The great England centre did not need the Irish wing's help; he simply kept on going and Angus Cameron had no difficulty in making the half-time tally 11-8.

After the resumption, the Lions lost Reg Higgins, who was playing an outstanding game, and it does say a lot for their character that the misfortune inspired rather than dispirited them. Perhaps it was the Morgan magic that did it because almost immediately after Higgins was helped off, he broke with tremendous speed, caught the defence in two minds, and flashed over with Basie van Wyk, who had done so much to neutralise him at Cardiff Arms Park just under three years before, looking on in helpless frustration. Next Van der Schyff was put under terrific pressure and the bounce of the ball deceived him cruelly twice in quick succession. There were tries by a rampant Jim Greenwood and the long-legged Tony O Reilly. All three second-half tries were converted by Cameron who, in the process, must have thought back briefly to the Murrayfield nightmare when he was captain of the most badly-beaten international team in history.

Leading 23-11, the Lions suddenly appeared to have everything tied up in a nice, neat bundle, but back came the Springboks with an opportunistic try after a kick from Gentles had Cameron going the wrong way.

A moment to remember. A dejected Jack van der Schyff hangs his head as he realises that he has missed the conversion that could have given the Springboks a last-minute victory over the Lions in the first test at Ellis Park. Referee Ralph Burmeister and Tommy Gentles watch the ball swing outside the far upright.

Ivor Hanes

NN'S BREAD
AISE & DELICIOUS JELLIES

Van der Schyff could not convert, but in the final minute of the match Chris Koch showed once again what a tremendous forward he could be. He picked up some 20 metres from the line and dodged, weaved and crashed through a swarming defence to score a try that made those heavily-weighted temporary pavilions sway as the massive crowd screamed their happiness. This time Van der Schyff converted and with what was about half-a-minute of injury time remaining, Stephen Fry picked up a loose ball and flipped it to Theunis Briers. The Paarl farmer had two men to beat, Pedlow and Cameron, but with that quite amazing ability to swerve inside at top speed, he beat them both to flash over, somewhere midway between the corner flag and the posts.

The conversion was not from a too difficult angle but the incredible tension of the moment was the thing to overcome. The huge scoreboard read 23-22 to the Lions and then the last numeral abruptly disappeared as the scorer, undoubtedly a Springbok supporter, prepared to make it read 23-24.

Tommy Gentles placed the ball for Van der Schyff with the referee, Ralph Burmeister, resting on his haunches a few paces behind and to the left of the kicker so that he would have a clear view to the centre of the crossbar.

The tall fullback, then playing for Western Transvaal, took four steps back and then ran up, for the kick that would decide the result. It was a moment I and probably 90 000 others will always be able to recall at will. The instant his boot struck the ball we knew that it was going to swing outside the left-hand post and that the Springboks had lost. His head down in utter dejection, Van der Schyff turned away as the Lions, standing behind the goalline, jumped for joy. If ever a man was desperately lonely in spite of the thousands of people around him it must have been Jack Henry van der Schyff on the afternoon of August 6, 1955.

Craven, Fry, Van der Schyff, Van Vollenhoven, the whole Springbok team were in disgrace all of a sudden with a rugby public, the majority of whom did not even know what they were agitating about. It should have been so easy to take a defeat like that with good grace, but instead there was a perverse desire to blame rather than to criticise constructively. Thankfully, sanity returned fairly quickly although Craven and Fry throughout that year remained the targets of abuse to those cranks who can never learn the meaning of sportsmanship.

It is a pity they were not present when Philip Nel, the 1937 Springbok, came to Craven after the match and said: "Danie, we came to within one point of beating them with players who have never been together in a team before. The foundations are there for the next test."

Nel's words were to prove prophetic.

Some of the letters received by Craven and his co-selectors were simply disgusting, but here and there was at least a glimmer of humour. Craven remembers the telegram that read: "Still room for another seven. Old Age Home, Pretoria"!

The embattled national selectors, Craven, Mellish, Bill Zeller, Maurice Zimerman and Basil Kenyon had only two further opportunities of seeing the Lions in action before they had to knuckle down to the unenviable task of appointing a team for the vital Newlands test; this while a barrage of criticism and advice poured down on them from all sides.

The British team beat Boland 11-0 but did not play all that well and on the Tuesday before the test, had to give everything they had to score a 20-17 victory over the Western Province Universities. The Maties and the Ikeys are traditional rugby enemies, but whenever they combine they seem to have an instinctive ability to dovetail and their performance against the 1955 Lions was particularly outstanding. Brilliantly led by James Starke, they scored four tries to four and Pedlow's better placekicking saved the touring team. It is hardly surprising that 11 of the students eventually gained Springbok

Karel Thomas van Vollenhoven dives over the line for the second of his three historic tries in the second test at Newlands. Jim Greenwood's tackle is too late to stop the flying Springbok.

Die Burger

colours.

It took the selectors five hours of debate before they could reach consensus on their team for the second test. Roy Dryburgh took over from the hapless Van der Schyff at fullback, while Tom van Vollenhoven was switched from centre to left-wing and Sias Swart, who had done well in the first test, had to make way for him. Wilfred Rosenberg, a dentistry student at the University of Witwatersrand who was born in Cape Town, but spent his boyhood years in Australia, became Des Sinclair's new centre partner. Jaap Bekker, Northern Transvaal's man-of-muscle, took over from Amos du Plooy while Albertus Johannes (Bertus) van der Merwe, a member of a famous Worcester rugby family, replaced Colin Kroon to begin what was to be an illustrious career as Springbok hooker. Basie van Wyk, one of the greatest of post-war looseforwards, lost his place to the tall, symmetrically-built Matie, Dawie Ackermann, and the prematurely bald Basie was destined never to play again for South Africa.

The rugby public did not approve of the team at all and the selectors and the players were attacked bitterly from virtually all quarters. The Springboks, managed by Boy Louw, did their preparations in virtual seclusion and outside telephone calls and visits from friends or fans were practically prohibited.

Stephen Fry had equipment brought from Stellenbosch and with the help of Craven, the players were given a clear idea of what was expected of each one. There were many quiet team talks and a firm decision that the tactics would be traditional; a softening-up process by the forwards in the first half and then attacks from a sound foundation after half-time.

In this atmosphere the Springboks built up a remarkable spirit and determination. Their critics had done them a favour; they were prepared to fight to the death. Wilf Rosenberg recalled once how an inebriated hanger-on managed to sidle up to him and Van Vollenhoven at the hotel on the evening before the test.

"Van Vollenhoven," he spat at the 20-year-old Pretoria policeman. "How're you going to catch O'Reilly? You can't even catch a cold, man!"

Van Vollenhoven did not bother to reply, but later he did mention the incident again to Rosenberg, who was a close friend of his, and vowed: "Wilf, tomorrow I'm going to clobber O'Reilly!" Coming from this most modest of sportsmen, it was an indication of the Springbok mood.

This time it was the British team who sang on the bus on their way to the ground where 46 000 spectators were waiting while the Springboks slumped in silence, each man wrapped up in his own thoughts. In the dressing-room under the new Grand Stand pavilion at Newlands, Stephen Fry was too tense to address his team and he asked Craven to do it for him. A few minutes later the two teams were on the field and Mike Slabber, the referee, whistled them into action as the crowd crammed into Newlands, released their pent-up emotions with a roar that echoed from the slopes of Devil's Peak.

Cameron got an early penalty for the Lions, but it was soon clear that the Springboks were not going to allow any team to beat them that day. The forwards, with each man working with a fierce urgency, gave the Lions no mercy and they gradually established their superiority.

Near the end of the first half Gentles and Fry broke well and from the loose scrum that followed Des Sinclair cross-kicked towards the centre of the field. The ball travelled a bit too far for his forwards and three Lions, including the dangerous O'Reilly, were waiting for it with Van Vollenhoven alone facing them. The Springbok left-wing did the only thing he could. He swooped down on his three opponents and with a perfectly-timed leap, plucked the ball out of the air, landed on his feet with cat-like agility and was streaking for the goalline before the Lions quite realised what was happening. Van Vollenhoven still had the fullback, Cameron, to beat, but this presented no problems to one of the fastest Springboks ever to wear

Wilf Rosenberg

Daan Retief

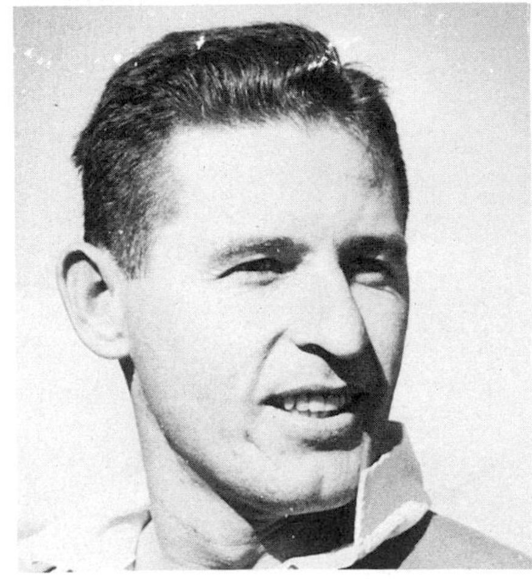

Roy Dryburgh

Des Sinclair

Tommy Gentles

Dawie Ackermann

the green-and-gold. The conversion failed, and poor placekicking was in fact to be the only weakness revealed by the Springboks in the whole match.

Immediately after half-time it was obvious that Fry had decided that the time was ripe for attack and within nine minutes Karel Thomas Van Vollenhoven had become the first Springbok since Boetie McHardy and Jan Stegmann against Ireland in 1912, to notch up a hat-trick in a test, and the first to achieve the feat in South Africa.

For his second try Van Vollenhoven ran fully 40 yards and for his third he beat O'Reilly hands-down with a feint and swerve and again left Cameron standing with his bewildering ability to change direction at top speed.

Rosenberg was the next to score after Sinclair had flashed through a gap between Butterfield and Davies. Then more history was made when Roy Gladstone Dryburgh, after a perfectly-executed scissors movement between Rosenberg and Sinclair, became the first Springbok fullback since Percy Alport in 1910 (also against Britain and on the same ground) to score a try in a test. Dryburgh managed to convert his own try; the first successful kick from the Springboks in the match. A break by Ulyate gave Briers a chance to score his team's sixth try and then the Lions, at last, struck back when Morgan made an opening for an unconverted try by Butterfield.

Before the end Ackermann managed to celebrate his test debut with a try, converted by Dryburgh, to push the score to 25-6 and although Bryn Meredith added three more points to his team's total with a brave try in the final minute after good work by Butterfield and Greenwood, the much-maligned Springboks were the most convincing winners of one of the most crucial international matches of all time.

Sports fans are fickle and all of a sudden the Springboks were again national heroes. Countless youngsters rushed to their barbers for a "Van Vollenhoven crew-cut" and if there were any critics left, they sulked in silence.

The Springboks made only one change for the third test in Pretoria, replacing Tommy Gentles with Coenraad (Popeye) Strydom of Free State. The Friday before the match Daan Retief had to withdraw because of injury, however, and his place was taken by George Phillip (Butch) Lochner, a young crash-tackling eighthman

Bryn Meredith, the hard-working Lions hooker, is held in a vice-like grip by Salty du Rand in this scene from the second test. Tony O'Reilly is waiting for Meredith's pass.

The Cape Times

Above: The agony of defeat. Daan Retief, the brilliant Springbok eighthman who had to withdraw from the team shortly before the third test in Pretoria because of injury, seeks solace from a pondering Danie Craven on the touchline at Loftus Versfeld. It had just become clear to both Craven and Retief that the Lions were heading for victory.

Left: Agony of a different kind. Tony O'Reilly, one of the stars in the Lions team, gasps with pain as he is carried off the field after being injured in the final test in Port Elizabeth.

Below: The series is saved and an embattled Springbok captain can relax again. Stephen Fry, his wife Betty and his brother Dennis, an immaculate flyhalf, who was a member of the 1951/52 Springbok team.

from Stellenbosch. Injuries forced several changes in the Lions line-up and Cliff Morgan led the side when Robin Thompson also dropped out because of injury.

The Springboks played a slovenly game while the Lions, shrewdly guided by Morgan who kicked more often than he passed, made few mistakes and deserved their 9-6 victory. Fry's men were sluggish, for some reason or other, and the best example of this came midway in the the first half when Rosenberg, whose tackling was a highlight of the series, flattened Phil Davies. The ball rolled loose, creating a perfect opportunity for the South African loose forwards. Instead it was the ever-alert Butterfield who snapped it up and dropped a beautiful goal. Many people thought that Davies had actually passed the ball off the ground and that a penalty should have gone to the Springboks but it was not a match South Africa deserved to win anyway.

The Lions followed dull and effective tactics while the Springboks completely failed to find their feet. Butterfield also scored the only try of the match with Doug Baker adding a penalty. Dryburgh scored all of South Africa's points with two penalties, one of them a magnificent dropped goal.

Once again a torrent of abuse was directed at Craven and Fry with many of the poison pen letters now also acquiring political overtones; some apparently felt that there were too many "English-speaking" players in the team! Fry even received an anonymous letter threatening him with death should he be captain again for the decisive test in Port Elizabeth. There is an ugly face to sport when enthusiasm becomes fanaticism and too much of it was seen in the turbulent winter of 1955.

The selectors, quite rightly, refused to be stampeded and except for the return of Gentles and Retief, they did not do any tampering to the team. The Lions on the other hand made a fatal error by dropping the feared Phil Davies and compounding the error by switching O'Reilly from his usual position to the mid-field.

This time both teams were equally well motivated. The Lions had the unprecedented opportunity to win a series in South Africa for the first time since 1896, while the Springboks had to prove to a large section of their own people that they were worthy representatives of their country.

For most of the first half it looked as if the visitors simply had to win. They launched one attack after the other and only desperate defence and a fair amount of luck kept them out. Finally Greenwood did go over after a clever kick by Gareth Griffiths which Pedlow converted. But it was Pedlow's inability to judge the high ball properly, that enabled the Springboks to make it 5-3 at halftime. The ball was floating towards the Irish wing when Briers, so outstanding in this series, simply swept it from under his nose to beat Baker and score.

In the second half, with the Springbok forwards again gradually gaining the ascendancy, Ulyate tried the same kick once more and Briers made no mistake for his fifth try in four tests; a record on South African grounds. A break by Gentles, with Fry and Claassen in brilliant support, then gave Ulyate a try converted by Dryburgh and the Lions' hopes of making history were dashed. Van Vollenhoven was next to score after a short, sharp burst for the corner flag and a dropped goal from Ulyate made it 17-5.

There was a brief fight-back from the Lions and O'Reilly scored, but was so injured in the process that he had to leave the field. Then the Springbok forwards took complete command. Only desperate defence and the bounce of the ball kept the South Africans from scoring. With only a minute or so to go Daan Retief got his try under the crossbar after an interception by Van Vollenhoven and strong running from Ackermann. Dryburgh converted to make the final score 22-8. The South Africans scored a record 16 tries in the series while the Lions notched 10. The total of 26 is the highest number of tries to be scored in a series involving the Springboks.

And so ended one of the most exciting of all tours to South Africa. The Lions not only managed to draw the series, but they also earned the affection and respect of South Africans with their sportsmanship on and their friendliness off the field.

It is hardly surprising that several thousand South Africans turned up at the airport to say goodbye on the morning they left. The Lions responded in typical fashion by singing *Sarie Marais*, *Sospan Fach* and *Now is the hour* before they disappeared into the aircraft.

FALTERING CHAMPIONS

Destined for defeat

An unfortunate altercation between Salty du Rand (left) and Jan Pickard during the trials cost Du Rand the captaincy of the 1956 Springbok team and set off a chain reaction of decisions that affected the destiny of the touring side.

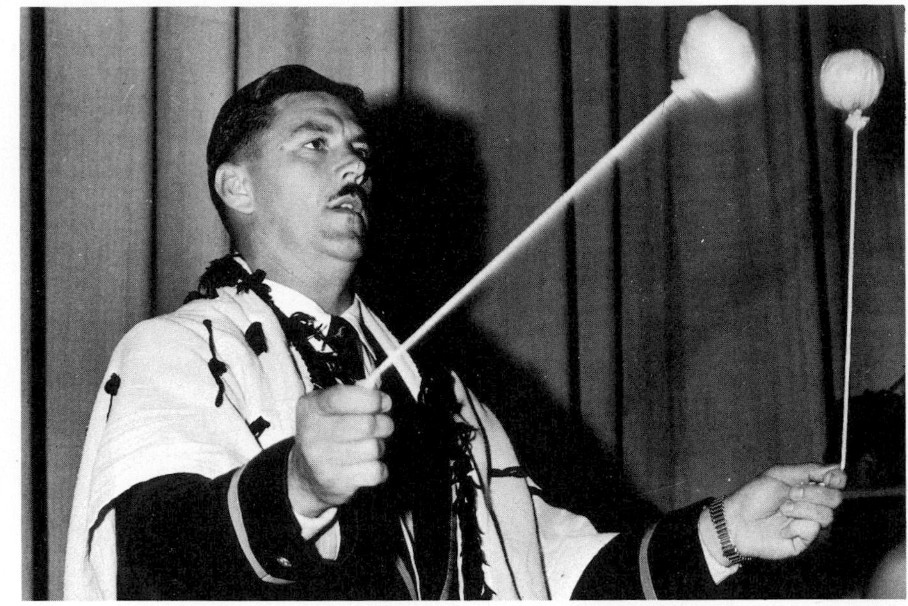

Basie Viviers, past his best, was appointed captain of the 1956 Springboks. Here Viviers, a man of great charm, demonstrates his prowess with the "pois" during a Maori ceremony at Rotorua. He is wearing a Maori cloak.

If 1949 was known to disgruntled New Zealanders as the year of Okey Geffin's boot then 1956 is remembered by many South Africans for the merciless efficiency with which Kevin Skinner used his fists.

Geffin's kicking and Skinner's punching have become part of rugby folklore and have obscured the many other factors that influenced the outcome of the two series.

New Zealand's pride was badly bruised by their four test defeats in South Africa in 1949 and like Cato, the single-minded Roman senator of more than 2 000 years ago who ended all his speeches with the demand that Carthage should be destroyed, their rugby administrators spent the next few years calling for the demolition of the Springboks to wipe out the disgrace.

It was to be nearly seven years before they got the opportunity and by that time the All Blacks were more than ready to take revenge for what Okey Geffin, Hennie Muller and, as many of them firmly believed, our referees, had done to Fred Allen and his Forty-niners.

All players with the remotest chance of wearing the black jersey were given special training schedules and diet charts and coaches went to great lengths to create a mental attitude which could best be described as one of relentless determination. In later years the New Zealand authorities were to admit this only with some understandable embarrassment, but back in 1956 the approaching test series against the Springboks was regarded as a holy war which simply had to be won. The general public was as worked up about the tour as the players were and there was certainly too much tension in the air for the atmosphere to be healthy.

The Springboks' problems began when Salty du Rand, in a rash moment, punched Jan Pickard on the nose in an hotel room altercation during the week of trials matches in Cape Town. His indiscretion eliminated Du Rand as the tour captain and scrambled the cards for the national selectors. Stefanus Sebastian (Basie) Viviers, an affable veteran with admirable qualities but certainly at that stage of his career no longer a player of international standard, was given the captaincy in what appeared to have been a compromise move.

Jack van der Schyff, whose powerful touchkicking would have been so valuable on the tour, was sacrificed to make place for Viviers and, with the wisdom of hindsight, several other selection blunders were committed.

Some critics afterwards thought that too many players in the team were "too soft" but, while it was true that there were a few who were rather frail, no-one in his right mind could describe Springboks like Du Rand, Jaap Bekker, Chris Koch, Harry Newton Walker, Daan Retief, Butch Lochner, Johan Claassen, Bertus van der Merwe or Jan Pickard as "softies". It just so happened that the 1956 Springboks ran into a bunch of All Blacks who were prepared to be killed rather than to be beaten. It was a state of mind not foreign to Springboks over the years either, but no matter how hard Dr. Danie Craven tried, he could not get his team up to quite the same level of motivation. By then he had been elected president of the South African Rugby Board but he was also manager of the side.

It was, incidentally, the first-ever Springbok touring team without at least one pair of brothers in it!

A rash of injuries which started with Basie van Wyk breaking his leg even before his first match on the Australian part of the tour, had a lot to do with the Springboks' failures.

For the first time a South African team had travelled by air and many thought that this was the reason for an epidemic of hamstring problems which bothered key players throughout the tour and caused two replacements, wing Theunis Briers and flanker James Starke, to be called for. The team also had its problems with refereeing decisions and the outspoken Craven got into hot water for commenting on this issue. It was the sort of thing all touring teams have to contend with, however, and, in retrospect, it is probably fair to say that the 1956 Springboks lost the series because they were playing inspired opponents in their own backyard.

The traditional visit to Australia was unhappy, although the Springboks were undefeated and won both tests. Bertus van der Merwe, who was to be one of the stars of the tour, had to hear the news that his little boy had died back in the Boland and not long afterwards Ian Kirkpatrick had to be told of the death of his father. Then Basie van Wyk broke his leg at a practice, an accident which ended the career of this marvellous player, and a long lineup of other Springboks suffered injuries of varying degrees of seriousness. The only real highlight of the Australian part of

The amazing Bekker family. Dolf, Martiens and Jaap played rugby for South Africa, sister Corrie was a Springbok athlete and Daan *(far right)* represented his country in the boxing ring.

Martin Gibbs, Pretoria

the tour was Roy Dryburgh's feat of scoring six tries against Queensland, still a Springbok record.

On their arrival in New Zealand the Springboks were stunned by the fanatical interest in the game and even more startled when Waikato clobbered them in a brawling match on a rain-soaked field. It was in this game that they made the acquaintance of massive Donald Barrie Clarke, whose booming boot notched eight of his side's 14 points and which even defied the strong wind which blew throughout the match. They were to see a lot more of Don Clarke, who as a fullback and placekicker was to play such a dominating role in world rugby for the next eight years.

The Springboks won all their other fixtures up to the first test in Dunedin where Ron Jarden, one of the best wings in rugby history, virtually beat South Africa on his own in an injury-plagued match. Jan du Preez and Dawie Ackermann failed to see out the game for the Springboks while New Zealand lost prop Mark Irwin. Clive Ulyate, at flyhalf for South Africa, kicked away almost every ball he received from his over-worked and depleted pack and Jeremy Nel, the big Matie centre whom the All Blacks

Above: Harry Newton Walker and his father Alf, who hold the distinction of being the first father and son to gain Springbok colours. Alf played for South Africa in 1921 and 1924 and Harry in 1953 and 1956.

Right: Roy Dryburgh in the act of scoring one of his record number of six tries against Queensland during the Australian part of the 1956 tour.

eyed uneasily throughout the tour, never had an opportunity to test the defence.

Roy Dryburgh, playing at fullback as both Viviers and Johnny Buchler were injured, scored a penalty for the Springboks and centre Bennett (Peewee) Howe a try, after brilliant work by Popeye Strydom and the veteran Paul Johnstone. The All Blacks' points came from a try by Tiny White, a gaunt but great forward, which Jarden converted and it was the balding wing who also swooped onto a pass between Ackermann and Johnstone and outstripped the cover defence with majestic grace to score under the posts to give himself an easy conversion.

In between the first and second tests the Springboks also lost to Canterbury and their prospects suddenly looked very bleak indeed. Nevertheless, they won the second test at Wellington in spite of going into the battle with Basie Viviers nursing an injury and with the arctic conditions all in favour of the home side.

The Springbok forwards, with Jan Pickard giving solidarity and weight at No. 8 and leaving Butch Lochner free to rattle the opposing backs with his crushing tackles, played magnificently. Chris Koch, Bertus van der Merwe, Piet du Toit and Jaap Bekker dominated the scrums, Johan Claassen earned praise as the finest lock forward ever to visit New Zealand and Salty du Rand, Pickard and Daan Retief kept it tight and hard. It was once again a bruising affair with Du Rand and Bekker looking like the victims of a road accident by the time the final whistle blew.

In fact, Bekker was so badly concussed that he had to spend 24 hours in hospital for observation. In the dressingroom after the match, he had no idea what he was doing and frequently had to be restrained as he lashed out blindly at well-wishers. Not only the forwards played it hard; Paul Johnstone, the South African wing, and his counterpart, Morrie Dixon, had several sharp arguments as well.

The Springboks' points came from tries by Retief (converted with a miraculous kick by Viviers) and Du Rand, while Ross Brown gave the All Blacks an unconverted try.

The South African victory rocked New Zealand rugby; the thought that the 1949 disasters might go unavenged after all, horrified them. They decided that the Springbok frontrankers, Bekker and Koch, would have to be tamed if the All Blacks were to win the series. The New Zealanders were convinced that Bekker and Koch, by using what they called "bullocking tactics, heaving, hacking and wrestling" were splitting the All Blacks' frontrow. They pointed to the fact that Mark Irwin had received severe chest injuries in the first test and that Frank McAtamney was lucky to come out of the second test relatively unscathed.

More pertinent was probably the knowledge that Bekker and Koch were giving the Springboks a very definite advantage with their strength and know-how and the New Zealand selectors were determined that something should be done about this. They decided to recall Kevin Lawrence Skinner, a 28-year-old veteran from the 1949 side, who had prematurely retired.

The trouble was that Skinner was also once the amateur heavyweight boxing champion of New Zealand and this gave an extra dimension to subsequent events in the controversial third test in Christchurch. South Africans are adamant to this day that Skinner came into the New Zealand frontrow basically to punch

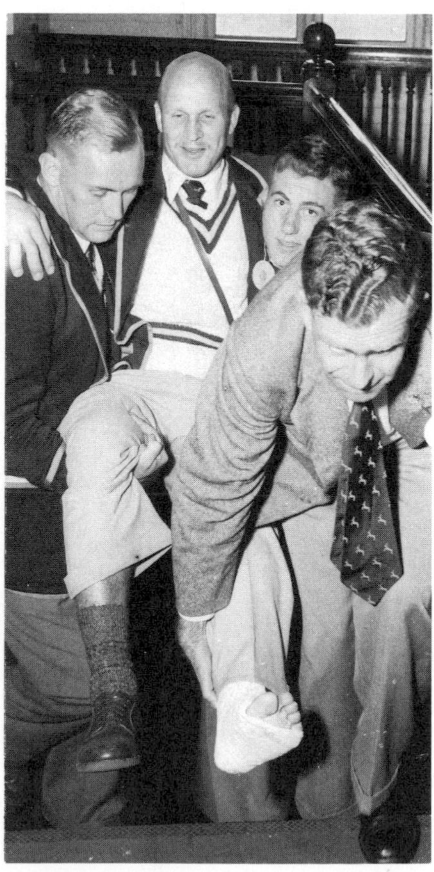

Basie van Wyk, the veteran Springbok flanker, broke a leg at a practice shortly after the team's arrival in Australia. Here he is being carried to his hotel room after leaving hospital.

first Koch and then Bekker into submission. As evidence they point to the fact that after Koch had been tamed, Skinner deliberately switched positions with Ian Clarke to "take care of Bekker". There is no doubt that both Springbok frontrankers were hit, and hit often, but, in all fairness, the punching was not confined between Skinner, Koch and Bekker. Boots and fists flew indiscriminately in the first half and the referee, Bill Fright, a former policeman, could do little more than issue warnings and penalties.

The game was appallingly savage and within the first eight minutes Don Clarke, playing in his first test, had scored six points from penalties, the first one given against Chris Koch, who had been hit in the first lineout for aiming a haymaker at Skinner. After 15 minutes the All Blacks led 11-0, when Morrie Dixon scored a try, with Clarke, who was actually successfully concealing a knee injury, converting. There was a lot of arguing about this kick afterwards as the Springboks were quite convinced that the ball had not gone over; a view supported by, among others, the well-known New Zealand sportswriter Terry McLean.

In the second half there was so much brawling that the referee spoke to Bob Duff, the All Blacks' captain, and Basie Viviers and ordered them to control their men. Things then settled down to a grim but fairly legitimate battle of attrition and for a few glorious moments it looked as if the Springboks would pull it off after all.

Tom van Vollenhoven picked up a fly-kick from Jarden, who proved to be human after all, and darted through, switching direction as suddenly as only he could, to throw off the cover defence. A well-timed pass to Butch Lochner left the All Blacks completely stranded and Viviers converted with a nicely-judged kick practically from touch. Only a few minutes later, Tommy Gentles broke brilliantly, passed to Ackermann, then on to Bekker and finally to Du Rand before the ball travelled to Wilf Rosenberg. The black-haired centre, hampered so often on the tour by injury, cut through to score after a spectacular dive for the line. Viviers again converted to bring the Springboks to within one point of their opponents' total.

It was then that Don Clarke showed that he was more, so much more, than just a goalkicking robot. His touch kicks swallowed large tracts of land from the Springboks and wore down the South African forwards. In the final few minutes the All Blacks were right on top and Jarden, after an amazing exhibition of agility, and then Tiny White, scored unconverted tries to give New Zealand a convincing 17-10 victory.

The Springboks were very upset afterwards. Koch and Bekker looked as if they had been in the boxing ring and there were dark threats that Skinner could expect retribution in the fourth test. Later, Bekker's delightful sense of humour returned and in his book *The Battle for the Rugby Crown*, McLean recounts how the bull-necked Northern Transvaler innocently asked someone whether Skinner intended going to the Olympic Games.

"No, he has long ago retired from boxing," came the answer. "Pity,"

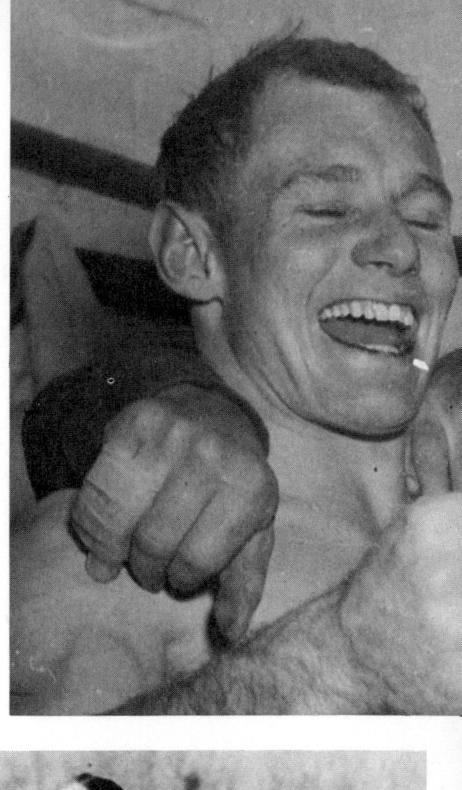

Right: A band of happy Springboks in the dressingroom after the victorious second test. *From the left:* Clive Ulyate, Basie Viviers, Daan Retief, Bertus van der Merwe and Butch Lochner. The crash-tackling Lochner did much to rattle the New Zealand backline throughout the series.

Die Huisgenoot

Below: Ron Jarden, the splendid All Black wing of the 1950's, caused the Springboks many headaches. Here he catches Paul Johnstone on the wrong foot and sets off in the curving, graceful style he was renowned for.

Die Huisgenoot

Right: Johan Claassen, who showed maturity far beyond his years, played some of the best rugby of his career in the grim tests against the All Blacks in 1956. Here he seems to take on the whole opposing pack.

Below: Kevin Skinner, outstanding New Zealand frontranker and, incidentally, a former heavyweight boxing champion, entered the arena after the second test. The Springboks suspected that he was selected with the specific purpose of "fixing" Chris Koch and Jaap Bekker.

Above: Jaap Bekker and Kevin Skinner being warned by the referee during the relentless third test. Controversy raged for years over the many ugly incidents which marred this match. New Zealand captain Bob Duff is on the right.

Left: Donald Barrie Clarke, one of the greatest matchwinners in modern rugby history, made his debut against the 1956 Springboks. His mighty boot gave opponents nightmares for years to come.

Right: Rugby the hard way. Jaap Bekker's face is swollen and covered in blood after one of the many vicious encounters on the 1956 tour.

Die Vaderland

replied Bekker drily. "He'd win his division."

It also became a team joke among the Springboks that boxing classes would be arranged as part of the practices with Brian Pfaff, who was a schoolboy champion at Hilton College, doing the coaching.

The final test, Eden Park, Auckland, was as bitterly fought as the epic third but except when New Zealand's Tiny White was severely injured by what some considered a deliberate kick in the back, was comparatively free of the type of extreme viciousness which marred the Lancaster Park battle. Both packs ploughed after the ball with a furious intensity and Peter Frederick Jones, a massive fisherman-farmer from North Auckland, played with such fierce dedication that he stood out even in such company. Don Clarke, once more, was the deciding factor with two long-range penalties and a conversion of a try by Jones, a remarkable individual effort in which he beat Viviers and then outpaced Jeremy Nel and Daan Retief.

The final few minutes of the match was packed with tension, and at one stage there was a brief but dangerous flare-up when White was injured and had to be helped off the field. Mr. Fright's stern warning to both teams again prevented further trouble.

It was too late to really matter, but the Springboks did get some consolation by scoring the last try of the 1956 series. Briers ran strongly and Starke nearly got to the ball after the Paarl wing had cleverly chipped ahead. The All Black centre Gray snapped up the loose ball, but he was tackled hard and Peewee Howe picked up and flipped infield to Dryburgh, on the right wing, who scored, Viviers converted to make the final score 11-5.

"It is all yours," Danie Craven told the cheering masses afterwards. And so it was. The All Blacks had avenged the defeats of 1949 and now it was the turn of the Springboks to lick their wounds and to scheme for the next encounter.

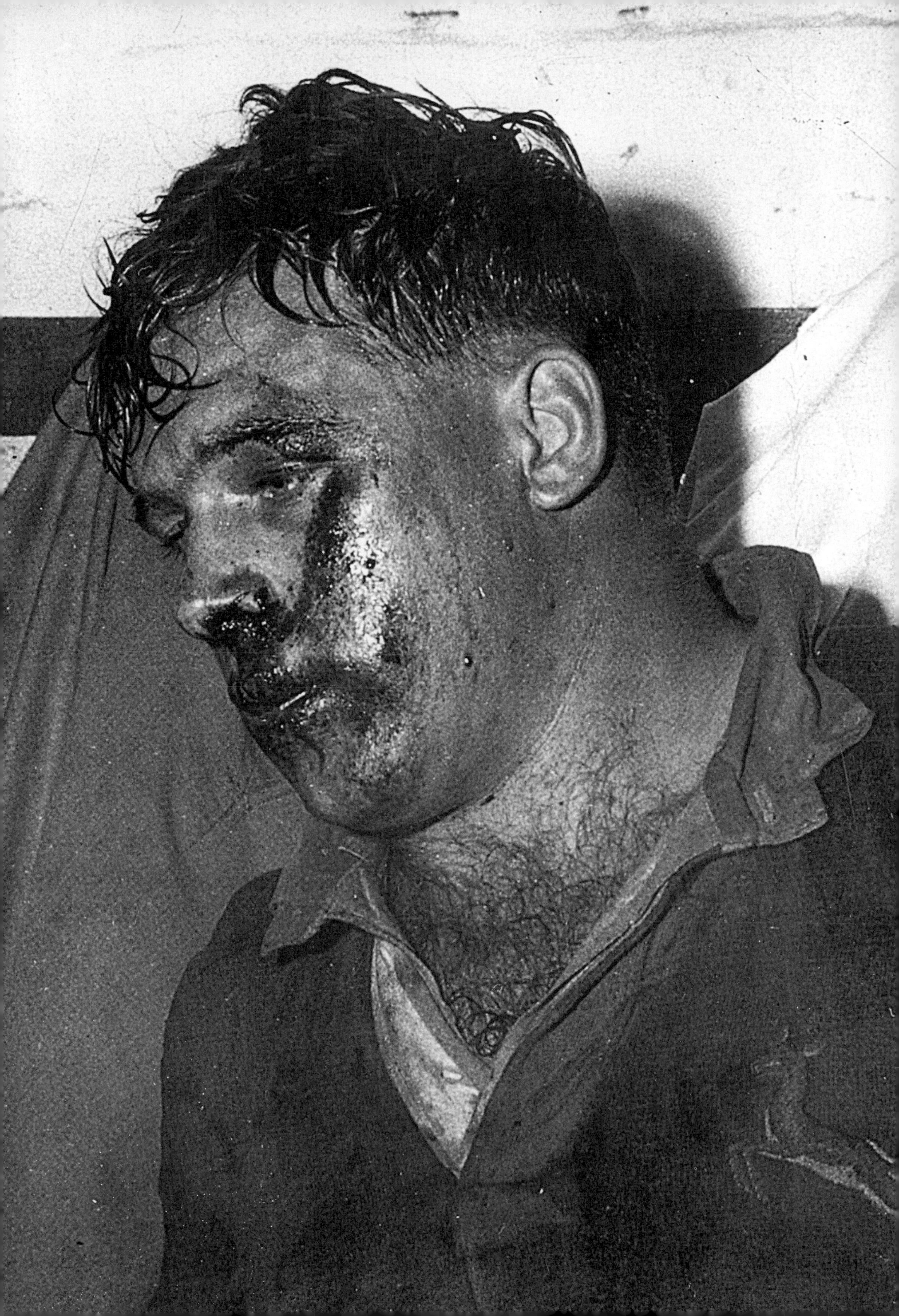

4/ THE TURBULENT YEARS

Australia 1961 – 1971

Below: Jannie Engelbrecht evades Beres Ellwood to score in the first test against the 1961 Wallabies at Ellis Park. It was a great day for the Springboks.

John Edward Thornett wore the Australian colours on 118 occasions and between water polo, surfing and the acquiring of several scientific and engineering degrees, he also squeezed in nearly 200 other matches which qualify for inclusion in the category of first-class rugby.

Only once in all those games did the blond Sydney forward pray to hear the final whistle and that was in the first of the two tests between the Wallabies and the Springboks, at Ellis Park, Johannesburg, in 1961.

This is how Thornett described what happened that afternoon in his book *"This World of Rugby":*

"We went into this match a little cockier than we should have been after a couple of good wins against provincial sides and we were absolutely overwhelmed. I have never had such a feeling of helplessness on a football field as when wave after wave of Springbok players poured through our defences. It was my first test as a frontranker and I remember that we were pushed back so fast in some scrums that even when we won the ball, Ken Catchpole had to dive to escape being trampled on by our own scrum which seemed to be almost running back.

"We had expected a dour struggle

Wallaby wing Mike Cleary gets hold of Springbok left-wing Hennie van Zyl during the second of the two-match series at Port Elizabeth in 1961. But it was a poor tackle and the lanky van Zyl jerked himself over the line to score. In the Ellis Park test Van Zyl notched three tries to join the select band of Springboks who have scored hat-tricks in a test.

Eastern Province Herald

against opponents who would play tight, safe football, but the landslide started 10 minutes after the start when one of the South Africans threw a long Fijian-style one-handed pass to a team-mate standing unmarked on the opposite side of the field. Our backs were non-plussed and the Springboks scored.

"From then on they scored try after try, with Keith Oxlee at five-eighth, the centres Mannetjies Roux and John Gainsford, and Jannie Engelbrecht and Hennie van Zyl on the wings, forming the most devastating attacking combination I have encountered.

"The Springboks' forward power and the altitude of Johannesburg soon absorbed all our energy. All we could do was to try and keep down the scoring against us; but whatever we attempted seemed to end with the Springboks breaking through again. The scrums were like South African charges and near the end, with my shoulder red raw from the pounding my opposite number had given me, I kept telling myself there couldn't be many more scrums. But in the last minute or two there must have been six. I had a tremendous feeling of relief as the whistle went to end the game because it meant South Africa couldn't score any more — the only time I have ever felt quite like that. They scored eight tries that day, a remarkable feat in a test."

Thornett and his fellow-Wallabies on that short two-test tour of 1961 were unfortunate enough to meet a Springbok team, the nucleus of which had been forged in a full year of continuous international competition, including a series against the All Blacks and a tour of the United Kingdom and France. Just about every Springbok who played against Catchpole's team was not only superlatively fit and confident, but with the added advantage of being test-hardened in spite of comparative youth. In 1961, at least, the Springboks had as much right to call themselves the world champions as their illustrious predecessors of the late 1930's and the early 1950's.

The Springboks established a record for a home test by scoring eight tries, of which only two were converted, and Hennie van Zyl joined the select band of Boetie McHardy, Jan Stegmann and Karel van Vollenhoven by accomplishing a hat-trick. The South Africans gave an exhilarating performance of sound but uninhibited rugby and the Wallabies could scrape up only a solitary penalty in reply. Even during the brief spell when Keith Oxlee, who had been superb at flyhalf, had to go off the field to have a head-wound attended to, the splendid machine never spluttered as Mannetjies Roux substituted with aplomb.

The Springboks were not nearly as efficient — or as motivated — for the second test in Port Elizabeth and they could only total three tries in their 23-11 victory. It would have been miraculous had they been able to maintain the standard they had set at Ellis Park; it was a peak of perfection seldom reached.

Thornett led the next Australian team to visit South Africa and his 1963 Wallabies became the first touring team to beat the Springboks in two consecutive tests since 1896.

His was an Australian team with a difference. Gone was the unpredictability, and the flair which used to impress us so much that we always wanted to follow suit and frequently came to grief as a result. In its place was a new approach; the 1963 Wallabies rarely took risks, their backs were defenders first and foremost and unless they received the ball quickly and cleanly they did not attempt to attack.

Sturdy and intelligent forwards and

Above: Tiny Naude, a fine lock forward whose mighty boot helped his team so often, made his international debut against the 1963 Wallabies.

The Cape Times

Left: John Thornett, likeable captain of the 1963 Wallabies, meets the then State President, The Hon. C. R. Swart.

Right: Ken Catchpole, a brilliant scrumhalf, gets his line moving as Doug Hopwood pops up from behind the Springbok scrum and Lofty Nel prepares to give chase.

a brilliant scrumhalf in Ken Catchpole were the pillars on which the team was built.

Kenneth William Catchpole was then 24 years old and on his performances on the 1963 tour, particularly in the second and third tests (he missed the first because of a hand injury), he must be ranked among the best scrumhalves of all time. He had both the physical and mental agility demanded by his position and his judgment rarely failed him. "Catchy", as his teammates called him, gave his flyhalf an impeccable service, he could break or kick when the situation called for it and on the defence he was simply wonderful. His nursing made the talented 19-year-old Phil Hawthorne a top-class international flyhalf overnight and it was obvious that whenever Hawthorne was partnered by Kenneth ("Nipper") McMullen, he was often exposed as still having a lot to learn. In the tests, with Catchpole behind the scrum, Hawthorne hardly ever made a mistake, however, and his two dropgoals in the tests were lovely efforts.

The Australian forwards were well-drilled by coach Alan Roper, a man who knew and appreciated the value of a solid scrum but whose policy of "take no risks, make no mistakes" was criticised by some members of the touring party.

Apart from the amazing Catchpole, the stars of the side were the trio of loose forwards, Greg Davis, Jules Guerassimoff and John O'Gorman.

Gregory Victor Davis, balding at the age of 23, was actually a New Zealander who had played in All Blacks trials as a centre before settling in Sydney. He had a Kiwi attitude to the game and never allowed himself to be pushed around. His quick raids from the side of the scrum and powerful tackling caused the Springboks a lot of headaches and in the second test at Newlands, in particular, he gave Keith Oxlee a torrid time. The Springbok flyhalf was, in fact, dropped for the third test, a mistake the selectors rectified by restoring him to the fourth test team.

Guerassimoff, of White Russian descent and known as "Julie", was the Boland Coetzee type of flanker. He played it tight and hard and though not nearly as spectacular as Davis, did an enormous amount of work. O'Gorman, the other member of the trio, was somewhat similar in style, a defensive eighthman who covered well and always seemed to be on the spot to either smother an attack or to help a teammate who had run into trouble.

Stewart Boyce was the most accomplished wing threequarter in the side although he lacked the pace of his partner John Williams, who as a sprinter had been considered for the Australian track team to the 1962 Commonwealth Games. Ian Moutray and Beres Ellwood were fair centres. Moutray, a deeply religious young man, often addressed church associations. He was a tackler in the Ryk van Schoor mould. In the match against Northern Transvaal he brought down the mighty Frik du Preez with such force that the Springbok lock tore the ligaments in his foot and could play in only one of the tests in the series. Moutray's problem was that he lacked the other skills and he only played in the second test.

John Thornett whose exceptionally attractive appearance and unfailing courtesy charmed the South African rugby public, was a strong leader of a most well-behaved party and although the standard of play from both sides was seldom memorable, it was a pleasant tour unmarred by squabbles, squeals and deliberate fouling.

The South African selectors did more than their usual share of chopping and changing in the series. It was almost a game of musical chairs as outstanding players were often dropped only to be brought back again. Abie Malan, who had led the Springboks in the first two tests, was axed for the third, Avril Malan taking over. When the Springboks lost this test, Abie Malan was reinstated for the final test. Such uncertainty about the all-important captaincy was not the sort of thing to promote confidence in the Springbok camp.

The Springboks nevertheless won the first test in Pretoria 14-3, a match which marked the international debut of Tommy Bedford, Gert Cilliers, Trix Truter, substituting for the injured Engelbrecht, and the veteran frontranker Dick Putter. Cilliers and Bedford (on the flank) celebrated their debut with a try each.

A groin injury kept Cilliers out of the second test at Newlands and

Engelbrecht was brought back while Stompie van der Merwe came in for the injured Frik du Preez. Mannetjies Roux replaced Truter and Wang Wyness took over from Dave Stewart who had played well at Loftus Versfeld.

The Springboks were given a penalty try in the seventh minute of the match after Engelbrecht had sprinted nearly the length of the field before chipping the ball over the Australian goal-line. Bedford, following up, was held without the ball by Ellwood and the referee, Toy Myburgh, awarded the first and still the only penalty try ever to be given in a test in South Africa. A series of injuries, with scrumhalf Piet Uys' dislocated shoulder the most serious, undoubtedly disrupted the Springbok rhythm, but the Wallabies nevertheless looked the better side on the day. Catchpole and Davis were magnificent and O'Gorman, Guerassimoff, Rob Heming and Thornett played their hearts out to score a well-deserved 9-5 victory. Catchpole's tactical kicking in the final 10 minutes, when he kept the Springboks on their heels, was perfect.

Abie Malan, Doug Hopwood, Keith Oxlee, Mannetjies Roux, Piet Uys (injured), Wang Wyness, Lofty Nel and Dick Putter were all dropped for the third test at Ellis Park. Ronnie Hill, Dave Stewart and Gert Cilliers were recalled and Norman Riley, at flyhalf, Nelie Smith, scrumhalf, Hannes Marais, tight-head prop, Johan (Haas) Schoeman, flank, and Josua (Poens) Prinsloo, eighthman, were given colours for the first time.

Avril Malan decided on keeping the game as tight as possible, hoping that the Springboks would gain control up front. The plan failed because

Above: Piet Visagie, the Springbok flyhalf who dominated the undistinguished 1969 series against the Wallabies by scoring a record 43 points.

The Natal Mercury

Right: Demonstrators often interrupted the Springbok matches in Australia in 1971. Here the players watch as one finds himself confronted by a mounted policeman.

the Australian forwards actually had the better of things throughout and Catchpole again had a field day. His work on the defence was particularly good and he so inspired his team-mates that the South Africans failed to get even one try, all nine points coming from penalties by Nelie Smith. Terry Casey, the quiet-spoken Australian full-back, put over a dropped goal, a penalty and he also converted Williams' try to give his team a winning margin of two points.

With Smith and Riley committed to kicking, the Springboks threequarters were rarely asked to do anything else except chase and defend. The spontaneous way in which the Springboks afterwards gathered in their opponents' dressingroom to congratulate them was, frankly, about the only thing they did right all afternoon.

With South Africa in danger of losing the series the selectors dropped no less than seven players for the final test. Avril Malan, Hill, Marais, Prinsloo and Fanie Kuhn (after wearing the Springbok jersey with distinction in 17 consecutive tests), Jannie Engelbrecht and Norman Riley were all axed. Oxlee, Hopwood, Abie Malan (back as captain), Putter, Mof Myburgh, Tiny Naude and Corra Dirksen were the replacements. Naude, a mobile lock forward who had provided one of the highlights of the tour with a huge 69-yard penalty goal for Western Province against the visitors, and Dirksen, a powerful Northern Transvaal wing who only the previous season was a lowly-regarded club centre, were the new "caps".

The day before the test in Port Elizabeth, Australian manager Bill McLaughlin was heard to remark to rugby writer A. C. Parker, that "the coves are as sharp as they've ever been", but he obviously did not realise exactly how keyed-up his opponents were.

Abie Malan very sensibly decided not to repeat the Ellis Park mistake of trying to play 10-man rugby. He and Hennie Muller, whom he had asked to help him with the coaching, stressed to the team that they must not allow themselves to be too inhibited. Malan's relaxed confidence had the desired effect and the Springboks generally played their best rugby of the series.

With only eight minutes of the match to go, the score was still 6-all, but then a penalty by Oxlee nosed the Springboks into the lead and the Wallabies seemed to panic. Malan, Naude and Gainsford added tries in quick succession. Rather against the run of play, the Springboks eventually won 22-6 to share the series. Oxlee scored 10 points with two penalty goals and two conversions and Naude, whose booming boot was to play such a dramatic part in several tests to come, also added a penalty.

Greg Davis brought out the next Wallabies team to South Africa in 1969 and this time the Springboks won all four tests and the visitors altogether lost 11 out of 26 matches. It was, in all conscience, the dullest series probably ever to be played in this country.

"They came as middleweights to take on the heavyweights", Maxwell Price wrote in *"Wallabies Without Armour"*, his book on the tour. "They could not shove and batter through in the manner of the robust Springboks; they had no iron front, they lacked the reinforced steel and concrete of rugby where they needed it most. They sorely needed the heavy guns up front to pave the way for the excellent talent behind. . . ."

It was an accurate summing-up of the tour. The Springboks had simply too much all-round strength and with flyhalf Piet Visagie scoring a record total of 43 points in the series, the South Africans were never in any danger. Not only did the Wallabies lack the forward power they had in 1963 or, for that matter, when the Springboks met them on their own grounds in 1965, but they also did not have the services of a strategist of the calibre of Ken Catchpole. Johnny Hipwell, their No. 1 scrum-half, was a good player indeed, but he did not have the incisiveness of his predecessor and he certainly was also handicapped by the fact that he seldom had the kind of protective screen from behind which Catchpole could cook up his schemes.

The 1969 tour did produce some highlights of course. The now fully matured Piet Visagie's marvellous kicking in the tests, for instance, and Rupert Rosenbloom's feat of scoring 11 dropped goals in 14 matches, a record that will take some beating. Altogether the Wallabies totalled 16 dropgoals in their 26 matches, more than any previous touring team.

Visagie, Mannetjies Roux, Syd Nomis, Jan Ellis, Jannie Engelbrecht, and Eben Olivier each scored two tries in the series and it was rather fitting that Engelbrecht, a wing whose likes we have not seen since his retirement, ended his career by scoring twice in the second international in Durban, the final test of his career. He scored eight tries in his 33 tests, a South African record he shares with John Gainsford who had played in the same number of tests.

A nagging groin injury had handicapped him so much that the selectors had no option but to drop him in favour of his young fellow-Matie, Gert Muller, for the third test at Newlands.

Frik du Preez was another giant dropped after the second test, but he soon proved the selectors wrong and he carried on for another four international series before he himself decided that he had had enough.

With Dawie de Villiers able to play in only two of the tests, Tommy Bedford substituted capably on the other two occasions and the Wallabies had no counter to the loose forward combination of Jan Ellis, Piet Greyling and Bedford or the solidity of Mof Myburgh, Gys Pitzer and Hannes Marais in the frontrow. With Visagie outstanding at flyhalf Eben Olivier and Mannetjies Roux were steady centres and Muller and Nomis always looked better than their opponents. H. O. de Villiers, at fullback, was invariably in total control of the situation, but for some inexplicable reason his flair for surprise attack was never exploited.

The Springboks played conventional rugby in the first three tests, with a slightly more adventurous approach in the fourth. They won 30-11, 16-9, 11-3 and 19-8, scoring 13 tries to two and 76 points to 31. It could hardly have been a more convincing triumph but the opposition was too dull and the Springboks too conservative for the public imagination to be gripped.

In 1971 a Springbok team boarded a Boeing 707 to tour Australia; for the first time the Wallabies would not just be fitted in during a stop-over on the way to the real thing in New Zealand. The 13-match itinerary provided for three tests and there was no doubt that Hannes Marais was given the best available team.

Political demonstrators, backed by the Australian trade unions, made almost as much noise as they did on the 1969/70 tour of the United Kingdom, but a rather tougher reaction from the police prevented them from being as effective as a destructive force. The Springboks, many of whom were veterans of the campaign in Britain, learnt quickly enough to accept the situation with wry amusement and the demonstrations hardly affected them on the field.

For the first time in history a Springbok team completed an overseas tour without a single defeat. They scored 76 tries, 42 conversions, 24 penalties and four dropped goals for a total of 396 points in 13 matches, which included the three tests. Their opponents totalled 102 points in reply with the Springbok goal-line crossed on only eleven occasions.

Hannes Marais, with his powerful but friendly personality and infectious smile, kept the morale of his team at a high level and Johan Claassen and Flappie Lochner, the coach and manager respectively, fitted well into the picture. Tommy Bedford and Gert Muller returned home after being injured early on the tour, but in both positions the reserve strength was more than just adequate.

Hannes Viljoen, the Natal wing, notched five tries against Western Australia and he ended up with a tour total of 16 in 10 matches. Ian McCallum, Piet Visagie and the extremely talented young Dawie Snyman scored 84, 55 and 54 points respectively.

The Springboks played attractive rugby, but without undue frills. Attacks were launched from solid foundations, but there was plenty of opportunity and encouragement for individualism. One of the six tries scored against New South Wales, virtually an international combination, illustrates best how Marais and his men managed to blend the correct with the bright.

This is how the sports commentator and TV personality Kim Shippey described it in his book *"The Unbeatables"*:

"Ian McCallum started it within his own 25, reaching out to retrieve an impossible ball as it floated towards the Members' Stand.

"He got it, cleverly kept his balance, and then, instead of belting the ball down the touchline, he opened up across field to his left. Hannes Viljoen took over and further unsettled an already shaken defence.

"Then Hannes Marais came inside Viljoen to take a pass to the right. The Springbok captain showed a turn of speed we didn't know he possessed. It was as though he had a smoke bomb in his pocket. Now the forwards were in command. They swept infield with Marais shovelling the ball into the hands of Piet Greyling.

"In support of him was the long-striding newcomer, Morne du Plessis. No-one doubted for a moment that he would hold the pass. He took it with outstretched arms 15 yards from the line and dived for the far left corner.

"At the celebration dinner at the Squire Inn that evening Charles Blunt (president of the Australian Rugby Union) described it as the greatest try he had ever seen. 'What's more', he said, 'it was the most complete exhibition of rugby football I have ever experienced' ".

With the exception that Theo (Sakkie) Sauermann was replaced in the frontrow by Martiens Louw after the first test, South Africa kept the same combination for the series. They were: Ian McCallum; Hannes Viljoen, Joggie Jansen, Peter Cronje, Syd Nomis, Piet Visagie, Joggie Viljoen; Martiens Louw, Piston van Wyk, Hannes Marais (capt.), Piet Greyling, Frik du Preez, John Williams, Jan Ellis and Morne du Plessis. There were strong challengers for several of the positions of course, with Thys Lourens rather unlucky not to have been preferred to Piet Greyling.

The Springboks won the first test 19-11 with tries by the two Viljoens and Ellis, two conversions and a penalty by Ian McCallum and a dropped goal by Visagie. The second test was taken 14-6 with Visagie going over for two tries and Hannes Viljoen one. McCallum succeeded with a conversion and a penalty. Cronje, Visagie and Ellis scored tries, all three converted by Visagie who also put over a penalty, to give the Springboks an 18-6 victory over Australia in the final test.

Frik du Preez, that living legend of South African rugby, had announced before the last test in Sydney that he intended retiring from the game and Marais, with typical thoughtfulness,

Frik du Preez makes a typical bullocking run in the last test of the 1971 series in Australia. This magnificent player announced his retirement immediately after the match. On Du Preez's left is Hannes Viljoen, the Natal wing who scored 16 tries on the tour. Piet Greyling is on the far left of the picture.

Gert Hattingh, Die Transvaler

asked him to lead the Springboks onto the field for the game.

Afterwards at a team function to celebrate the successful end to the tour, Flappie Lochner, Johan Claassen and Hannes Marais made moving speeches and then everybody turned to Frik du Preez. But after 38 tests and six overseas tours during which he earned almost as big a reputation for his ready wit as his amazing ability, the old veteran could find nothing to say. He leant against a wall, turning a beer can slowly between his fingers as his teammates waited in silence. And as Kim Shippey wrote:

"In silence they showed their respect for him, and in silence he acknowledged their adulation. It was the most eloquent non-speech I've ever heard. . . ."

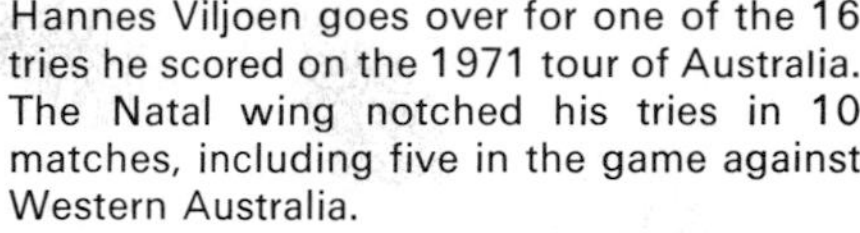

Hannes Viljoen goes over for one of the 16 tries he scored on the 1971 tour of Australia. The Natal wing notched his tries in 10 matches, including five in the game against Western Australia.

Die Huisgenoot

Above: Hannes Marais gives the thumbs-up signal at the end of the 1971 series. As the first captain to lead a Springbok team on an undefeated tour overseas the burly front-ranker had every right to smile.

Right: A great player leaves the international scene and a new star rises to prominence. Frik du Preez, as casual as ever, stretches his legs during the stop-over at Mauritius on the return journey from Australia to South Africa. In the background is Morné du Plessis, a young player whose success on his first tour stamped him as a great Springbok of the future.

Gert Hattingh, Die Transvaler

ELCOME TO MAURI

THE TURBULENT

Britain 1960 – 1970

EARS

The rain is a grey curtain in front of you; a gale drives particles of ice like a thousand constant pin-pricks into your face. Cardiff is wet, indescribably wet, and cold, bitterly cold, on the morning of December 3, 1960.

In a few hours Avril Malan and his Springboks are due to meet Wales on Cardiff Arms Park and you look at the field, lying there like a soaked green blanket with the chocolate-coloured water of the River Taff lapping at the edges, and you wonder whether it will be necessary for the South Africans to leave the cosy lounges of the Seabank Hotel in Porthcawl about 30 miles away. A test match can surely not be played under such conditions.

But your Welsh companions laugh at your gloomy predictions; to live with the unchained elements has been their heritage for many centuries. It is with relish that the older ones tell you about great battles fought on that same field under similar, if not worse conditions.

Later, from the comparative comfort of a seat in the press box you marvel at the fact that there are 53 000 people, with only a little more than one-fifth of them under cover, packed around the ground. A brass band is playing and they are singing, even as the wind lashes at them and rain streams down from the sulky sky. A beautiful voice seems to be God's gift to those who came from the scarred valleys of Wales; no other nation can sing as stirringly, as spontaneously, as the Welsh and they do it best when they are massed together to support their red-jerseyed rugby team. They do not just sing *"Land of my Fathers"*; their emotions lift it to the level of a prayer and you, the outsider, are left with something special to remember for the rest of your life.

The two teams, the Springboks still wearing their green tracksuits for last-minute protection against the weather, are on the field for the anthems. The members of the band do their honest best with "*Die Stem van Suid-Afrika*" and "*God Save the Queen*" but after the first few strains you hardly hear them again as the huge crowd take over their anthem, affirming their claim to a special identity.

The next 80 minutes were to prove the greatness of Avril Malan's 1960/61 Springbok team in Britain because more than just speed, strength and skill were needed to win on a day like that. The deciding factor was an uncompromising refusal to be beaten.

By the time the game was under way for five minutes, the ground could hardly be seen. There was water wherever you looked with two brave packs of mud-covered forwards straining and heaving to gain a few inches at a time, the steam rising from their struggling bodies.

Wales had won the toss and Terry Davies had decided to give the Springboks the advantage of playing with the wind in the first half. There was a big controversy over this in Welsh rugby circles afterwards but Avril Malan would almost certainly have made the same decision; this was one time where there was no doubt that the weather was likely to get worse rather than better during the match. The Springboks adopted the obvious tactics and Wales were often driven into desperate situations with the wind carrying any kind of kick deep into their territory and, too often, into the dead-ball area.

The ball quickly became shapeless and slippery and handling was impossible. Placekicking was even more difficult and the Springboks missed several opportunities as Jock Taylor, a schoolteacher from Scotland and the referee, spotted irregularities committed by the Welshmen as they kept the South Africans at bay. Hopwood, Jannie Engelbrecht, Mannetjies Roux and Ian Kirkpatrick in turn, came close to scoring after somehow managing to control the cake of black soap masquerading as a ball. For a long time it did not look however as if the Springboks would be able to establish a lead to draw on when it would be their turn to play into the teeth of the wind.

But, in the 21st minute, the Welsh scrumhalf O'Connor infringed at a scrum practically in front of his posts and Avril Malan handed the ball to Keith Oxlee. The Natal flyhalf, who was so outstanding against Wilson Whineray's All Blacks a few months earlier, had not yet gained the international renown as a placekicker he was later to enjoy and the few shivering Springbok supporters hardly dared to hope that the kick would succeed.

Oxlee, his dark hair plastered over his forehead, slammed his right boot into the soggy ball and lifted it high enough for the wind to send it tumbling over the crossbar for the first successful kick of his test career. Of all the many kicks from which this shrewd tactician and undoubted matchwinner was to score points for South Africa in the next few years, it was probably the least graceful, but certainly one of the most valuable.

Only three points up at half-time and with Johan Claassen handicapped by a painful ankle injury, the Springboks faced the grim prospect of playing against the elements as well as the inspired Welshmen in the second half.

The first 15 minutes after the resumption Wales, past masters of the art of rugby in the rain, laid siege to the Springbok line. Making expert use of the whipping wind with kicks of every description, they had the South Africans reeling and it seemed only a matter of time before the slender lead would be overtaken.

Then, suddenly and almost miraculously, the Springbok forwards pulled themselves together; really a wonderful tribute to the leadership qualities of young Avril Stefan Malan. From Fanie Kuhn, Ronnie Hill and Piet du Toit in the frontrow, to Doug Hopwood at eighthman, the pack seemed to realise that it was entirely up to them to win the test.

Whenever Hill heeled, Hopwood would either pick up himself or take the ball from that brave scrumhalf Piet Uys, playing in his first test. The seven other forwards would immediately rally around Hopwood as he bullocked ahead, making as much ground as possible. Possession was vital and yet to have used it in the normal way would have been to tempt fate. To have kicked would have been useless; the wind would simply have blown the ball towards their own tryline. The only answer was to keep the ball among the forwards or under control on the ground, where it would skid crazily over the puddles as the players slid and slithered in pursuit. All 16 forwards were covered in mud; it was in their hair, eyes, ears and nostrils and frequently Mr. Taylor had to call a halt so that the players could have their eyes attended to.

Preceding pages: Two brave packs slogged it out in the mud of Cardiff Arms Park when the Springboks beat Wales 3–0 on December 3, 1960. Here the referee's whistle has stopped a maul as Piet du Toit and Hugo van Zyl of South Africa and Danny Harris and Roddy Evans, of Wales, look on. The strain of the grim battle can be read in their expressions.
The Cape Times

The backs on both sides were drenched and bedraggled; for once they were playing in the supporting role only. It was so cold that some of them had to hammer their thighs with their fists to keep the circulation going. Once Mannetjies Roux, that impetuous little fighter, climbed into a loose scrum just to get a little action and whenever there was an interruption in play, some of the backs would scurry towards the forwards to use their bigger teammates as temporary protection against the cold. Lionel Wilson, who was as superb as always when the chips were down, once found that he was too frozen to get his arms into position to catch the ball and he had to allow it to bump off his chest into touch. But through it all, the Welsh crowd continued to sing and to encourage their team.

Doug Hopwood endured terrific punishment but in the process he made it possible for the Springboks to win. Time and again he took the ball from the scrum and then drove into the Welsh pack, keeping possession, gaining ground and leaving no room for error. He was the centre of the whirling mass of mud-smeared, steaming bodies and it was hardly surprising that the spinal weakness which had plagued him since he had lifted a heavy weight as a teenager, began to give him severe pain in the last few minutes and was to force him into a hospital bed for several weeks after the match. At one stage Mr. Taylor, noticing that the touch-lines and goal-lines had disappeared under water, had asked Terry Davies whether he was prepared to abandon the game. Davies, who by then must have known that his forwards were in a vice-grip they could never have shaken off, nevertheless refused, and the relentless battle ran its full course. It was a triumph for the Springbok forwards but the 3-0 victory proved something even more important. It showed that Avril Malan's often-maligned 1960/61 touring team to the United Kingdom and France had character and courage in the true tradition of Springbok rugby.

Generally speaking, they were not a popular team. The British public and press criticised them frequently for playing stodgy, unattractive rugby and even for not being particularly friendly off the field.

The side had the misfortune of striking one of the worst British winters in living memory and often conditions simply did not allow sweeping threequarter attacks, especially since so many of the opponents encountered, relied heavily on spoiling tactics. With an abundance of forward talent available, the tour management consisting of Avril Malan, Dick Lockyear, Ferdie Bergh and Boy Louw, consequently preferred building their pattern around the pack and the threequarters were, in the conventional sense, forced to play second fiddle.

Doug Hopwood played the best rugby of his great career on the tour and Hugo van Zyl and Martin Pelser were nearly up to his standard. Fanie Kuhn, Piet (Spiere) du Toit, Ronnie Hill, Abie Malan, Mof Myburgh, Frik du Preez, Avril Malan, Johan Claassen, Stompie van der Merwe, to name only a few, were brilliant players then either at the height of their powers, or just beginning to approach it. Among the backs, scrumhalf Dick Lockyear was past his best and his placekicking rather disappointing but he had an outstanding deputy in Piet Uys. Keith Oxlee, Dave Stewart, Ian Kirkpatrick, John Gainsford, Mannetjies Roux, Jannie Engelbrecht, Michel Antelme, Hennie van Zyl and Lionel Wilson were invariably steady and often brilliant. Bennie van Niekerk, Giepie Wentzel and Charlie Nimb were too injury-ridden to hit their best form and with forward Doug Holton unable to complete the tour, Bobby Johns and Ben-Piet van Zyl were

Cardiff Arms Park is completely flooded only a few hours after the end of the 1960 test against Wales.

Overleaf: Avril Malan, captain of the 1960/61 touring team to Britain and France and one of the dominating rugby personalities of his time.

Doug Hopwood

Martin Pelser

Lionel Wilson

Johan Claassen

sent over as late replacements. Except at the end of the tour, injuries and illness did not seriously hamper the team however, and, like Bennie Osler and his team of 30 years before, it was a case of the side deciding on the recipe which suited them best and then sticking to it, regardless of criticism.

No-one can deny that their playing pattern was successful. Malan and his men stayed undefeated until the very last match of the tour of Britain. Even then, had they been at full strength it is virtually certain that they would have beaten an out-of-character Barbarians team who, for the occasion it seemed, approached the game as if it was a test match. The Springboks' record of one defeat and two draws in 34 matches over nearly four months in Britain and France, is ample testimony of their ability.

The test against Wales was the highlight of the tour in spite of the fact that it was hardly spectacular and had drama rather than thrills. The match against England was the most disappointing; dull, lacking in spirit generally and played in a rather unpleasant atmosphere. Vivian Jenkins, the 1938 Lions fullback, picturesquely, but accurately described it as "about as exciting as a couple of hippopotami sawing logs, and not as novel...."

Both teams seemed committed to the same monotonous kicking tactics and neither looked prepared to risk anything. Hopwood won the match for the Springboks with a typically clever try, two minutes before half-time, when he received from Claassen after a wheeled scrum, dummied, and then broke inside to catch the England defence in a hopeless tangle. Frik du Preez, playing in his first test on the flank in the place of the injured Pelser, converted with a magnificent kick.

The noisy jeering of a section of the crowd at Twickenham made this the least memorable match of the tour. Once, when Du Preez was taking a placekick, he was given a slow handclap that visibly unnerved him and the London *Times* afterwards called it "worse than a lack of sportsmanship; it is rank bad manners".

It was a mild forerunner of the smoke bombs, slogans and worse the Springboks of nearly a decade later were to contend with.

The game against Scotland at Murrayfield was by far the best of the series as a spectacle and also for the type of rugby played. It marked Johan Claassen's 20th test appearance and he suitably celebrated the occasion with his first try in an international match. The Springboks other points in a 12-5 victory came from yet another try by Hopwood, who throughout the tour had the talent scouts for the professional clubs rushing about waving cheque books, and two penalties by Du Preez, whose remarkable natural talents were already obvious.

Ronnie Dawson's inspired Irish team put up the most exciting battle of the series in the test at Lansdowne Road, Dublin, with the Springboks winning after a push-over try by Hugo van Zyl in injury time. The South Africans made this a tough one for themselves, with the backs missing several scoring opportunities. Eventually, after lying level throughout the match with a try by Gainsford against a penalty by Tom Kiernan, the Springbok pack, from a five-yard scrum, put all their weight, muscle, sinew and will-to-win into one irresistible shove that pushed the Irish forwards well over their tryline. All the hard-working Paarl flanker had to do was to fall on the ball. Lockyear, no longer anywhere near the scrumhalf or the placekicker he was against the All Blacks only about six months earlier, managed to convert the try, with the ball glancing off the upright and over the crossbar.

Doug Hopwood, who played the best rugby of his great career on the 1960/61 tour picks himself up after scoring his match-winning try in the test against England. Piet Uys and Hennie van Zyl are on standby.

The tour was generally free of blatant rough play with the exception of the match against Cardiff, and the first few minutes of the test against France.

The smaller and lighter Cardiff pack made a cardinal error when they tried to intimidate the Springboks and the retribution was swift and more than they or their supporters had bargained for.

Piet du Toit had teeth marks to show afterwards while Johan Claassen had scratches around his eyes which could only have been caused deliberately. Hopwood, a clean player if ever there was one, was hit in the opening minute of the match by Dai Hayward, a black-haired vacuum cleaner salesman who had the good grace to apologise afterwards. The Springboks retaliated furiously and the referee, Mr. Gwynne Walters, had his hands full. The crowd of more than 50 000 barracked him and the touring team at every opportunity, particularly when he awarded a penalty try against Cardiff near the end of the match which the Springboks won 13-0.

Exaggerated and biased newspaper reports threatened to make a big issue out of the miserable mess but it blew over fairly quickly as subsequent games proved that the Springboks were not really out to kill and maim. Mannetjies Roux, the stocky little Matie centre and wing, earned an overnight reputation as a murderous tackler in this match and he was particularly criticised for what many considered a late tackle on Alun Priday, the Cardiff fullback.

By a co-incidence, Mr. Walters was also the man in charge when the Springboks played France at Colombes Stadium, a few miles from Paris.

In the first scrum Hugo van Zyl was kicked, Martin Pelser had his cheek split by a punch and Piet du Toit received a blow against the head. Mr. Walters immediately penalised Moncla for having kicked Van Zyl but the Springboks were incensed and for a few minutes there was bedlam on the field.

Avril Malan tried to stop his team from retaliation but they were in too ugly a mood to listen to a captain for whom they normally had the greatest respect. Fortunately the referee took a firm stand at this point and he told both captains that he would have no hesitation in abandoning the game should the fighting continue. The rest of the match was a superb struggle between two extremely powerful teams and, in retrospect, a scoreless draw was about the fairest reflection of the proceedings. Johan Claassen and Avril Malan dominated the lineouts but in the tight scrums and in the loose the blue-jerseyed Frenchmen gave as good as they got. The French forwards, in fact, won several vital tight head heels against the powerful Springbok frontrow of Kuhn, Abie Malan, and du Toit. Dave Stewart, at flyhalf, was off-form and even Lionel Wilson often failed to find touch. The biggest surprise of the match was the way in which Jacques Bouquet nailed John Gainsford every time he touched the ball. The big Springbok was already then being described as the best centre in the world but Bouquet was quite unconcerned about the South African's fame. To this day, Gainsford gives him credit as the most difficult opponent he encountered in the 33 tests of his career.

Although the 1960/61 touring team to Britain and France had several members who deserve to be rated with the best Springboks of all time, the side as a whole was efficient more often than brilliant.

But it was not efficiency or even brilliance that carried them to victory over Wales in the mud of Cardiff Arms Park. It was courage and character and of all their triumphs it was this one that made them a team to remember.

Hennie van Zyl hurls Andy Mulligan, the Irish scrumhalf, to the ground in the test against Ireland. In the background is John Gainsford, one of the other stars of the tour. The Springboks won 8–3.

The Springboks of 1969/70 had to get used to sights like these. Demonstrators and policemen followed them wherever they went and smoke bombs, abuse and tin tacks interrupted their matches.

THE DEMO TOUR

With regiments of demonstrators chanting a message of hate from the terraces and with tin-tacks and smoke bombs on the playing fields, Dawie de Villiers and his Springboks completed their tour of the United Kingdom in the winter of 1969/70 under conditions no South African team must ever be subjected to again.

The tour will be remembered for the Springboks' dignity and restraint under pressure and provocation and for the moral courage and determination of their opponents and their hosts who refused to be intimidated by the most violent campaign ever to be conducted against a group of sportsmen. It will be remembered, also, for the brave and patient British policemen who bore the brunt of abuse even more directly than the Springboks.

Whatever convictions motivated the demonstrators were obscured by their uncouth behaviour; the slogans devalued by their spitting and cursing.

Judged against a background of harrassment on and off the field, the team's record of 15 wins out of 24 matches with four draws and five defeats, is remarkably good but it cannot compare with the achievements of previous South African teams to have visited Britain on a full-scale tour and for the first time the Springboks failed to win any of the tests against the Home Countries.

Apart from the interference on the actual field of play which, of course, hampered their opponents as much as it did them, the Springboks had a multitude of other problems. For the sake of security, they had to spend much of their time practically locked up in heavily guarded hotels with bomb hoaxes, noisy picketing and even the attempted hijacking of one of the team buses just before the test against England, disturbing their peace of mind and making proper preparations impossible.

Plain bad luck hounded the Springboks even more relentlessly than the demonstrators did. No less than four players were knocked out of the tour by injury and had to be replaced with substitutes flown over from South Africa while several key men were incapacitated at one time or another. An ironic twist of fate was the fact that left-wing Gert Muller like Hennie van Zyl, his predecessor in the same position in Britain in 1961, had to receive the news of his father's death while on the tour. Muller flew home to attend the funeral and then rejoined the side.

The total loss of form of Piet Visagie, the team's first-choice placekicker and most experienced flyhalf, was a severe blow. It is conceivable that had Visagie been at his best the Springboks would have done better, as many points were missed through erratic placekicking. Dawie de Villiers, who early on in the tour had successfully converted a penalty goal against Swansea, kicked extremely well against the Barbarians in the final match and he should have used himself more often in this capacity.

The tour management handled a difficult job well although Avril Malan's coaching methods were often criticised. He was pilloried in particular for assigning throw-ins at lineouts to the hookers instead of following the time-honoured practice of letting the wings do it.

It is possible that such innovations should not have been imposed on a team already faced with so many difficulties, but Malan has since been vindicated and the throw-in is now automatically part of the hooker's function.

Dawie de Villiers' leadership under such abnormal conditions was faultless and he was admirably backed by Tommy Bedford, an Oxford graduate who had the added advantage of being thoroughly familiar with Britain. De Villiers' instinctive ability to combine tact with firmness contributed immeasurably to the fact that the team never cracked under the pressure and managed to remain dignified and courteous in the face of unbelievable

Dawie de Villiers, outstanding captain of the embattled Springboks, with four of his stalwarts. *From the left:* Don Walton, Dawie de Villiers, H. O. de Villiers, Tommy Bedford and Frik du Preez.

provocation.

Bedford played some of the best rugby of his career and had injury not limited Jan Ellis to only nine appearances, which meant that he lacked real match fitness until just before the end of the tour, the Ellis-Bedford-Greyling combination might have been an even more decisive factor in the tests. Although Piet van Deventer, Albie Bates and Mike Jennings also played consistently well throughout, they were never up to the same standard of a trio as experienced as Bedford, Ellis and Greyling. Among the tight forwards Hannes Marais further enhanced his well-earned reputation as one of the finest frontrankers in world rugby, but generally the Springbok packs found themselves up against teams who were re-discovering the value of solidity up front, a trend which was shortly to enable British rugby to dominate the international arena.

Visagie's poor form gave Mike Lawless the opportunity he had been denied since his unhappy debut against France in 1964 when he was unfairly saddled with all of the blame for an inept performance by most of his teammates. Lawless, an introverted and strong-willed personality, proved himself to be one of the steadiest players in the side, with an unruffled poise and total mastery of the basic skills of the game.

The Springbok mid-field presented problems throughout the tour. Tonic Roux, although more talented as a fullback, was the most reliable centre, with J. P. van der Merwe showing glimpses of promise. Mannetjies Roux, who was rushed over from his Victoria West farm to replace the injured Johann van der Schyff, did not really have an opportunity to settle down and he played in only one test.

Eben Olivier unfortunately also never approached the form that made him South Africa's most dangerous centre threequarter against France in 1967 and who fitted in so well with Mannetjies Roux in the final test against the Lions in 1968.

All four wings, Gert Muller, Andrew van der Watt, Syd Nomis and Renier Grobler were outstanding. Muller, hit by injury and bereavement, played in only five matches, including two tests, but notched five tries with his rare blend of speed and raw power, while Andy van der Watt and Syd Nomis were always dangerous on the attack but even more valuable with their skill and tenacity on the defence. The comparatively inexperienced Grobler, destined to die when three S.A.A.F. jet aircraft were destroyed in a multiple crash against the slopes of Table Mountain so shortly after the team's return, was not overshadowed by his more famous colleagues and it was a pity that such above-average players were so often starved of opportunities. Van der Watt, with his astonishing acceleration, and Nomis, who at his peak had all the attributes of an international wing of the highest class, should certainly have been used more often and more effectively than they were.

H. O. de Villiers, after being injured early on in the tour, nevertheless played in 16 out of the 24 matches and established himself, by consensus between opponents, critics and the British public alike, as the most brilliant player in the side. He, Jan Ellis, Syd Nomis, Dawie de Villiers and Tommy Bedford were afterwards singled out by most British rugby writers as the stars of the team, but it was H. O., as dynamic on the field as he was self-effacing off it, who was regarded as the only one without a serious challenger should a World XV have been selected at the time. H. O.'s only weakness was his inconsistency as a placekicker; throughout his career he was as liable to miss the easiest kick as he was to succeed with the most difficult.

The test against Scotland was won and lost up front where Peter Stagg, at 6ft 8 probably the tallest man ever to play in international rugby, was virtually impossible to counter in the lineouts and Frank Laidlaw, with the aid of that master scrummager Ian McLauchlan, the future "Mighty Mouse" of the 1974 Lions, made Charlie Cockrell's debut a miserable one by clearly winning the hooking duel.

It was a scrappy affair, generally, as Piet Visagie and Scottish fullback Ian Smith took turns at missing penalty kicks. Visagie finally succeeded with one while Smith also had a solitary success in the second half. Less than ten minutes from the end the Scotland threequarters ripped the South African defence to shreds and Ian Smith came from the blue to take a long pass which left the cover defence with no hope of stopping the long-striding fullback on his way to scoring the try that gave Scotland their 6–3 victory.

Wallace Reyburn, a veteran New Zealand journalist who was awarded the O.B.E. for his work as a front-line correspondent during World War II, once wrote that the only time he had ever seen a referee acknowledging a score while three feet up in the air, was when Kevin Kelleher signalled the try that beat the Springboks against England at Twickenham on December 20, 1969.

The score came from a maul on the Springbok goal-line late in the second half with the South Africans clinging grimly to an 8–6 lead. The England hooker, John Pullin, hovered outside the ruck and when the ball rolled out to Dawie de Villiers, he dived for it. All the Springboks vowed that their captain got the touchdown but Kelleher, who in all fairness, was perfectly in position according to photographs of the incident, gave the decision in England's favour. Bob Hiller's conversion made it 8-11 and although the Springboks tried all they knew, they failed to prevent England from scoring their first-ever win over South Africa. Hiller's team had the luck of the devil in the last few minutes. On one occasion the ball shaved the upright from a dropkick by Visagie and only the bounce of the ball foiled Andy van der Watt after a perfect crosskick by Dawie de Villiers. Bob Hiller, incidentally, made history in this match by scoring England's first-ever penalty against the Springboks in 63 years of playing against each other.

The demonstrators were probably at their venomous worst in Ireland. To quote what Reyburn wrote in his book *"There was Also Some Rugby"*:

"The genuine anti-apartheid demonstrators were surrounded by as fine a rabble as you could wish to see, representing every breed of political and religious trouble-maker, trade union agitators, Sinn Fein, Young Socialists, communists, Britain-haters, Maoists, anarchists. . . .

"The switchboard at the Springboks' hotel was jammed by anonymous callers pouring out a flood of obscenities directed against the team, calls which the operators didn't put through, except to give samples to anyone in the hotel who wanted to know why it was so difficult to get the switchboard's attention. . . ."

Bomb scares were so frequent that the Springboks stopped worrying about such alarms and even after Dawie de Villiers had agreed to being interviewed by Bernadette Devlin, a Member of the British Parliament who had turned up in Dublin because, in her own (censored) words "These. . . . demonstrators aren't being tough enough with the . . . . . . Springboks", there was no relief for the beleaguered South Africans.

Reyburn describes how Tommy Bedford and the former Irish international Sam Walker went for a drink in what they thought would be a quiet pub.

"A girl at the bar prodded Bedford in the back with her umbrella and

Left: Demonstrations and defeats are momentarily forgotten as Tonie Roux, Andre de Wet and Dawie de Villiers soak themselves in a communal bath.

Above: Andrew van der Watt, whose official achievements on the athletic track support the argument that he was the fastest wing ever to wear the Springbok jersey, forces his way over for a try at Aldershot.

Die Burger

chanted, 'Fascist....! Fascist....!' He asked her to stop, but despite the fact that it was a more difficult chant to get one's tongue around than the usual 'fascist pig' she continued throughout his stay...."

The famous humorist Spike Milligan, a keen rugby fan, also attended the Springboks' match against Ireland. When the demonstrators recognised him they insisted that he join the parade. Grabbing a megaphone he marched along shouting "I'm a fascist bastard, I'm a fascist bastard!" His "deceit" was eventually discovered, his megaphone confiscated and, as he put it: "My career as a demonstrator came to an end."

The Springbok forwards gave one of their best performances in the test against Ireland, but Dawie de Villiers was off-form and Mike Lawless, Tonie and Mannetjies Roux, also made many mistakes. Had this not been the case, Ireland would surely have been beaten as Nomis and Van der Watt were in particularly good form while H. O. de Villiers, to quote Reyburn: "showed that he was ready to be upgraded from the category of one of the stars of the team to *the* star...."

A poor pass from Mannetjies Roux gave Mike Gibson the chance to send Alan Duggan through for a beautiful try, converted by the veteran Tom Kiernan, but H. O. cut the lead to only two points by putting over a long-range penalty kick before half-time. This, incidentally, was South Africa's 100th penalty goal in all tests.

With Bedford, Greyling and Ellis working together smoothly and Frik du Preez showing something of the ability that made him one of the greatest forwards of his time, the Springboks seemed certain to clinch the affair in the second half. Piet Greyling duly scored after half-an-hour of narrow escapes for Ireland and H. O. made it 8-5.

This was still the score after the full 40 minutes of the second half had run its course, but referee Grierson allowed an extra eight minutes of injury time. In the eighth and last minute Alan Duggan intercepted a wild pass and when cornered, he cross-kicked towards the mid-field. Jan Ellis gathered the kick in front of his own posts and surrounded by Irishmen and with no immediate support in sight, Ellis, rather than concede a try under the posts, had no option but to hold on and to refuse to let the ball go after having been tackled. He was penalised, of course, and Kiernan levelled the score, the whistle ending the match immediately afterwards.

Fortune seldom smiled on the 1969/70 Springboks. The test against Wales was also drawn, and again the equalising score came in injury time.

The Springbok forwards outplayed Wales, with Charlie Cockrell raking against the head on no less than five occasions and Ellis, Greyling and

Bedford simply superb on attack and defence. As usual in tests between these two countries at Cardiff Arms Park, it rained throughout the game, but there was no wind to speak of and both teams were enterprising.

Dawie de Villiers and Mike Lawless split the defence several times, both dovetailing well with Ellis to keep Wales pinned down in their own half. A penalty-goal by H. O. de Villiers opened the score, but Gareth Edwards made it 3-all at half-time by also somehow managing to lift the soggy ball over the crossbar. After the resumption, Jan Ellis who gave one one of the best performances of his 38-test career, broke away on three occasions and the third time Dawie de Villiers and Lawless rounded off the movement with swift and sure passing to send Nomis over for an unconverted try.

The Celts call it *hwyl* and the word describes that something extra only Welsh rugby players can draw on when they are fighting against the odds. With five minutes to go and doomed to defeat, Edwards and his mud-smeared men launched a series of sustained attacks and it was the Springboks' turn to slither and slide in desperate defence.

In the second minute of injury time Barry John, the famous Welsh flyhalf, kicked deep into South African territory. When the ball came out of the ruck it popped safely into the hands of Gareth Edwards who sliced through a gap to score just in from the corner flag. With the tally 6-all, the final result was all up to Edwards' conversion. The Springboks, stunned by the jinx that so remorselessly pursued them throughout the tour, stood with bowed heads and hunched shoulders, hardly daring to look as the Welsh scrumhalf lined up the ball. But the kick was missed, the match drawn, and even the referee, Air Commodore G. C. Lamb, remarked afterwards that it would have been a travesty of justice had the conversion succeeded. The result, a draw, meant that the Springboks stayed unbeaten in encounters against Wales.

In the final match of the tour, against the Barbarians, the Springboks struck the form that had evaded them for so long. The smoke- and flour-bombs, the tin-tacks on the field and the obscene insults screamed from the ramps, were ignored as the two teams, playing in the finest spirit of the game, made sure that at least a few fond memories would remain of a tour that so often resembled a nightmare.

David Duckham, Rodger Arneil, Keith Fairbrother and Alan Duggan scored magnificent tries for the Baa-Baas while Jan Ellis, who went over twice, and Andy van der Watt notched tries for the Springboks. Mike Lawless also dropped a goal and Dawie de Villiers was on target with three conversions and a penalty.

The second try by Jan Ellis has

Above: Brilliant Gareth Edwards snatched victory from the Springboks in injury time with a try for Wales. Hannes Marais is just too late to stop Edwards from going over for the equalising score.

Left: Gert Muller was plagued by injury and bereavement during the tour but whenever he did play, the burly Matie was at his superlative best. Here he goes over for one of his five tries on the tour.

Right: Syd Nomis was an outstanding success. This picture shows him scoring South Africa's only try in the test against Wales.

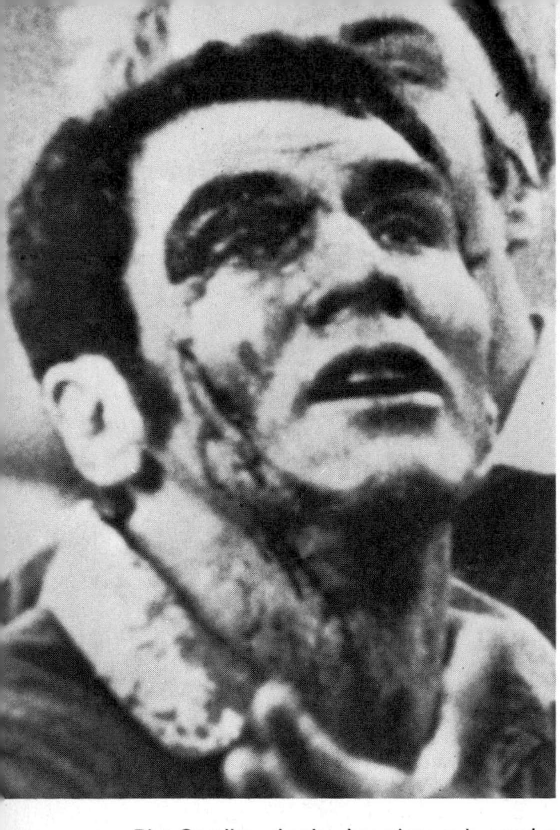

been called one of the best ever to have been scored by a forward at Twickenham. Grabbing a loose-rolling ball, the freckled flanker dummied twice, leaving several defenders confused and bewildered before he jinked past J. P. R. Williams to cross the line without a finger having been laid on him.

At a dinner that night the late Brigadier Hugh Llewellyn Glyn Hughes, the 78-year-old president of the Barbarian Football Club, made Dawie de Villiers an honorary member, an honour traditionally bestowed on the captains of touring teams to visit Britain.

In two world wars Brigadier Hughes had won the D.S.O. with two Bars, the Military Cross and the *Croix de Guerre avec palme* among other awards for conspicuous gallantry and he knew more about bravery than most.

Perhaps that is why he took the unprecedented step of also presenting each member of the Springbok team with a Barbarian monogram, including four extra for the players who had been injured and who had returned home before the end of the tour.

It was an old soldier's way of paying homage to courage in adversity.

Piet Greyling, destined to play such a major role in defeating the All Blacks a few months later, played consistently well throughout the controversial tour. Demonstrations did not bother him and neither did the sight of his own blood.

Below: One of the most controversial incidents of the tour. Referee Kevin Keleher signals a try by John Pullin for England, ruling that the hooker had got to the ball before Dawie de Villiers. The Springbok captain looks up in amazement and Piet Visagie, on the far left, rushes up to protest. This much-discussed try gave England her first-ever victory over South Africa.

Right: Keith Oxlee, a match-winning flyhalf from Natal, who dominated the 1962 series.

Die Huisgenoot

Colour overleaf:

Jannie Engelbrecht, one of the greatest wings of all time.

Stewart Colman

Mike Gibson and Gareth Edwards carry Dawie de Villiers off the playing field of Twickenham after the Springboks had beaten the Barbarians in their best performance of the tour. De Villiers and a rampant Jan Ellis were particularly outstanding.

The Lions/Home Countries in SA 1961 – 1974

Mini-skirts were still to be discovered but mini-tours were much in vogue in 1961. Ireland and Australia paid brief visits to South Africa and just for once, test rugby was played in a more or less relaxed manner.

Even the trials match the selectors organised before the one and only test against Ronnie Dawson's Irishmen at Newlands, was marked by good humour rather than the usual, unavoidable, tension. More than 30 of the trialists had just returned from a tour of nearly four months in Britain and France, and the test side obviously had to be built around them. John Gainsford and Jannie Engelbrecht were injured and out of contention but there were any number of outstanding candidates for the vacancies.

The tour veterans finding themselves suddenly in opposition to each other, had to devise new signals and one, designed by the A-team to confuse their old teammates, led to probably the only occasion in history where a Springbok trials match was interrupted because all 16 forwards had burst out laughing.

Piet Uys, at scrumhalf, was supposed to call out the name of an animal whenever he wanted the ball thrown in deep at a lineout and a bird when it was to be a short throw-in. Michel Antelme, whose land surveyor's mind often seemed pre-occupied with mathematical problems when it should have been concentrated on the task at hand, had the ball in his hands and the lineout was ready.

"Ostrich!", Uys instructed.

"Ostrich?", Antelme asked, looking puzzled and as vague as only he could be. "Hey, what's that, an animal or a bird?"

With Avril Malan also out because of injury, Johan Claassen was given the captaincy against Ireland and the only new Springbok was Colin Greenwood, a fleet-footed Western Province centre. All the other players selected were members of the team which had toured Britain and France, although it was to be a first test appearance for Charlie Nimb, Ben-Piet van Zyl and Piet van Zyl.

The Irishmen, who had foolishly insisted that the international be the first match on the itinerary, were outclassed and they were fortunate that the final score was only 24-8 in favour of Claassen's Springboks.

Dave Stewart, who had previously played flyhalf and fullback for South Africa, was smoothly effective at centre and both Greenwood and Ben-Piet van Zyl, a wing of blistering pace, were given every opportunity. Each scored two tries and Charlie Nimb, a most talented young flyhalf who, like Greenwood, shortly afterwards succumbed to the lure of the professional game, not only kicked immaculately but he dovetailed enterprisingly with Stewart, his Villagers clubmate and the tough and quick-thinking Piet Uys.

Lionel Wilson injured his shoulder severely in the second half and Stewart had to take over from him, with Ben-Piet van Zyl moving to centre and Doug Hopwood, who had been outstanding at No. 8, going to the wing position. The enforced reshuffle saved Ireland from being massacred as the Springboks who had led 13-0 at half-time, could add only eleven more points, two tries by Ben-Piet van Zyl, one after a devastating break by Uys and a penalty goal from inside his own half by Nimb, who also converted one of the tries.

All Ireland's points were scored in the second half and all of them by Tom Kiernan, their fullback, with a penalty, a try and a conversion. Kiernan, with Springboks Percy Allport and Roy Dryburgh, is still one of only three fullbacks to have scored a try in a test in South Africa, all at Newlands. There were, incidentally, no less than four Van Zyls in the Springboks team, Hennie, Ben-Piet, Piet and Hugo, which must have been a record and certainly a nightmare to the radio commentators.

The Springboks were even more enterprisingly aggressive in the two tests against Ken Catchpole's Wallabies in that same season (discussed more fully elsewhere in this book) and, generally speaking, 1961 was a vintage year for South African rugby. The slump of the late 1950's was all but forgotten; since the beginning of 1960 the Springboks had lost only one out of 13 tests, scoring 10 victories and being held to a draw twice.

Arthur Robert Smith, long-jump champion, veteran international wing-threequarter and known at Caius College, Cambridge, as a mathematician of exceptional ability, was selected to lead the 1962 Lions challenge in South Africa. The fair-haired, impeccably-mannered Scot had been here before as a member of the famous 1955 side but injury had sidelined him for most of the tour. Smith was a member of the 1958 Barbarians team to tour South Africa and he also came out with the Scottish side which visited this country in 1960. His 60-yard run for a try for the Baa-baas against Transvaal at Ellis Park in 1958 alone stamped him as a wing of the highest class.

He was given a pack of massive forwards; outstanding players with the experience to go with their brawn; men like the indefatigable Bryn Meredith and Syd Millar, Michael Campbell-Lamerton, Keith Rowlands, Willie-John McBride, Bill Mulcahy, Kingsley Jones, Budge Rogers, Haydn Morgan and Alun Pask. Dickie Jeeps, getting on in years but still a shrewd and brave scrumhalf was first choice for this vital position and he and Richard Sharp, a tall, blond flyhalf from Oxford University, were expected to make the maximum use of the abundance of possession the forwards were certain to get. Part of the prediction came true. Unlike most British teams of the past who usually had to make the most of a less than fair share of the ball, the 1962 Lions had no such problems. Their inside backs lacked sparkle, however, and they never came near to matching their predecessors of 1955 or 1938 for attacking ideas. David Hewitt, a centre who did

Right: Dave Stewart, the versatile Western Province Springbok, who gave one of his best international performances as a centre against Ireland in 1961.

Below: Colin Greenwood, wearing a white jersey in deference to the Irish visitors, scores the first of his two tries against Ireland at Newlands in 1961.

well against New Zealand in 1959, was bothered by injury, Ken Jones invariably tried to do too much on his own and Mike Weston and Gordon Waddell were steady rather than brilliant.

Richard Sharp played exceptionally well at the start of the tour and it could be that the injury he suffered against Northern Transvaal in the match just before the first test had meant the elimination of the one player who could have lifted the backline from comparative mediocrity to something a little more in the tradition of Lions of the past.

Sharp's injury caused a violent row as the British press representatives and some members of the team, thought that he had been deliberately put out of action by Mannetjies Roux, the Springbok centre and wing who was then a S.A.A.F. pilot and playing for Northern Transvaal. Sharp was on the field for less than five minutes. Receiving the ball, the lanky, lantern-jawed flyhalf, tried to cut through with a typical dummy to the inside and, as he did so, Roux hit him with a flying tackle that fractured his cheekbone. Roux has always insisted that Sharp had ducked into his tackle and that it was an unfortunate accident.

"I met Sharp some time afterwards and he told me right away that my tackle was fair," Roux told me years later. "He was on the point of kicking, but realised that I would charge down the ball and, instead, he tried to duck away from me. This brought his head in line with my tackle."

Sharp personally never made any accusations against Roux and since he had always been such an outspoken person, his silence is rather revealing. After the Barbarians had become the first — and only — team to beat Avril Malan's Springboks in Britain in 1961, Sharp certainly did not keep his misgivings about the match to himself.

"There was much of the Roman arena that day and I shall always remember the roar from the crowd when Haydn Mainwaring tackled Avril Malan" he wrote later. "It was one of those moments when I for one had doubts about the game as a game. . . . I think that I should add that I have never kicked so much in a top level game and that I heard not a single word of criticism. . . ."

The injury sidelined Sharp for five weeks and meant that he missed the first two tests, certainly a heavy blow to the tourists. Gordon Waddell, whose father Herbert was a member of Cove-Smith's 1924 side, took over. A clever and sturdy flyhalf, he lacked speed and preferred to use his boot and did not present many problems on the attack.

Jannie Engelbrecht and Dave Stewart, both obvious choices for the Springbok team, were injured and their places for the first test at Ellis Park were taken by Roux and a newcomer, Melville (Wang) Wyness, of Western Province. Ormond Taylor, a Natal wing, and Mof Myburgh, the huge Northern Transvaal prop who in later years was to prove his value so often, also made their international debut in the match.

The two packs were so evenly matched that neither side could ever really get going. A few minutes before half-time Ken Jones kicked for touch, Roux fielded and, switching direction twice, gave to John Gainsford who showed astonishing accelleration for a man of his size to cut through for

Above: Experienced test players John Gainsford and Doug Hopwood flank Dawie de Villiers after the Matie scrumhalf had spurted from club player to international in the space of four weeks.

Above, left: Arthur Smith, captain of the 1962 Lions in South Africa.

Left: Richard Sharp, outstanding 1962 Lions flyhalf. A tackle by Mannetjies Roux laid him low before the first test and caused a nasty row.

Right: Alun Pask, the great Lions loose-forward, gets three fingers to the ball for a try against Western Province at Newlands. A youthful Dawie de Villiers is too late to prevent the score.

The Cape Times

a spectacular try in the corner. Late in the second half Jones made amends for his earlier indiscretion with a try of his own and the result of 3-all was generally regarded as a fair reflection of the game.

The Springbok selectors made several changes for the second test in Durban. Wyness retained his place but Taylor and Myburgh were dropped. Avril Malan and Hugo van Zyl were also left out and Frik du Preez locked the scrum with Claassen, Chris Bezuidenhout went into the frontrow and Hannes Botha and Louis Schmidt were on the flanks. Engelbrecht, as expected, came back into the team and Roux, who always preferred the centre position, was shunted from the right- to the left-wing.

The most interesting newcomer to the side was Dawie de Villiers, the flaxen-haired Matie scrumhalf who had made a remarkable recovery from injury, to earn Western Province, Junior Springbok and Springbok colours, all within the space of one month.

It turned out to be one of those grimly-fought tests, clouded by controversy. At half-time there was still no score but late in the second half Keith Oxlee, the Springbok flyhalf who was such a major factor in the series, put over a penalty kick after Keith Rowlands had tackled Du Preez from an offside position. There was no argument about this one but all hell broke loose over what happened in the last few seconds of the game.

There was a scrum on the South African goalline and the Springboks were pushed back and over, for the two packs to collapse in a tangled mound of bodies. Rowlands and all of his teammates were convinced that he had scored a push-over try but the referee, Ken Carlson, ruled that since he had not seen the try being scored, he could not award it. There was intense bitterness over his decision and Rowlands, long after the match, still had tears in his eyes from frustration and disappointment.

A fully recovered Richard Sharp returned to the Lions side for the third test, at Newlands, but the less impetuous Waddell might have been more useful to Arthur Smith and his competent pack. His appraisal of his threequarters was probably more realistic than Sharp's. The Springboks had made only one change this time, bringing back Hugo van Zyl and dropping Louis Schmidt.

There was tremendous interest in the match and at one stage riots threatened at the gates of Newlands. Scores of people were arrested and many of them were found to be carrying knives and other dangerous weapons; prompt police action certainly saved Newlands from what could have been dangerous crowd reactions. The official attendance was 54 843, still the largest crowd in the history of Newlands and more than 4 000 people had to be turned away at the gates.

With Bryn Meredith proving once and for all why he was regarded as the best hooker of his era, the Lions forwards dominated the tight phases but in the loose Hannes Botha, playing the finest rugby of his career, Hugo van Zyl and Doug Hopwood gave the Springboks the edge.

At half-time the score was 3-all, with Oxlee having succeeded with a penalty after Sharp had put over a dropgoal. Their excellent efforts were overshadowed, nevertheless, by an

Left: Piet Uys, a brilliant scrumhalf of the early 1960s.

amazing run by Jannie Engelbrecht after Gainsford had given him the ball just outside the Springbok "25". The Stellenbosch flyer left everybody standing with a burst of sustained speed worthy of an Olympic Games sprinter and Tom Kiernan, coming across to take him on the cornerflag, never had a chance. The huge crowd's roar turned into a rumbling groan when the referee, Dr. Bertie Strasheim, ruled that Gainsford's pass had been forward, however, and that Engelbrecht's superhuman effort had been in vain. Later on in the match Engelbrecht also used his exceptional pace to prevent a certain try when he flashed across the field to neutralise a ball that had been grubbered over the goalline.

The man of the match, however, was Keith Oxlee who, for the second successive test, scored all of the South African points. His try in the second half was a model of quick thinking and it secured the series for his team.

An ill-advised attempt by Sharp to start a move on his tryline gave the Springbok flyhalf his chance. Ken Jones was flattened by Wang Wyness and Oxlee grabbed the loose ball, dodged inside and then sped sharply towards the touchline, beating a baffled cover defence by his quick changes of direction. He calmly converted his own try and the Lions never looked like getting back into the picture after this set-back and the final score was 8-3.

Piet Uys replaced the injured Dawie de Villiers for the final test in Bloemfontein and Ronnie Hill took over from Abie Malan, who had been thoroughly out-hooked by Meredith at Newlands.

It was a hot afternoon with an unpleasant wind periodically driving miniature dust storms across the field, a ground hard and barren at the end of a harsh Free State winter.

Up to referee Toy Myburgh's half-time whistle, the Lions were holding their own, although the Springboks were leading 10-6. Mannetjies Roux had scored a good try after a break by Wyness while earlier on a thrust by Gainsford, in turn, had given Wyness a try.

Oxlee, who could not have put a foot wrong that day had he tried, had no problems with the conversions, while a penalty by John Willcox and an unconverted try by Ronnie Cowan made up the touring side's half-time score.

After the resumption Gainsford slashed through three defenders for the only try of the day that Oxlee could not convert. The Lions, still very much in the picture, replied promptly with a try by Rowlands, converted by Willcox, but, after a penalty by Oxlee, the Springboks suddenly looked as good an attacking side as any in the history of the game.

It was Frik du Preez who sparked it off. Gathering a pass from Engelbrecht, the Northern Transvaal lock burst away on a thrilling run in which he swept aside half-a-dozen defenders. With superb timing, he ran into the final tackle before flipping the ball to his left for Hugo van Zyl to score. Oxlee converted and when he also converted a try by Johan Claassen after good combining between Hugo van Zyl and Doug Hopwood, the Springboks had added 13 points in six minutes. A penalty goal shortly afterwards pushed the flyhalf's personal tally for the match to 14 points and left him in sight of Okey Geffin's long-standing record.

With only a few minutes to go, Mannetjies Roux received a long pass on the half-way line and with electrifying speed he shot past Ronnie Cowan and then cut sharply in-field to leave several Lions floundering in his wake. With only the fullback left to beat, Roux revealed his instinctive genius. Instead of going for the corner-flag and running the risk of Willcox bumping him into touch, he ran straight at the full-back and swerved past him with such bewildering ease that Willcox realised the futility of it all and did not even attempt a tackle. Roux rounded off his spectacular run with an exuberant dive over the line for what must surely rate with the best tries ever to have been scored in test rugby.

Oxlee placed the ball for the conversion, not even knowing then that he needed the two points to become the Springbok who had scored the most points in a test. The wind kept blowing the ball over and eventually Hopwood had to hold it down for the flyhalf's kick. It was on target, from the moment the boot hit the ball.

A moment later Mike Campbell-Lamerton, a burly Scot who had been one of the most popular members in Smith's team, broke away from a line-out to score the final try before referee Myburgh's whistle sent more than 60 000 happy spectators flowing towards the exits. The Springboks had scored six tries in their 34-14 victory and Keith Oxlee had succeeded with seven out of the eight kicks he had aimed at the posts. Dickie Jeeps, who captained the Lions in the final test as Smith was injured, had actually correctly predicted the Springboks' winning margin. In an interview before the test he said: "We have already lost the series and there is no point in playing it safe. We'll either win by 10 points or lose by 20!"

Victory over the Springboks has eluded Wales from the first time the two teams clashed back in 1906 but the men from the valleys had strong hopes of beating the hoodoo when they paid a short visit to South Africa in 1964. They had a strong side and, equally important, the South African season had just started and Wales were expected to have a vital advantage in fitness.

In the first half of the only test,

Above: John Gainsford at his greatest. The burly Springbok centre outpaces Niall Brophy and is about to swerve past John Willcox on his way to a superb try in the first test against the Lions at Ellis Park in 1962.

played in Durban, it looked as if the experts had, for once, predicted correctly. The Springboks were just not combining properly and with Brian Price outstanding in the lineouts and Clive Rowlands and Dave Watkins dovetailing slickly at halfback, the South Africans were distinctly lucky to be level at 3-all at half-time. A penalty by Oxlee was cancelled out by a penalty for Wales from Keith Bradshaw.

With only 20 minutes to go Lionel Wilson, who had saved his team repeatedly in a match of many errors, caught a poor clearing kick from Grahame Hodgson near his halfway line and just in from touch. For once in his long test career, the normally conservative Wilson gambled. He put everything he had into a dropkick and, from that acute angle and nearly half the length of the field away from the posts, he sent the ball sailing safely over the crossbar. It did more than add three points to the South African score; it also inspired the Springboks and disheartened the Welshmen. In the less than 20 minutes remaining, Hannes Marais, Doug Hopwood and Nelie Smith scored tries, all converted by Oxlee who also stabbed over a penalty and Wales were beaten 3-24, their biggest defeat ever against South Africa. Hopwood's try meant that he became the first and so far only Springbok to have notched a try against each of the four Home Countries.

In 1964 the South African Rugby Board celebrated its 75th anniversary by inviting some of the best rugby players from all parts of the world to play in a series of festival matches. The games and more specifically the after-match gatherings were good for diplomatic relations. Carefree, running rugby was the order of the day and perhaps it was only a co-incidence that the Springboks were to lose eight of their next 10 tests.

Against France in 1967 there was an improvement, uneven but obvious, as detailed in the chapter on our battles with the Tricolors.

It was with mixed feelings, nevertheless, that South Africa welcomed the ninth Lions touring team in 1968.

Thomas Joseph Kiernan, the experienced Irish fullback whose profession as a chartered accountant seemed so apt in the light of the many points he was to score on the tour, was placed in charge of a team which looked enormously strong on paper. Injuries handicapped the Lions from the start, however, and the loss of Barry John, the Welsh flyhalf, midway through the first half of the first test must have had an incalculable effect on them. Gareth Edwards, the young Welsh scrumhalf destined for future greatness, played in only eight matches because of hamstring problems. Edwards, strangely enough, was not all that highly regarded by the majority of his 1968 teammates, who considered him selfish and inclined to "keep the good ball for himself". Roger Young, the extremely capable other scrumhalf in the side, was also hampered by injury and their best centre, Gerald Davies, could only play in one test because of torn ankle ligaments.

With Barry John out, Mike Gibson who was expected to give thrust in mid-field, had to play flyhalf and this further disrupted the pattern. In fact, there were so many injuries that three replacements had to be flown over from Britain and any assessment of Kiernan's team must be done with all these misfortunes borne in mind. Even then the final judgment has to be that this was a side which promised more than it delivered.

Their general record was excellent with Transvaal the only provincial side to beat them, but tours are judged on the results of test matches and in these they failed badly. They drew the second test but lost the other three and could score only one try against eight by the Springboks. Take away Tom Kiernan's unbelievable contribution of 35 out of the Lion's total of 38 points, and it is painfully obvious that this was a team with an almost total lack of thrust.

The tour was marred by controversy with the Lions' manager, David Brooks, expressing his dissatisfaction with South African referees in such intemperate terms that he harmed rather than enhanced the image of British rugby. Brooks also failed to maintain proper discipline in the team and there were several incidents of vandalism in hotels and of other puerile behaviour. On the credit side, there was little rough play and although John O'Shea, the Cardiff tighthead prop, was sent off the field by referee Bert Woolley in the match against Eastern Transvaal at Springs, there was nothing but sympathy for this most likeable player. O'Shea took his punishment with good grace and it was he who gave Mr. Woolley a ticket for the third test.

Ronnie Dawson, the Lions' coach and an intelligent, dedicated man, tried but failed to convince his players that there is usually a huge difference between a South African provincial side and the Springbok team. This hard fact of life the undefeated Lions had to discover for themselves in the first test at Loftus Versfeld.

Rodney Gould, thc Natal fullback who had been chosen in the place of the injury-ridden, out-of-form H. O. de Villiers, was the only new "cap" in the side led by Dawie de Villiers. Dawie's own selection was severely criticised in some quarters but he silenced his critics with an outstanding display.

The Springboks proved to be far too good for the Lions and the score of 25-20 was not a fair reflection at all. Tiny Naude, Dawie de Villiers and Frik du Preez scored tries and Visagie added two penalty goals and two conversions while Naude also succeeded with two enormous penalty goals. Willie-John McBride scored a try for the Lions and Kiernan, kicking like a machine, put over five penalty goals and the conversion.

Frik du Preez's try was the highlight of a match riddled by errors. Receiving from his old friend Mof Myburgh at a lineout, Du Preez

slipped round the front, brushing off several half-hearted tackles before bursting clear. Kiernan made a brave attempt to stop him but the Lions fullback was sent cartwheeling into touch as the great Springbok lock barged over for a try only a player of his unique gifts could possibly have scored.

Barry John suffered a broken collarbone after a tackle by Jan Ellis midway through the first half and when Mike Gibson replaced him, the curly-haired Irishman became the first substitute in a test, the new law having just come into effect.

Kiernan's 17 points established a record as the most to be scored by an individual in a test against South Africa and the conversion of his first penalty goal, in fact, gave him his 100th point in internationals.

The second test, in Port Elizabeth, was an awful affair made worse by the unseemly haggling over the appointment of Mr. Hansie Schoeman as the referee. The Lions wanted Mr. Walter Lane, of Natal, instead of one of the officials on the panel—Piet Robbertse, Cas de Bruyn, Wynand

Right: Springbok centre Wang Wyness cuts through in the final test of the 1962 series in Bloemfontein. Next to him is Mannetjies Roux who scored a fantastic try in this match.

Below: Dickie Jeeps, one of the great scrumhalves of his time, sends the ball to his backs. About to pounce is Hannes Botha, the Springbok flank, who was in outstanding form in the 1962 series.

Malan and Max Baise. The colourful Baise had done a good job in the first test but the tour management, aware of a ruling that no referee can officiate in more than two tests in a series, wanted to hold him in reserve, so to speak, for a later occasion. The South African Rugby Board then stepped in and named Schoeman as a compromise appointment.

The Springboks, with hard-working Thys Lourens in the place of the injured Piet Greyling, held a territorial advantage throughout the match but one mistake after the other prevented them from scoring. The Lions defended well but their task was made easier by the Springbok threequarters who were slow, unenterprising and guilty of the most elementary errors. Piet Visagie and Tiny Naude collected a penalty each and Kiernan, once again outstanding, scored all of his side's points with two penalties.

Jannie Engelbrecht was injured in a friendly game just before the third test at Newlands and he was replaced by Gertjie Brynard while Mannetjies Roux returned to the team at centre and Syd Nomis replaced Corra Dirksen, who had lost the terrific form he had shown against France the previous season. It was Nomis' first test on the left wing but he was to retain this position for the next 22 tests in succession.

For once there was no argument, either before or after the game. The Lions were satisfied with Max Baise's refereeing and their forwards with McBride and Peter Stagg particularly effective in the lineouts, held their own for the first time. There was some mild grumbling over the fact that Gys Pitzer had knocked out his opposite number John Pullin with a punch thrown right in front of the grandstand, but Mr. Baise was unsighted at that moment and there was nothing he could do about it. The Springboks insisted that Pullin had provoked Pitzer and the Lions manager, considering the fact that he so readily complained about other matters, was remarkably unconcerned about the incident.

The Springboks clinched the series 11-6 through a good try by Thys Lourens, a penalty goal and a conversion by Visagie and a penalty, as usual from the "outfield", by that most valuable forward Tiny Naude. Kiernan once again did all the scoring for his team with two immaculately-taken penalty goals.

Although the result of the match no longer held much significance, more than 60 000 spectators nevertheless packed Ellis Park for the final test. They were rewarded by the best rugby of the series, all of it coming from the Springboks.

Visagie, who in this game was to show the first signs of the gradually-gained confidence which was to make him such a fine international flyhalf, only just missed a first-minute try after a good break and Brynard was also called back after the referee, Dr. Strasheim, had spotted a forward pass. Except for the lineouts where Delme Thomas, Willie McBride and Peter Stagg did well, the Springbok pack had matters in hand and the backs were given many opportunities. Mannetjies Roux ripped the defence to shreds with a brilliant run in which he left Gibson and Kiernan standing and the marvellous little Springbok saved a certain try a few minutes later when he tackled Maurice Richards on the line.

A penalty by the infallible Kiernan halted the Springbok onslaught for a while but Tommy Bedford, the Springbok eighthman who played one of the best matches of his long and controversial career, attacked from deep in his own half of the field, De Villiers and Brynard came to his aid, and under intense pressure, centre Bresnihan sent a poor kick straight into the hands of Gould who dropped a lovely goal.

After half-time Ellis and Eben Olivier, who for the first time approached the form he showed against France the season before, and Syd Nomis added tries with Visagie converting two of them. Kiernan, scoring all his team's points for the third successive time, replied with a penalty and an entertaining game, played in a fine spirit, ended with the Springboks winning 19-6.

It was hardly a memorable tour

Top right: Frik du Preez bursts away for his amazing try in the first test against the 1968 Lions. Mof Myburgh, a magnificent front-ranker, is up to help if needed.

Right: Dawie de Villiers and Thys Lourens give chase after Gordon Connell had passed from a scrum. Jim Telfer looks on.

Left: Tom Kiernan, the captain of the 1968 Lions and one of the most accurate place-kickers ever to visit South Africa.

but Kiernan's splendid kicking, Frik du Preez's explosive run at Loftus Versfeld, a couple of Tiny Naude's enormous placekicks and the scintillating running of Mannetjies Roux in the final test did give it a few moments of distinction.

In the Northern Hemisphere winter of 1969 the Springboks visited Britain in what turned out to be a bizarre tour, discussed in more detail elsewhere. The next contact with a team from the Home Countries in South Africa therefore had to wait until 1972 when John Pullin brought an England side out on a short tour.

They were not highly regarded after poor performances in the Five Nations tournament of the previous season, but they remained undefeated throughout a seven-match tour and scored a stunning 18-9 victory over South Africa at Ellis Park in the only test. They also made history by meeting a team of Coloured players from the South African Rugby Federation at Athlone, Cape Town, and a Black team in Port Elizabeth, setting a precedent for all future touring teams to follow.

Piet Greyling led a combination of Springboks who seemed hopelessly unsure of themselves. Dawie Snyman collected all the South African points with three penalties but several easy kicks were fluffed while England, with unspectacular competence, grabbed every scoring chance. Fullback Sam Doble converted a try by wing

John Ruby

Willie-John McBride, a leader to respect. His 1974 Lions swept unbeaten through South Africa.

Alan Morley and also booted four penalties to establish the highest points total by an individual player in tests between the two countries since Dougie Morkel scored six points for Billy Millar's Springboks in 1913.

The alarm bells were ringing for South African rugby but a loud chorus of excuses muffled the sound and precious few heard it.

Willie-John McBride's Lions of 1974 became the first touring team to beat the Springboks in a four-match series in South Africa in 78 years. The final test was drawn but the Lions won the first three with such convincing ease that the harsh truth had to be faced at last. McBride and his magnificently-drilled team could well have been the best side ever to visit this country but they were made to look even better by Springboks who always seemed to be on their heels; demoralised and disorganised.

Georges Mazzocut, an impartial observer from France, was moved to the following comment in *L'Equipe:*

"The price of a Springbok skin, once so highly valued, is of very little value at this time....who wants a goat's head above his mantelpiece..?"

A harsh statement, perhaps not entirely fair to either the brilliant Lions or the embattled Springboks, but with enough truth in it to hurt.

The greatness of the 1974 Lions cannot be denied. It was a team without weakness from frontrow to fullback; led by an outstanding captain in William John McBride, coached by a dedicated man in Syd Millar and guided by the ideal tour manager in Alun Thomas, who had the good sense not to interfere in the running of the team.

They were a new breed of Lions. The sound fundamentals were no longer being sacrificed for flair and individualism but had instead been elevated to the point of prime importance. Millar believed in the old truism that tests are won in the frontrow and that cohesion up front is essential. He had played in South Africa on three tours and, on his own admission, had acquired the Springbok approach to the game. The fact that he had noticed a defection from that philosophy on the part of the South Africans he had kept to himself; throughout the preparation of the team in England and out here before the tour actually started, he had continued to stress the difficulty of the task ahead. "To beat the Springboks in their own country is more difficult than beating the All Blacks in New Zealand," he had constantly warned. "Conditions in New Zealand are similar to those we are used to. On South Africa's hard fields and under that bright sun, the ball will behave a lot more strangely."

Millar's efforts ensured that no Lions team had ever been better prepared for a tour of South Africa. Willie-John McBride, a stern-faced Ulsterman mentally and physically as firm and strong as an ancient oak, provided the leadership that gave the team the character and dedication no amount of coaching could have brought. Millar and McBride came from the same club, Ballymena, and they shared the same attitude, the same desire to avenge the humiliating defeats they had endured together on previous tours.

British rugby had undergone a transformation since the lacklustre days of 1968. It was better organised and officials, players and coaches had become a lot more concerned with winning than they had ever been before. The first fruits of the new approach were plucked when they beat the All Blacks on their own fields in 1971 and McBride's men, in spite of having undertaken the tour in the face of the official disapproval of their government and the vociferous criticism of anti-South African factions, were proud, almost arrogant, in their self-confidence.

John Gainsford, the great Springbok threequarter of the 1960's, summed them up best when he told sportswriter, Neville Leck:

"They were mentally tougher, physically harder, superbly drilled and coached and disciplined and united. They were dedicated fellows who were trained to peak fitness, who were prepared like professionals and who were ready to die on the field for victory. They were rugged, even ruthless competitors who played their rugby to win and who were not squeamish about resorting to obstruction, gamesmanship and even the use of their fists and boots to achieve their end."

The thorough preparation beforehand must have been the main reason why the team suffered so few serious injuries on the tour. Alan Old, the England flyhalf was incapacitated by a late tackle against the Proteas, but not before he had scored 37 points against S.W.D., a record for an individual player in a single match on a tour of South Africa, and veteran Mike Gibson had to be flown over to join the team, and that was the only time the tour management had to call for aid. Gordon Brown, the outstanding lock, suffered a broken hand in the third test and had to be replaced by Chris Ralston for the final international while Phil Bennett played in the third test with a foot so badly gashed that he had to leave the placekicking to Andy Irvine who had replaced Billy Steele on the wing for that express purpose. It is a fact that no team in recent years was bothered less by the bogey of injuries to key players.

An indication of how seriously the Lions approached their task was the fact that they were all fitted out with special gum shields and knee guards and that they also took two "slow sodium" tablets a day to counter the loss of salt through unaccustomed perspiration in South Africa's hotter climate.

All the preparation in the world cannot make world-beaters out of mediocrities, however, and in the final analysis the 1974 Lions were successful because there was such an abundance of talent in the side. Hannes Marais, who was brought from retirement to lead the Springboks, afterwards admitted that it took the Springboks until the final test before they could go some way towards countering the Lions in the scrums where the amazing Ian ("Mighty Mouse") McLauchlan proved to be the finest scrummaging technician ever to visit South Africa.

McLauchlan, a short and squat prop, was regarded by the Springboks as the "brains" of the Lions' pack and he, hooker Bobby Windsor and the massive Fran Cotton formed an invincible frontrow. Gordon Brown was the best lock on either side throughout the series and McBride, apart from his inspiring leadership, was nearly as solid. Fergus Slattery, Roger Uttley and Mervyn Davies made up a formidable looseforward combination who used the sound springboard provided by their hard-working colleagues to wreak destruction amongst their opponents' halves and threequarters. It was, in short, the kind of pack the finest Springbok teams used to have.

Behind that magnificent set of forwards the Lions enjoyed the services of the best scrumhalf in the world, Gareth Owen Edwards, now a matured international player whose long and quick passing, speed and strength on the break and marvellous tactical kicking, had his opponents groping blindly throughout the series. Phil Bennett was nearly as brilliant at flyhalf where he always gave the impression of a man knowing what he intended to do and his place-and dropkicking made him one of the finest matchwinning flyhalves to have visited South Africa.

Centres Dick Milliken and Ian McGeechan were reliable rather than outstanding but John James Williams, the diminutive "J. J.". was not a Commonwealth Games sprinter for nothing. His phenomenal speed and his intelligence on the field, made this Llanelli physical education instructor one of the most potent attacking weapons in McBride's armoury. His total of four tries is the most by any player in a series against South Africa, and is only one short of the record number scored by Theunis Briers in 1955. Andy Irvine who took over from Billy Steele on the right-wing in the last two tests was also a player of exceptional talent and his eclipse of Gert Muller, a wing so feared by the 1970 All Blacks, underlined not only his skill but also his courage.

Gareth Edwards might have been the outstanding star of the team but J. P. R. Williams, the tall Welsh fullback with the long, flowing hair and the distinctive white sweatband was not far behind, if behind he was. John Peter Rhys Williams spelt danger for the Springboks every time he touched the ball and with his weight and pace he sliced through defenders as if they did not exist. Williams, like Edwards, was the best player in his position in the world in 1974 and, again like his countryman, he was fully aware of the fact. He played with supreme confidence and his aggressiveness on at least one occasion led to a potentially explosive situation. The punches he rained on Tommy Bedford's face after a tackle in the match against Natal nearly caused a riot when some spectators invaded the field to avenge the attack on Natal's most popular player.

The Lions never hesitated to use their fists or boots when they felt it necessary and at their captain's call of "Ninety-nine" just about every member of the team would select an opponent and start belabouring him. "We will take no prisoners" and "Let's get in our retaliation first" were phrases often used in their team talks and one of the reports in *L'Equipe* referred to the third test as *un combat de rue*, a fight in the street.

McBride and Millar, remembering their previous visits to South Africa, had primed their men to expect the hardest games of their lives in the tests. It must have come as an anti-climax to these highly-motivated competitors when the Springboks proved to be nowhere near as tough as they had expected. After 10 minutes of the first test, played at Newlands in muddy conditions, Millar predicted that his team would win the series. It took him only that long to realise that the South Africans, who had been masters of scrummaging for so long, had forgotten the art. Edwards could cook up all sorts of tricks behind his scrum while his forwards held the Springboks in the proverbial vice. In the light of subsequent events the Springboks actually fared reasonably well in the first encounter and three penalty goals by Bennett and a drop by Edwards, against a drop by Dawie Snyman, made up the score of 12-3

The mighty J. P. R. Williams in action. John Rubython

in their favour.

The South African selectors then became panicky and made the first of many mostly inexplicable changes which in the end were to lead to 33 different players being used in the four tests; 21 of them gaining their colours for the first time. It was certainly not the best method of building up a team with a hope of beating a side as splendidly-drilled as the Lions. The second test was lost 9–28, South Africa s biggest-ever defeat, and no less than 11 changes were made for the next international.

The selectors at this stage seemed to have lost control of the situation. There certainly was no reason to axe John Williams, the best lineout forward in South Africa, or to go into the third test without any mobility up front. With both scrumhalves Roy McCallum and Paul Bayvel injured, the selectors with an astonishing lack of logic, chose Gerrie Sonnekus in preference to experienced specialists like Barry Wolmarans or Gert Schutte. Sonnekus, an eighthman who played briefly as a scrumhalf and subsequently successfully returned to the scrum at provincial level, was literally thrown to the Lions. After doing reasonably well in the first half, the Springboks crumbled and were beaten 9–26, the second biggest defeat in our history! It was the roughest test of the series with both sides dishing out and taking fearful punishment and it was hardly surprising that the Springbok lock Moaner van Heerden, who had a particularly fiery first-half, was so badly injured that he had to be replaced by Kevin de Klerk. In the second half the Lions more or less did as they pleased against a Springbok team who had run out of steam.

The selectors were more conservative when they chose their team for the final test and a minimum of changes were made. There was some continuity and pattern for the first time and the Springboks responded by holding the Lions to a 13-all draw. For once the Lions, who were beginning to lose their motivation after the long tour, were not quite so slick and by swinging the scrum, the Springboks were able occasionally to put Edwards under pressure.

It was a dramatic, controversial test and the 75 000 spectators who paid a record R500 000 were at least spared the sight of seeing the Springboks humiliated as they were in the second and third internationals.

The referee, Mr. Max Baise, had an afternoon of agonising decisions and he left the field at the end of the match with Phil Bennett on his heels, hurling abuse at him.

Mr. Baise's disputed decisions affected both teams, however, and a draw was probably the best result. Roger Uttley was awarded a try which the Springboks felt he should not have been given. Chris Pope, the South African right wing, was quite adamant that he had dotted down before the tall Lions flanker could get to the ball and a photograph published later supported the University of Cape Town medical student's claim. It showed Pope putting the ball down with Uttley still in the process of diving for it.

In the final minute of the match J. P. R. Williams launched a fantastic run which split the Springbok defence before he passed inside to Slattery. As Slattery dived for the line, Peter Cronje slammed into him and it appeared as if the Lions flanker had pressed the ball on the Springbok centre's thigh instead of grounding it. The referee was unsighted and in accordance with the rules, he gave the Lions a five-yard scrum instead of a try. They were extremely upset about the decision and some outright insults were directed at Mr. Baise. Cronje, who had scored the Springboks' only try of the series earlier in the match after a powerful burst by Pope, afterwards said that he had also thought that Slattery should have been given the score. Referees are only human and if Mr. Baise did indeed err on both counts, the one mistake cancelled out the other and the result of the match remains a fair one. Cronje's try, incidentally, was the first 4-point try to be scored by the Springboks.

The final test gave the Springboks some compensation but the Lions were emphatically the better side in the series and it was South Africa's most comprehensive defeat since Bill MacLagan's pioneers made a clean sweep of it back in 1891.

Above: Andy Irvine receives congratulations from Thomas Magxala, the captain of the Leopards, after scoring 20 points.

John Rubython

Below: Smiles all round as Dr. Danie Craven visits the triumphant Lions in their dressingroom at the end of the tour.

John Rubython

Overleaf: Frik du Preez at home in the saddle while Abie Malan seems amused. Two mighty Springbok forwards enjoying an outing.

Die Huisgenoot

Right: Gareth Edwards, the best scrumhalf in the world in 1974.

John Rubython

Dawie de Villiers, outstanding player and inspiring captain.

Die Huisgenoot

France 1958 – 1975

Jan Ellis, one of the finest loose-forwards in Springbok history. Ellis played in 38 tests for South Africa.

John Rubython

Lucien Mias, who wandered through the hotel corridors the night before France won the 1958 series against the Springboks at Ellis Park.

At just about the time Bill Mclagan and his first British team to tour South Africa disembarked at Cape Town in 1891, a French journalist wrote an article warning his countrymen against playing *"le football"*.

"It is a brutal British game," the Parisian preached in his journal. "The ball is a heavy projectile and when propelled by a vigorous English kick is at least as dangerous as the ball of a revolver. . . ."

Frenchmen do not like to be told what to do or not to do and the warning fell on deaf ears. The game soon took root in France, or in some parts of it rather, but the growth was stunted for many years because of a total lack of discipline among players or administrators. "Rugby is a quarrel perfectly expressed," the novelist Jacques Perret once wrote and the problem was that French players fought each other with the same relish with which they tackled opponents.

Paul Roos, the captain of the first-ever Springboks to visit Britain and France, tried to explain to them the virtues of team spirit as far back as 1907, but the lesson took a long time to sink in. So long, in fact, that French rugby was for many years something hardly to be discussed in decent company. Frenchmen gave the world the phrase *"esprit de corps"* but the moment they had an oval ball in their hands they invariably forgot the meaning of it.

Jean Prat appeared on the scene immediately following World War II and it was he who finally managed to bring discipline into French rugby; who made his fellow players realise that the game is played best when it is seen as the perfect society in microcosm with different elements performing a variety of tasks in unison for the common good. Prat brought home to his players that strength of character is the basic requirement for success in international rugby; that a player must sublimate his own ego in the interests of his team. Once this new approach was accepted — and it was not done at the expense of flair and individual genius — France soon developed into a major power in world rugby.

In 1952 Hennie Muller, leading what some consider the best Springbok combination in history, slammed France into abject defeat on their own ground, but two years later the Tricolors, carrying the symbol of the rooster on their blue jerseys, had beaten the All Blacks and were more than holding their own against the four Home Countries, England, Scotland, Wales and Ireland.

The rooster, as a symbol of French defiance of foreign supremacy dates back to 52 B.C. when Caesar, to the dismay of thousands of generations of schoolboys to come, decided to conquer what was then known as Gaul. He encountered stern opposition from a chieftain called Vercingetorix whose guerilla tactics earned him the admiration of the Romans, who likened his gallant men to fighting roosters. Vercingetorix was flattered enough to order everyone under his command to wear the emblem of a rooster on their chests.

The symbol did not bring the Gaul chief much luck. He was eventually captured and taken to Rome where he was put on exhibition as a sort of tourist attraction. When the novelty wore off, the Romans executed him. The popular comic strip of today was almost certainly inspired by Vercingetorix's exploits of more than 2 000 years ago.

In 1958 a French team visited South Africa for the first time and Denis Lalanne of *L'Equipe* referred to it in his magnificently-written book *Le Grand Combat du Quinze de France* as the "A.D.I for French rugby", the true year of birth for the game as far as he and his compatriots were concerned.

Michel Celaya was the tour captain but he was injured early on and it was mainly Lucien Mias who led the team to five wins, two draws and three defeats. Much more important to them was the fact that they drew one of the test matches and won the other, thereby becoming the first visiting side to beat the Springboks in a series in South Africa in over 60 years.

The language barrier presented some problems but, generally speaking, the South African public was fascinated by the darting unorthodoxy of the visitors in blue.

The pugnacity and toughness of forwards like Jean Barthe, Alfred ("The Rock") Roques, Francois Moncla, Bernard Mommejat, Jean Carrere, Aldo Quaglio and others shook the South Africans and backs like Pierre Danos, Roger Martine, Pierre Lacaze, Jean Dupuy and Henri Rancoule delighted the spectators with the most impudent moves.

Rugby writers who had never seen French rugby players before were quite stunned at the basic differences between them and the Springboks, or players from any of the Anglo-Saxon countries for that matter. Lucien Mias, a doctor by profession, always seemed to be arguing endlessly and loudly with his players and the night before the Ellis Park test he polished off a bottle of rum. He then wandered around the corridors of the Langham Hotel until the early hours and yet he turned in a superlative performance against the Springboks. With Barthe, Mommejat and Roques, he was one of the best forwards on the field, and they had the South African pack slowed down to a trot by the time the referee, Chris Ackermann, ended the match.

It was a team packed with courageous players, no-one more so than Pierre ("The Butterfly") Lacaze who substituted for the injured Michel Vannier in both tests, and who played at Ellis Park with several novocaine injections in his ankle. This did not prevent him from scoring a penalty and a dropgoal.

The first test, at Newlands, was frankly dull with the Springboks being barracked by their own supporters as Ian Kirkpatrick, at flyhalf, adopted kick-first, think-later, tactics.

Pierre Danos, once summed up his rugby philosophy by saying: "There are two kinds of players; those who play pianos and those who shift them". His performances on the tour left no

Above: Jeremy Nel, outstanding centre in New Zealand in 1956, attempts a cross-kick in the first test against France in 1958 at Newlands. In the background is Ian Kirkpatrick.

Below: Dawie Ackermann, an effective flanker against the Lions in 1955 and the All Blacks in 1956, tries vainly to barge past a French defender. In the background is Alan Skene.

doubt to which school he belonged; France's only points at Newlands came from a perfectly-executed drop-goal by the slender French scrumhalf. Danos also often said that he never kicked for goal unless he was sure of success and the fact that he did not fail once on the three occasions he attempted dropkicks on the tour, seems to prove that he knew what he was talking about.

The Springboks' only points came from a try by Butch Lochner, one of the few South African players who distinguished himself that season, and the Newlands match ended in a 3-all draw.

The second test, at Ellis Park, was more exciting. The Frenchmen had suffered a crushing defeat against a combined Western Province-Boland -South Western Districts side at Wellington shortly before the international encounter, and the South Africans had been lulled into a false sense of security. As was the case in the first test, they again erred by over-estimating the French backs and under-estimating their forwards. The Springbok pack failed to master the fiery French forwards and they also lost the battle of tactics. A scintillating break by Jeremy Nel, the burly centre who played so well on the 1956 tour of New Zealand but who had been shifted to the flyhalf position, led to the only South African score, a try by wing Lofty Fourie and converted by fullback Mickey Gerber. A penalty and a dropgoal by Lacaze and a drop from Roger Martine made the game safe for the Tricolors.

The French dressingroom afterwards was a sight to see. Several of the players were weeping with joy with Martine totally overcome by emotion. When Danie Craven and Louis Babrow, who had often helped the visitors with advice on the tour, walked in to congratulate them, the team gave them a touching ovation. Craven and Babrow made some staunch friends for South African sport with their gesture; friendships which were to bear fruit in the difficult years to follow when France so often stepped into the breach whenever tours from other countries failed to come off because of political pressure.

The next time the Roosters and the Springboks met were at Colombes Stadium in 1961 and neither side could score in a rousing battle described more fully in the chapter on Avril Malan's touring team to the United Kingdom and France. Three years later Michel Crauste brought out a team to play South Africa in a single test at Springs and they won 8-6 in what had frequently been described as the worst international match yet to have been seen in this country.

The Tricolors, at that stage, really

Right: The only test between France and the 1961 Springboks ended in a scoreless draw after an absorbing struggle in Paris. Here a French forward makes sure of good possession as Avril Malan and Johan Claassen try to get to him. On the right is Fanie Kuhn and Dick Lockyear.

Below: Michel Antelme and John Gainsford flash charming smiles as they help a mannequin with her choice of hat during a visit to *Chez Dior* in Paris in 1961.

seemed to have the Springboks taped; whenever they met, the South Africans looked disorganised and leaden-footed. This was certainly the case at Springs in 1964 when wing Christian Darrouy scored a try and Pierre (Monsieur Le Drop) Albaladejo added a conversion and a penalty. Dave Stewart, with his usual unobtrusive efficiency, notched all the Springbok points with a try and a penalty.

France undertook their first full-scale tour of this country in 1967 and it coincided with a critical stage in South African rugby history. Including the 1964 debacle at Springs the Springboks had lost eight out of nine test matches and their chances of regaining their self-confidence against opponents they had been unable to fathom on four successive occasions over a period of nearly 10 years, looked slim.

France was riding the crest of the wave after having won the Five-Nations tournament, an achievement considered so highly that their skipper Christian Darrouy sent an after-match message to General de Gaulle reading simply: "Mission accomplished". The championship became theirs through powerful forwards and the Camberabero brothers, Lilian and Guy, as the half-backs.

Tiny Guy Camberabero, protected by his scrumhalf-brother and some of the toughest and best forwards in the game, scored the points with the computer-like precision of his boot, and as a general rule the threequarters were neglected. Lilian could not make the trip to South Africa but "The Flea" was fully expected to do to South Africa what he did so efficiently in the Five-Nations tournament: stabbing over penalties and dropgoals whenever his pack could bring him within potting range.

Darrouy's team was particularly strong up front with players like Jean-Michel Cabanier, Benoit Dauga (one of the best forwards in rugby history), Walter Spanghero, Jacques Fort (who was effectively the skipper of the side), Alain Plantefol (who was involved in virtually all of the brawls which were to make the tour such a rough, controversial one), and the fast and intelligent Christian Carrere.

Fullbacks Claude Lacaze (like his older brother Pierre, he was known as "Butterfly") and Pierre Villepreux, with centres Claude Dourthe and Jean Trillo, were the most impressive backs but the 10-man pattern employed by the Frenchmen did not give their threequarters much scope.

As for South Africa, a new panel of selectors under the chairmanship of the invariably calm and courteous Flappie Lochner, refused to accept the commonly-held view that the Springboks were doomed once again. They selected eight newcomers for the first test in Durban, then stuck

Above: Benoit Dauga, a giant in the history of rugby.

Below: Guy Camberabero, whose deadly kicking was a constant threat to the 1967 Springboks.

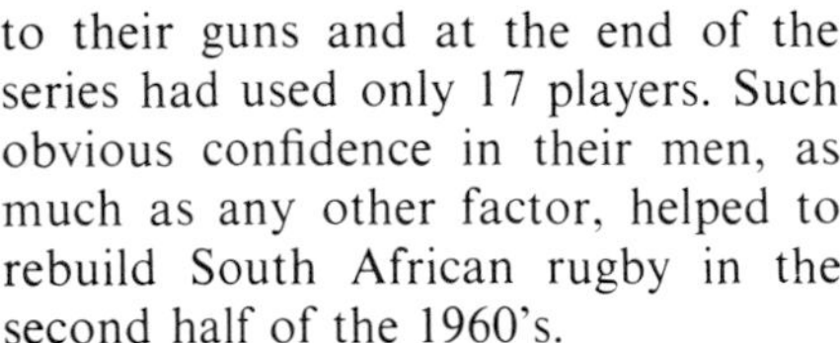

H. O. de Villiers on the rampage in his first test. His remarkable ability to launch counter attacks stunned the Frenchmen. With him is his captain, Dawie de Villiers.

Jimmy Soullier

to their guns and at the end of the series had used only 17 players. Such obvious confidence in their men, as much as any other factor, helped to rebuild South African rugby in the second half of the 1960's.

The four tests were crammed into less than a month and this probably accounts for the fact that the standard of play dipped sharply after the first two matches.

The Springboks made a brilliant start to the series in Durban. Led with verve and fire by Dawie de Villiers, they played with such assurance and enterprise that the Frenchmen were run ragged and could scrape together only three points against 26 for South Africa.

In the dark-haired, powerfully-built H. O. de Villiers, the Springboks proved to have a new fullback who was as unpredictably dangerous as any Frenchman. Henry Oswald de Villiers, who was to play in 14 tests before injury so tragically ended his international career at the age of 25, was a trump card against a team like France in particular. The Frenchmen never before had to contend with a Springbok fullback who believed firmly in counterattack rather than the safe kick to touch. In spite of what they said later, they never did solve the problem he represented; unless it was to make darn sure not to kick in his direction the way they did in the first two tests. In addition to his instinctive aggression, H. O. also had wonderfully safe hands, a quick brain, raw courage and the sheer physical strength to break tackles or to flatten forwards.

Eben Olivier, an extremely nimble centre with remarkable acceleration and a bobbing running style also came as a nasty shock to the Frenchmen and Corra Dirksen, the stocky, fearless, Northern Transvaal wing was a downright nightmare to them. John Gainsford and Jannie Engelbrecht and to a lesser extent, Dawie de Villiers, gave the backline the guiding hand of experience and Piet Visagie, De Villiers' new partner, made no mistakes, was an excellent kicker and a valuable defender. The freckle-faced flyhalf from Griqualand West had to endure a lot of criticism in the initial stages of his career because his approach was considered too negative, but he was to go on to play in 25 tests, to score 130 points, and to be accurately acclaimed as just about the perfect pivot in the merciless world of international rugby.

The Springbok pack also surprised the Frenchmen. The new hooker, Gys Pitzer, not only did his job

Eben Olivier, the agile Stellenbosch centre, also often foxed the French defence with his dodging, weaving style of running.

superbly well but he also proved himself to be one of the toughest men ever to pull the green and gold jersey over his head. Boxing ability should hardly be a qualification for a rugby player but some members of the 1967 French team often enough confused the two sports for it to have been an advantage in that hotly contested series.

The Durban test also marked the debut of Piet Greyling, who immediately dovetailed perfectly with Jan Ellis on the other flank, and the partnership became one of the mainstays of Springbok rugby in a record number of 24 tests. Albie de Waal, the selectors' choice at No. 8 had a good enough series before fading abruptly from the scene but the tight-forwards, Tiny Neethling, Tiny Naude and Gawie Carelse (replaced by Frik du Preez in the 4th test) made solid contributions for years to come.

The South African rugby public was so numbed by the long run of defeats that the Springbok team for the first test caused hardly any reaction. A. C. Parker afterwards wrote that the actual announcement of the team at a function in Durban was, with the exception of a few cheers for H. O. and Ellis, greeted "in stony silence".

Within five minutes of the start of the test, Corra Dirksen steamed inside from the leftwing position to take the ball from Dawie de Villiers. Without even making a pretence at side-stepping or swerving past any opponent, he ploughed through and over next to the posts, with H. O. de Villiers making it five points. The Tricolors replied promptly with an unconverted try by Claude Dourthe but rough play gave H. O. the chance to make the score 8-3 with a penalty.

Less than 15 minutes before half-time, the Springboks ripped the heart out of the French resistance with a sudden try from the blue. H. O. de Villiers, running at full speed, snapped up a poor clearance a few yards from touch, dummied once, bumped off two defenders, and then ran just far enough to bring his forwards on-side before kicking ahead with unerring accuracy. The French fullback, Lacaze, and the cover defence had no chance of saving the situation. Jan Ellis over-ran the ball but Piet Greyling was just behind him to pick up and score. H. O., his handsome features creased with the lines of concentration, steered the difficult conversion kick high over the crossbar as he did again a few minutes later when Jan Ellis also carved through a demoralized defence.

After half-time, Greyling scored his second try to make his debut really memorable and H. O., already the darling of Newlands, became a national hero as he again added two more points. The game then deteriorated as sporadic fighting broke out among the forwards and Spanghero was briefly knocked out by a punch which was apparently not even intended for him. With 15 minutes to go, Dirksen again treated the French defence with contempt to score an unconverted try and the game ended with the Springboks having scored a remarkably comfortable 26-3 victory over the European champions.

The second test in Bloemfontein was not quite so easy and it was not until the second half that the Springbok forwards gained enough of a grip to drive through to victory.

At half-time the Springboks had only a long-range penalty from Tiny Naude to show for all their hard work and on several occasions only H. O. de Villiers stood between France and a score. Once, with three Frenchmen coming at him and no other defenders in sight, H. O. risked life and limb by successfully diving onto Dourthe's boot as he tried to grubber-kick the ball towards the goalline. The other bright star in the Springbok line-up was Eben Olivier, who scored a brilliant individualistic try in the second half, and who had the defence groping blindly more than once. He handed Corra Dirksen his third try of the series on a plate after one such break and not long afterwards Jannie Engelbrecht was sent on his way with only fullback Villepreux to beat. The willowy Stellenbosch wing left the Frenchman standing with a typical outside swerve and, with H. O. converting, the Springboks won 16-3.

Guy Camberabero, with 10 points out of a total of 19, six of them from two smooth dropkicks, steered France to an upset victory in the third test at Ellis Park. It was Claude Lacaze's remarkable dropped penalty goal from the half-way line, however, that stands out in memory as the highlight of a game in which nothing went right for the Springboks. Eben Olivier once again scored a try with his bewildering ability to vary his pace but the rest of the South African points came from two penalties from way out by that veteran stalwart, Tiny Naude and a try by Ellis, converted by Visagie to make the final score 19–14 in favour of France. It was, incidentally, the first time Visagie had scored in a test.

John Gainsford, after having played in 33 tests and having scored a record total of eight tries, lost his place for the 4th test at Newlands to make way for Syd Nomis, later to become one of the best wings in the world. Gainsford, although then only 29 years old, had already shown signs of fading the previous season and he was certainly no longer the most feared centre in the world. He had suddenly seemed to lose the speed which was always so startling for such a tall, heavy, man and that once devastating inside break could no longer cut the line with the ease of old. He was one of the truly great players of his era, however, and John Leslie Gainsford will never be forgotten.

The final test ended in a draw and the game, played in a whipping wind, had no flow or pattern and referee Piet Robbertse dished out no less than 26 penalties to the two sides. Camberabero and H. O. succeeded with a penalty each and the other points came from a try by Spanghero for France and a fantastic dropgoal from a difficult angle and practically on the halfway line by Piet Visagie. Generally, the Springbok half-backs did not play well, though, and Dawie de Villiers was given far too little protection by his forwards. The match, once again, had moments of bad temper and Frik du Preez and Alain Plantefol had an argument that resulted in the Frenchman receiving a black eye. The two players made their peace in the dressingroom afterwards and exchanged jerseys to prove their goodwill.

Although the Springboks could not sustain the brilliant form they showed in the first two tests, the series at least did prove that South African rugby was pulling out of the nose-dive. Brilliant new players had come to the fore and pride and self confidence had returned after the horrible disasters of 1965.

South Africa and France did not have long to wait before they clashed again. In 1968 the Springboks beat Tom Kiernan's disappointing Lions and three months afterwards left for a short six-match tour of France. Dawie de Villiers' team lost one of the matches against South-West France, South Africa's first-ever defeat on French soil, but won both tests. Jannie Engelbrecht scored five tries in his five matches on the tour, a Springbok record in France. Engelbrecht, South Africa's best wing for nearly a decade, at the time already held the record for the most tries by a Springbok on a tour of

Above: Piet Greyling, destined to become one of the best Springbok forwards of his era, dives over for one of the two tries he scored in his debut. Albie de Waal (left) and Gys Pitzer, in support, also shone in their first test in Durban in 1967.

The Sunday Times

Right: Several members of the 1968 Springbok team to France were of French descent. Here they are, *from left:* Hannes Marais, Tonie Roux, Mannetjies Roux, Dawie de Villiers, Eben Olivier, H. O. de Villiers, Frik du Preez and Tiny Naude.

Corra Dirksen, the powerful Springbok wing, who was feared by his French opponents in 1967.

New Zealand established when he notched 15 in 15 matches on the 1965 tour. Piet Visagie, who was at his match-winning best on the 1968 tour of France, scored 20 points (out of a South African total of 26) against Auvergne-Limousin which is still the highest individual score by a Springbok in France.

It was also Visagie's ice-cool temperament and deadly boot that won the first test at Bordeaux. Visagie placed four penalty kicks to score all of South Africa's points against France's nine, which came from three tries. Benoit Dauga, playing at lock, got two of the tries.

The second test, in Paris, was a thriller with the Springboks trailing after first Puget, and then Paries, had succeeded with dropgoals. The Springboks were playing against a bitterly-cold wind and the French forwards were rampant in the first half. The utter fearlessness of H. O. de Villiers under an absolute barrage of up-an-unders and some desperate all-round defensive work, somehow kept the Springbok goalline intact and by the end of the first half some of France's fury seemed to be spent. It was then that Visagie, who played some of the best rugby of his career on this tour, put over a perfectly-judged penalty. Just on half-time an incorrect decision by the referee, Paddy D'Arcy, robbed Syd Nomis of a try scored after a well-controlled grubber by the Springbok flyhalf.

Twenty minutes after the resumption, Mannetjies Roux snapped up a rolling ball and after Nomis and Olivier had done their share, Frik du Preez passed to Engelbrecht who swerved out and then jinked inside, for one of the best of the eight test tries he was eventually to leave next to his name in the record books. Not long afterwards, Dawie de Villiers broke cleanly from a scrum and, revealing his exceptional pace, he ran right through without a hand being laid on him. Visagie converted this one and then came a try which Syd Nomis must have relived in many a nightmare in the years to come.

Eben Olivier tackled Claude Dourthe near the French line and Nomis flashed up to dribble it over the line for what should have been an easy try. Instead Nomis stumbled.... fell....struggled up....and fell again as cramp in the leg suddenly all but paralysed him. As the defence thundered up, Nomis continued his slow-motion progress towards the ball and he collapsed on it only in the nick of time. Visagie again converted and the Springboks eventually won 16-11 after a fantastic come-back by France had been rounded off with Ellie Cester going over next to the posts.

In 1971 France paid yet another short visit to South Africa when Christian Carrere brought out a strong side with one of its members, Roger Bourgarel, a nine-day wonder because he was the first Black player to be seen in action against the Springboks on a South African field. The novelty soon wore off and the slightly-built wing will be remembered not for the colour of his skin but for twice having stopped Frik du Preez in full cry for the line.

The South Africans won the first test in Bloemfontein 22-9 with the immaculate left boot of Ian ("Mighty Mac") McCallum contributing 13 of the points. It was the 34th test match for Frik du Preez, one of the most colourful and most idolised of all Springboks, and once, for a few dramatic seconds, it looked as if the big Northern Transvaal lock would score a try to celebrate the fact that he had become the most-capped South African up to that time. It was Bourgarel who somehow knocked him off-balance on the corner flag and the Free State crowd expressed their approval of his courage in no uncertain terms. To have tackled Frik du Preez under any circumstances took a very brave brave man; to have stopped him at full speed in a test, bordered on the foolhardy!

The best player on the field that day, however, was a member of the losing side. Benoit Dauga, the lanky, bearded French eighthman gave a magnificent performance but it was not enough to win the day for his country.

The second test in Durban was spoilt by an ugly brawl midway through the first half. It erupted shortly after Jo Maso had to leave the field with an injury after being crash-tackled from behind by Joggie Jansen. His replacement, Dourthe, climbed into McCallum immediately after play was resumed and he viciously kicked the Springbok fullback who was nowhere near the ball. Piet Greyling immediately sped to McCallum's aid and a general free-for-all ensued with both teams equally guilty of disgraceful behaviour.

The fighting was eventually stopped but flared up again briefly, before good sense prevailed for the rest of a match which was bitterly contested but conducted more or less according to the rules. The result was an 8-all draw and Frik du Preez was foiled for a second time by the tenacious Bourgarel. This time the craggy-faced Springbok had actually shaken off three opponents and was pounding towards the tryline when Bourgarel got hold of his jersey and slowed him down long enough for the cover defence to bring him down.

The Frenchmen played excellent rugby throughout their short visit, with Dauga towering over all his opponents as the best eighthman of his era. Claude and Walter Spanghero, Jean-Claude Skrela, Jack Cantoni, Roland Bertranne, and Jean Trillo also shone in a team which was always entertaining. From a South African viewpoint, the first test marked the debut of John Williams, a lanky lineout specialist, frontranker Theo Sauermann, scrumhalf Joggie Viljoen and centre Peter Cronje.

Three years later, their confidence badly shaken by Willie-John McBride's 1974 Lions who mauled them in three of the four tests on South African soil, Hannes Marais took a rather subdued Springbok team to France. They won both tests, 13-4 and 10-8, and were beaten only once when West France defeated them on a muddy ground. Nevertheless the Springboks were not entirely convincing. French rugby was also going through a period crisis as their defeats against Rumania, Ireland and Wales had proved.

The emergence of Morne du Plessis as a mature international player was one of the few benefits of the tour and Robert Cockrell and Moaner van Heerden also showed signs of developing into test players of the highest class. The tour ended the career of Hannes Marais, one of the true giants of South African rugby, and had it not been for the solitary defeat at Angouleme, he would have gone into retirement with the unique distinction of being the only Springbok captain ever to have led undefeated teams on two overseas tours.

Among the backs Dawie Snyman was often brilliant, sometimes erratic. Willem Stapelberg, a Pretoria detective, was an unqualified success and Carel Fourie, on the other wing, did well enough and also proved to have a good boot for long-range penalties. Johan Oosthuizen and Ian Robertson showed glimpses of real class but Gerald Bosch, a match-winning kicker too seldom revealed the other attributes expected of an international flyhalf. His provincial scrumhalf Paul Bayvel had a good tour but he was certainly not a new Dawie de Villiers.

Dawie de Villiers and Gawie Carelse have a brief chat at half-time during the second test in France in 1968. The Springboks won the first test 12-9 and the second 16-11.

Stapelberg's try in the first test at Toulouse was the highlight of the tour. This is how Neville Leck described it in the *Cape Times* afterwards:

"In the 19th minute of the game Johan Oosthuizen kicks ahead. A French defender catches the ball but is promptly flattened by Marais. The Bok forwards pour in over the ball, bunched together in a tight green knot. The ball spews back from the heaving Springbok machine and in a flash Paul Bayvel has spun the ball to Gerald Bosch and Bosch is flipping it inside to Jan Ellis. It is a perfect pass. Ellis rips through the gap, hammers forward, 10, 15, 20 yards. He is stopped, but his trusty pack-mates roar in behind him, forming a perfect wedge. The ball shoots back again. This time Morne du Plessis, running at top speed, takes it and throws out a perfect pass to Ian Robertson. Robertson lets go immediately to Dawie Snyman who has slipped into the Boks backline like a shadow. Snyman waits just long enough to draw Roland Bertranne, then lets go. Next thing Willem Stapelberg, given the overlap, has blazed the remaining 15 yards and dived into history. . . ."

There were minor political demonstrations against the visit of the Springboks and the team was frequently criticised for being "anti-social". Several of the matches were extremely rough and Carel Fourie, an aggressive wing, was the man the spectators loved to hate; the role filled for so long on overseas tours by fiery little Mannetjies Roux. After a few of the tougher matches, the Springboks were described in several newspapers as "Buffaloes" and a "Savage Horde", and one sportswriter claimed that they were a poor side who had to choose between "finesse and force, and chose force". Nobody took these charges very seriously as rugby in France is never a garden party affair.

Five months later South Africa and France were at it again. It was to be a short but strenuous tour with 11 matches, including two tests, to be crammed into less than one month. Most of the top French players could not make the trip and their sportswriters, with their rather typical tendency to exaggerate, described the touring team as a gathering of lambs destined to be slaughtered. They were beaten, all right, but it was no slaughter of the innocents and 1975 became a particularly significant year in South African rugby history.

The simple announcement of the team established a record of some sort when not one, but two captains were appointed. Richard Astre and Jacques Fouroux were both given equal responsibility and authority and although the touring party seemed to be definitely divided into two camps, the unprecedented set-up seemed to work somehow. The team of largely untried youngsters adapted with remarkable ease and, probably because most French players are so well-schooled in the basics, they revealed astonishing versatility. Jean-Pierre Romeu scored 71 points on the tour, the highest individual total by a French player in South Africa, beating the aggregates of such legendary match winners as Pierre Albaladejo and Guy Camberabero.

Two mileposts in South African rugby history were reached during the tour. In the second test in Pretoria, Gerald Raymond Bosch, often criticised for his general performances at flyhalf but undoubtedly the most consistently accurate placekicker of his era, scored 22 points to notch the highest individual total by a Springbok in an official international match.

And when Morne du Plessis, the tall, angular Western Province eighthman was given the Springbok leadership, it was the first time that the son of a Springbok captain had followed in his father's footsteps to earn the same honour. Morne's father, Felix, had led South Africa in three winning tests against the All Blacks in 1949.

Du Plessis, a product of Grey College, Bloemfontein, and the University of Stellenbosch, had all the qualifications for the assignment and was really an obvious choice. A player with an abundance of natural talent, he is a relentless competitor with as much iron in his soul as any of his illustrious predecessors. He is without a doubt the dominating personality in South African rugby of the mid-70's.

Du Plessis, incidentally, is dramatic proof of Dr. Danie Craven's well-known theory that athletic ability is hereditary. Morne's father was a Springbok rugby captain, his mother a Springbok hockey captain and his uncle on his maternal side, Horace Smethurst, was a Springbok soccer captain. Nic du Plessis, the rugby Springbok of the 1920's was his father's uncle.

The two tests against France in 1975 were both handled by Mr. Norman Sanson, a London-based Scot, the first time that a neutral referee officiated in South Africa.

Mannetjies Roux, unpredictable genius

Ian McCallum, immaculate placekicker

John Gainsford, speed and power

Frik du Preez, living legend

Tommy Bedford, fiery and intelligent

Hannes Marais, solid as a rock

Above: H. O. de Villiers, played in 14 tests in a short but illustrious career as Springbok fullback.

Die Huisgenoot

The 1975 French team also made more significant history by, apart from playing against the Leopards, a team consisting of Black players, and the Proteas, a combination of coloured players, they also became the first team to play a South African Invitation XV selected from all races. The match took place at Newlands on June 7 when Morne du Plessis led a team which included two players from the Proteas and two from the Leopards, to a thrilling 18-3 victory.

The names of these four pioneers will always have a special place of honour in rugby's hall of fame. They were Morgan Cushe, a 26-year-old clerk from Uitenhage and a lively, if smallish, flanker, Toto Tsotsobe, a 22-year-old worker in a Port Elizabeth tyre factory and a driving wing, John Noble, 21 years old and a very fast wing who worked as a messenger at the University of Stellenbosch, and Harold (Turkey) Shields, a 24-year-old truck driver from the Strand, who can hold his own in most frontrows.

South Africa's first-ever racially mixed team, played well indeed and a packed Newlands gave the alert John Noble a stirring ovation when he followed up a cleverly-placed grubber by Dawie Snyman to score. It was South African rugby's first glimpse of a new dawn, heralding an era which could lead to achievements matching and perhaps even surpassing those of the past.

The first test, in Bloemfontein, was a strange affair with the Springboks winning 38-25 for an amazing match aggregate of 63 points. It equalled the world record match aggregate established when Wales beat France 49-14 in 1910. At one stage the Springboks led 35-9 but then they inexplicably lost their grip and the lighter French forwards came into

Above: Carel Fourie, a strong and aggressive wing, was one of the stars of the 1974 Springbok team to tour France.
John Rubython

Above, right: Nothing can stop Willem Stapelberg, the big Pretoria detective, on his way to the line for a brilliant try during the 1974 series in France. John Rubython

Right: The French touring team of 1975 became the first international side to play a mixed South African XV. Here John Noble, who scored a fine try, attempts to control a rolling ball in the face of a challenge from Amade and Aguirre. Pierre Goosen is in the background. John Rubython

Left: Gerald Bosch, the Transvaal flyhalf, whose accurate boot made him one of the game's greatest matchwinners. In the final test against the 1975 French team in Pretoria, Bosch scored 22 points to establish a South African test record.
John Rubython

their own. The South Africans were never in any danger of losing but their shocking slump in the final 20 minutes cast a shadow over the brilliant first 60 minutes of the match when players like Dawie Snyman, Johan Oosthuizen, Peter Whipp, Gerald Bosch, Paul Bayvel, Kleintjie Grobler, Robert Cockrell, Moaner van Heerden, Kevin de Klerk and Morne du Plessis were outstanding.

Brawling marred the second test, at Loftus Versfeld, and there was a fearsome toll of injuries. Moaner van Heerden was taken off the field in the 69th minute with his cheek flayed open and his hand fractured while French forwards Michel Palmie, Robert Paparemborde and Patrice Peron all had to receive medical attention for chest and rib injuries,

The first 20 minutes after half-time were as torrid as any in the history of the game but the Springboks kept their cool a little better than their opponents and they deserved their 33-18 victory. The referee, Mr. Sanson, awarded no less than 34 penalties and Gerald Bosch, kicking with computer-like efficiency, succeeded with six and also converted tries by Fourie and Du Plessis. Carel Fourie also slammed over a massive penalty from the halfway line.

The turning point of the match came after Moaner van Heerden had been led off the field, bleeding profusely. Instead of losing their heads and trying to take violent revenge, the Springboks controlled themselves while the Frenchmen continued with their mad-dog tactics, conceding three successive penalties with futile fouling. Gerald Bosch converted the first two into points and Carel Fourie made sure of the third. It spelt the end of France's challenge.

Above: Dawie Snyman, an outstanding Springbok of the mid-1970s, kicks for touch against the 1974 Frenchmen. Up in support are veteran Jan Ellis and brilliant newcomers Morné du Plessis and Johan Oosthuizen.

John Rubython

THE TURBULENT YEARS

All Blacks 1960 – 1976

Richard James Conway is not remembered in South Africa as one of the great All Blacks; even the few among us who recall his name will never mention it with the awe and admiration reserved for a Kevin Skinner, a Colin Meads, a Bob Scott, a Don Clarke or a Bryan Williams.

And yet, what "Red" Conway did to ensure his place in Wilson Whineray's touring team to South Africa in 1960, illustrates the unbelievable intensity of the rugby rivalry between the Springboks and the All Blacks. During the New Zealand trials Conway's fourth finger of his right hand turned septic after an injury and his doctor told him that it would not be healed in time for him to make the tour. A specialist suggested, probably in jest, that an amputation would mean quicker mending. Without hesitation the red-haired Otago carpenter had the finger amputated and he played in three of the four tests of the series.

The 1960 tour very nearly did not come off as there were strong protests against the exclusion of Maori players. It was, in fact, to be the last tour by New Zealand to South Africa for ten years, by which time the embarrassing situation had been changed with Maoris as welcome as anyone else.

Wilson Whineray commanded an extremely strong combination which in Don Clarke, Ian Nev MacEwan, Colin Meads, Kelvin Tremain and Peter Jones had players who simply must be rated among the best from any country, in any era.

Whineray, himself, was a born leader of men; firm but tactful. A receding hair line made the 25-year-old Aucklander look older than his age and he had a deceptively soft appearance for an international prop forward. His tussles with Piet (Spiere) du Toit, the immensely powerful Springbok frontranker whose pushing method the All Blacks regarded as illegal, proved, however, that the New Zealander was perfectly capable of looking after himself. A former Universities heavyweight boxing champion, Whineray never used his fists on the field to intimidate opponents, which is further testimony to his fine character.

He had retained his love for boxing, and was most knowledgeable about the lore of the ring while he also liked soccer, a game he played before switching to rugby. Whineray's after-match speeches were invariably warm and chivalrous but it was the team manager, Tom Pearce, who really could enliven the dullest function. Pearce, the son of a sea captain, revealed an astonishing general knowledge of subjects as diverse as skin-diving and cooking and he could, and unfailingly did, find a quote from the classics to suit any occasion.

The star of the team, the player everyone in South Africa wanted to see in action, was Donald Barrie Clarke, the tall fullback who had made his international debut against the Springboks four years earlier, and had since developed into the deadliest placekicker of his time. Quite unconcerned with his world-wide fame, Clarke turned out to be one of the most relaxed members of a side — a great deal more affable than most.

Colin Earl Meads and Kelvin Robin Tremain were then poised on the edge of greatness but already formidable men. A nagging groin injury prevented Peter Jones, whom the 1956 Springboks rated so highly, from being the force he should have been. Jones was outstanding against a powerful Northern Transvaal but altogether he could only play in 11 of the matches on tour, this in spite of even going to a faith healer for help. Jones, whose blunt description of the rugged fourth test against the Springboks in 1956 over a public broadcasting system will remain a classic in the annals of pungent comment, was Don Clarke's unofficial bodyguard. He effectively shielded "Camel" as some members of the team called the fullback, from the worst onslaughts of his fans and accepted responsibility for his boots.

This was not as ridiculous a function as it sounds. Clarke wore specially-made size 11½ boots and these

Don Clarke, New Zealand's renowned matchwinner and one of the most acclaimed sportsmen ever to visit South Africa.
Die Burger

were highly-prized by souvenir hunters all over the rugby-playing world and were stolen at an alarming rate. Clarke lost a broken-in pair just before one of the tests and he has said that this was one occasion where he felt the boots were stolen in an attempt to make him less effective.

In his biography *"The Boot"*, Clarke told Pat Booth: "Secret raids on my boots were nothing new. They started when I was an unknown and just before that Ranfurly Shield match at Whangarei which began it all in 1951.

"E. T. Welch, then playing for Bay of Plenty, had his kicking boots stolen only a few hours before his match against North Auckland and had to play in several sizes too big. He tipped me off, and I left a pair of boots easily available for theft — and they went as expected. But they were an old practice pair. My match boots came up, locked in the Clarke car with my parents, on the day of the match!"

Once Peter Jones, all 18 stone of him, took over the job of guarding Clarke's boots on the tour he had no further problems with theft. He went through boots at a remarkable rate, however, and, so it was reported at the time, used up six pairs in 20 matches over a period of just over three months.

The South Africans were well prepared for the tour, following a successful visit by the Junior Springboks to the Argentine and on early-season test against Scotland which served as an opportunity to blood several players who were to wear the green-and-gold with distinction for a long time. The test, a so-so affair in Port Elizabeth, was won 18-10 with Des van Jaarsveldt becoming the first Rhodesian ever to skipper the Springboks.

The All Blacks, as usual, swept through the various provincial teams. Free State beat them 9-8, however, and Combined Services won 8-3 after brilliant performances by then relatively unknown players like Piet Uys, Mof Myburgh, Frik du Preez and Andrew Janson.

In several of the matches rough play was a feature and the whole thing reached boiling point in the match against Eastern Province, a game ever after to be known as the "Battle of Boet Erasmus" in dubious honour of the then brand-new stadium where it was played. The Eastern Province Rugby Union, renowned as one of the most hospitable in South Africa, had gone out of their way to be nice to the tourists, even to the extent of paying for a birthday party for Whineray, but on the field it was a different story. The Eastern Province props, Hambley Parker and Doug Holton, were both extraordinarily strong and their opposite numbers, Eric Anderson and Ian Clarke, objected to their methods.

Soon there was general fighting among the forwards and old-timers afterwards described it as one of the dirtiest matches to have been played in South Africa with players on both sides suffering unnecessary injuries. Some press representatives with the tourists made dire predictions of "blood baths" to follow but fortunately nothing came of this and the tour was actually remarkably free of what are normally euphimistically described as "incidents". Tom Pearce, a man of tempestuous temper, conducted a low-key running battle with the press for some time, but it was mainly hairsplitting, taken seriously only by the people who were involved. In the light of what has been happening in

test matches all over the world in the 1970's, the "Battle of Boet Erasmus" these days would hardly rate the label of a skirmish.

Looking back on the tour, the All Blacks probably produced their best form outside the tests when they battered Transvaal into a 19-3 defeat. The Transvaal team were extremely strong with 12 members of the side either Springboks or Junior Springboks and a thirteenth, centre Eddie Barlow, destined for cricket fame, a sport in which he was to become one of the most illustrious performers in the world. Transvaal were hopelessly outclassed by the All Blacks, however, with Conway, MacEwan, Meads, Tremain, Horsley and the halfback pair of pugnacious Kevin Briscoe and mop-haired Steve Nesbit in superb form.

Roy Dryburgh, a veteran from the 1956 team, was selected to lead the Springboks in the first test and he, Chris Koch and Johan Claassen were the most experienced players in a side which included six newcomers and six who had limited test experience. Hennie Muller, the player so dreaded by the All Blacks in 1949, was later invited by Dryburgh to assist him with the coaching but there was no pressure from the selectors or the South African Rugby Board on the Natal fullback to take this step.

That first test, before more than 75 000 spectators at Ellis Park, established the reputations of several Springboks. Among them were Hennie van Zyl, an extremely tall, clumsy-looking wing who, at his peak, was almost impossible to stop, Michel Antelme, fast and intelligent on the other wing, and two outstanding combinations, Ian Kirkpatrick and John Gainsford at centre, and Keith Oxlee and Dick Lockyear at halfback. Hugo van Zyl and Martin Pelser proved to be flankers of the highest class and Avril Malan, making his test debut at the age of 23, looked and acted the part of a future Springbok captain.

Keith Oxlee, John Gainsford and Avril Malan played dominating roles in world rugby for the next few years but, although his career was relatively short, the man the All Blacks would have liked most to have had in a black jersey with a silver fern on his breast, was Hendrik Jacobus Martin Pelser. This 26-year-old Transvaal flanker, who had lost an eye in a boyhood accident, and was withdrawn to the point of shyness, has probably never had an equal for sheer tenacity, toughness and aggression. Take the

word of Colin Meads for that. Here is what he said about Pelser 14 years after playing against him:

"Martin Pelser, the one-eyed Springbok. What a player he was! One of the hardest, most skilful players in any position I have played against. Without making it a back-handed compliment I would say that Pelser was just a bloody pain in the neck to the All Blacks of 1960. I mean that in the best possible way. He gave our half-back Kevin Briscoe a hell of a time and right through the tour these two were mighty scratchy with each other. But he stood no nonsense from Kel Tremain and me, either. On that tour I played mostly as a loose forward. Kel and I looked after the back of the lineout. It was a sort of co-operative venture — you push and I'll jump. But when Kel pushed Pelser, Pelser belted him. Then when it was for me to look after Pelser while Kel jumped, he didn't hesitate. As the ruck formed he chased me round the side of it. There was I, diplomatically trying to hide myself, when he belted me, too. I'd have loved to have had him on my side. . . ."

Pelser's feud with Briscoe, a chunky, cheeky, little chap who had a knack of annoying his opponents, was one of the interesting sidelights of the tour. It was more or less a draw until the fourth test when Pelser laid him out with a left-hook so perfectly timed that even the New Zealanders expressed admiration for the punch. According to strictly unofficial after-match statements, several All Blacks thought that Briscoe had only himself to blame.

Hugo van Zyl, a handsome, highly-articulate, businessman from Paarl, packed on the other side of the scrum and with his unobtrusive efficiency he formed a tremendous partnership with the more dynamic Pelser. When they were later joined by the equally skilled and talented Doug Hopwood at eighthman, South Africa again had a loose forward trio comparable to the legendary Van Wyk-Fry-Muller combination.

The Springboks, as is invariably the case when the All Blacks are on a tour of South Africa, went into the first test as underdogs but long before half-time it was obvious that they would win. A brilliant try by Hennie van Zyl, very early in the match, seemed to shatter their self assurance and Whineray's men could not get back into the game.

The try was the result of a much-practiced version of the old ruse whereby the blindside wing is brought in to take the ball from the scrumhalf to breach the first line of defence. The Springboks used it from a scrum given to them just inside New Zealand territory, Abie Malan duly hooked and Michel Antelme, who was hanging slightly behind Oxlee, rocketed in, between the flyhalf and Gainsford, to take the pass at full speed. By the time Antelme had linked up with Kirkpatrick at outside centre, only Don Clarke was left to beat. Kirkpatrick drew Clarke in masterly fashion and then passed to Hennie van Zyl, who galloped over for a try Dryburgh converted.

Whineray then made one of the few tactical errors of his career. Instead of trying to regain the initiative he went on the defensive and delegated Conway to help the backs.

The Springbok pack, with virtually only seven forwards in opposition, took complete command and the All Blacks should really have lost by a bigger margin than 13-0. In the second half they were fooled again by Antelme cutting into the line and

Above, left: Colin Meads, symbol of All Black power on two tours of South Africa.

Far left: Chris Koch started his international career against the All Blacks in 1949. He ended it against them 11 years later.

Left: Piet "Spiere" du Toit, tilling his Boland farm. The quiet-spoken Du Toit proved to be one of the strongest front-rankers ever to play for South Africa.
Die Burger

Right: Hennie van Zyl, the tall and slender Transvaal wing, who scored two tries in the first test against the 1960 All Blacks at Ellis Park. Here Don Clarke vainly tries to head him off.

swift passing gave Hennie van Zyl a slight start on his opposite number Russell Watt. The left-wing, whose height and bony build always made him look as if he was running on stilts, shook off Watt's challenge and then with an amazing display of determination, he fought his way through Don Clarke, Conway and Briscoe to score his second try in the corner. Lockyear converted with the first of the several vital kicks he was to put over in the series and, not long afterwards, he added three more points with an equally difficult penalty kick.

The All Blacks' only excuse was that the Rand's high altitude had knocked them out and it must be admitted that it was a rare sight to see every member in a team looking as if he had suddenly lost form. Whineray even received a letter from a crank afterwards suggesting that the All Blacks had been doped!

Don Clarke towered over everybody else in the second test at Newlands; not only did he score eight of his team's winning total of 11 points but it was his fantastic touchkicking that enabled the New Zealand forwards to turn the table on the Springboks. He, himself, considers it to this day as his best performance.

"The ball seemed drawn to me as if on the end of a string," he said years later. "From the opening whistle I was gaining 60 yards with touchfinders".

Clarke scored a penalty, a perfectly-executed left-footed dropgoal, and he converted a try by Colin Meads, but it was his touchkicking that was unforgettable. In those days the ball could still be kicked out on the full and Clarke simply slammed it into space and it would go soaring towards the South African corner-flag. It was the best all-round kicking performance I, personally, have ever seen and I have witnessed nothing since to equal it. South Africa's only points came from Keith Oxlee, who scored a typically clever try. When Don Clarke converted Meads' try he reached his 100th point on the tour and he eventually ended up with a total of 175, the most by any player on a tour of South Africa. The conversion also brought the total of points scored against South Africa to 500. By a strange coincidence South Africa's 500th test point was also scored at Newlands, in the final international against the 1938 Lions.

The Springbok selectors made drastic changes for the third test. Dryburgh, who had been playing on borrowed time after a two-year battle with injuries, lost his place to Lionel Wilson, of Western Province, and the captaincy went to Avril Malan who, at the age of 23, became the youngest man ever to lead South Africa, a record he still holds.

Chris Koch, one of the chosen few in our rugby history of whom it can truthfully be said that they became legends in their own lifetime, finally faded from the scene after 11 seasons of international rugby. Fanie Kuhn, a blond and powerful Transvaler, took his place and filled it admirably for several years while Abie Malan went back to the middle of the front-row after the magnificent veteran, Bertus van der Merwe, had been given a last chance in the Newlands test. Lofty Nel, tall, tough and always hard-working, made way for Doug Hopwood, a burly eighthman who could run and handle as well as any threequarter and who went on to become one of the really great Springbok forwards of the 60's.

The choice of Lionel Wilson at fullback was severely criticised. He was virtually unknown and had detractors even in his own province, but how wrong he was to prove his critics. His unflinching courage under any kind of pressure soon made him

Above: Martin Pelser, a relentless competitor who was deeply respected by the All Blacks, and Kevin Briscoe, the touring team's tough scrumhalf, conducted their own feud throughout the 1960 series. This picture shows Pelser arriving just too late to collar his foe. Kel Tremain, Lofty Nel and Wilson Whineray are in the background.

one of the most widely-respected of all Springboks and he went on to play in 27 tests for South Africa, more than any other fullback to wear the green jersey.

The third test was an amazing affair. There were six minutes to go, South Africa was leading 11-3, and the huge Bloemfontein crowd was getting ready to celebrate. Then the All Blacks staged a fantastic come-back.

Until that moment all the New Zealanders had to show for themselves were three points from a penalty by Clarke. The Springbok score came from a try by Oxlee — his second successive one in tests—and a conversion and two penalty goals by Lockyear, one of the most valuable players on either side in this series.

Then the Springboks were penalised not far from the New Zealand quarter of the field. Whineray, noticing that the Springboks were slow in falling back, quickly took a tap kick and the referee duly gave them an extra 10 yards. It was still an enormous distance from the Springbok posts, but Clarke was told to have a go.

The All Black fullback admitted afterwards that for once he had doubts about his ability as he lined up the ball. He had just recovered from 'flu and the pace of the test had taken its toll.

"That feeling of uncertainty stayed with me even after my boot hit the ball," he said. "The impact was not true and my doubts mounted in the split second it took for the ball to begin its flight. Yet something happened, something beyond my doing, for when it was about 20 yards on its flight, the ball seemed to change direction, seemingly drawn to the goalposts so far away. On and on it flew until, almost unbelievably, the flags went up."

The Springboks were still leading by five points but in the final minute Terry Lineen snapped up a bad pass from Briscoe and gave to Kevin Laidlaw who kicked ahead for Frank McMullen to chase. The ball bounced high but perfectly for the All Black wing who took it in full stride and crashed over in the corner. The result then depended on the conversion and Clarke calmly placed it from an acute angle with what coach Jack Sullivan afterwards described as the man from Waikato's greatest kick of his career. Clarke, strangely enough, was not particularly impressed by it. In his biography he wrote: "When I went through the routine of setting the ball up and striding through, the whole affair had a feeling of formality about it. There's no doubt about it, when you're playing well, kicking goals is easy....it's when you're below form that they become more and more difficult — as I was to discover on a fateful tour four years later...."

By snatching a dramatic draw when all had seemed lost, the All Blacks managed to level the series and the fourth test in Port Elizabeth became the vital crunch.

Jan Pieter Engelbrecht, a tall Matie wing who could run with such consummate grace and whose all-round ability was to earn him 33 test caps, eight test tries and 44 tries altogether in the green-and-gold, was selected to replace Michel Antelme for the test. Jannie, who had made his international debut against Scotland earlier in the season, developed tonsilitis however, and Antelme was brought back. Antelme was a most competent wing, but he sometimes revealed an inexplicable lethargy which prevented him from developing his full potential.

The only other change was an enforced one. Johan Claassen after playing in 16 successive tests, was injured and Northern Transvaal's Hendrik Stefanus van der Merwe, known to all and sundry as "Stompie", had the unenviable task of substituting for one of the giants of South African rugby. Van der Merwe, in fact, was to give a superb performance and Claassen's absence was not really felt.

It was one of those tense, merciless tests, played in a nasty wind and it was won for the Springboks by their wonderful forwards and the superb kicking of Dick Lockyear, a scrum-half who had been ignored for years and who had only gained his colours at the age of 29.

Keith Oxlee saved a certain try within minutes of the beginning when he just managed to ankle-tap Frank McMullen who was flying towards the goalline for what appeared to be a certain try. The All Black wing was knocked off balance and he fell short before reaching out and planting the ball behind the line. Mr. Ralph Burmeister, a referee with a splendid record, was on the spot and instead of giving the All Blacks a try, he awarded a penalty against them. There was to be a brief storm of controversy over this but Whineray's men were, generally speaking, not the squealing kind and the incident was not used as an excuse for defeat.

The Springbok forwards were invincible that afternoon at Boet Erasmus Stadium, as they drove forward with tremendous will and Martin Pelser and Hugo van Zyl rattled the All Black halfbacks into mistakes. Don Clarke gave them an early lead with a penalty but Lockyear levelled the score with a penalty of his own, a quite remarkable kick since it was into a treacherous wind.

Early in the second half the Springboks clinched the series. There was a scrum near the All Blacks posts and a hurried few words between Lockyear and Pelser before the South African scrumhalf let the ball in.

The Springboks heeled, half wheeled, Lockyear ran wide and it was Pelser who picked up and threw everything he had into making those two precious strides to the tryline. He was tackled, sure enough, but it was not enough to hold his hurtling body and he scored his try, next to the upright. Lockyear converted and this time the Springboks were not going to fritter away a lead. There were a few narrow escapes as Clarke came close with huge kicks into the wind but when the final whistle ended the match and the series, the Springboks had won 8-3.

The 1960 All Blacks were a mighty side. South Africa was fortunate that she had the Springboks to match, and beat them.

1965

The big clock at Lancaster Park, Christchurch, New Zealand, showed less than three minutes to go before the end of the third test between the 1965 Springboks and the All Blacks.

In a thrilling fight-back, the underdog South Africans had turned a half-time score of 5-16 into 16 points all. Then Lionel Wilson was tackled from an off-side position and the Springboks were given a penalty, not far from the All Blacks posts, but near the touchline. Victory or defeat, it all depended on the kick.

Jacobus Pieter (Tiny) Naude, the tall, magnificently-built Western Province lock-forward, stepped up to prepare for a personal date with destiny. His sweat-soaked green jersey and white shorts were caked with mud and his boots felt heavier than usual as they squelched into the soft, yielding surface.

Wing three-quarter Gertjie Brynard was wiping the ball against his chest to remove some of the clinging clay. His alert eyes were hooded to hide the scheming look as he whispered

A mud-covered Tiny Naude is hugged by Lofty Nel, a split-second after he had succeeded with the kick that won the third test for the 1965 Springboks.

Above: Morné du Plessis, South Africa's most outstanding player of recent years, shakes off the attentions of Sid Going before passing to Western Province scrumhalf Divan Serfontein. Du Plessis guided Western Province to a thrilling triumph over the 1976 All Blacks and then led South Africa to victory in the series. This brilliant action shot was taken by Jim McLagan, Chief Photographer of The Argus.

Gerrie Germishuys, a Free State wing of great pace, was one of the big Springbok successes against the 1976 All Blacks.

John Rubython

urgently: "Tiny, look at those guys sauntering back! They've had it. Make it a short one, I'm sure I can beat them to the line!"

Brynard, whose agility and sniping speed had brought him two glorious tries that afternoon, considered the odds against him catching the defence napping to be no higher than the odds stacked against anyone succeeding with a kick from a patch of slush, with a heavy, shapeless ball and from a difficult angle. But Tiny Naude had made up his mind. The responsibility of ending a long run of Springbok defeats was to be his and his alone.

He placed the ball flat on the imprint left by referee Alan Taylor's heel. For a fleeting moment he was grateful for the advice he had been given by someone not to tee the ball the usual inch above the ground, as he would have done on the harder South African fields. In New Zealand that would have meant hitting it too low as his own considerable weight caused him to sink slightly into the soft earth.

As he stepped back for his run-up he consciously forced his lungs and heart to slow down to an easy, even rhythm. The noise, even a courteously quiet crowd of 54 000 simply must make as tension builds up to an unbearable pitch, receded as he closed his mind to all but the job he had to do. Head down, body perfectly balanced, the right leg swung firmly in the follow-through. Only then did he look up to follow the flight of the ball; it was going low and straight and Tiny Naude knew that he had not failed his team.

His pent-up feelings exploded in a great shout and even as he shouted, his team-mate Lofty Nel was there to grab him in a bear-hug of joy and triumph.

One minute had passed since Naude was handed the ball. Both the longest and the shortest minute he will probably ever know in his life; a mere sixty clicks on the stadium clock, but it was long enough to provide a fitting climax to one afternoon the 1965 Springboks can remember with pride.

It was the year South African rugby plumbed the depths. Eight tests were played in 1965; against Scotland, Ireland, two against Australia and four against New Zealand, and the Springboks won only one of them.

The first warning signals of a decline were already flashing the year before when France won a dismal match at Springs; a game so poor that it was described by some as the worst test ever to be seen in this country.

Early in 1965 Avril Malan took a Springbok team on a short tour of Ireland and Scotland and they returned without having scored a single victory. It was an unfortunate venture from the beginning, soured by an unfortunate haggling over the captaincy. The selectors' choice was Doug Hopwood who had led the Western Province superbly in the Currie Cup tournament, but they were overruled by the South African Rugby Board and the job was given to Malan. The Springboks departed in an atmosphere of acrimony and although powerful enough on paper, the side floundered through the tour, an unhappy combination without aim or spirit.

Shortly after their return, the team to tour Australia and New Zealand had to be selected. A week of trials at Newlands produced nothing startling and, taking into account the

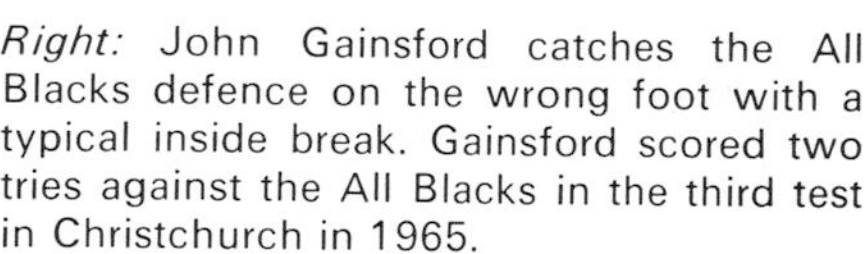

Right: John Gainsford catches the All Blacks defence on the wrong foot with a typical inside break. Gainsford scored two tries against the All Blacks in the third test in Christchurch in 1965.

Left: Gert Brynard hurls himself over the line for one of his two tries against the All Blacks in the thrill-packed third test in 1965.

usual toll exacted by injury and retirement, the selectors relied on the best available talent.

Dawie de Villiers, at 24, became the youngest Springbok captain since Avril Malan was given the honour in 1960 and no one could have seriously doubted his qualifications for the task. De Villiers was an outstanding scrumhalf whose speed and incisiveness compensated for the occasional lapses in his service. He had overcome a serious knee injury which had prompted his surgeon to advise him against playing again and courage, both physical and moral, was always to be his strongest attribute on and off the field.

Highly intelligent and a sophisticated speaker, Dawie commanded the respect of his team through a combination of natural charm and total sincerity. His tactical appreciation of the game was frequently criticised, but he was nevertheless an inspiring captain with a tough streak which was not easy to detect behind his boyish good looks and unfailing courtesy.

The 29-year-old Nelie Smith, then past his best and also a scrumhalf, was given the vice-captaincy and this was not a sound move. Not that Smith could not do the job, but because it left the forwards without an appointed leader and it is a bad principle anyway to have two players in the same position who are holding the reins. Hennie Muller, the scourge of the 1949 All Blacks, was the appointed coach and it was to be a frustrating tour for the former "Windhond". He vainly advocated a more definite playing pattern and he also felt that too many of the players were not dedicated enough and, to put it bluntly, were too "soft". The team's active social life and the happy-go-lucky attitude of more than just a few players horrified and disillusioned a man to whom a Springbok blazer meant so much.

Dawie de Villiers was placed in charge of an impressive lineup, manned by some of the finest players of their era. Among the backs there were steady Lionel Wilson at fullback, Jannie Engelbrecht, certainly one of the greatest wings of all time, John Gainsford, who was generally regarded as the best centre in the world, that mercurial genius Mannetjies Roux, versatile Gert Brynard, Keith Oxlee, one of the outstanding flyhalves in Springbok history, but fading rapidly by that time, Jannie Barnard, whose remarkable potential was never to be fully realised, and newcomers like Syd Nomis and the late replacement, Eben Olivier, who both went on to gain international fame in the years to follow.

Among the forwards there were individual stars like Frik du Preez, Abie Malan, Tiny Naude, Don Walton, Doug Hopwood, Andrew Janson, Andy MacDonald, Sakkie van Zyl, Lofty Nel, Hannes Marais, Johan (Haas) Schoeman and youthful Jan Ellis. The controversial but brilliant Tommy Bedford was prevented by injury from taking any active role in the tests and Hopwood, the best eighthman of his time, was plagued even more than usual by the back injury he had to live with throughout his illustrious career.

The Australian leg of the tour was an unmitigated disaster. The Springboks failed to understand some inexplicable refereeing decisions and they were more than once unhappy with the hotel accommodation offered to them. On one occasion a deputation from the dissatisfied players forced a transfer to another hotel and it is said that Syd Nomis, who is Jewish, once found himself confronted with a menu on which the only meat dish was pork!

Impartial observers from New Zealand agreed that the refereeing in Australia left much to be desired and with this added handicap the Springboks not only lost to New South Wales but also could not win either of the two tests against one of the strongest teams ever to be fielded by Australia. In the process it also became obvious that while the Springboks had plenty of pace and enterprise up front and behind the scrum, their forwards lacked cohesion and had little hope of coping with the relentless driving they could expect from New Zealand's best packs. The gloomy predictions proved to be correct. Colin Meads later described the performances of the Springbok forwards of 1965 as "loose and shiftless" and it is a fact that in at least two of the four tests the All Blacks forwards were in complete command and that they held the edge throughout the series.

This often forced the Springbok backs, whose capabilities on the attack the New Zealanders frankly feared, to try and strike from an unsound platform. Mistakes simply had to be made under such circumstances and the All Blacks, absolute masters of second-phase attack and splendid opportunists, were always quick to capitalise.

Nevertheless the Springboks were unlucky not to have drawn the first test, played at Wellington in a wind approaching gale strength. The All Blacks had it in their favour in the first half, but the Springbok defence,

Two of the Springbok stars of the bitterly-contested 1970 series against the All Blacks. Gert Muller is on the attack and he has Joggie Jansen at his side.

Die Burger

with Roux and Gainsford particularly deadly, stood up well and the All Blacks led only 6-0 at half-time. New Zealand thoroughly deserved the first-half try by wing Bill Birtwistle, but there was a great deal of doubt about Kelvin Tremain's try a few seconds from half-time. Dawie de Villiers had tackled Mick Williment and the ball had appeared to pop out of his hands towards the Springbok line when the ever-alert "Bunny" Tremain snapped it up to dive over. A dropgoal by Keith Oxlee halved the lead after the resumption, but the All Blacks held on to win. The Springbok forwards simply could not get enough clean possession for their threequarters while New Zealand, in turn, did not have backs talented enough to make maximum use of what they got.

The second test was played in Dunedin, on a field turned into a swamp by steady rain and the Springboks failed dismally to adapt to the conditions. The All Black forwards were on top from the kick-off and the Springbok pack was given a thorough beating. Had it not been for a heroic performance by Lionel Wilson, at fullback, the final score would certainly have been bigger than 13-0. Lionel Geoffrey Wilson never once in his test career let his country down, but it was in the mud of Carisbrook that he proved beyond all doubt his right to be counted among the great Springbok fullbacks.

Wilson's courageous performance so deeply impressed the All Blacks that Wilson Whineray, their skipper and a man who must rate among the best international captains in the history of the game, paid a special tribute to the Springbok in his after-match speech. Lionel Wilson and Frik du Preez were later named as two of the five Players of the Year by New Zealand critics.

Dawie de Villiers, who did not play in the disastrous second test because of injury, returned for the third international and several other overdue changes were made. Oxlee, who had reached the end of the trail after serving South Africa so well and for so long, had to make way for little Jannie Barnard, Naude replaced Piet Goosen, Don Walton took over from Abie Malan, Lofty Nel was switched to the side of the scrum in place of Haas Schoeman and, at last, Doug Hopwood was brought back as eighthman. It was never announced officially, but by common consent, Hopwood was also given the job of leading the pack.

This is how New Zealand's Alex Veysey described the third test in *Colin Meads, All Black,* a book he wrote with Meads:

"If ever a country needed a test victory to salve its hurt pride in itself it was South Africa. When the Springboks took the field on a sludgy surface at Lancaster Park, Christchurch, the country had lost seven matches on the trot. Pride seemed doomed to dip to its nadir when at half-time New Zealand led 16-5, a launching pad, it seemed, for utter rout. It was a Springbok team which had more than enough problems during the tour. There was not a tight binding of thought and allegiance at senior player-coach level and this in itself was shockingly uncharacteristic of South African rugby. It was also one strong reason why it seemed that at 16-5 down at half-time, there was no psychological spring from which a new life could be drawn.

"Meads believes that quite a magnificent first spell try by John Gainsford sowed the seed of hope in at least one Springbok breast — and this was an all-important one because it belonged to the captain Dawie de Villiers. At half-time while De Villiers delivered his message to the players — Forwards, give us the ball to play with; the backs can win it — the New Zealanders quite unconsciously relaxed. . . ."

At this point in the book Meads took over the narrative:

"Even though you tell yourself the job is still to be done there is an automatic mental reaction to a position such as 16-5 at half-time in a test match. Had it been 6-3 we might have won the match. As it was, De Villiers was proved right and the South African backs cut us up. Every man did his piece; while De Villiers was steady and reliable, outside him, Jannie Barnard, John Gainsford, Mannie Roux, Gert Brynard were inspired. Suddenly, after Brynard had scored a try early in the second spell and then another nine minutes later, we were on the back foot and once you get into this sort of rut, it's damned hard to get out of it. By the time Gainsford had scored another try it was 16-16 and one of the great triumphs of rugby was in sight. But we hoisted ourselves back into it by controlling play till just two or three minutes from time. Then I got myself offside and watched in despair as Tiny Naude kicked the goal from out of the slush. . . ."

Naude's moment of glory was described at the start of the chapter but unfortunately for South Africa the revival was short-lived. Soon they were once again in a slump, worse than ever before, and when they lost the fourth test 3-20, it was the biggest hiding the Springboks had ever suffered against the All Blacks.

Springbok centre Johan Oosthuizen is airborne as he intercepts a pass between the All Blacks centres to score a stunning try in the third test at Newlands in 1976.

Terry Shean, The Sunday Times

New Zealand's captain, Wilson Whineray, was rather worried about the Springbok backs before the final test. He worked out an elaborate scheme with coaches Neil McPhail and Fred Allen to contain De Villiers and his threequarters, but it was never necessary to employ the plan. The All Blacks forwards again dominated the proceedings with such absolute authority that the Springboks were forced to attack from poor possession and from dangerous positions near their own line. They made numerous mistakes in the process and the All Blacks had a field day, scoring five tries to none and winning with almost contemptuous ease.

Over to Colin Meads again: "I must say the comparative mediocrity of much of the Springbok play on that whole tour surprised me. *It was so out of character with South African rugby as I knew it. . . .*"

The full story of the 1965 Springboks is perhaps best told in that final sentence in a judgement passed by a respected opponent.

During the tour the political pressure South African sport had been subjected to for several years, reached breaking point with a statement by Dr. H. F. Verwoerd, then Prime Minister of the Republic, that Maoris would not be welcome in any New Zealand team to visit this country. The future was to prove different, but at that stage it looked as if the long and tradition-rich rivalry between the All Blacks and the Springboks had come to an end.

The year 1965 was indeed a terrible one for South African rugby.

1970

Like a pilot checking his instruments before take-off, Ian Duncan McCallum methodically but briskly went through his ritual.

First he studied the ball to find the side with the best kicking surface. Not all the seams of a ball are equally straight and he selected the best one for sighting as he lined up for the target nearly 65 yards away — the longest penalty kick he had ever attempted. When All Blacks frontranker Jazz Muller incurred the disapproval of referee Bert Woolley and 65 000 Ellis Park spectators, Springbok captain Dawie de Villiers had flipped the ball to his fullback with instructions to give his forwards a breather. The 26-year-old University of Cape Town student had decided he might as well give the All Blacks a fright in the process.

There was no teeing up. McCallum, unlike so many other placekickers believes that a slight indentation dug with the heel is enough to hold the point of the ball.

He made sure that his toes were right at the front of the boot. To be certain, he tap-kicked twice into the tough Highveld turf.

Then he checked that the toe of his left boot was clean, without even a particle of grass on it that could make the impact less true and perhaps affect the flight of the ball.

It was going to be a tough kick. For this one, McCallum calculated, he would have to add two steps to his normal run-up which was usually either four or five.

Left: Ian McCallum, a slightly-built University of Cape Town medical student, whose splendid placekicking destroyed all hopes the 1970 All Blacks had of winning the series.

Wessel Oosthuizen/Die Vaderland

Right: The veteran Mannetjies Roux displayed magnificent form against the 1970 All Blacks. Here he slips past Grahame Thorne and is about to pass to Gert Muller, whose three tries in the series is still a record for a Springbok against the All Blacks.

Die Huisgenoot

When the distance is long, a good placekicker hits the ball faster, not harder than he does normally. The longer run-up increases the speed and therefore the momentum.

All these preparations took seconds, not minutes, and McCallum had no time to think of anything but the job in hand. Self-confidence — and years of practice — are what count once the ball has been placed.

Laces pointing goalwards and upright, the ball was lined up for the kick. Making sure his left foot was perfectly in line with the seam of the ball and the posts, McCallum moved back, off this foot, with his eyes always on the ball. He paused and inhaled deeply. Then he took a short step forward, again off the left foot, and launched himself on his perfectly balanced run-up to the ball.

The huge crowd was silent as, pendulum-like, McCallum's leg swung till the boot hit the ball. The follow-through was unfettered and complete. Then came the roar, first only from those sections where the unerring flight could be spotted first and finally from all sides of the stadium as the flags shot skywards to salute one of the greatest placekicks in the history of the game.

The time was six minutes past four on September 12, 1970 and it was McCallum's miracle kick that then and there killed the All Blacks' hopes of retaining their unofficial rugby championship of the world....

After his retirement Colin Meads, New Zealand's legendary "Pine Tree" and certainly one of the greatest forwards the rugby world has known, described to Alex Veysey, his biographer, his feelings on playing in South Africa.

"This is what it has all been about, this is South Africa and these are the players you most want to beat. That is the feeling inside you, as an All Black, when you play in South Africa," he said. "If you're ever going to play good rugby, you'll play it in South Africa. The atmosphere demands it of you....To beat South Africa in South Africa! What a dream it was...."

Springboks, of course, feel the same way about the All Blacks and that is why tests between the two countries have such a special importance. Only once in 55 years of fierce competition have the Springboks been able to win a test series in New Zealand and for the All Blacks such an achievement in South Africa continues to be a dream to be realised some day.

If ever a side looked capable of beating the Springboks on their own fields, it was the one brought out here by Brian Lochore in 1970. They were the acknowledged world champions and the hard core of "Unsmiling Giants" who had so convincingly conquered South Africa, Britain and France in the 'sixties were still together although two such remarkable forwards as Ken Gray and Kelvin Tremain were missing in the line-up.

They steamrollered over one provincial side after the other and players like Meads, Lochore, Strahan, McLeod, Kirkpatrick, Murdoch, Sutherland, Muller, Williams, Thorne, Going and McCormick, to single out only a few, looked every inch the great All Blacks they were.

Meads, that gnarled veteran of the 1960 tour, suffered a broken arm in a brawl-marred match against Eastern Transvaal and for a while it looked as if he would not play again on the tour. At the time it seemed as if the All Blacks would hardly need his mighty services to be able to smash the national team with the same ease with which they crumpled the provincial opposition. As it turned out, Meads, with the aid of typical stoicism and an arm guard, did play in the final two tests, but not even he could save his team from the humiliation of losing three out of the four international matches.

The tests between Lochore's 1970 All Blacks and the Springboks under Dawie de Villiers must, however, count among the most tense, gruelling and desperately fought in the history of rugby in South Africa.

The Springboks won the series, three matches to one. They scored 59 points to 35, seven tries against four. When somebody flips through the record books 50 years from now, these cold statistics will make it look as if it was all so easy. But, as is so often the case, bare statistics could never tell the full story.

Everyone who saw the four titanic struggles will have a personal storehouse of memories to treasure and to trot out in the years to come. To me, the turning-point of the whole series came in the first few minutes of the first test at Loftus Versfeld.

The All Blacks' magnificent performances against the provincial opposition and their unbeaten record stretching over five years, all helped to build them up into giants surrounded by an aura of almost mystical invincibility and hardly any hope was held out for the Springboks who had fared so poorly on the demo-plagued tour of Britain.

The Springboks had to prove quickly, to themselves as much as to their gloomy supporters, that the All Blacks were only human after all. Fittingly, it was skipper Dawie de Villiers himself who opened the first

Above: Bryan Williams, a superb wing, was one of the stars of the 1970 All Blacks. Outstanding sports photographer John Rubython took this picture of Williams brushing aside Nelson Babrow, the Western Province centre, in the match at Newlands.

Below: The second test against the All Blacks at Newlands in 1970 was an uncompromising battle. Piston van Wyk, the Springbok hooker, was badly hurt in the second half and had to be replaced by Robbie Barnard. This picture shows a dazed and bloodied Van Wyk being led off by First Aid officials.

John Rubython

crack in a wall that had looked so impregnable.

It happened in the fourth minute of the game. There was a scrum not far from the All Blacks 25-yard line, the ball was held and Piet Greyling kicked it through and over the tryline. Like a green-and-gold flash, Dawie streaked after it and the try was his. One wonders what the outcome of the series would have been had the All Blacks been first to draw blood.

From that moment onwards there was confidence in the Springbok team and only three minutes later Joggie Jansen, wearing the Springbok jersey for the first time, showed that he, already, was no longer awed by his opponents' reputation.

All Black flyhalf Wayne Cottrell received from a set scrum and, moving to the blindside, he tried to probe for an opening. As he was about to pass, the big Free Stater hit him squarely with a shoulder-first tackle in the midriff and Cottrell was flattened as effectively as if he had been run over by a truck. Cottrell was never the same again and 22-year-old Joachim Scholtz (Joggie) Jansen went on to terrorise the All Blacks midfield in the tradition of Jimmy White and Ryk van Schoor.

When Piet Visagie, who played with flawless efficiency in all four tests, shortly afterwards snapped over a left-footed dropgoal on the run, reaching his century of test points in the process, the transformation of the Springboks from a collection of no-hopers into a team of winners, was complete.

I will also never forget Ian McCallum putting over a magnificent 55-metre penalty after Chris Laidlaw was trapped offside. The slightly-built baby-faced McCallum was to score 35 points in the four tests, breaking Okey Geffin's 21-year-old record, and the All Blacks must have hated the sight of him and his immaculate left-footed placekicking, by the time the series was over!

Then there was Bryan Williams' glorious try for the All Blacks when, with hardly any room to move in, he beat three Springboks and ran himself right into the hearts of all rugby lovers in South Africa.

A lightning interception and a try by Syd Nomis, Piet Greyling refusing to show even the slightest sign of the excruciating pain he must have suffered after a rib injury — these are other highlights I will remember from the first test.

It was the vital match of the series

for the Springboks; the one they simply had to win to regain their self confidence and, in winning it, they laid the foundation for taking the rubber.

The second test at Newlands will probably be remembered for the rough play more than anything else. I doubt if any test has ever been played in a more tense atmosphere than this one. The forwards piled into one another as if they were on suicide missions and there were rucks so fierce that it sickened many in the crowd. From one such maul, Springbok hooker Piston van Wyk was led off the field with blood streaming down his face and onto his chest and the First Aid officials helping him looked as if they were wearing red gloves.

There was the notorious incident when Syd Nomis was knocked unconscious by All Blacks fullback Fergi McCormick, and other ugly moments when the players swung savage punches and aimed brutal kicks at each other with complete contempt for the authority of the referee.

A dramatic, exciting match nevertheless, with the Springboks holding a narrow lead after a strong comeback in the second half. Then veteran centre Mannetjies Roux, who was in severe pain after a kick in the back, was judged to have tackled Bill Davis from an offside position and McCormick gave his team a one-point win with a penalty kicked from a comfortable angle.

The Springboks had their easiest victory of the series in the third test at Port Elizabeth where the highlights were two magnificent tries by the Stellenbosch wing Gert Muller and, again, the wonderful kicking of McCallum.

Muller's first try came after the Springboks had trapped Fergi McCormick, whose blood they were after from the start, with the ball. From the ruck Dawie de Villiers slipped away on a devastating break to send Muller over for his first test try. Later an All Blacks fumble gave Mannetjies Roux an opportunity to set Muller off on another powerful run for his second try. But the match was also unforgettable for the deadly tackle with which Piet Greyling slammed McCormick into the ground with less than a minute gone.

It was a great series for Greyling, tall, dark and handsome, and his partner on the other flank, red-haired, tearaway Jan Ellis from South West Africa. Their speed to the point of break-down ruined the All Blacks efficiency in creating second phase possession, and probably contributed as much to South Africa's triumph as did McCallum's kicking and, never forget it, Dawie de Villiers' inspiring leadership.

The third test was a triumph also for Lofty Nel and Mof Myburgh, two veterans brought back by the selectors to a chorus of criticism from the experts and the sportswriters.

The All Blacks had a lot to do with their own defeat. Their selection blunders cost them any advantage they had after their Newlands victory and the omission of Alan Sutherland up front and the switching of Bryan Williams from wing to centre, were moves welcomed by the Springboks.

The South Africans went into the final test as favourites to win for the first time in the series. Win they did, but only after more than 80 minutes of pulsating action that left the crowd of 65 000 limp and emotionally drained.

Two players dominated the game, Ian McCallum for South Africa and Gerald Kember for New Zealand. Between them they scored 28 of the 37 points on the scoreboard and the kick of the match was the Zambia-born McCallum's enormous effort from at least 65 yards just before half-time. McCallum's placekicking in the series was so good that the All Blacks coach Ivan Vodanovich praised him later as the kicker with the best technique he had ever seen, a view I share even now that we are in the era of round-the-corner kickers.

In addition to McCallum's spectacular placekicking in the final test those who saw this match are not likely either to forget Piet Visagie's clever break and try in the first five minutes or Gert Muller's bulldozer run after Jansen had toppled Kember with one of his dive bomber tackles. This was a tackle that had a very definite bearing on the outcome of the match. The score was 17-14 and the All Blacks forwards, playing with frenzied fury, were in the ascendancy. Then Kember came into the line from fullback and the next instant the Free State agricultural student hit him with such force that the ball jumped out of his hands and there was Mannetjies Roux, that supreme opportunist, to snap it up, make the defence hesitate and then pass to Muller. Muller, a compact bundle of muscle with the speed to match his power, beat two defenders on his way to score and it must have been a mortal blow to New Zealand's hopes of salvaging the series.

Bryan Williams, the good-looking black-haired teenager of Samoan descent who became such a favourite of all South African fans, supplied another memory to treasure when he picked up a pass from Sid Going and ran through with impudent ease for a try behind the posts.

And perhaps the most memorable scene of all. The final whistle and captain Dawie de Villiers, his mission accomplished, had time for one little jump of joy before he was lifted high in triumph by his teammates. Seconds later hundreds of spectators poured onto the field and, swaying precariously but happily on many willing shoulders, the Springbok heroes were carried to the dressingroom.

As Nelson said after the battle of the Nile: "Victory is not a name strong enough for such a scene".

1976

For Morne du Plessis the highway to valour has indeed led through many disasters, as the poet once wrote about Hector in the ancient days of Troy. Had he not the tenacity to equal his phenomenal talent, Du Plessis could so easily have been just another one of those Springboks who came and went in the unhappy 1970's, leaving little more than a name and a date in the annals.

Instead of that the tall, gangling, Vereeniging-born Western Province captain has shrugged away disappointment, unfair criticism and downright maliciousness to emerge unchallenged as South Africa's greatest player at a crucial stage in our rugby history. The detractors who have hounded him since he became the 101st Matie to gain Springbok colours when he was selected for the tour of Australia in 1971, have been reduced to a grumbling minority and it has become obvious that in Morne du Plessis we have the ideal man to fill a vital role as South African rugby enters a new era.

Du Plessis was born on October 21, 1949, only a few months after his father, Felix, had led the Springboks to three successive victories over Fred Allen's All Blacks. His mother Pat, who in her day captained a Springbok hockey team, once told sportswriter George Gerber that she was so heavily pregnant with Morne when she watched her husband's team play so well in the famous second test at Ellis Park, that she needed two seats for herself!

Growing up in such a household (in addition to the honours earned by his parents his uncle, Horace Smethurst, was a South African soccer captain), it was hardly surprising that Morne would have a wide-ranging interest in all sports. At the Klerksdorp Primary School he captained both the cricket and the rugby teams, he was Victor Ludorum in athletics, a swimming champion and he won every conceivable tennis title.

Later, at Grey College, Bloemfontein, he concentrated on rugby and cricket and as a fast bowler for the South African Schools XI in 1967, he hit the winning runs against Rhodesia's senior team. In later years he had a brief spell in the Western Province cricket side but by that time rugby had won the battle for his affections.

At Grey College, Du Plessis in spite of his exceptional height, initially played at flyhalf, centre and fullback before being switched to lock but once he arrived at Stellenbosch he was promptly moved to the flank by Dr. Danie Craven. Mr. Jannie Krige, who has been coaching the junior Maties for more than two decades, has often said that Morne was possibly the best player under the age of 20 he had ever prepared for bigger things.

As a National Serviceman in the South African Navy, Du Plessis won the Admiral's Award for his performances in cricket, rugby and golf, a game he plays to a nine-handicap. While at Stellenbosch, where he eventually graduated with an honours degree in industrial psychology, Du Plessis captained the Western Province under-20 rugby team and he was not yet 21 when he first won senior provincial colours. A year later he became a member of Hannes Marais' invincible team to Australia.

Du Plessis was axed from the Springbok team after the dismal defeat by the Lions in the second test in 1974 and he admits that for a brief period his confidence was shattered. With typical grit and self-discipline, this rather withdrawn man who does not hesitate to speak his mind when he feels it necessary, sorted out his problems in his own way and a year later he followed in his father's footsteps when he captained the Springboks against France. By that time he had left Stellenbosch whom he had led for several seasons and he therefore became the first member of the Villagers Club to lead South Africa since Bennie Osler in 1931.

As an eighthman for Western Province and the Springboks, Du Plessis has an unique style which can probably be best described as a hybrid between that of Doug Hopwood and that of the great French player Benoit Dauga. His instinctive ability is backed up by utter dedication; it is unlikely that any player of his era works harder to maintain peak fitness. He is, quite frankly, a fierce competitor and his ability to take care of himself in the most bitter war of attrition has been proved often enough.

The spirit of a lesser man than Morne du Plessis would have been broken by often quite ridiculous criticism made worse by the same blind personal condemnation which made the "campaigns" against Jannie Engelbrecht in the early 1960's so ugly. Du Plessis has, for instance, been attacked, virtually in the same breath for being "too soft" and "too rough". Fortunately for South African rugby, this sort of thing has rarely influenced the people who really matter and Du Plessis, like Engelbrecht before him, was given the opportunities to prove himself thoroughly in the heat of battle.

When Andy Leslie brought his All Blacks to South Africa in 1976 Du Plessis was the obvious choice for captain with Thys Lourens his only serious challenger for the job. Lourens, Northern Transvaal's shrewd leader, a sterling player and a man of fine character whom fortune has often treated unkindly, had his age counting against him and it is doubtful whether he or any of the others mentioned at the time were ever seriously in the race. The issue was settled once and for all anyway by the manner in which Du Plessis inspired his Western Province team to a thrilling win over the All Blacks at Newlands.

The Springboks won the series 3-1 but the All Blacks were distinctly unlucky in the final test and instead of jubilation, South Africans were left with a vague feeling of unease. Not enough was accomplished, either against France the previous season or against New Zealand, to completely dispel the gloom caused by the appalling performances against the 1974 Lions.

The tests were hard and merciless in the accepted tradition of clashes between these two implacable rivals but with rare exceptions, there was no enterprise from behind the scrum.

Barry Glasspool, sports editor of the Sunday Times, summed it up well in *"One in the Eye"*, a book he wrote after the tour:

"Total commitment to the capabilities of a freakishly brilliant goal-kicker (Gerald Bosch) whose form otherwise had slumped alarmingly, but who operated behind a screen of aggressive forward play, meant that the exciting talents of runners like Gerrie Germishuys, Peter Whipp and Johan Oosthuizen were largely unexploited.

"With the exception of that breathtaking first test try by Germishuys which rounded off a backline thrust of sheer uncomplicated artistry, the Springboks hardly put together another worthwhile backline move for the rest of the series."

Glasspool suggests that the coaching responsibility for all future Springbok teams be given back to the captain and considering the success Du Plessis has had in this capacity in restoring the dented prestige of Western Province, it is certainly a move worth making.

The Springbok forwards did a sound enough job against the All Blacks. Moaner van Heerden, Jan (Boland) Coetzee, Kevin de Klerk and Morne du Plessis were always good and frequently outstanding and the Transvaal frontranker Johan Strauss was of inestimable value in the crucial third test at Newlands.

Threequarters like Peter Whipp, who was dropped for the second test for no apparent reason, Johan Oosthuizen, Gerrie Germishuys and Chris Pope were neglected, however, as either Paul Bayvel, at scrumhalf, or Gerald Bosch, at flyhalf, kicked away possession. Bayvel had an erratic season while Bosch lacked the delicate judgment required of an international flyhalf.

Gerald Bosch is a courageous player with safe hands, the temperament for the big occasion, and he is indisputably the most successful place- and dropkicker in South African rugby history, as a glance at the statistics will prove. His tactical kicking, particularly on a hard ground, is also excellent and it all adds up to a formidable array of qualities. Unfortunately, probably because he had been straitjacketed from the start by his phenomenal talent for kicking, Bosch seems constitutionally unable to play a balanced game.

If he had the ability to know when and how to employ his threequarters with snap and decisiveness, Gerald Raymond Bosch would have ranked with the great flyhalves in history.

The strain of test rugby shows on the face of Morné du Plessis, as the Springbok captain waits for the ball at the back of the lineout in the third test of the 1976 series against the All Blacks.

John Rubython

But his mental make-up has been programmed for 10-man rugby only and in an era where Springbok packs can no longer guarantee their backs the major portion of possession against international teams, it is an approach which fails as often as it succeeds. Hypothetically at least, Springbok backs like Whipp, Oosthuizen, Germishuys and Pope could perhaps have accomplished with tries what Bosch did with his boot had they been given enough opportunities against the All Blacks.

Looking at the records only, there is no doubt that Bosch was the deciding factor in the 1976 series, played between two teams who were otherwise so evenly matched. He scored 33 out of the Springboks' total of 55 points and the lack of a goal-kicker of his stature was the All Blacks' biggest weakness. With 89 points scored in only nine tests, the important role this affable sports shop owner who also has his own race-horse — his colours are green and gold, of course — has played in Springbok rugby in the mid-70's cannot be minimised whatever criticism might be levelled at him.

Controversy over refereeing decisions cast a shadow over the tour but the All Blacks had only themselves to blame. The South African Rugby Board had offered them the services of neutral referees but their own authorities had declined, probably because acceptance would have created a precedent with future touring teams to New Zealand expecting the same privilege. To halt the perpetuation of "feuds", the wait until-we-get-you-in-our-backyard attitude, it is high time that the use of neutral referees became compulsory.

The wrangle after the final test left a particularly sour taste. Throughout the match the All Blacks showed their annoyance with Mr. Gert Bezuidenhout, a referee whom they had praised after they had won the second test, had criticised after they had lost the third and were prepared to draw and quarter long before his whistle ended the last test.

When Oosthuizen prevented Bruce Robertson from chasing a rolling ball he might well have reached in the in-goal area before the covering Gerald Bosch and Peter Whipp, the All Blacks expected a penalty try. Mr. Bezuidenhout was not certain that Robertson would have got to the ball before the defence and, acting according to the rules, he gave New Zealand a penalty instead. It was the final straw as far as the All Blacks were concerned and Andy Leslie, who had proved to be a most tactful tour captain up till then, bluntly described the match as a "hollow Springbok victory" in a television interview immediately after the game.

Their anger was understandable as many good judges had agreed that a penalty try should have been awarded but their general dismissal of their defeats as being mainly due to refereeing decisions can never be accepted. The All Blacks also received their share of penalties which could have been converted into points but both Sid Going and Bryan Williams were erratic and the tour management seemed to have no confidence in Laurie Mains, the only specialist kicker in their party.

The balding and pugnacious Sid Going, and the reliable Doug Bruce formed a most capable half-back combination while Peter ("Pole") Whiting was the best lock-forward on either side. Ian Kirkpatrick, was still an outstanding flanker in spite of his age and Joe Morgan, Duncan Robertson (who should never have been switched to fullback), and loose-forward Kevin Eveleigh were consistently competent. Bryan Williams, who was so brilliant in 1970, seemed to have lost his edge however, and Gerrie Germishuys, if anything, looked more dangerous than his famous opponent. Grant Batty, a small and bustling wing, was severely handicapped by injury but he did enough to earn the respect of opponents and spectators alike. Generally speaking, it was a team, however, which could not bear comparison with any of their predecessors.

The Springbok backs gave their best performance of the series in the first test in Durban when Gerrie Germishuys scored a try to remember after everyone, from Bayvel to Ian Robertson, who had slipped into the line from fullback, had done his job with passes as swift and precise as could be found outside the pages of a text book.

A slashing break by Bayvel initiated the Springboks' other try of the match, scored by Edrich Krantz after the young Free Stater who was making his international debut, had kept his head admirably as he snapped up a flicked-away ball on the try-line.

Ian Robertson, the versatile Rhodesian who substituted for the ailing Dawie Snyman at fullback, put over a dropped goal to crown a quite outstanding display and Bosch, who had been ill during the week preceeding the test, added a penalty and a conversion to make the final score 16-7. The Springbok flyhalf, in fact, had to be replaced by substitute De Wet Ras a few minutes before the end.

Lyn Jaffray scored New Zealand's sole try after a superbly individualistic effort from Grant Batty while Bryan Williams contributed a penalty to his team's total. Although the score indicates a convincing victory for the Springboks there was actually little to choose between the two sides with only tremendous work on the defence by Boland Coetzee, Moaner van Heerden, Morne du Plessis, Peter Whipp and Johan Oosthuizen halting powerful drives by the New Zealand forwards.

The Springbok selectors wielded the axe with abandon when they selected the side for the second test in Bloemfontein. Peter Whipp, so brilliant in Durban, was dropped and Ian Robertson, a success at fullback, was pushed into his place at centre to allow the out-of-form Dawie Snyman to return to the team at fullback. Krantz, who had done well in his debut, was nevertheless dropped for the more experienced Chris Pope while Jan Ellis, who had obviously reached the end of the line, had to make way for Martinus Theunis Steyn Stofberg, a 21-year-old Free State forward of immense, if raw, potential. Ellis had played in 38 tests and shares with Frik du Preez the distinction of being the most-capped Springbok ever.

The All Blacks never looked like losing the second test. Sid Going was at his considerable best and apart from nursing his pack and his backs, he scored two penalty goals and a conversion and also harrassed the life out of his opposite number Paul Bayvel. Joe Morgan broke through for an excellent try and Doug Bruce, making good use of Going's impeccable service, dropped a goal. All the Springboks could produce were three penalty goals by Gerald Bosch.

It was an even more bruising, and far less enterprising, test than the first one and the Springboks lost their best lineout forward John Williams with a gruesome injury to his nose in the second half. He was replaced by Kevin de Klerk and the big Transvaal lock made sure of his place for the rest of the series with a furious display. The Springboks were generally subdued, however, and too many key-players faltered and fumbled for them to be a serious threat at any stage of the match.

South Africa won the vital third test at Newlands because of a truly great performance by Morne du Plessis who so inspired his team that they completely wiped out the bad memory of their groping incompetence at Bloemfontein. Play was rough to the point of being vicious and Du Plessis afterwards looked as if he had fought a losing battle for the world heavyweight championship. But, then, hardly a player came out of this match without scars of some sort or other.

The Springbok frontrow of Rampie Stander, veteran Piston van Wyk, and the barrel-chested Johannesburg carpenter Johan Strauss, as well as the second-row men, De Klerk and Van Heerden, were magnificent while Boland Coetzee with typical courage, skill and sheer doggedness, gave a rampaging Du Plessis all the support he needed. Even the young Stofberg, in company as rough as he is ever likely to encounter, showed that he was not a boy trying to do a man's job.

Oosthuizen, with a try after a perfectly-timed interception followed by electrifying acceleration, Bosch with two penalties and a conversion and a dropgoal, three minutes from the end, by Dawie Snyman gave the Springboks their 15 points. Bruce Robertson, with an opportunistic try after Germishuys had got himself in a tangle near his own line, and Bryan Williams, with two penalties, made the All Blacks' total of 10 points.

John Reason, of the London *Daily Telegraph*, summarised the fourth test accurately when he wrote:

"The final test of this series was, sadly, a game which is all too typical of international rugby. It was a brutally hard, bludgeoning business, repeatedly interrupted by stoppages for deliberately inflicted injuries.

"It contained the minimum of movement and there were blood and bandages everywhere...."

Prolonged complaining over the referee and some of his decisions overshadowed the Springboks' 15-14 victory and it was repeatedly claimed that the South Africans had been lucky to have won. It is true that the All Blacks scored two tries to one and that Bosch with two penalties, a drop-goal and a conversion, had made all the difference. Going and Kirkpatrick scored tries for the All Blacks while "Klippies" Kritzinger went over for the Springboks' only try.

But Morne du Plessis put it in perspective when he said afterwards:

"Sure we were lucky, but I've also played in games where the opposition had been lucky. It's part of the game...."

But it is a pity that the 1976 series could not have ended on a more positive note.

After all, when the two teams disappeared into the tunnel under the huge grandstand at Ellis Park, the curtain closed on what will one day be known as only an era in our rugby history. An era which lasted for 85 years, leaving all South Africans a legacy of achievement in the rugby arenas of the world. It is a precious heritage and it is there for all of us to share and to build on so as to ensure that there will be more, much more, for the generations to come.

Jan (Boland) Coetzee, the courageous and tenacious Western Province flanker, was one of the most consistent Springboks in the 1976 series. Here he drives past the scrum in the first test in Durban as the veteran Jan Ellis looks on. Ellis reached the end of the trail in 1976.

John Rubython

SOUTH AFRICAN INTERNATIONAL RUGBY RECORDS (1891-1976)

INTERNATIONAL MATCHES

SOUTH AFRICA VS. BRITISH ISLES

Matches played 36: South Africa 17 victories, British Isles 13, 6 drawn

Year	Venue	S.A. Result	South Africa T.	C.	P.	D.	British Isles T.	C.	P.	D.
1891	Port Elizabeth	Lost 0—4	0	0	0	0	2	1	0	0
	Kimberley	Lost 0—3	0	0	0	0	0	0	0	1m
	Newlands	Lost 0—4	0	0	0	0	2	1	0	0
Series: S.A. played 3; W0, L3, D0		0—11	0	0	0	0	4	2	0	1m

N.B. In 1891 the value of a try was 1 point. m=Drop from a mark: value 3 points.

Year	Venue	S.A. Result	South Africa T.	C.	P.	D.	British Isles T.	C.	P.	D.
1896	Port Elizabeth	Lost 0—8	0	0	0	0	2	1	0	0
	Johannesburg	Lost 8—17	2	1	0	0	3	2	0	1
	Kimberley	Lost 3—9	1	0	0	0	1	1	0	1
	Newlands	Won 5—0	1	1	0	0	0	0	0	0
Series: S.A. played 4: W1, L3, D0		16—34	4	2	0	0	6	4	0	2
1903	Johannesburg	Draw 10—10	2	2	0	0	2	2	0	0
	Kimberley	Draw 0—0	0	0	0	0	0	0	0	0
	Newlands	Won 8—0	2	1	0	0	0	0	0	0
Series: S.A. played 3; W1, L0, D2		18—10	4	3	0	0	2	2	0	0
1910	Johannesburg	Won 14—10	4	1	0	0	2	0	0	1
	Port Elizabeth	Lost 3—8	1	0	0	0	2	1	0	0
	Newlands	Won 21—5	4	3	1	0	1	1	0	0
Series: S.A. played 3; W2, L1, D0		38—23	9	4	1	0	5	2	0	1
1924	Durban	Won 7—3	1	0	0	1	1	0	0	0
	Johannesburg	Won 17—0	4	1	1	0	0	0	0	0
	Port Elizabeth	Draw 3—3	1	0	0	0	1	0	0	0
	Newlands	Won 16—9	4	0	0	1	2	0	1	0
Series: S.A. played 4; W3, L0, D1		43—15	10	1	1	2	4	0	1	0
1938	Johannesburg	Won 26—12	4	4	2	0	0	0	4	0
	Port Elizabeth	Won 19—3	3	2	2	0	1	0	0	0
	Newlands	Lost 16—21	3	2	1	0	4	1	1	1
Series: S.A. played 3; W2, L1, D0		61—36	10	8	5	0	5	1	5	1
1955	Johannesburg	Lost 22—23	4	2	2	0	5	0	0	0
	Newlands	Won 25—9	7	2	0	0	2	4	1	0
	Pretoria	Lost 6—9	0	0	2	0	1	0	1	1
	Port Elizabeth	Won 22—8	5	2	0	1	2	1	0	0
Series: S.A. played 4; W2, L2, D0		75—49	16	6	4	1	10	5	2	1
1962	Johannesburg	Draw 3—3	1	0	0	0	1	0	0	0
	Durban	Won 3—0	0	0	1	0	0	0	0	0
	Newlands	Won 8—3	1	1	1	0	0	0	0	1
	Bloemfontein	Won 34—14	6	5	2	0	3	1	1	0
Series: S.A. played 4; W3, L0, D1		48—20	8	6	4	0	4	1	1	1
1968	Pretoria	Won 25—20	3	2	4	0	1	1	5	0
	Port Elizabeth	Draw 6—6	0	0	2	0	0	0	2	0
	Newlands	Won 11—6	1	1	2	0	0	0	2	0
	Johannesburg	Won 19—6	4	2	0	1	0	0	2	0
Series: S.A. played 4; W3, L0, D1		61—38	8	5	8	1	1	1	11	0
1974	Newlands	Lost 3—12	0	0	0	1	0	0	3	1
	Pretoria	Lost 9—28	0	0	2	1	5	1	1	1
	Port Elizabeth	Lost 9—26	0	0	3	0	3	1	2	2
	Johannesburg	Draw 13—13	1	0	3	0	2	1	1	0
Series: S.A. played 4; W0, L3, D1		34—79	1	0	8	2	10	3	7	4

SOUTH AFRICA VS. NEW ZEALAND

Matches played 34: South Africa 19 victories, New Zealand 13, 2 drawn

Year	Venue	S.A. Result	South Africa T.	C.	P.	D.	New Zealand T.	C.	P.	D.
1921	Dunedin	Lost 5—13	1	1	0	0	3	2	0	0
	Auckland	Won 9—5	1	1	0	1	1	1	0	0
	Wellington	Draw 0—0	0	0	0	0	0	0	0	0
Series: S.A. played 3; W1, L1, D1		14—18	2	2	0	1	4	3	0	0
1928	Durban	Won 17—0	1	0	2	2	0	0	0	0
	Johannesburg	Lost 6—7	0	0	1	1m	0	0	1	1
	Port Elizabeth	Won 11—6	3	1	0	0	2	0	0	0
	Newlands	Lost 5—13	1	1	0	0	1	0	2	1
Series: S.A. played 4; W2, L2, D0		39—26	5	2	3	3m	3	0	3	2

m Includes 1 drop from a mark: value 3 points. (Value of dropped goal: 4 points)

Year	Venue	S.A. Result	South Africa T.	C.	P.	D.	New Zealand T.	C.	P.	D.
1937	Wellington	Lost 7—13	1	0	0	1	1	0	2	1
	Christchurch	Won 13—6	2	2	1	0	2	0	0	0
	Auckland	Won 17—6	5	1	0	0	0	0	2	0
Series: S.A. played 3: W2, L1, D0		37—25	8	3	1	1	3	0	4	1
1949	Newlands	Won 15—11	0	0	5	0	1	1	1	1
	Johannesburg	Won 12—6	2	0	1	1	0	0	1	1
	Durban	Won 9—3	0	0	3	0	1	0	0	0
	Port Elizabeth	Won 11—8	1	1	1	1	2	1	0	0
Series: S.A. played 4; W4, L0, D0		47—28	3	1	10	2	4	2	2	2
1956	Dunedin	Lost 6—10	1	0	1	0	2	2	0	0
	Wellington	Won 8—3	2	1	0	0	1	0	0	0
	Christchurch	Lost 10—17	2	2	0	0	3	1	2	0
	Auckland	Lost 5—11	1	1	0	0	1	1	2	0
Series: S.A. played 4; W1, L3, D0		29—41	6	4	1	0	7	4	4	0
1960	Johannesburg	Won 13—0	2	2	1	0	0	0	0	0
	Newlands	Lost 3—11	1	0	0	0	1	1	1	1
	Bloemfontein	Draw 11—11	1	1	2	0	1	1	2	0
	Port Elizabeth	Won 8—3	1	1	1	0	0	0	1	0
Series: S.A. played 4; W2, L1, D1		35—25	5	4	4	0	2	2	4	1
1965	Wellington	Lost 3—6	0	0	0	1	2	0	0	0
	Dunedin	Lost 0—13	0	0	0	0	3	2	0	0
	Christchurch	Won 19—16	4	2	1	0	3	2	1	0
	Auckland	Lost 3—20	0	0	1	0	5	1	0	1
Series: S.A. played 4; W1, L3, D0		25—55	4	2	2	1	13	5	1	1
1970	Pretoria	Won 17—6	2	1	2	1	1	0	1	0
	Newlands	Lost 8—9	1	1	1	0	2	0	1	0
	Port Elizabeth	Won 14—3	2	1	2	0	0	0	1	0
	Johannesburg	Won 20—17	2	1	4	0	1	1	4	0
Series: S.A. played 4; W3, L1, D0		59—35	7	4	9	1	4	1	7	0
1976	Durban	Won 16—7	2	1	1	1	1	0	1	0
	Bloemfontein	Lost 9—15	0	0	3	0	1	1	2	1
	Newlands	Won 15—10	1	1	2	1	1	0	2	0
	Johannesburg	Won 15—14	1	1	2	1	2	0	1	1
Series: S.A. played 4; W3, L1, D0		55—46	4	3	8	3	5	1	6	2

SOUTH AFRICA VS. AUSTRALIA

Matches played 28: South Africa 21 victories, Australia 7

Year	Venue	S.A. Result	South Africa T.	C.	P.	D.	Australia T.	C.	P.	D.
1933	Newlands	Won 17—3	4	1	1	0	0	0	1	0
	Durban	Lost 6—21	1	0	1	0	4	3	1	0
	Johannesburg	Won 12—3	2	1	0	1	1	0	0	0
	Port Elizabeth	Won 11—0	2	1	1	0	0	0	0	0
	Bloemfontein	Lost 4—15	0	0	0	1	3	1	0	1
Series: S.A. played 5; W3, L2, D0		50—42	9	3	3	2	8	4	2	1

Year	Venue	S.A. Result		South Africa				Australia			
				T.	C.	P.	D.	T.	C.	P.	D.
1937	Sydney	Won	9—5	2	0	1	0	1	1	0	0
	Sydney	Won	26—17	6	4	0	0	3	1	2	0
Series: S.A. played 2; W2, L0, D0			35—22	8	4	1	0	4	2	2	0
1953	Johannesburg	Won	25—3	5	2	2	0	0	0	1	0
	Newlands	Lost	14—18	4	1	0	0	4	3	0	0
	Durban	Won	18—8	4	3	0	0	1	1	1	0
	Port Elizabeth	Won	22—9	2	2	2	2	1	0	2	0
Series: S.A. played 4; W3, L1, D0			79—38	15	8	4	2	6	4	4	0
1956	Sydney	Won	9—0	2	0	1	0	0	0	0	0
	Brisbane	Won	9—0	2	0	0	1	0	0	0	0
Series: S.A. played 2; W2, L0, D0			18—0	4	0	1	1	0	0	0	0
1961	Johannesburg	Won	28—3	8	2	0	0	0	0	1	0
	Port Elizabeth	Won	23—11	3	1	3	1	1	1	2	0
Series: S.A. played 2; W2, L0, D0			51—14	11	3	3	1	1	1	3	0
1963	Pretoria	Won	14—3	2	1	2	0	1	0	0	0
	Newlands	Lost	5—9	1*	1	0	0	1	0	1	1
	Johannesburg	Lost	9—11	0	0	3	0	1	1	1	1
	Port Elizabeth	Won	22—6	3	2	3	0	0	0	1	1
Series: S.A. played 4; W2, L2, D0			50—29	6	4	8	0	3	1	3	3
**Penalty try*											
1965	Sydney	Lost	11—18	2	1	1	0	2	0	4	0
	Brisbane	Lost	8—12	2	1	0	0	0	0	4	0
Series: S.A. played 2; W0, L2, D0			19—30	4	2	1	0	2	0	8	0
1969	Johannesburg	Won	30—11	5	3	3	0	1	1	2	0
	Durban	Won	16—9	3	2	1	0	0	0	3	0
	Newlands	Won	11—3	2	1	1	0	0	0	1	0
	Bloemfontein	Won	19—8	3	2	2	0	1	1	1	0
Series: S.A. played 4; W4, L0, D0			76—31	13	8	7	0	2	2	7	0
1971	Sydney	Won	19—11	3	2	1	1	1	1	2	0
	Brisbane	Won	14—6	3	1	1	0	0	0	1	1
	Sydney	Won	18—6	3	3	1	0	1	0	1	0
Series: S.A. played 3; W3, L0, D0			51—23	9	6	3	1	2	1	4	1

SOUTH AFRICA VS. FRANCE

Matches played 16: South Africa 9 victories, France 3, 4 drawn

Year	Venue	S.A. Result		South Africa				France			
				T.	C.	P.	D.	T.	C.	P.	D.
1913	Bordeaux	Won	38—5	9	4	1	0	1	1	0	0
1952	Paris	Won	25—3	6	2	1	0	0	0	0	1
1958	Newlands	Draw	3—3	1	0	0	0	0	0	0	1
	Johannesburg	Lost	5—9	1	1	0	0	0	0	1	2
Series: S.A. played 2; W0, L1, D1			8—12	2	1	0	0	0	0	1	3
1961	Paris	Draw	0—0	0	0	0	0	0	0	0	0
1964	Springs	Lost	6—8	1	0	1	0	1	1	1	0
1967	Durban	Won	26—3	5	4	1	0	1	0	0	0
	Bloemfontein	Won	16—3	3	2	1	0	0	0	1	0
	Johannesburg	Lost	14—19	2	1	2	0	2	2	1	2
	Newlands	Draw	6—6	0	0	1	1	1	0	1	0
Series: S.A. played 4; W2, L1, D1			62—31	10	7	5	1	4	2	3	2
1968	Bordeaux	Won	12—9	0	0	4	0	3	0	0	0
	Paris	Won	16—11	3	2	1	0	1	1	0	2
Series: S.A. played 2; W2, L0, D0			28—20	3	2	5	0	4	1	0	2
1971	Bloemfontein	Won	22—9	2	2	3	1	1	0	2	0
	Durban	Draw	8—8	1	1	0	1	1	1	0	1
Series: S.A. played 2; W1, L0, D1			30—17	3	3	3	2	2	1	2	1

Year	Venue	S.A. Result		South Africa				France			
				T.	C.	P.	D.	T.	C.	P.	D.
1974	Toulouse	Won	13—4	1	0	3	0	1	0	0	0
	Paris	Won	10—8	1	0	2	0	2	0	0	0
Series: S.A. played 2; W2, L0, D0			23—12	2	0	5	0	3	0	0	0
1975	Bloemfontein	Won	38—25	5	3	4	0	4	3	1	0
	Pretoria	Won	33—18	2	2	7	0	1	1	3	1
Series: S.A. played 2; W2, L0, D0			71—43	7	5	11	0	5	4	4	1

SOUTH AFRICA VS. SCOTLAND

Matches played 8: South Africa 5 victories, Scotland 3

Year	Venue	S.A. Result		South Africa				Scotland			
				T.	C.	P.	D.	T.	C.	P.	D.
1906	Glasgow	Lost	0—6	0	0	0	0	2	0	0	0
1912	Edinburgh	Won	16—0	4	2	0	0	0	0	0	0
1932	Edinburgh	Won	6—3	2	0	0	0	1	0	0	0
1951	Edinburgh	Won	44—0	9	7	0	1	0	0	0	0
1960	Port Elizabeth	Won	18—10	4	3	0	0	2	2	0	0
1961	Edinburgh	Won	12—5	2	0	2	0	1	1	0	0
1965	Edinburgh	Lost	5—8	1	1	0	0	1	1	0	1
1969	Edinburgh	Lost	3—6	0	0	1	0	1	0	1	0

SOUTH AFRICA VS. IRELAND

Matches played 8: South Africa 6 victories, Ireland 1, 1 drawn

Year	Venue	S.A. Result		South Africa				Ireland			
				T.	C.	P.	D.	T.	C.	P.	D.
1906	Belfast	Won	15—12	4	0	1	0	3	0	1	0
1912	Dublin	Won	38—0	10	4	0	0	0	0	0	0
1931	Dublin	Won	8—3	2	1	0	0	0	0	1	0
1951	Dublin	Won	17—5	4	1	0	1	1	1	0	0
1960	Dublin	Won	8—3	2	1	0	0	0	0	1	0
1961	Newlands	Won	24—8	5	3	1	0	1	1	1	0
1965	Dublin	Lost	6—9	1	0	1	0	1	0	2	0
1970	Dublin	Draw	8—8	1	1	1	0	1	1	1	0

SOUTH AFRICA VS. WALES

Matches played 7: South Africa 6 victories, Wales 0, 1 drawn

Year	Venue	S.A. Result		South Africa				Wales			
				T.	C.	P.	D.	T.	C.	P.	D.
1906	Swansea	Won	11—0	3	1	0	0	0	0	0	0
1912	Cardiff	Won	3—0	0	0	1	0	0	0	0	0
1931	Swansea	Won	8—3	2	1	0	0	1	0	0	0
1951	Cardiff	Won	6—3	1	0	0	1	1	0	0	0
1960	Cardiff	Won	3—0	0	0	1	0	0	0	0	0
1964	Durban	Won	24—3	3	3	2	1	0	0	1	0
1970	Cardiff	Draw	6—6	1	0	1	0	1	0	1	0

SOUTH AFRICA VS. ENGLAND

Matches played 7: South Africa 4 victories, England 2, 1 drawn

Year	Venue	S.A. Result		South Africa				England			
				T.	C.	P.	D.	T.	C.	P.	D.
1906	Crystal Palace	Draw	3—3	1	0	0	0	1	0	0	0
1913	Twickenham	Won	9—3	1	0	2	0	1	0	0	0
1932	Twickenham	Won	7—0	1	0	0	1	0	0	0	0
1952	Twickenham	Won	8—3	1	1	1	0	1	0	0	0
1961	Twickenham	Won	5—0	1	1	0	0	0	0	0	0
1969	Twickenham	Lost	8—11	1	1	1	0	2	1	1	0
1972	Johannesburg	Lost	9—18	0	0	3	0	1	1	4	0

SOUTH AFRICA'S OVERALL TEST RECORD

Since playing the first test against the British Isles in Port Elizabeth in 1891, South Africa has played 146 official international matches, and the complete record of all these matches, up to and including the Test matches played against New Zealand in 1976 is:

	Played	Won	Lost	Drawn	For	Agst.
vs. British Isles	36	17	13	6	394	315
vs. New Zealand	34	19	13	2	340	299
vs. Australia	28	21	7	0	429	229
vs. France	18	11	3	4	291	151
vs. Scotland	8	5	3	0	104	38
vs. Ireland	8	6	1	1	124	48
vs. Wales	7	6	0	1	61	15
vs. England	7	4	2	1	49	38
	146	89	42	15	1 792	1 133

LEADING SOUTH AFRICAN SCORERS
TEST MATCHES

(Players who have scored a total of 20 or more points in Test Matches)

		Tests	*Tries*	*Conv.*	*P.G.*	*D.G.*	*Pts.*
1.	Piet Visagie (1967—71)	25	6	20	19	5	130
2.	Gerald Bosch (1974—)	9	—	7	23	2	89
3.	Keith Oxlee (1960—65)	19	5	14	14	1	88
4.	Ian McCallum (1970—74)	11		10	14	—	62
5.	Gerry Brand (1928—38)	16	—	13	7	2	55
6.	Okey Geffin (1949—51)	7	—	9	10	—	48
7.	Tiny Naude (1963—68)	14	2	4	11	—	47
8.	Bennie Osler (1924—33)	17	2	6	4	4	46
9.	Dougie Morkel (1906—13)	9	3	7	5	—	38
10.	Freddy Turner (1933—38)	11	4	4	3	—	29
11.	Roy Dryburgh (1955—60)	8	3	5	3	—	28
12.	H. O. de Villiers (1967—70)	14	—	7	4	—	26
13.	Jannie Engelbrecht (1960—69)	33	8	—	—	—	24
14.	John Gainsford (1960—67)	33	8	—	—	—	24
15.	Ferdie Bergh (1931—38)	17	7	—	—	—	21
16.	Jan Ellis (1965—)	38	7	—	—	—	21
17.	Dick Lockyear (1960—61)	6	—	4	4	—	20
18.	Dawie Snyman (1972—)	9	—	1	4	2	20

LEADING S.A. TRY SCORERS: TEST MATCHES

(Figures in parentheses are the number of test matches played)

John Gainsford	8 (33)	Jack Morkel	4 (5)
Jannie Engelbrecht	8 (33)	Freddy Turner	4 (11)
Ferdie Bergh	7 (17)	Tom van Vollenhoven	4 (7)
Jan Ellis	7 (38)	Daan Retief	4 (9)
Boetie McHardy	6 (5)	Salty du Rand	4 (21)
Basie van Wyk	6 (10)	Hugo van Zyl	4 (17)
Hennie van Zyl	6 (10)	Gert Muller	4 (14)
Mannetjies Roux	6 (27)	Bob Loubser	3 (7)
Syd Nomis	6 (25)	Dougie Morkel	3 (9)
Piet Visagie	6 (25)	Kenny Starke	3 (4)
Jan Stegmann	5 (4)	Louis Babrow	3 (5)
Dai Williams	5 (8)	Tjol Lategan	3 (11)
Chris Koch	5 (22)	Hennie Muller	3 (13)
Theuns Briers	5 (7)	Chum Ochse	3 (7)
Keith Oxlee	5 (19)	Roy Dryburgh	3 (8)
Doug Hopwood	5 (22)	Corra Dirksen	3 (10)
Eben Olivier	5 (16)	Dawie de Villiers	3 (25)
Piet Greyling	5 (25)	Peter Cronje	3 (7)

INDIVIDUAL APPEARANCES
TEST MATCHES

The following players have represented South Africa in 15 or more Test Matches:

F. C. H. du Preez	38	J. A. du Rand	21
J. H. Ellis	38	S. P. Kuhn	19
J. F. K. Marais	35	K. Oxlee	19
J. L. Gainsford	33	M. M. Louw	18
J. P. Engelbrecht	33	G. F. Malan	18
J. T. Claassen	28	J. L. Myburgh	18
L. G. Wilson	27	B. L. Osler	17
F. du T. Roux	27	W. F. Bergh	17
D. J. de Villiers	25	G. H. van Zyl	17
T. P. Bedford	25	P. J. Nel	16
P. J. Visagie	25	G. H. Brand	16
S. H. Nomis	25	D. H. Craven	16
P. J. F. Greyling	25	A. S. Malan	16
A. C. Koch	22	E. Olivier	16
D. J. Hopwood	22	H. P. J. Bekker	15
		J. F. B. van Wyk	15

CAPTAINS IN TEST MATCHES

Thirty-five different players have captained South Africa in 146 test matches as follows:

22 — D. J. de Villiers
11 — J. F. K. Marais
10 — A. S. (Avril) Malan
9 — H. S. V. Muller, J. T. Claassen
8 — P. J. Nel
6 — M. du Plessis
5 — W. A. Millar, B. L. Osler, S. S. Vivier(s)
4 — P. K. Albertyn, P. J. Mostert, D. H. Craven, S. P. Fry, G. F. (Abie) Malan, C. M. Smith
3 — F. T. D. Aston, P. J. Roos, W. H. (Boy) Morkel, F. du Plessis, T. P. Bedford
2 — B. H. Heatlie, D. F. T. Morkel, R. G. Dryburgh
1 — H. H. Castens, R. C. Snedden, A. Richards. A, Frew, J. M. Powell, H. W. Carolin, F. J. Dobbin, B. J. Kenyon, J. A. du Rand, D. C. van Jaarsveldt, P. J. F. Greyling.

N.B. *T. B. (Theo) Pienaar, captain of the 1921 Springbok team in Australia and New Zealand did not play in a test match.*

SOUTH AFRICAN RECORDS ON OVERSEAS TOURS
RECORD OF THE TOURS

		P	W	L	D	F	A	S.A. Tries
In United Kingdom	1906—07	28	25	2	1	553	79	130
	1912—13	26	23	3	0	403	96	94
	1931—32	26	23	1	2	407	124	86
	1951—52	27	26	1	0	499	143	103
	1960—61	30	28	1	1	476	110	111
	1969—70	24	15	5	4	323	157	59
In Ireland and Scotland	1965	5	0	4	1	37	53	7
In France	1913	1	1	0	0	38	5	9
	1952	4	4	0	0	63	24	17
	1961	4	3	0	1	91	22	21
	1968	6	5	1	0	84	43	12
	1974	9	8	1	0	170	74	23
In Australia	1921	4	4	0	0	83	38	20
	1937	9	8	1	0	342	65	74
	1956	6	6	0	0	150	26	29
	1965	6	3	3	0	184	53	39
	1971	13	13	0	0	396	102	76
In New Zealand	1921	19	15	2	2	244	81	54
	1937	17	16	1	0	411	104	87
	1956	23	16	6	1	370	177	79
	1965	24	19	5	0	485	232	105
Total played by S.A. overseas		311	261	37	13	5 809	1 808	1 235
Test matches played in S.A.		90	53	27	10	1 187	779	183
All matches played by S.A.		401	314	64	23	6 996	2 587	1 418

BIGGEST WINS

The biggest wins scored by South Africa on a tour of each country is as follows:

Country	*Tour*	*Opponents*	*S.A. won*
Australia	1937	Western Districts	63—0
New Zealand	1965	N. Z. Universities	55—11
United Kingdom	1906—07	Northumberland	44—0
United Kingdom	1951—52	SCOTLAND	44—0
France	1913	FRANCE	38—5

BIGGEST DEFEATS

The biggest defeats of a South African team on a tour of each country is as follows:

Country	*Tour*	*Opponents*	*S.A. Lost*
New Zealand	1965	Wellington	6—23
New Zealand	1965	NEW ZEALAND (4th Test)	3—20
United Kingdom	1906—07	Cardiff	0—17
Australia	1937	New South Wales	6—17
France	1968	South West France	3—11

MOST TRIES BY S.A. IN A MATCH ON TOUR

The most tries scored by South Africa in a match on a tour or each country is as follows:

Country	*Tour*	*Opponents*		*Result*	*S.A. Tries*
Australia	1937	Newcastle	S.A. won	58—8	16
New Zealand	1965	N.Z. Universities	S.A. won	55—11	13
United Kingdom	1906—07	Northumberland	S.A. won	44—0	12
France	1913	FRANCE	S.A. won	38—5	9

MOST TRIES AGAINST S.A. IN A MATCH ON TOUR

The most tries scored against South Africa in a match on a tour of each country is as follows:

Country	*Tour*	*Opponents*		*Result*	*Opp. Tries*
Australia	1937	New South Wales	S.A. lost	6—17	5
New Zealand	1965	NEW ZEALAND (4th Test)	S.A. lost	3—20	5
United Kingdom	1932	Midland Counties	S.A. lost	21—30	5
France	1961	Coast of Basque	S.A. won	36—9	3
France	1968	FRANCE (1st Test)	S.A. won	12—9	3

BEST INDIVIDUAL TOUR RECORD

The most total points scored by a Springbok player on a tour of each country is as follows:

Country	*Tour*	*Player's record*
New Zealand	1937	G. H. Brand scored 100 pts. in 13 games.
Australia	1937	G. H. Brand scored 90 pts. in 7 games.
United Kingdom	1951—52	A. O. Geffin scored 89 pts. in 12 games.
France	1974	G. R. Bosch scored 55 pts. in 7 games.

MOST POINTS IN A MATCH

The most points scored in a match by a Springbok player on a tour of each country is as follows:

Country	*Tour*	*Opponents*	*Player's Record*
Australia	1971	South Australia	P. J. Visagie scored 25 pts.
New Zealand	1937	Manawatu	G. H. Brand scored 21 pts.
France	1968	Auvergne-Limousin	P. J. Visagie scored 20 pts.
United Kingdom	1906—07	Yorkshire	H. W. Carolin scored 16 pts.

ANALYSIS OF POINTS IN TESTS

	SOUTH AFRICA					OPPONENTS				
	T.	C.	P.	D.	M.	T.	C.	P.	D.	M.
vs. British Isles	70	35	31	6	—	51	21	27	10	1
vs. New Zealand	44	25	38	11	1	45	18	31	9	—
vs. Australia	79	38	31	7	—	28	15	33	5	—
vs. France	43	24	32	3	—	20	10	11	10	—
vs. Scotland	22	13	3	1	—	8	4	1	1	—
vs. Ireland	29	11	4	1	—	7	3	7	—	—
vs. Wales	10	5	5	2	—	3	—	2	—	—
vs. England	6	3	7	1	—	6	2	5	—	—
	303+	154	151	32*	1	168+	73	117	35*	1

**9 of the dropped goals scored by South Africa and 8 by their opponents count 4 points each. All other dropped goals count 3 points each.*
+14 of the tries scored by South Africa and 24 by their opponents count 4 points each. 4 of the tries scored by the British Isles in 1891, count 1 (one) point each. All other tries count 3 points each.

S.A. RECORDS IN INTERNATIONAL MATCHES

BIGGEST WINS IN A TEST MATCH

The biggest wins scored by South Africa in a Test Match against each country is as follows:

Opponents	*Venue*	*Date*	*S.A. won:*
Scotland	Edinburgh	24 Nov. 1951	*44—0
Ireland	Dublin	30 Nov. 1912	38—0
France	Bordeaux	11 Jan. 1913	38—5
Australia	Johannesburg	5 Aug. 1961	28—3
Wales	Durban	23 May 1964	24—3
British Isles	Bloemfontein	25 Aug. 1962	34—14
New Zealand	Durban	30 June 1928	17—0
England	Twickenham	2 Jan. 1932	7—0

**International record.*

BIGGEST DEFEATS IN A TEST MATCH

The biggest defeat of a South African team in a Test Match against each country is as follows:

Opponents	*Venue*	*Date*	*S.A. lost*
British Isles	Pretoria	22 June 1974	9—28
New Zealand	Auckland	18 Sept. 1965	3—20
Australia	Durban	22 July 1933	6—21
England	Johannesburg	3 June 1972	9—18
Scotland	Glasgow	17 Nov. 1906	0—6
France	Johannesburg	29 July 1967	14—19
Ireland	Dublin	10 Apr. 1965	6—9
Wales	*South Africa have not lost a test match to Wales; the closest that S.A. has been to defeat was in the 6—6 draw in Cardiff in 1970, when Wales missed a conversion in the last seconds of the match.*		

MOST TRIES BY S.A. IN A TEST MATCH

The most tries by South Africa in a test match against each country is as follows:

Opponents	*Year*	*Venue*	*Result*	*S.A. Tries*
Ireland	1912	Dublin	S.A. won 38—0	10
France	1913	Bordeaux	S.A. won 38—5	9
Scotland	1951	Edinburgh	S.A. won 44—0	9
Australia	1961	Johannesburg	S.A. won 28—3	8
British Isles	1955	Newlands	S.A. won 25—9	7
New Zealand	1937	Auckland	S.A. won 17—6	5
Wales	1906	Swansea	S.A. won 11—0	3
Wales	1964	Durban	S.A. won 24—3	3
England	*South Africa have never scored more than one try in a test match against England.*			

MOST TRIES AGAINST S.A. IN A TEST MATCH

The most tries scored against South Africa in a test match by each country is as follows:

Opponents	*Year*	*Venue*	*Result*	*Opp. Tries*
British Isles	1955	Johannesburg	S.A. lost 22—23	5
British Isles	1974	Pretoria	S.A. lost 9—28	5
New Zealand	1965	Auckland	S.A. lost 3—20	5
Australia	1933	Durban	S.A. lost 6—21	4
Australia	1953	Newlands	S.A. lost 14—18	4
France	1975	Bloemfontein	S.A. won 38—25	4
Ireland	1906	Belfast	S.A. won 15—12	3
England	1969	Twickenham	S.A. lost 8—11	2
Scotland	1906	Glasgow	S.A. lost 0—6	2
Scotland	1960	Port Elizabeth	S.A. won 18—10	2
Wales	*have never scored more than one try in a test match against South Africa.*			

MOST POINTS IN A TEST MATCH

The most points scored by a Springbok in a test match against each country is as follows:

Opponents	*Year*	*Venue*	*Player's Record*	
France	1975	Pretoria	G. R. Bosch scored	22 points
British Isles	1962	Bloemfontein	K. Oxlee scored	16 points
New Zealand	1949	Newlands	A. O. Geffin scored	15 points
Australia	1969	Johannesburg	P. J. Visagie scored	15 points
Scotland	1951	Edinburgh	A. O. Geffin scored	14 points
Wales	1964	Durban	K. Oxlee scored	12 points
Ireland	1912	Dublin	J. A. Stegmann scored	9 points
Ireland	1912	Dublin	E. E. McHardy scored	9 points
Ireland	1961	Newlands	C. F. Nimb scored	9 points
England	1972	Johannesburg	D. S. L. Snyman scored	9 points

MOST POINTS IN A TEST MATCH AGAINST S.A.

The most points scored against South Africa in a test match by a player from each country is as follows:

Opponents	*Year*	*Venue*	*Player's Record*	
British Isles	1968	Pretoria	T. J. Kiernan scored	17 points
New Zealand	1970	Johannesburg	G. F. Kember scored	14 points
England	1972	Johannesburg	S.A. Doble scored	14 points
France	1975	Pretoria	J. P. Romeu scored	14 points
Australia	1965	Sydney	B. J. Ellwood scored	12 points
Ireland	1961	Newlands	T. J. Kiernan scored	8 points
Scotland	1960	Port Elizabeth	A. R. Smith scored	7 points
Wales	1970	Cardiff	G. O. Edwards scored	6 points

MOST POINTS IN A SERIES OF TEST MATCHES

The most points scored by a Springbok player in a series of test matches against each country is as follows:

Opponents	*Year*	*Where played*	*Player's Record*	
*Australia	1969	South Africa	*P. J. Visagie scored	43 points
New Zealand	1970	South Africa	I. D. McCallum scored	35 points
France	1975	South Africa	G. R. Bosch scored	35 points
British Isles (Lions)	1962	South Africa	K. Oxlee scored	27 points

**International Record*

NOTE: The most points scored by a Springbok in the four test matches played during a tour of the United Kingdom is 16 by A. O. Geffin in 1951—52.

MOST TRIES IN A SERIES OF TEST MATCHES

The most tries scored by a Springbok player in a series of test matches against each country is as follows:

Opponents	*Year*	*Where played*	*Player's Record*	
British Isles (Lions)	1955	South Africa	T. P. D. Briers scored	5 tries
Australia	1961	South Africa	H. J. van Zyl scored	4 tries
France	1967	South Africa	C. W. Dirksen scored	3 tries
New Zealand	1970	South Africa	G. H. Muller scored	3 tries

NOTE: The most tries scored by a Springbok in the four test matches played during a tour of the United Kingdom is 5—by J. A. Stegmann in 1912—13.

MOST POINTS IN A TEST SERIES AGAINST S.A.

The most points scored against South Africa, in a series of test matches, by a player from each country is as follows:

Opponents	*Year*	*Where played*	*Player's Record*	
British Isles (Lions)	1968	South Africa	T. J. Kiernan scored	35 points
New Zealand	1960	South Africa	D. B. Clarke scored	19 points
Australia	1965	Australia	B. J. Ellwood scored	18 points
France	1975	South Africa	J. P. Romeu scored	14 points

MOST TRIES IN A TEST SERIES AGAINST S.A.

The most tries scored against South Africa, in a series of test matches, by a player from each country is as follows:

Opponents	*Year*	*Where played*	*Player's Record*	
British Isles (Lions)	1974	South Africa	J. J. Williams scored	4 tries
New Zealand	1965	New Zealand	K. R. Tremain scored	3 tries
Australia	1953	South Africa	K. Cross scored	2 tries
Australia	1953	South Africa	E. Stapleton scored	2 tries
France	1968	France	B. Dauga scored	2 tries
France	1975	South Africa	R. Paparemborde scored	2 tries

MOST TRIES ON A TOUR

The most tries scored by a Springbok player on a tour of each country is as follows:

Country	*Tour*	*Player*	*Tries scored*
United Kingdom	1906—07	J. A. Loubser	22 tries in 20 games
Australia	1971	J. T. (Hannes) Viljoen	16 tries in 10 games
New Zealand	1965	*J. P. Engelbrecht	15 tries in 15 games
France	1968	J. P. Engelbrecht	5 tries in 5 games

**Engelbrecht scored 20 tries on the combined tour of Australia and New Zealand in 1965.*

MOST TRIES IN A MATCH

The most tries scored in a match by a Springbok player on a tour of each country is as follows:

Country	*Tour*	*Opponents*	*Player and Tries scored*	
Australia	1956	Queensland	R. G. Dryburgh	6 tries
New Zealand	1921	Comb. Auckland	W. C. Zeller	4 tries
New Zealand	1956	Nelson-Marlborough Golden Bay-Motueka	K. T. van Vollenhoven	4 tries
France	1968	Littoral—Prov.	J. P. Engelbrecht	4 tries
United Kingdom	1906—07	East Midlands	A. C. Stegmann	4 tries
United Kingdom	1912—13	Glamorgan	J. A. Stegmann	4 tries
United Kingdom	1931—32	Durham and Northumberland	J. H. v.d. Westhuizen	4 tries
United Kingdom	1931—32	Midland Counties	M. Zimerman	4 tries
United Kingdom	1969—70	N. & M. Scotland	G. H. Muller	4 tries

LEADING SOUTH AFRICAN SCORERS: ALL MATCHES

(Players who have scored more than 50 points in all official tour matches including test matches played both away and in South Africa).

		Games	*Tries*	*Conv.*	*P.G.*	*D.G.*	*Pts.*
1.	Gerry Brand	46	2	100	25	3	293
2.	Piet Visagie	44	8	36	40	8	240
3.	Keith Oxlee	48	11	45	23	3	201
4.	Basie Vivier(s)	31	5	45	17	3	165
5.	Dougie Morkel	40	9	37	13	—	140
6.	Ian McCallum	17	2	28	24	—	134
7.	Jannie Engelbrecht	67	44	—	—	—	132
8.	Gerald Bosch	14	—	15	31	3	132
9.	Freddy Turner	24	18	26	7	1	131
10.	Wynand Mans	19	14	30	6	1	123
11.	Okey Geffin	17	1	26	22	—	121
12.	Roy Dryburgh	20	15	13	15	—	116
13.	Bennie Osler	30	7	17	7	8	108
14.	Dick Lockyear	20	—	32	11	—	97
15.	Jan Ellis	74	32	—	—	—	97
16.	John Gainsford	71	31	—	—	—	93
17.	Tiny Naude	28	6	9	18	—	90
18.	Frik du Preez	87	12	15	7	—	87
19.	Dawie Snyman	21	6	13	8	4	82
20.	H. O. de Villiers	29	2	22	10	—	80
21.	Gerhard Morkel	33	—	33	3	1	79
22.	Paddy Carolin	18	6	15	3	4	73
23.	Paul Johnstone	35	14	7	4	—	68
24.	Bob Loubser	23	22	—	—	—	66
25.	Tom van Vollenhoven	23	20	—	—	1	63
26.	Boetie McHardy	17	20	—	—	—	60
27.	Anton Stegmann	16	18	—	—	—	54
28.	Hennie van Zyl	24	18	—	—	—	54
29.	Dai Williams	18	17	—	—	—	51

LEADING S.A. TRY SCORERS: ALL MATCHES

(Players who have scored 10 or more tries in all official tour matches including test matches played both away and in South Africa. Figures in parentheses are the number of matches played).

Jannie Engelbrecht	44 (67)	Wynand Mans	14 (19)
Jan Ellis	32 (74)	Gert Brynard	14 (21)
John Gainsford	31 (71)	Andy van der Watt	14 (22)
Bob Loubser	22 (23)	Jan Stegmann	13 (15)
Boetie McHardy	20 (17)	Bill Zeller	13 (14)
Tom van Vollenhoven	20 (23)	Pat Lyster	13 (11)
Anton Stegmann	18 (16)	Mannetjies Roux	13 (56)
Freddy Turner	18 (24)	Ponie van der Westhuizen	12 (16)
Hennie van Zyl	18 (24)	Daan Retief	12 (21)
Dai Williams	17 (18)	Frik du Preez	12 (87)
Chum Ochse	16 (22)	Hannes Marais	12 (75)
Hannes Viljoen	16 (10)	Jack Hirsch	11 (18)
Roy Dryburgh	15 (20)	Buks Marais	11 (18)
Mike Antelme	15 (25)	Martin Saunders	11 (14)
Doug Hopwood	15 (53)	Chris Koch	11 (46)
Syd Nomis	15 (54)	Trix Truter	11 (16)
Gert Muller	15 (20)	Keith Oxlee	11 (48)
Attie van Heerden	14 (17)	Japie le Roux	10 (9)
Morris Zimerman	14 (18)	Apie van der Hoff	10 (9)
Ferdie Bergh	14 (41)	Wally Mills	10 (13)
Louis Babrow	14 (16)	Johnny Bester	10 (14)
Paul Johnstone	14 (35)	Eben Olivier	10 (34)

INDIVIDUAL APPEARANCES
ALL MATCHES

(All official tour matches and test matches)

The following players have represented South Africa in 40 or more matches; i.e. official tour matches and test matches.

F. C. H. du Preez	87	J. A. du Rand	47
J. F. K. Marais	75	P. J. Nel	46
J. H. Ellis	74	G. H. Brand	46
J. L. Gainsford	71	A. C. Koch	46
J. P. Engelbrecht	67	G. F. Malan	44
L. G. Wilson	58	P. J. Visagie	44
J. T. Claassen	57	A. I. Kirkpatrick	43
J. L. Myburgh	57	P. J. F. Greyling	43
F. du T. Roux	56	W. F. Bergh	41
S. H. Nomis	54	D. F. T. Morkel	40
D. J. Hopwood	53	P. J. Mostert	40
D. J. de Villiers	53		
M. M. Louw	49		
P. S. du Toit	49		
K. Oxlee	48		
T. P. Bedford	48		

INTERNATIONAL TOURING TEAMS IN SOUTH AFRICA
RECORD OF THE TOURS

		P.	*W.*	*L.*	*D.*	*F.*	*A.*	*Tries For*
British Isles: (Lions)	1891	19	19	0	0	224	1	89
	1896	21	19	1	1	310	45	64
	1903	22	11	8	3	231	138	49
	1910	24	13	8	3	290	236	68
	1924	21	9	9	3	175	155	45
	1938	23	17	6	0	407	272	79
	1955	24	18	5	1	418	271	94
	1962	24	15	5	4	351	208	62
	1968	20	15	4	1	377	181	55
	1974	22	21	0	1	729	207	107
Scotland:	1960	3	2	1	0	61	45	13
Ireland:	1961	4	3	1	0	59	36	8
Wales:	1964	4	2	2	0	43	58	5
England:	1972	7	6	0	1	166	58	23
New Zealand: (All Blacks)	1928	22	16	5	1	339	144	70
	1949	24	14	7	3	230	146	43
	1960	26	20	4	2	441	164	75
	1970	24	21	3	0	687	228	135
	1976	24	18	6	0	610	291	89
Australia: (Wallabies)	1933	23	12	10	1	299	195	67
	1953	27	16	10	1	450	413	92
	1961	6	3	2	1	90	80	15
	1963	24	15	8	1	303	233	46
	1969	26	15	11	0	465	353	78
France: (Tricolours)	1958	10	5	3	2	137	124	26
	1964	6	5	1	0	117	55	18
	1967	13	8	4	1	209	161	30
	1971	9	7	1	1	228	92	42
	1975	11	6	4	1	282	190	41

BIGGEST WINS

The biggest wins scored by each country during a tour of South Africa is as follows:

Country	*Tour*	*Opponents*	*Tour Team won:*
British Isles	1974	South Western Districts	97—0
New Zealand	1970	North East Cape	85—0
France	1971	Western Transvaal	50—0
England	1972	Griqualand West	60—21
Australia	1953	Western Transvaal	50—12
Australia	1969	O.F.S. Country Dist.	47—9

BIGGEST DEFEATS

The biggest defeats of each country during a tour of South Africa is as follows:

Country	*Tour*	*Opponents*	*Tour Team Lost*
France	1958	Comb. W.P.—Boland-S.W.D.	8—38
Australia	1953	Orange Free State	3—28
Australia	1961	SOUTH AFRICA (1st Test)	3—28
British Isles	1955	Eastern Province	0—20
British Isles	1962	SOUTH AFRICA (4th Test)	14—34
New Zealand	1928	SOUTH AFRICA (1st Test)	0—17
Wales	1964	SOUTH AFRICA	3—24

MOST TRIES IN A MATCH BY A TOURING TEAM IN SOUTH AFRICA

The most tries scored in a match by each country during a tour of South Africa is as follows:

Country	*Tour*	*Opponents*	*Tour team Won:*	*Tour team's Tries:*
New Zealand	1970	North East Cape	85—0	17
British Isles	1974	South West. Dist.	97—0	16
France	1971	Western Transvaal	50—0	12
Australia	1953	Western Transvaal	50—12	12

MOST TRIES IN A MATCH AGAINST A TOURING TEAM IN SOUTH AFRICA

The most tries scored in a match against a touring team from each country in South Africa is as follows:

Country	*Tour*	*Opponents*			*Opp. Tries*
Australia	1961	SOUTH AFRICA (1st Test)	Aust. lost	3—28	8
British Isles	1955	SOUTH AFRICA (2nd Test)	B.I. lost	9—25	7
France	1958	Comb. W.P.—Boland-S.W.D.	Fr. lost	8—38	5
France	1967	SOUTH AFRICA (1st Test)	Fr. lost	3—26	5
France	1975	SOUTH AFRICA (1st Test)	Fr. lost	25—38	5
New Zealand	1960	Central Universities	N.Z. won	21—12	4
New Zealand	1976	Quaggas-Barbarians	N.Z. won	32—31	4
New Zealand	1976	Northern Transvaal	N.Z. lost	27—29	4

BEST INDIVIDUAL TOUR RECORD BY A VISITING PLAYER IN SOUTH AFRICA

The most total points scored on an International tour of South Africa by a player from each country is as follows:

Country	*Tour*		*Player's Record*
New Zealand	1960	D. B. Clarke	scored 175 pts. in 20 games.
British Isles	1974	A. R. Irvine	scored 156 pts. in 15 games.
Australia	1969	J. P. Ballesty	scored 89 pts. in 17 games.
France	1975	J-P. Romeu	scored 71 pts. in 7 games.
England	1972	S. A. Doble	scored 47 pts. in 5 games.

NOTE:
The 47 points scored by England's S. A. Doble is the best tour record by a player from any of the four Home Unions during their respective tours of South Africa.

MOST POINTS IN A MATCH BY A VISITING PLAYER IN SOUTH AFRICA

The most points scored on an International tour of South Africa by a player from each country is as follows:

Country	*Tour*	*Opponents*		*Player's Record*
British Isles	1974	S.W. Districts	A. G. B. Old	scored 37 pts.
New Zealand	1970	N.E. Cape	G. F. Kember	scored 34 pts.
England	1972	Griqualand W.	A. G. B. Old	scored 24 pts.
Australia	1969	O.F.S. Country	B. A. Weir	scored 20 pts.
France	1967	S. W. Districts	J. L. Dehez	scored 19 pts.

NOTE: The 24 points scored by England's A. G. B. Old is the best individual match record by a player from any of the four Home Unions during their respective tours of South Africa.

MOST TRIES ON A TOUR OF SOUTH AFRICA

The most tries scored on an International tour of South Africa by a player from each country is as follows:

Country	*Tour*		*Player's Record*
British Isles	1891	R. L. Aston	scored 30 tries in 19 games
New Zealand	1970	G. S. Thorne	scored 17 tries in 19 games
Australia	1953	G. R. Horsley	scored 14 tries in 12 games
France	1971	R. Bertranne	scored 7 tries in 6 games

MOST TRIES IN A MATCH ON A TOUR OF SOUTH AFRICA

The most tries scored in a match on an International tour of South Africa, by a player from each country is as follows:

Country	*Tour*	*Opponents*		*Player's Record*
British Isles	1974	S.W. Dist.	J. J. Williams	scored 6 tries
Australia	1953	Western Tvl.	G. R. Horsley	scored 4 tries
New Zealand	1970	N.E. Cape	G. S. Thorne	scored 4 tries
France	1971	Western Tvl.	R. Bertranne	scored 4 tries

MOST POINTS IN A MATCH AGAINST AN INTERNATIONAL TOURING TEAM IN SOUTH AFRICA

The most points scored in a match by a South African player against an International touring team from each country is as follows:

Country	*Tour*	*Opponents*		*Player's Record*
France	1975	SOUTH AFRICA (2nd Test)	G. R. Bosch	scored 22 pts.
Australia	1969	Western Tvl.	P. J. Durand	scored 18 pts.
British Isles	1962	SOUTH AFRICA (4th Test)	K. Oxlee	scored 16 pts.
New Zealand	1976	S.A. Inv. XV	W. J. de W. Ras	scored 16 pts.

SPRINGBOK BROTHERS

Twenty-five sets of brothers have represented South Africa at Rugby Football. They are:

M. (Oupa) VERSFELD — 1891, and C. (Hasie) VERSFELD — 1891.
J. M. (Jacky) POWELL — 1891–1903, and A. W. (Bertie) POWELL — 1896.
C. G. (Charlie) VAN RENEN — 1891–96, and W. (Willie) VAN RENEN — 1903.
Allan REID — 1903, and H. G. (Bert) REID — 1906.
J. S. (Japie) LE ROUX — 1906, and P. A. (Pietie) LE ROUX — 1906.
D. F. T. (Dougie) MORKEL — 1906–13, and W. S. (Sommie) MORKEL — 1906.
A. F. W. (Artie) MARSBERG — 1906, and P. A. (Peter) MARSBERG — 1910.
P. J. (Paul) ROOS — 1903–06, and G. D. (Gideon) ROOS — 1910.
*F. P. (Freddie) LUYT — 1910–13, R. R. (Dick) LUYT — 1910–13, and J. D. (John) LUYT — 1912–13.
J. D. (Japie) KRIGE — 1903–06, and W. A. (Willie) KRIGE — 1912–13.
A. C. (Anton) STEGMANN — 1906, and J. A. (Jan) STEGMANN — 1912–13.
P. G. (Gerhard) MORKEL — 1912–21, and J. W. H. (Jackie) MORKEL — 1912–13.
H. W. (Henry) WALKER — 1910, and A. P. (Alf) WALKER — 1921–24.
H. J. (Harry) MORKEL — 1921, and J. A. (Royal) MORKEL — 1921.
B. L. (Bennie) OSLER — 1924–33, and S. G. (Stanley) OSLER — 1928.
J. C. VAN DER WESTHUIZEN — 1928–32, and J. H. (Ponie) VAN DER WESTHUIZEN — 1931–32.
M. M. (Boy) LOUW — 1928–38, and S. C. (Fanie) LOUW — 1931–38.
S. P. (Stephen) FRY — 1951–55, and D. J. (Dennis) FRY — 1951–52.
H. P. J. (Jaap) BEKKER — 1952–56; R. P. (Dolf) BEKKER — 1953, and M. J. (Martiens) BEKKER — 1960.
†P. W. (Piet) WESSELS — 1951–52, J. W. (John) WESSELS — 1965.
J. H. (Jannie) BARNARD — 1965, and R. W. (Robbie) BARNARD — 1969–71.
I. D. (Ian) McCALLUM — 1970–74, and R. J. (Roy) McCALLUM — 1974.
D. S. L. (Dawie) SNYMAN — 1971–76, and J. C. P. (Jackie) SNYMAN — 1974.
T. T. (Polla) FOURIE — 1974, and C. (Tossie) FOURIE — 1974–75.
C. H. (Charlie) COCKRELL — 1969–70, and R. J. (Robert) COCKRELL — 1974–76.

**The three Luyt brothers hold the unique record of all having played together in three test matches — against Scotland, Wales and England, on the 1912–13 tour.*
†A third brother, Koos Wessels played for the Junior Springboks, all three brothers were hookers.

SPRINGBOK FATHERS AND SONS

†A. P. (Alf) WALKER — 1921–24, and H. N. (Harry) WALKER — 1953–56.
C. B. (Cecil) JENNINGS — 1937, and M. W. (Mike) JENNINGS — 1969–70.
*Felix DU PLESSIS — 1949, and Morne DU PLESSIS — 1971–76.
M. A. (Mauritz) VAN DEN BERG — 1937, and D. S. (Derek) VAN DEN BERG — 1974–76.
*Both father and son also captained South Africa in test matches. Felix in 1949 and Morne in 1975 and 1976.
†Alf Walker's brother Henry also played for South Africa (See "Springbok Brothers").

"VITAL STATISTICS"

J. L. "Mof" MYBURGH is the heaviest player to have represented South Africa, tipping the scales at 123 Kilos. (270 lbs.) during the Springbok tour of 1969–70 in Britain.
W. D. "Billy" SENDIN was the lightest player, having weighed only 60 Kilos (132 lbs.) on the Springbok tour of Australia and New Zealand in 1921.
J. G. "John" WILLIAMS (1971) is the tallest player being 1,99 metres (6'. 6½") in height.
T. A. "Tommy" GENTLES is the shortest player at 1,6 metres (5' 3").
J. A. "Lofty" NEL is the oldest player to have represented South Africa. Nel, born in August 1934, was 36 years and one month old, when he played against the 1970 All Blacks.
D. O. "Dai" WILLIAMS was the youngest player, being 18 years and 4½ months old when sent out as a replacement to join the 1931–32 Springbok touring team in Great Britain.
F. G. "Freddie" TURNER was the youngest Springbok to play in a test match, being 19 years and 3½ months old when he played in the first test against Australia in 1933.

COMPLETE LIST OF SPRINGBOKS
1891—1976
(International Record)

N.B.
(i) This list of Springboks also includes players who were selected for a touring team, but did not play in a test match.
(ii) Provincial Unions in parenthesis are those in which the player was resident when first obtaining his Springbok "Colours", i.e. either for a touring team, or in a test match in South Africa.
(iii) International records, e.g. 1955 Br. 2, 3. means that player played in the second and third tests against the British Isles in 1955.
(iv) (s) signifies substitute.
Legend—Br. = British Isles; A. = Australia; NZ = New Zealand; E = England; W = Wales; I = Ireland; S = Scotland; Fr = France

	International Record	*Tests*	*Tries*	*Pts.*
ACKERMANN, D. S. P. (W.P.)	1955 Br. 2, 3, 4; 1956 A. 1, 2; NZ. 1. 3; 1958 Fr. 2	8	1	3
ALBERTYN, P. K. (S.W.D.)	1924 Br. 1, 2, 3, 4	4	1	3
ALEXANDER, E. (G.W.)	1891 Br. 1, 2	2	—	—
ALLEN, P. B. (E.P.)	1960 S	1	—	—
ALLPORT, P. (W.P.)	1910 Br. 2, 3	2	1	3
ANDERSON, J. A. (W.P.)	1903 Br. 3	1	—	—
ANDERSON, J. H. (W.P.)	1896 Br. 1, 3, 4	3	—	—
ANDREW, J. B. (Tvl.)	1896 Br. 2	1	—	—
ANTELME, J. G. M. (Tvl.)	1960 NZ. 1, 2, 3, 4; 1961 Fr.	5	—	—
APSEY, J. T. (W.P.)	1933 A. 4, 5; 1938 Br. 2	3	—	—
ASHLEY, S. (W.P.)	1903 Br. 2	1	—	—
ASTON, F. T. D. (Tvl.)	1896 Br. 1, 2, 3, 4	4	—	—
AUCAMP, J. (W.T.)	1924 Br. 1, 2	2	1	3
BAARD, A. P. (W.P.)	1960—61 I	1	—	—
BABROW, L. (W.P.)	1937 A. 1, 2; NZ. 1, 2, 3	5	3	9

	International Record	Tests	Tries	Pts.
BARNARD, J. H. (Tvl.)	1965 S; A. 1, 2; NZ. 3, 4	5	—	—
BARNARD, R. W. (Tvl.)	1969—70 tour of U.K. No tests; 1970 NZ. 2(s); 1971 tour of Aust. no tests	1	—	—
BARNARD, W. H. M. (N.T.)	1949 NZ. 4; 1951 W.	2	—	—
BARRY, J. (W.P.)	1903 Br. 1, 2, 3	3	1	3
BASTARD, W. E. (N)	1937 A. 1; NZ. 1. 2. 3; 1938 Br. 1, 3	6	2	6
BATES, A. J. (W.T.)	1969—70 E., 1970 NZ. 1, 2; 1971 tour of Aust. no tests; 1972 E	4	—	—
BAYVEL, P. C. R. (Tvl.)	1974 Br. 2, 4; Fr. 1, 2; 1975 Fr. 1, 2; 1976 NZ. 1, 2, 3, 4	10	—	—
BEDFORD, T. P. (N)	1963 A. 1, 2, 3, 4; 1964 W. Fr. 1965I; A. 1, 2; 1968 Br. 1, 2, 3, 4; Fr. 1, 2; 1969 A. 1, 2, 3, 4; 1969—70 S. E. I. W.; 1971 Fr. 1, 2; 1971 tour of Aust.—no tests	25	1	3
BEKKER, H. P. J. (N.T.)	1952 E. Fr.; 1953 A. I. 2, 3, 4; 1955 Br. 2, 3, 4; 1956 A. 1, 2; NZ. 1, 2, 3, 4,	15	1	3
BEKKER, M. J. (N.T.)	1960 S	1	—	—
BEKKER, R. P. (N.T.)	1953 A. 3, 4	2	1	3
BERGH, W. F. (S.W.D.)	1931—32 W. I. E. S.; 1933 A. 1, 2, 3, 4, 5; 1937 A. 1, 2; NZ. 1, 2, 3; 1938 Br. 1, 2, 3	17	7	21
BESTBIER, A. (O.F.S.)	1974 Fr. 2 (s)	1	—	—
BESTER, J. L. A. (W.P.)	1937 tour of A. & N.Z.—no tests; 1938 Br. 2, 3,	2	2	6
BESTER, J. J. N. (W.P.)	1924 Br. 2, 4	2	1	3
BESWICK, A. M. (Bor.)	1896 Br. 2, 3, 4	3	—	—
BEZUIDENHOUT, C. E. (N.T.)	1962 Br. 2, 3, 4	3	—	—
BEZUIDENHOUT, N. S. E. (N.T.)	1972 E; 1974 Br. 2, 3, 4; Fr. 1, 2; 1975 Fr. 1, 2	8	—	—
BIERMAN, J. N. (Tvl.)	1931 I	1	—	—
BISSET, W. M. (W.P.)	1891 Br. 1, 3	2	—	—
BOSCH, G. R. (Tvl.)	1974 Br. 2; Fr. 1,2; 1975 Fr. 1, 2 1976 NZ. 1, 2, 3, 4	9	—	89
BOSMAN, N. J. S. (Tvl.)	1924 Br. 2, 3, 4	3	—	—
BOTHA, J. (Tvl.)	1903 Br. 3	1	—	—
BOTHA, J. P. F. (N.T.)	1960—61 tour of U.K.—no tests; 1962 Br. 2, 3, 4	3	—	—
BOTHA, P. H. (Tvl.)	1965 A. 1, 2	2	—	—
BOYES, H. C. (G. W.)	1891 Br. 1, 2	2	—	—
BRAINE, J. S. (G.W.)	1912 tour of U.K.—no tests	—	—	—
BRAND, G. H. (W.P.)	1928 NZ. 2, 3; 1931—32 W. I. E. S; 1933 A. 1, 2, 3, 4, 5; 1937 A. 1, 2; NZ. 2, 3; 1938 Br. 1	16	—	55
BREDENKAMP, M. (G.W.)	1896 Br. 1, 3	2	—	—
BREWIS, J. D. (N.T.)	1949 NZ. 1, 2, 3, 4; 1951—52 S. I. W. E. Fr.; 1953 A. 1	10	1	18
BRIERS, T. P. D. (W.P.)	1955 Br. 1, 2, 3, 4; 1956 NZ. 2, 3, 4	7	5	15
BRINK, D. J. (W,P,)	1906 S. W. E.	3	—	—
BROODRYK, J. A. (Tvl.)	1937 tour of A. & NZ.—no tests	—	—	—
BROOKS, D. (Bor.)	1906 S.	1	—	—
BROWN, C. (W.P.)	1903 Br. 1, 2, 3	3	—	—
BRYNARD, G. S. (W.P.)	1965 A. 1; NZ. 1, 2, 3, 4; 1968 Br. 3, 4	7	2	6
BUCHLER, J. U. (Tvl.)	1951—52 S. I. W. E. Fr.; 1953 A. 1, 2, 3, 4; 1956 A. 2	10	—	8
BURDETT, A. F. (W.P.)	1906 S. I.	2	—	—
BURGER, W. A. G. (Bor.)	1906 S. I. W.; 1910 Br. 2	4	—	—
BURMEISTER, A. R. (W. P.)	1906 tour of U.K.—no tests	—	—	—
CARELSE, G. (E.P.)	1964 W; Fr.; 1965 I. S.; 1967 Fr. 1, 2, 3; 1968 Fr. 1, 2; 1969 A. 1, 2, 3, 4; 1969 S.	14	—	—
CARLSON, R. A. (W.P.)	1972 E	1	—	—
CAROLIN, H. W. (W.P.)	1903 Br. 3; 1906 S. I.	3	—	—
CASTENS, H. H. (W.P.)	1891 Br. 1.	1	—	—
CHIGNELL, T. W. (W.P.)	1891 Br. 3.	1	—	—
CILLIERS, G. D. (O.F.S.)	1963 A. 1, 3, 4; 1965 tour of I. & S.—no tests	3	1	3
CLAASSEN, J. T. (W.T.)	1955 Br. 1, 2, 3, 4; 1956 A. 1, 2; NZ. 1, 2, 3, 4; 1958 Fr. 1, 2; 1960 S.; NZ. 1, 2, 3; 1960—61 W. I. E. S. Fr.; 1961 I.; A. 1, 2; 1962 Br. 1, 2, 3, 4	28	2	10
CLARKE, W. H. (Tvl.)	1933 A. 3	1	—	—
CLARKSON, W. A. (N)	1921 NZ. 1, 2; 1924 Br. 1	3	—	—
CLOETE, H. A. (W.P.)	1896 Br. 4.	1	—	—
COCKRELL, C. H. (W.P.)	1969—70 S. I. W.	3	—	—
COCKRELL, R. J. (W.P.)	1974 Fr. 1, 2; 1975 Fr. 1, 2; 1976 NZ. 1, 2	6	1	4
COETZEE, J. H. H. (W.P.)	1974 Br. 1; 1975 Fr. 2(s); 1976 NZ. 1, 2, 3, 4	6	—	—
CONRADIE, S. C. (W.P.)	1965 tour of S. &. I.—no tests	—	—	—
COPE, D. (Tvl.)	1896 Br. 2.	1	—	2
COTTY, W. (G.W.)	1896 Br. 3.	1	—	—
CRAMPTON, G. (G.W.)	1903 Br. 2.	1	—	—
CRAVEN, D. H. (W.P.)	1931—32 W. I. S.; 1933 A. 1, 2, 3, 4, 5; 1937 A. 1, 2, NZ. 1, 2, 3; 1938 Br. 1, 2, 3	16	2	6
CRONJE, C. J. C. (E.T.)	1965 tour of A. & NZ. no tests	—	—	—
CRONJE, P. A. (Tvl.)	1971 Fr. 1, 2; A. 1, 2, 3; 1974 Br. 3, 4	7	3	10
CRONJE, S. N. (Tvl.)	1912 tour of U. K.—no tests	—	—	—

	International Record	Tests	Tries	Pts.
CROSBY, J. H. (Tvl.)	1896 Br. 2.	1	—	—
CROSBY, N. J. (Tvl.)	1910 Br. 1, 3	2	—	—
CURRIE, C. (G.W.)	1903 Br. 2.	1	—	—
D'ALTON, G. (W.P.)	1933 A. 1	1	—	—
DANEEL, G. M. (W.P.)	1928 NZ. 1, 2, 3, 4; 1931—32 W. I. E. S.	8	2	6
DANEEL, H. J. (W.P.)	1906 S. I. W. E.	4	—	—
DANNHAUSER, G. (Tvl.)	1951—52 tour of U.K.—no tests	—	—	—
DAVIDSON, M. (E.P.)	1910 Br. 1	1	—	—
DE BRUYN, J. (O.F.S.)	1974 Br. 3; 1974 tour of Fr.—no tests	1	—	—
DE JONGH, H. P. K. (W.P.)	1928 NZ. 3	1	1	3
DE KLERK, I. J. (Tvl.)	1969—70 E. I. W.	3	—	—
DE KLERK, K. B. H. (Tvl.)	1974 Br. 1, 2, 3(s); 1974 tour of Fr.—no tests; 1975 Fr. 1, 2; 1976 NZ. 2(s), 3, 4	8	—	—
DE KOCK, A. (G.W.)	1891 Br. 2.	1	—	—
DE KOCK, J. S. (W.P.)	1921 NZ. 3; 1924 Br. 3	2	—	—
DELANEY, E. T. (G. W.)	1912 tour of U.K.—no tests	—	—	—
DELPORT, W. H. (E.P.)	1951—52 S. I. W. E. Fr; 1953 A. 1, 2, 3, 4	9	2	6
DE MELKER, S. C. (G.W.)	1903 Br. 2; 1906 E.	2	—	—
DE NYSSCHEN, C. J. (N)	1956 tour of A. & NZ.—no tests	—	—	—
DEVENISH, C. (G.W.)	1896 Br. 2.	1	—	—
DEVENISH, G. ST. L. (Tvl.)	1896 Br. 2	1	—	—
DEVENISH, M. (Tvl.)	1891 Br. 1.	1	—	—
DE VILLIERS, D. J. (W.P.)	1962 Br. 2, 3; 1965 I.; NZ. 1, 3, 4; 1967 Fr. 1, 2, 3, 4; 1968 Br. 1, 2, 3, 4; Fr. 1, 2; 1969 A. 1, 4; 1969—70 E. I. W.; 1970 NZ. 1, 2, 3, 4	25	3	9
DE VILLIERS, D. I. (Tvl.)	1910 Br. 1, 2, 3	3	1	3
DE VILLIERS, H. A. (W.P.)	1906 S. W. E.	3	—	—
DE VILLIERS, H. O. (W.P.)	1967 Fr. 1, 2, 3, 4; 1968 Fr. 1, 2; 1969 A. 1, 2, 3, 4; 1969—70 S. E. I. W.	14	—	26
DE VILLIERS, I. B. (Tvl.)	1921 tour of A. & NZ.—no tests	—	—	—
DE VILLIERS, P. du P. (W.P.)	1928 NZ. 1, 3, 4; 1931—32 E.; 1933 A. 4; 1937 A. 1, 2; NZ. 1	8	—	—
DEVINE, D. (Tvl.)	1924 Br. 3; 1928 NZ. 2	2	—	—
DE VOS, D. J. J. (W.P.)	1965 S.; 1969 A. 3; 1969—70 S.; 1971 tour of Aust.—no tests	3	—	—
DE WAAL, A. N. (W.P.)	1967 Fr. 1, 2, 3, 4	4	—	—
DE WAAL, P. (W.P.)	1896 Br. 4.	1	—	—
DE WET, A. E. (W.P.)	1969 A. 3, 4; 1969—70 E.	3	—	—
DE WET, P. (W.P.)	1938 Br. 1, 2, 3	3	—	—
DE WILZEM, C. J. (O.F.S.)	1956 tour of A. & NZ.—no tests	—	—	—
DINKELMANN, E. E. (N.T.)	1951—52 S. I. E. Fr; 1953 A. 1, 2	6	2	6
DIRKSEN, C. W. (N.T.)	1963 A. 4; 1964 W; 1965 I. S; 1967 Fr. 1, 2, 3, 4; 1968 Br. 1, 2	10	3	9
DOBBIN, F. J. (G.W.)	1903 Br. 1, 2; 1906 S. W. E.; 1910 Br. 1; 1912 S. I. W.	9	1	3
DOBIE, J. A. R. (Tvl.)	1928 NZ. 2	1	—	—
DOLD, J. B. (E.P.)	1931—32 tour of U.K.—no tests	—	—	—
DORMEHL, P. J. (W.P.)	1896 Br. 3, 4	2	—	—
DOUGLASS, F. W. (E.P.)	1896 Br. 1.	1	—	—
DRYBURGH, R. G. (W.P.)	1955 Br. 2, 3, 4; 1956 A. 2; NZ. 1, 4; 1960 NZ. 1, 2.	8	3	28
DUFF, B. (W.P.)	1891 Br. 1, 2, 3	3	—	—
DUFFY, B. A. (Bor.)	1928 NZ. 1	1	—	—
DU PLESSIS, F. (Tvl.)	1949 NZ. 1, 2, 3	3	—	—
DU PLESSIS, M. (W.P.)	1971 A. 1, 2, 3; 1974 Br. 1, 2; Fr. 1, 2; 1975 Fr. 1, 2; 1976 NZ. 1, 2, 3, 4	13	1	4
DU PLESSIS, N. J. (W.T.)	1921 NZ. 2, 3; 1924 Br. 1, 2, 3.	5	—	—
DU PLESSIS, P. G. (N.T.)	1972 E.	1	—	—
DU PLOOY, A. J. J. (E.P.)	1955 Br. 1.	1	—	—
DU PREEZ, F. C. H. (N.T.)	1960—61 E. S.; 1961 A. 1, 2; 1962 Br. 1, 2, 3, 4; 1963 A. 1; 1964 W.; Fr.; 1965 tour of I. & S.—no tests; 1965 A. 1, 2; NZ. 1, 2, 3, 4; 1967 Fr. 4; 1968 Br. 1, 2, 3, 4; Fr. 1, 2; 1969 A. 1, 2; 1969—70 S. I. W.; 1970 NZ. 1, 2, 3, 4; 1971 Fr. 1, 2; A. 1, 2, 3	38	1	11
DU PREEZ, J. G. H. (W.P.)	1956 NZ. 1	1	—	—
DU RAND, J. A. (R)	1949 NZ. 2, 3; 1951—52 S. I. W. E. Fr.; 1953 A. 1, 2, 3, 4; 1955 Br. 1, 2, 3, 4; 1956 A. 1, 2; NZ. 1, 2, 3, 4	21	4	12
DURAND, P. J. (W.T.)	1969—70 tour of U.K.—no tests	—	—	—
DU TOIT, A. F. (W.P.)	1928 NZ. 3, 4	2	—	—
DU TOIT, B. A. (Tvl.)	1937 tour of A. & NZ.—no tests; 1938 Br. 1, 2, 3	3	1	3
DU TOIT, P. A. (N.T.)	1949 NZ. 2, 3, 4; 1951—52 S. I. W. E. Fr.	8	2	6
DU TOIT, P. S. (W.P.)	1956 tour of A. & NZ.—no tests; 1958 Fr. 1, 2; 1960 NZ. 1, 2, 3, 4; 1960—61 W. I. E. S. Fr.; 1961 I.; A. 1, 2	14	—	—
DU TOIT, S. R. (W.P.)	1931—32 tour of U.K.—no tests	—	—	—
DUVENHAGE, F. P. (G.W.)	1949 NZ. 1, 3	2	—	—

Name	International Record	Tests	Tries	Pts.
ELLIS, J. H. (S.W.A.)	1965 NZ. 1, 2, 3, 4; 1967 Fr. 1, 2, 3, 4; 1968 Br. 1, 2, 3, 4; Fr. 1, 2; 1969 A. 1, 2, 3, 4; 1969—70 S. I. W.; 1970 NZ. 1, 2, 3, 4; 1971 Fr. 1, 2; A. 1, 2, 3; 1972 E. 1974 Br. 1, 2, 3, 4; 1976 NZ. 1.	38	7	21
ELLIS, M. (Tvl.)	1921 NZ. 2, 3; 1924 Br. 1, 2, 3, 4	6	—	—
ENGELBRECHT, J. P. (W.P.)	1960 S.; 1960—61 W. I. E. S. Fr.; 1961 A. 1, 2; 1962 Br. 2, 3, 4; 1963 A. 2, 3; 1964 W.; Fr.; 1965 I. S.; A. 1, 2; NZ. 1, 2, 3, 4; 1967 Fr. 1, 2, 3, 4; 1968 Br. 1, 2; Fr. 1, 2; 1969 A. 1, 2	33	8	24
ETLINGER, T. E. (W.P.)	1896 Br. 4	1	—	—
FERRIS, H. H. (Tvl.)	1903 Br. 3	1	—	—
FORBES, H. H. (Tvl.)	1896 Br. 2	1	—	—
FORREST, H. M. (Tvl.)	1931—32 tour of U.K.—no tests	—	—	—
FOURIE, C. (E.P.)	1974 Fr. 1, 2; 1975 Fr. 1, 2	4	1	10
FOURIE, T. T. (S.E.T.)	1974 Br. 3; 1974 tour of Fr.—no tests	1	—	—
FOURIE, W. L. (S.W.A.)	1958 Fr. 1, 2	2	1	3
FRANCIS, J. A. J. (Tvl.)	1912—13 S. I. W. E. Fr.	5	2	6
FRANCIS, M. G. (O.F.S.)	1931—32 tour of U.K.—no tests	—	—	—
FREDERICKSON, C. A. (Tvl.)	1974 Br. 2	1	—	—
FREW, A. (Tvl.)	1903 Br. 1	1	1	3
FRONEMAN, I. L. (Bor.)	1933 A. 1	1	—	—
FRY, D. J. (W.P.)	1951—52 tour of U.K.—no tests	—	—	—
FRY, S. P. (W.P.)	1951—52 S. I. W. E. Fr.; 1953 A. 1, 2, 3, 4 1955 Br. 1, 2, 3, 4	13	—	—
GAGE, J. H. (O.F.S.)	1933 A. 1	1	—	—
GAINSFORD, J. L. (W.P.)	1960 S.; NZ. 1, 2, 3, 4; 1960—61 W. I. E. S. Fr.; 1961 A. 1, 2; 1962 Br. 1, 2, 3, 4; 1963 A. 1, 2, 3, 4,; 1964 W. Fr.; 1965 I. S.; A. 1, 2; NZ. 1, 2, 3, 4; 1967 Fr. 1, 2, 3	33	8	24
GEEL, P. J. (O.F.S.)	1949 NZ. 3	1	—	—
GEERE, V. (Tvl.)	1931—32 tour of U.K.—no tests 1933 A. 1, 2, 3, 4, 5	5	—	—
GEFFIN, A. O. (Tvl.)	1949 NZ. 1, 2, 3, 4; 1951.—52 S. I. W.	7	—	48
GENTLES, T. A. (W.P.)	1955 Br. 1, 2, 4; 1956 NZ. 2, 3; 1958 Fr. 2	6	—	—
GERAGHTY, E. M. (Bor.)	1949 NZ. 4	1	—	—
GERBER, M. C. (E.P.)	1958 Fr. 1, 2; 1960 S.	3	—	8
GERICKE, F. W. (Tvl.)	1960 S.	1	1	3
GERMISHUYS, J. S. (O.F.S.)	1974 Br. 2; 1976 NZ. 1, 2, 3, 4.	5	1	4
GIBBS, B. (G.W.)	1903 Br. 2	1	—	—
GOOSEN, C. P. (O.F.S.)	1965 NZ. 2	1	—	—
GORTON, H. C. (Tvl.)	1896 Br. 1	1	—	—
GOULD, R. L. (N.)	1968 Br. 1, 2, 3, 4; 1968 tour of Fr.—no tests	4	—	3
GRAY, B. G. (W.P.)	1931—32 W. E. S.; 1933 A. 5	4	—	—
GREENWOOD, C. M. (W.P.)	1961 I.	1	2	6
GREYLING, P. J. F. (O.F.S.)	1967 Fr. 1, 2, 3, 4; 1968 Br. 1; Fr. 1, 2; 1969 A. 1, 2, 3, 4,; 1969—70 S. E. I. W.; 1970 NZ. 1, 2, 3, 4; 1971 Fr. 1, 2; A. 1, 2, 3; 1972 E.	25	5	15
GROBLER, C. J. (O.F.S.)	1974 Br. 4; 1974 tour of Fr.—no tests; 1975 Fr. 1, 2	3	1	4
GROBLER, R. N. (N.T.)	1969—70 tour of U.K.—no tests	—	—	—
GUTHRIE, F. H. (W.P.)	1891 Br. 1, 3; 1896 Br. 1	3	—	—
HAHN, C. H. L. (Tvl.)	1910 Br. 1, 2, 3	3	1	3
HAMILTON, F. (E.P.)	1891 Br. 1	1	—	—
HANEKOM, M. v.d.S. (Bol.)	1956 tour of A. & NZ.—no tests	—	—	—
HARRIS, T. A. (Tvl.)	1937 NZ. 2, 3; 1938 Br. 1, 2, 3.	5	1	3
HARTLEY, A. J. (W.P.)	1891 Br. 3	1	—	—
HATTINGH, L. B. (O.F.S.)	1933 A. 2	1	—	—
HEATLIE, B. H. (W.P.)	1891 Br. 2, 3; 1896 Br. 1, 4; 1903 Br. 1, 3	6	—	6
HEPBURN, T. (W.P.)	1896 Br. 4	1	—	2
HILL, R. A. (R.)	1960—61 W. I; 1961 I.; A. 1, 2; 1962 Br. 4; 1963 A. 3	7	—	—
HIRSCH, J. G. (E.P.)	1906 I.; 1910 Br. 1	2	—	—
HOBSON, T. E. C. (W.P.)	1903 Br. 3	1	—	—
HOFFMAN, R. S. (Bol.)	1953 A. 3	1	—	—
HOFMEYR, S. R. (W.P.)	1937 tour of A. & NZ.—no tests	—	—	—
HOLTON, D. N. (E.P.)	1960 S.; 1960—61 tour of U.K.—no tests	1	—	—
HOPWOOD, D. J. (W.P.)	1960 S.; NZ. 3, 4; 1960—61 W. E. S. Fr.; 1961 I.; A. 1, 2; 1962 Br. 1, 2, 3, 4; 1963 A. 1, 2, 4; 1964 W.; Fr.; 1965 S.; NZ. 3, 4	22	5	15
HOWE, B. F. (Bor.)	1956 NZ. 1, 4	2	1	3
HOWE-BROWNE, N. F. (W.P.)	1910 Br. 1, 2, 3	3	—	—
IMMELMAN, J. H. (W.P.)	1912—13 Fr.	1	—	—
JACKSON, D. C. (W.P.)	1906 I. W. E.	3	—	—
JACKSON, J. S. (W.P.)	1903 Br. 2	1	—	—
JANSEN, J. S. (O.F.S.)	1970 NZ. 1, 2, 3, 4; 1971 Fr. 1, 2; A. 1, 2, 3; 1972 E.	10	1	3
JANSON, A. (W.P.)	1965 tour of A. & NZ.—no tests	—	—	—
JENNINGS, C. B. (Bor.)	1937 NZ. 1	1	—	—
JENNINGS, M. W. (Bol.)	1969—70 tour of U.K.—no tests	—	—	—
JOHNS, R. G. (W.P.)	1960—61 tour of U.K.—no tests	—	—	—
JOHNSTONE, P. G. A. (W.P.)	1951—52 S. I. W. E. Fr.; 1956 A. 1.; NZ. 1, 2, 4	9	2	11
JONES, C. H. (Tvl.)	1903 Br. 1, 2	2	—	—
JONES, P. S. T. (W.P.)	1896 Br. 1, 3, 4	3	1	3
JORDAAN, R. P. (N.T.)	1949 NZ. 1, 2, 3, 4	4	—	—
JOUBERT, S. J. (W.P.)	1906 I. W. E.	3	1	8
KAMINER, J. (Tvl.)	1958 Fr. 2	1	—	—
KELLY, E. W. (G.W.)	1896 Br. 3	1	—	—
KENYON, B. J. (Bor.)	1949 NZ. 4; 1951—52 tour of U.K.—no tests	1	—	—
KEEVY, A. C. (E.T.)	1951—52 tour of U.K.—no tests	—	—	—
KIPLING, H. G. (G.W.)	1931—32 W. I. E. S.; 1933 A. 1, 2, 3, 4 5	9	—	—
KIRKPATRICK, A. I. (G.W.)	1953 A. 2; 1956 NZ. 2; 1958 Fr. 1; 1960 S.; NZ. 1, 2, 3, 4; 1960—61 W. I. E. S. Fr.	13	—	—
KNIGHT, A. S. (Tvl.)	1912—13 S. I. W. E. Fr.	5	—	—
KOCH, A. C. (Bol.)	1949 NZ. 2, 3, 4; 1951—52 S. I. W. E. Fr.; 1953 A. 1, 2, 4; 1955 Br. 1, 2, 3, 4; 1956 A. 1; NZ. 2, 3; 1958 Fr. 1, 2; 1960 NZ. 1, 2	22	5	15
KOCH, H. V. (W.P.)	1949 NZ. 1, 2, 3, 4	4	—	—
KOTZE, G. J. M. (W.P.)	1967 Fr.; 1, 2, 3, 4	4	—	—
KRANTZ, E. F. W. (O.F.S.)	1976 NZ. 1	1	1	4
KRIGE, J. D. (W.P.)	1903 Br. 1, 3; 1906 S. I. W.	5	1	3
KRIGE, W. A. (W.P.)	1912—13 tour of U.K.—no tests	—	—	—
KRITZINGER, J. L. (Tvl.)	1974 Br. 3, 4; Fr. 1, 2; 1975 Fr. 1, 2; 1976 NZ. 4	7	1	4
KROON, C. M. (E.P.)	1955 Br. 1	1	—	—
KRUGER, T. L. (Tvl.)	1921 NZ. 1, 2; 1924 Br. 1, 2, 3, 4; 1928 NZ. 1, 2	8	—	—
KUHN, S. P. (Tvl.)	1960 NZ. 3, 4; 1960—61 W. I. E. S. Fr.; 1961 I.; A. 1, 2; 1962 Br. 1, 2, 3, 4; 1963 A. 1. 2, 3; 1965 I. S.	19	—	—
LA GRANGE, J. B. (W.P.)	1924 Br. 3, 4	2	—	—
LARARD, A. (Tvl.)	1896 Br. 2, 4	2	1	3
LATEGAN, M. T. (W.P.)	1949 NZ. 1, 2, 3, 4; 1951—52 S. I. W. E. Fr.; 1953 A. 1, 2	11	3	9
LAWLESS, M. J. (W.P.)	1964 Fr.; 1969—70 E. (s). I. W.	4	—	—
LAWTON, A. D. (W.P.)	1937 tour of A. & NZ.—no tests	—	—	—
LEDGER, S. H. (G.W.)	1912—13 S. I. E. Fr.	4	1	3
LE ROUX, J. S. (W.P.)	1906 tour of U.K.—no tests	—	—	—
LE ROUX, P. A. (W.P.)	1906 I. W. E.	3	—	—
LITTLE, E. M. M. (G.W.)	1891 Br. 1, 3	2	—	—
LOCHNER, G. P. (W.P.) (Butch)	1955 Br. 3; 1956 A. 1, 2; NZ. 1, 2, 3, 4; 1958 Fr. 1, 2	9	2	6
LOCHNER, G. P. (E.P.)	1937 NZ. 3; 1938 Br. 1, 2	3	1	3
LOCKYEAR, R. J. (G.W.)	1960 NZ. 1, 2, 3, 4; 1960—61 I. Fr.	6	—	20
LOMBARD, A. C. (E.P.)	1910 Br. 2	1	—	—
LOTZ, J. W. (Tvl.)	1937 A. 1, 2,; NZ. 1, 2, 3; 1938 Br. 1, 2, 3	8	1	3
LOUBSER, J. A. (W.P.)	1903 Br. 3; 1906 S. I. W. E.; 1910 Br. 1, 3	7	3	9
LOURENS, M. J. (N.T.)	1968 Br. 2, 3, 4; 1968 tour of Fr.—no tests; 1971 tour of Aust.—no tests	3	1	3
LOUW, J. S. (Tvl.)	1891 Br. 1, 2, 3	3	—	—
LOUW, L. H. (W.P.)	1912—13 tour of U.K.—no tests	—	—	—
LOUW, M. M. (W.P.)	1928 NZ. 3,4; 1931—32 W. I. E. S.; 1933 A. 1, 2, 3, 4, 5; 1937 A. 1, 2; NZ. 2, 3; 1938 Br. 1, 2, 3	18	1	3
LOUW, M. J. (Tvl.)	1971 A. 2, 3	2	—	—
LOUW, S. C. (W.P.)	1931—32 tour of U.K.—no tests; 1933 A. 1, 2, 3, 4, 5; 1937 A. 1,; NZ. 1, 2, 3; 1938 Br. 1, 2, 3	12	2	6
LUYT, F. P. (W.P.)	1910 Br. 1, 2, 3,; 1912—13 S. I. W. E.	7	2	8
LUYT, J. D. (E.P.)	1912—13 S. W. E. Fr.	4	—	—
LUYT, R. R. (W.P.)	1910 Br. 2, 3; 1912—13 S. I. W. E. Fr.	7	1	3
LYONS, D. (E.P.)	1896 Br. 1	1	—	—
LYSTER, P. J. (N)	1933 A. 2, 5; 1937 NZ. 1	3	—	—
MacDONALD, A. W. (R)	1965 A. 1; NZ. 1, 2, 3, 4	5	—	—
MACDONALD, D. A. (W.P.)	1974 Br. 2	1	—	—
MALAN, A. S. (Tvl.)	1960 NZ. 1, 2, 3, 4; 1960—61 W. I. E. S. Fr.; 1962 Br. 1; 1963 A. 1, 2, 3; 1964 W.; 1965 I. S.	16	—	—
MALAN, G. F. (W.P.) (Abie)	1958 Fr. 2; 1960 NZ. 1, 3, 4; 1960—61 E. S. Fr.; 1962 Br. 1, 2, 3; 1963 A. 1, 2, 4; 1964 W.; 1965 A. 1, 2; NZ. 1, 2	18	1	3
MALAN, P. (Tvl.)	1949 NZ. 4	1	—	—
MANS, W. J. (W.P.)	1965 I. S.; 1965 tour of A. & NZ.—no tests	2	1	5
MARAIS, F. P. (Bol.)	1949 NZ. 1, 2; 1951 S.; 1953 A. 1, 2	5	1	10
MARAIS, J. F. K. (W.P.)	1963 A. 3; 1964 W.; Fr.; 1965 I. S. A. 2; 1968 Br. 1, 2, 3, 4; Fr. 1, 2; 1969 A. 1, 2, 3, 4; 1969—70 S. E. I. W.; 1970 NZ. 1, 2, 3, 4; 1971 Fr. 1, 2, A. 1, 2, 3; 1974 Br. 1, 2, 3, 4; Fr. 1, 2	35	1	3
MARE, D. S. (Tvl.)	1906 S.	1	—	—
MARSBERG, A. F. W. (G.W.)	1906 S. W. E.	3	—	—
MARSBERG, P. A. (G.W.)	1910 Br. 1	1	—	—

	International Record	Tests	Tries	Pts.
MARTHEZE, W. C. (G.W.)	1903 Br. 2; 1906 I. W.	3	—	—
MARTIN, H. J. (Tvl.)	1937 A. 2	1	—	—
McCALLUM, I. D. (W.P.)	1970 NZ. 1, 2, 3, 4; 1971 Fr. 1, 2, A. 1, 2, 3; 1974 Br. 1, 2	11	—	62
McCALLUM, R. J. (W.P.)	1974 Br. 1; 1974 tour of Fr.—no tests	1	—	—
McCULLOCH, J. D. (G.W.)	1912—13 E. Fr.	2	—	—
McDONALD, J. A. J. (W.P.)	1931—32 W. I. E. S.	4	—	—
McEWAN, W. M. C. (Tvl.)	1903 Br. 1, 3	2	—	—
McHARDY, E. E. (O.F.S.)	1912—13 S. I. W. E. Fr.	5	6	18
McKENDRICK, J. A. (W.P.)	1891 Br. 3	1	—	—
MEINTJIES, J. J. (G.W.)	1912—13 tour of U.K.—no tests	—	—	—
MELLETT, T. (G.W.)	1896 Br. 2	1	—	—
MELLISH, F. W. (W.P.)	1921 NZ. 1, 3; 1924 Br. 1, 2, 3, 4	6	—	—
MENTER, M. A. (N.T.)	1968 tour of Fr.—no tests	—	—	—
MERRY, J. (E.P.)	1891 Br. 1	1	—	—
METCALF, H. D. (Bor.)	1903 Br. 2	1	—	—
MEYER, C. du P. (W.P.)	1921 NZ. 1, 2, 3	3	—	—
MEYER, P. J. (G.W.)	1896 Br. 1	1	—	—
MICHAU, J. M. (Tvl.) (Baby)	1921 NZ. 1	1	—	—
MICHAU, J. P. (W.P.)	1921 NZ. 1, 2, 3	3	—	—
MILLAR, W. A. (W.P.)	1906 E.; 1910 Br. 2, 3; 1912—13 I. W. Fr.	6	2	6
MILLS, W. J. (W.P.)	1910 Br. 2; 1912—13 tour of U.K.—no tests	1	1	3
MOLL, T. (Tvl.)	1910 Br. 2	1	—	—
MONTINI, P. E. (W.P.)	1956 A. 1, 2	2	—	—
MORKEL, A. O. (Tvl.)	1903 Br. 1; 1906 tour of U.K.—no tests	1	—	—
MORKEL, D. F. T. (Tvl.)	1906 I. E.; 1910 Br. 1, 3; 1912—13 S. I. W. E. Fr.	9	3	38
MORKEL, H. J. (Harry) (W.P.)	1921 NZ. 1	1	—	—
MORKEL, H. W. (Henry) (W.P.)	1921 NZ. 1, 2	2	—	—
MORKEL, J. W. H. (W.P.)	1912—13 S. I. W. E. Fr.	5	4	16
MORKEL, P. K. (W.P.)	1928 NZ. 4	1	—	—
MORKEL, P. G. (W.P.)	1912—13 S. I. W. E. Fr.; 1921 NZ. 1, 2, 3	8	—	16
MORKEL, J. A. (Royal) (W.P.)	1921 NZ. 2, 3	2	—	—
MORKEL, W. H. (Boy) (W.P.)	1910 Br. 3; 1912—13 S. I. W. E. Fr.; 1921 NZ. 1, 2, 3	9	2	6
MORKEL, W. S. (Tvl.)	1906 S. I. W. E.	4	—	—
MOSS, C. (N.)	1949 NZ. 1, 2, 3, 4	4	—	—
MOSTERT, P. J. (W.P.)	1921 NZ. 1, 2, 3; 1924 Br. 1, 2, 4; 1928 NZ. 1, 2, 3, 4; 1931—32 W. I. E. S.	14	1	6
MULDER, C. G. (E.T.)	1965 tour of A. & NZ.—no tests	—	—	—
MULLER, G. H. (W.P.)	1969 A. 3, 4; 1969—70 S. W.; 1970 NZ. 1, 2, 3, 4; 1971 Fr. 1, 2; 1971 tour of Aust.—no tests; 1972 E.; 1974 Br. 1, 3, 4	14	4	12
MULLER, H. S. V. (Tvl.)	1949 NZ. 1, 2, 3, 4; 1951—52 S. I. W. E. Fr.; 1953 A. 1, 2, 3, 4	13	3	16
MYBURGH, B. (E.T.)	1951—52 tour of U.K.—no tests	—	—	—
MYBURGH, F. R. (E.P.)	1896 Br. 1	1	—	—
MYBURGH, J. L. (N.T.)	1960—61 tour of U.K.—no tests; 1962 Br. 1; 1963 A. 4; 1964 W.; Fr.; 1968 Br. 1, 2, 3; Fr. 1, 2; 1969 A. 1, 2, 3, 4; 1969—70 E. I. W.; 1970 NZ. 3, 4	18	—	—
MYBURGH, W. H. (W.T.)	1924 Br. 1	1	—	—
NAUDE, J. P. (W.P.)	1963 A. 4; 1965 A. 1, 2; NZ. 1, 3, 4; 1967 Fr. 1, 2, 3, 4; 1968 Br. 1, 2, 3, 4; 1968 tour of Fr.—no tests	14	2	47
NEETHLING, J. B. (W.P.)	1965 tour of I. & S.—no tests; 1967 Fr. 1, 2, 3, 4; 1968 Br. 4; 1968 tour of Fr.—no tests; 1969—70 S.; 1970 NZ. 1, 2	8	—	—
NEILL, W. A. (Bor.)	1906 tour of U.K.—no tests	—	—	—
NEL, J. J. (W.P.)	1956 A. 1, 2; NZ. 1, 2, 3, 4; 1958 Fr. 1, 2	8	1	3
NEL, J. A. (Tvl.)	1960 NZ. 1, 2; 1963 A. 1, 2; 1965 A. 2; NZ. 1, 2, 3, 4; 1970 NZ. 3, 4	11	—	—
NEL, P. A. R. O. (Tvl.)	1903 Br. 1, 2, 3	3	—	—
NEL, P. J. (N.)	1928 NZ. 1, 2, 3, 4; 1931—32 W. I. E. S.; 1933 A. 1, 3, 4, 5; 1937 A. 1, 2; NZ. 2, 3	16	1	3
NIMB, C. F. (W.P.)	1960—61 tour of U.K.—no tests; 1961 I.	1	—	9
NOMIS, S. H. (Tvl.)	1965 tour of A. & NZ.—no tests; 1967 Fr. 4; 1968 Br. 1, 2, 3, 4; Fr. 1, 2; 1969 A. 1, 2, 3, 4; 1969—70 S. E. I. W.; 1970 NZ. 1, 2, 3, 4; 1971 Fr. 1, 2; A. 1, 2, 3; 1972 E.	25	6	18
NYKAMP, J. L. (Tvl.)	1933 A. 2	1	—	—
OCHSE, J. K. (W.P.)	1951—52 I. W. E. Fr.; 1953 A. 1, 2, 4	7	3	9
OELOFSE, J. S. A. (Tvl.)	1951—52 tour of U.K.—no tests; 1953 A. 1, 2, 3, 4	4	2	6
OLIVER, J. F. (Tvl.)	1928 NZ. 3, 4	2	—	—
OLIVIER, E. (W.P.)	1965 tour of A. & NZ.—no tests; 1967 Fr. 1, 2, 3, 4; 1968 Br. 1, 2, 3, 4; Fr. 1, 2; 1969 A. 1, 2, 3, 4; 1969—70 S. E.	16	5	15
OLIVIER, J. S. (W.P.)	1921 tour of A. & NZ.—no tests	—	—	—
OLVER, E. (E.P.)	1896 Br. 1	1	—	—
OOSTHUIZEN, J. J. (W.P.)	1974 Br. 1; Fr. 1, 2; 1975 Fr. 1, 2; 1976 NZ. 1, 2, 3, 4	9	2	8
OSLER, B. L. (W.P.)	1924 Br. 1, 2, 3, 4; 1928 NZ. 1, 2, 3, 4; 1931—32 W. I. E. S.; 1933 A. 1, 2, 3, 4, 5	17	2	46
OSLER, S. G. (W.P.)	1928 NZ. 1	1	—	—
OXLEE, K. (N.)	1960 NZ. 1, 2, 3, 4; 1960—61 W. I. S.; 1961 A. 1, 2; 1962 Br. 1, 2, 3, 4; 1963 A. 1, 2, 4; 1964 W.; 1965 tour of I. & S.—no tests; 1965 NZ. 1, 2	19	5	88
PARKER, W. H. (E.P.)	1965 A. 1, 2	2	—	—
PARTRIDGE, J. E. C. (Tvl.)	1903 Br. 1	1	—	—
PAYN, C. (N.)	1924 Br. 1, 2	2	—	—
PELSER, H. J. M. (Tvl.)	1958 Fr. 1; 1960 NZ. 1, 2, 3, 4; 1960—61 W. I. Fr.; 1961 I.; A. 1, 2	11	2	6
PFAFF, B. D. (W.P.)	1956 A. 1	1	—	—
PICKARD, J. A. J. (W.P.)	1951—52 tour of U.K.—no tests; 1553 A. 3, 4; 1956 NZ. 2; 1958 Fr. 2	4	—	—
PIENAAR, T. B. (W.P.)	1921 tour of A. & NZ.—no tests	—	—	—
PITZER, G. (N.T.)	1967 Fr. 1, 2, 3, 4; 1968 Br. 1, 2, 3, 4; Fr. 1, 2; 1969 A. 3, 4; 1969—70 tour of U.K.—no tests	12	—	—
POPE, C. F. (W.P.)	1974 Br. 1, 2, 3, 4; 1974 tour of Fr.—no tests; 1975 Fr. 1, 2; 1976 NZ. 2, 3, 4	9	1	4
POTGIETER, H. J. (O.F.S.)	1928 NZ. 1, 2	2	—	—
POTGIETER, R. (N.T.)	1969—70 tour of U.K.—no tests	—	—	—
POWELL, A. W. (G.W.)	1896 Br. 3	1	—	—
POWELL, J. M. (G.W.)	1891 Br. 2; 1896 Br. 3; 1903 Br. 1, 2	4	—	—
PRETORIUS, N. F. (Tvl.)	1928 NZ. 1, 2, 3, 4	4	—	—
PRINSLOO, J. (Tvl.)	1958 Fr. 1, 2	2	—	—
PRINSLOO, J. P. (Tvl.) (Boet)	1928 NZ. 1	1	—	—
PRINSLOO, J. (N.T.) (Poens)	1963 A. 3	1	—	—
PUTTER, D. J. (W.T.)	1963 A. 1, 2, 4	3	—	—
RAAFF, J. W. E. (G.W.)	1903 Br. 1, 2; 1906 S. W. E.; 1910 Br. 1	6	1	3
RAS, W. J. de W. (O.F.S.)	1976 NZ. 1(s)	1	—	—
REID, A. (W.P.)	1903 Br. 3	1	1	3
REID, B. C. (Bor.)	1933 A. 4	1	—	—
REID, H. G. (Tvl.)	1906 tour of U.K.—no tests	—	—	—
RENS, I. J. (Tvl.)	1953 A. 3, 4	2	—	19
RETIEF, D. F. (N.T.)	1955 Br. 1, 2, 4; 1956 A. 1, 2; NZ. 1, 2, 3, 4	9	4	12
REYNECKE, H. J. (W.P.)	1910 Br. 3	1	1	3
RICHARDS, A. R. (W.P.)	1891 Br. 1, 2, 3	3	—	—
RILEY, N. (E.T.)	1963 A. 3	1	—	—
RIORDAN, C. E. (Tvl.)	1910 Br. 1, 2	2	—	—
ROBERTSON, I. W. (R)	1974 Fr. 1, 2; 1976 NZ. 1, 2, 4	5	—	3
ROOS, G. D. (W.P.)	1910 Br. 2, 3	2	1	3
ROOS, P. J. (W.P.)	1903 Br. 3; 1906 I. W. E.	4	—	—
ROSENBERG, W. (Tvl.)	1955 Br. 2, 3, 4; 1956 NZ. 3; 1958 Fr. 1	5	2	6
ROSSOUW, D. H. (W.P.)	1953 A. 3, 4	2	1	3
ROUSSEAU, W. P. (W.P.)	1928 NZ. 3, 4	2	—	—
ROUX, F. du T. (W.P.)	1960—61 W.; 1961 A. 1, 2; 1962 Br. 1, 2, 3, 4; 1963 A. 2; 1965 A. 1, 2; NZ. 1, 2, 3, 4; 1968 Br. 3, 4; Fr. 1, 2; 1969 A. 1, 2, 3, 4; 1969—70 I.; 1970 NZ. 1, 2, 3, 4	27	6	18
ROUX, O. A. (N.T.)	1968 tour of Fr.—no tests; 1969—70 S. E. I. W.; 1971 tour of Aust.—no tests; 1972 E.; 1974 Br. 3, 4	7	—	—
SAMUELS, T. A. (G.W.)	1896 Br. 2, 3, 4	3	2	6
SAUERMANN, J. T. (Tvl.)	1971 Fr. 1, 2; A. 1; 1972 E; 1974 Br. 1	5	—	—
SAUNDERS, M. J. (Bor.)	1951—52 tour of U.K.—no tests	—	—	—
SCHLEBUSCH, J. J. J. (O.F.S.)	1974 Br. 3, 4; 1975 Fr. 2	3	—	—
SCHMIDT, L. U. (N.T.)	1958 Fr. 2; 1962 Br. 2	2	—	—
SCHOEMAN, J. (W.P.)	1963 A. 3, 4; 1965 I. S.; A. 1; NZ. 1, 2	7	—	—
SCHOLTZ, H. H. (W.P.)	1921 NZ. 1, 2	2	—	—
SCOTT, P. (Tvl.)	1896 Br. 1, 2, 3, 4	4	—	—
SENDIN, W. D. (G.W.)	1921 NZ. 2	1	1	3
SHAND, R. (G.W.)	1891 Br. 2, 3	2	—	—
SHERIFF, A. R. (Tvl.)	1937 tour of A. & NZ.—no tests; 1938 Br. 1, 2, 3	3	—	—
SHUM, E. H. (Tvl.)	1912—13 E.	1	—	—
SIEDLE, L. B. (N.)	1921 Tour of A. & NZ.—no tests	—	—	—
SINCLAIR, D. J. (Tvl.)	1951—52 tour of U.K.—no tests; 1955 Br. 1, 2, 3, 4	4	—	—
SINCLAIR, J. H. (Tvl.)	1903 Br. 1	1	—	—
SKENE, A. L. (W.P.)	1958 Fr. 2	1	—	—
SLABBER, L. J. (O.F.S.)	1965 tour of A. & NZ.—no tests	—	—	—
SLATER, J. T. (E.P.)	1924 Br. 3, 4; 1928 NZ. 1	3	2	6
SMITH, C. W. (G.W.)	1891 Br. 2; 1896 Br. 2, 3	3	—	—
SMITH, C. M. (O.F.S.)	1963 A. 3, 4; 1964 W.; Fr.; 1965 A. 1, 2; NZ. 2	7	1	12
SMITH, D. (G.W.)	1891 Br. 2	1	—	—
SMITH, G. A. C. (E.P.)	1938 Br. 3	1	—	—
SMOLLAN, F. C. (Tvl.)	1933 A. 3, 4, 5	3	—	—
SNEDDEN, R. C. (G.W.)	1891 Br. 2	1	—	—
SNYMAN, D. S. L. (W.P.)	1971 tour of Aust.—no tests; 1972 E.; 1974 Br. 1, 2(s); Fr. 1, 2; 1975 Fr. 1, 2; 1976 NZ. 2, 3	9	—	20
SNYMAN, J. C. P. (O.F.S.)	1974 Br. 2, 3, 4; 1974 tour of Fr.—no tests	3	—	18

	International Record	Tests	Tries	Pts.
SONNEKUS, G. H. H. (O.F.S.)	1974 Br. 3	1	—	—
SPIES, J. J. (N.T.)	1970 NZ. 1, 2, 3, 4; 1971 tour of Aust.—no tests	4	—	—
STANDER, J. C. J. (O.F.S.)	1974 Br. 4(s); 1974 tour of Fr.—no tests 1976 NZ. 1, 2, 3, 4;	5	—	—
STAPELBERG, W. P. (N.T.)	1974 Fr. 1, 2	2	2	8
STARKE, J. J. (W.P.)	1956 NZ. 4	1	—	—
STARKE, K. T. (W.P.)	1924 Br. 1, 2, 3, 4	4	3	13
STEENEKAMP, J. (Tvl.)	1958 Fr. 1	1	—	—
STEGMANN, A. C. (W.P.)	1906 S. I.	2	1	3
STEGMANN, J. A. (Tvl.)	1912—13 S. I. W. E. Fr.	5	5	15
STEWART, D. A. (W.P.)	1960 S.; 1960—61 E. S. Fr.; 1961 I.; 1963 A. 1, 3, 4; 1964 W.; Fr.; 1965 I.	11	1	9
STOFBERG, M. T. S. (O.F.S.)	1976 NZ. 2, 3	2	—	—
STRACHAN, L. C. (Tvl.)	1931—32 E. S.; 1937 A. 1, 2; NZ. 1, 2, 3; 1938 Br. 1, 2, 3	10	—	—
STRAUSS, J. H. P. (Tvl.)	1976 NZ. 3, 4	2	—	—
STRAUSS, S. S. F. (G.W.)	1921 NZ. 3	1	—	—
STRYDOM, C. F. (O.F.S.)	1955 Br. 3; 1956 A. 1, 2; NZ. 1, 4; 1958 Fr. 1	6	—	—
STRYDOM, L. J. (N.T.)	1949 NZ. 1, 2	2	—	—
SUTER, M. R. (N.)	1965 I. S.	2	—	—
SWANSON, P. S. (Tvl.)	1971 tour of Aust.—no test	—	—	—
SWART, J. J. N. (S.W.A.)	1955 Br. 1	1	1	3
TABERER, W. S. (G.W.)	1896 Br. 2	1	—	—
TAYLOR, O. B. (N.)	1962 Br. 1	1	—	—
THEUNISSEN, D. J. (G.W.)	1896 Br. 3	1	—	—
THOMPSON, G. (W.P.)	1912—13 S. I. W.	3	—	—
TINDALL, J. C. (W.P.)	1921 tour of A. & NZ.—no tests; 1924 Br. 1; 1928 NZ. 1, 2, 3, 4; 1931—32 tour of U.K.—no tests	5	—	—
TOD, N. S. (N.)	1928 NZ. 2	1	—	—
TOWNSEND, W. H. (N.)	1921 NZ. 1	1	—	—
TRENERY, W. (G.W.)	1891 Br. 2	1	—	—
TRUTER, D. R. (W.P.)	1924 Br. 2, 4	2	—	—
TRUTER, J. T. (N.)	1963 A. 1; 1964 Fr.; 1965 A. 2	3	1	3
TURNER, F. G. (E.P.)	1933 A. 1, 2, 3; 1937 A. 1, 2; NZ. 1, 2, 3; 1938 Br. 1, 2, 3	11	4	29
TWIGGE, R. J. (N.T.)	1960 S.	1	—	—
ULYATE, C. A. (Tvl.)	1955 Br. 1, 2, 3, 4; 1956 NZ. 1, 2, 3	7	1	6
UYS, P. de W. (N.T.)	1960—61 W. E. S.; 1961 I.; A. 1, 2; 1962 Br. 1, 4; 1963 A. 1, 2; 1968 tour of Fr.—no tests; 1969 A. 1(s), 2.	12	—	—
VAN BROEKHUIZEN, H. D. (W.P.)	1896 Br. 4	1	—	—
VAN BUUREN, M. C. (Tvl.)	1891 Br. 1	1	—	—
VAN DE VYVER, D. F. (W.P.)	1937 A. 2	1	—	—
VAN DEN BERG, D. S. (N.)	1974 tour of Fr.—no tests; 1975 Fr. 1, 2; 1976 NZ. 1, 2	4	—	—
VAN DEN BERG, M. A. (W.P.)	1937 A. 1; NZ. 1, 2, 3	4	—	—
VAN DER HOFF, A. (Tvl.)	1912—13 tour of U.K.—no tests	—	—	—
VAN DER MERWE, A. J. (Bol.)	1955 Br. 2, 3, 4; 1956 A. 1, 2; NZ. 1, 2, 3, 4; 1958 Fr. 1; 1960 S.; NZ. 2	12	—	—
VAN DER MERWE, A. V. (W.P.)	1931—32 W.	1	—	—
VAN DER MERWE, B. S. (N.T.)	1949 NZ. 1	1	—	—
VAN DER MERWE, H. S. (N.T.)	1960 NZ. 4; 1960—61 tour of U.K.—no tests; 1963 A. 2, 3, 4; 1964 Fr.	5	—	—
VAN DER MERWE, J. P. (W.P.)	1969—70 W.	1	—	—
VANDERPLANK, B. E. (N.)	1924 Br. 3, 4	2	—	—
VAN DER RYST, F. E. (Tvl.)	1951—52 tour of U.K.—no tests	—	—	—
VAN DER SCHYFF, J. H. (G.W.)	1949 NZ. 1, 2, 3, 4; 1955 Br. 1	5	—	10
VAN DER SCHYFF, P. J. (W.T.)	1969—70 tour of U.K.—no tests	—	—	—
VAN DER WATT, A. E. (W.P.)	1969—70 S.(s), E. I.; 1971 tour of Aust.—no tests	3	—	—
VAN DER WESTHUIZEN, J. C. (W.P.)	1928 NZ. 2, 3, 4; 1931—32 I.	4	1	3
VAN DER WESTHUIZEN, J. H. (W.P.)	1931—32 I. E. S.	3	—	—
VAN DEVENTER, P. I. (G.W.)	1969—70 tour of U.K.—no tests	—	—	—
VAN DRUTEN, N. J. V. (Tvl.)	1924 Br. 1, 2, 3, 4; 1928 NZ. 1, 2, 3, 4	8	2	6
VAN HEERDEN, A. J. (Tvl.)	1921 NZ. 1, 3	2	1	3
VAN HEERDEN, J. L. (N.T.)	1974 Br. 3, 4; Fr. 1, 2; 1975 Fr. 1, 2; 1976 NZ. 1, 2, 3, 4	10	—	—
VAN JAARSVELD, C. J. (Tvl.)	1949 NZ. I.	1	—	—

	International Record	Tests	Tries	Pts.
VAN JAARSVELDT, D. C. (R.)	1960 S.	1	1	3
VAN NIEKERK, B. B. (O.F.S.)	1960—61 tour of U.K.—no tests	—	—	—
VAN NIEKERK, J. A. (W.P.)	1928 NZ. 4; 1931—32 tour of U.K.—no tests	1	—	—
VAN REENEN, G. L. (W.P.)	1937 A. 2; NZ. 1	2	2	6
VAN RENEN, C. G. (W.P.)	1891 Br. 3; 1896 Br. 1, 4	3	—	—
VAN RENEN, W. (W.P.)	1903 Br. 1, 3	2	—	—
VAN RENSBURG, M. C. (Janse) (N.)	1969—70 tour of U.K.—no tests	—	—	—
VAN ROOYEN, G. W. (Tvl.)	1921 NZ. 2, 3	2	—	—
VAN RYNEVELD, R. C. B. (W.P.)	1910 Br. 2, 3	2	—	—
VAN SCHOOR, R. A. M. (R.)	1949 NZ. 2, 3, 4; 1951—52 S. I. W. E. Fr.; 1953 A. 1, 2, 3, 4	12	2	6
VAN STADEN, J. A. (N.T.)	1974 tour of Fr.—no tests	—	—	—
VAN VOLLENHOVEN, K. T. (N.T.)	1955 Br. 1, 2, 3, 4; 1956 A. 1, 2; NZ. 3	7	4	15
VAN VUUREN, T. F. (E.P.)	1912—13 S. I. W. E. Fr.	5	—	—
VAN WYK, C. J. (Tvl.)	1951—52 S. I. W. E. Fr.; 1953 A. 1, 2, 3, 4; 1955 Br. 1; 1956 tour of A. & NZ.—no tests.	10	6	18
VAN WYK, J. F. B. (N.T.)	1970 NZ. 1, 2, 3, 4; 1971 Fr. 1, 2; A. 1, 2, 3; 1972 E.; 1974 Br. 1, 3, 4; 1976 NZ. 3, 4.	15	—	—
VAN WYK, S. P. (W.P.)	1928 NZ. 1, 2	2	—	—
VAN ZYL, B. P. (W.P.)	1960—61 tour of U.K.—no tests; 1961 I.	1	2	6
VAN ZYL, C. G. P. (O.F.S.)	1965 NZ. 1, 2, 3, 4	4	—	—
VAN ZYL, G. H. (W.P.) (Hugo)	1958 Fr. 1; 1960 S.; NZ. 1, 2, 3, 4; 1960—61 W. I. E. S. Fr.; 1961 I.; A. 1, 2; 1962 Br. 1, 3, 4	17	4	12
VAN ZYL, H. J. (Tvl.)	1960 NZ. 1, 2, 3, 4; 1960—61 I. E. S.; 1961 I.; A. 1, 2	10	6	18
VAN ZYL, P. J. (Bol.)	1960—61 tour of U.K.—no tests; 1961 I.	1	—	—
VENTER, F. D. (Tvl.)	1931—32 W. S.; 1933 A. 3	3	—	—
VERSFELD, C. (W.P.)	1891 Br. 3	1	—	—
VERSFELD, M. (W.P.)	1891 Br. 1, 2, 3	3	—	—
VIGNE, J. T. (Tvl.)	1891 Br. 1, 2, 3	3	—	—
VILJOEN, J. F. (G.W.)	1971 Fr. 1, 2; A. 1, 2, 3; 1972 E.	6	2	6
VILJOEN, J. T. (N.)	1971 A. 1, 2, 3	3	2	6
VISAGIE, P. J. (G.W.)	1967 Fr. 1, 2, 3, 4; 1968 Br. 1, 2, 3, 4; Fr. 1, 2; 1969 A. 1, 2, 3, 4; 1969—70 S. E.; 1970 NZ. 1, 2, 3, 4; 1971 Fr. 1, 2; A. 1, 2, 3	25	6	130
VISSER, P. J. (Tvl.)	1933 A. 2	1	—	—
VIVIER(S), S. S. (O.F.S.)	1951—52 tour of U.K.—no tests; 1956 A. 1, 2; NZ. 2, 3, 4	5	—	11
VOGEL, M. L. (O.F.S.)	1974 Br. 2(s)	1	—	—
WAHL, J. J. (W.P.)	1949 NZ. 1	1	—	—
WALKER, A. P. (N.)	1921 NZ. 1, 3; 1924 Br. 1, 2, 3, 4	6	—	—
WALKER, H. N. (O.F.S.)	1953 A. 3; 1956 A. 2; NZ. 1, 4	4	—	—
WALKER, H. W. (Tvl.)	1910 Br. 1, 2, 3	3	—	—
WALTON, D. C. (N.)	1964 Fr.; 1965 I. S.; NZ. 3, 4; 1968 tour of Fr.—no tests; 1969 A. 1, 2; 1969—70 E.	8	—	—
WARING, F. W. (W.P.)	1931—32 I. E.; 1933 A. 1, 2, 3, 4, 5	7	2	6
WATT, H. H. (W.P.)	1937 tour of A. & NZ.—no tests	—	—	—
WEEPNER, J. S. (W.P.)	1921 tour of A. & NZ.—no tests	—	—	—
WENTZEL, G. J. (E.P.)	1960—61 tour of U.K.—no tests	—	—	—
WESSELS, J. J. (W.P.)	1896 Br. 1, 2, 3	3	—	—
WESSELS, J. W. (O.F.S.)	1965 tour of I. & S.—no tests	—	—	—
WESSELS, P. W. (O.F.S.)	1951—52 tour of U.K.—no tests	—	—	—
WHIPP, P. J. M. (W.P.)	1974 Br. 1, 2,; 1974 tour of Fr.—no tests; 1975 Fr. 1; 1976 NZ. 1, 3, 4	6	1	4
WHITE, J. (Bor.)	1931—32 W.; 1933 A. 1, 2, 3, 4, 5; 1937 A. 1, 2; NZ. 1, 2	10	2	10
WILLIAMS, A. E. (G.W.)	1910 Br. 1	1	—	—
WILLIAMS, D. O. (W.P.)	1931—32 tour of U.K.—no tests; 1937 A. 1, 2; NZ. 1, 2, 3; 1938 Br. 1, 2, 3	8	5	15
WILLIAMS, J. G. (N.T.)	1971 Fr. 1, 2; A. 1, 2, 3; 1972 E.; 1974 Br. 1, 2, 4; Fr. 1, 2; 1976 NZ. 1, 2.	13	—	—
WILSON, L. G. (W.P.)	1960 NZ. 3, 4; 1960—61 W. I. E. Fr.; 1961 I.; A. 1, 2; 1962 Br. 1, 2, 3, 4; 1963 A. 1, 2, 3, 4; 1964 W.; Fr.; 1965 I. S.; A. 1, 2; NZ. 1, 2, 3, 4	27	—	6
WRENTMORE, G. M. (W.P.)	1912—13 tour of U.K.—no tests	—	—	—
WYNESS, M. R. K. (W.P.)	1962 Br. 1, 2, 3, 4; 1963 A. 2	5	1	3
ZELLER, W. C. (N.)	1921 NZ. 2, 3	2	—	—
ZIMERMAN, M. (W.P.)	1931—32 W. I. E. S.	4	1	3